SARAH GILBERT WHITE SMITH
From an unsigned miniature portrait, at the age of 24 in 1837,
before her marriage to Asa B. Smith.
See text pages 41-42. From *Missionary Album*.

THE MOUNTAINS WE HAVE CROSSED

Diaries and Letters of the
Oregon Mission, 1838

Introductions and Editorial Notes by
Clifford Merrill Drury

*Introduction to the Bison Books Edition
by Bonnie Sue Lewis*

University of Nebraska Press
Lincoln and London

First Bison Books printing: 1999
Most recent printing indicated by the last digit below:
10   9   8   7   6   5   4   3   2   1

Library of Congress Cataloging-in-Publication Data
The mountains we have crossed: diaries and letters of the Oregon Mission,
1838 / introductions and editorial notes by Clifford Merrill Drury; introduction to the Bison Books edition by Bonnie Sue Lewis.
p.   cm.
Originally published as v. 3 of: First white women over the Rockies. Glendale,
Calif.: A. H. Clark, 1966.
Consists of the diary of Sarah White Smith and letters of Asa B. Smith, and
other documents relating to the 1838 reenforcement to the Oregon Mission.
Includes bibliographical references and index.
ISBN 0-8032-6621-9 (pbk.: alk. paper)
1. Women pioneers—Northwestern States Diaries.   2. Women missionaries—Northwestern States Diaries.   3. Pioneers—Northwestern States
Correspondence.   4. Missionaries—Northwestern States Correspondence.
5. Smith, Sarah Gilbert White, 1813–1855 Diaries.   6. Smith, Asa Bowen,
1809–1886 Correspondence.   7. Overland journeys to the Pacific.
8. Oregon—History—To 1859.   9. Missions—Oregon—History—19th
century.   10. Indians of North America—Missions—Oregon—History—19th
century.   I. Smith, Sarah Gilbert White, 1813–1855.   II. Smith, Asa Bowen,
1809–1886.   III. Drury, Clifford Merrill, 1897–   IV. First white women
over the Rockies. Volume 3.
F597.M78   1999
978'.02'082—dc21
99-23583   CIP

IN DEDICATION

This volume, together with the seven preceding volumes
on this subject, was written to keep alive the memory of
thirteen intrepid men and women who, inspired by the
high ideal of civilizing and Christianizing the natives,
dared to venture across the Rocky Mountains into the
Oregon country where they established
homes, schools, and churches.

Introduction to the Bison Books Edition

Bonnie Sue Lewis

When Presbyterian minister Clifford Drury gathered the letters and diaries of the first six women missionaries of the American Board of Commissioners of Foreign Mission's (ABCFM) Oregon mission, he could find no diary for the youngest member, Sarah Gilbert White Smith. Therefore, his two-volume work, originally entitled *First White Women Over the Rockies*, contained only eight pages on Sarah Smith based upon the four letters known to exist. With their publication, however, a descendent of Smith's alerted Drury to the existence of a copy of her diary in the Denver Public Library made by Sarah Smith's niece, Alice J. White. Released to Drury for publication, this diary became the basis for a third volume of the series and provides additional valuable source material concerning the overland journey and arrival in the Oregon Territory of these pioneer missionary women, their husbands, and the native peoples they hoped to serve and to save.

Much has been written of the frailties of the missionaries who set out in the early nineteenth century to bring Christianity and western civilization to the "benighted heathen" both overseas and in their own backyards. The missionary women have received special attention in recent works, such as Julie Roy Jeffrey's compelling look at Narcissa Whitman in *Converting the West* and Mary Zwiep's engaging study of the Hawaiian missionary women in *Pilgrim Path*. Dana Robert's *American Missionary Women* gives a sweeping overview of the roles missionary wives and single women played during an era of growing contact with native peoples. This timely republication of Drury's collection of firsthand accounts of the Oregon mission, primarily through the eyes of the women, will be welcomed by a new generation of historians who are revisiting the relationships between missionaries and Native Americans. It also strengthens the conclusion that the nature of nineteenth-century missions was far more complex than initially believed.

One of the more complicated issues of the Oregon mission was the personalities involved. The eighteen-month diary of Sarah Smith, published here and supplemented by several unpublished accounts and letters by the men of the mission, sheds light on the personality problems that became, in Drury's words, the Oregon mission's "great misfortune"

(22). It was, perhaps, Sarah Smith's misfortune to be married to one of the most contentious of the mission leaders, Asa Bowen Smith. Her diary, however, gives no indication that she found him objectionable. Indeed, she often mourned the fact that the trip west and the crowded conditions at the mission afforded little privacy to be alone with her husband until they moved to the isolated Kamiah valley.

It is clear that Smith's coworkers found him a difficult man. William Gray remarked that Smith's "prejudices were so strong that he could not be reasonable with himself," and that he lacked "Christian forbearance and confidence in his associates" (249). Mary Walker, who, with her husband Elkanah, shared the Smiths' tent for the journey west, noted more candidly in her diary that Smith was "short as pie crust" (77 n) and was constantly finding fault with the others (91 n). He was, by nearly every account, critical, impatient and condescending. Drury labels him a perfectionist (51) whose study skills made him the best linguist of the group even if his social skills were less than adequate.

It should not be surprising that the relationships among the mission personnel were somewhat messy. Sarah and Asa Smith were one of four couples and a single man that were sent out to Oregon in 1838 as reinforcements to the 1836 mission team of Dr. Marcus and Narcissa Whitman and Rev. Henry and Eliza Spalding. Like the first members of the mission, the reinforcement team were all newlyweds who reflected the high idealism and strong convictions born of the nineteenth-century revivals known as the Second Great Awakening. These were powerfully motivated women and men whose spiritual enthusiasm led most of them to choose a missionary career first and a marriage partner second. Their faith in God and this mission rarely wavered. Their understanding of their role was seldom questioned. As Sarah penned upon arrival in Oregon, "[s]oon I hope to engage in the duties of missionary life, instructing the ignorant, relieving the distressed & leading to virtue the degraded host" (109). Despite a 1900-mile journey by horseback (sidesaddle, no less) that began on her wedding day, honeymooning in the same small tent as another newly-married couple, and subsisting on meager provisions, Sarah's zeal for mission work remained.

The need to present a picture of missionary life back home that would not alarm the family nor cut off the support of the American Board complicated matters further. Despite homesickness, illness and privation, Sarah frequently assured her family that she was happy and did "not regret the life I have chosen" (121–22). The words often have a hollow ring. It is little wonder. The ABCFM required only evidence of piety and reasonable health of its missionaries who were then sent off with simply a sermon of exhortation. Unrealistic expectations, little preparation to understand another culture, severe trials and poor health took their toll. In an isolated cabin among the Nez Perces, where Sarah and Asa spent most of their two years with the Oregon mission, she was known as the "weeping one" (187). Never robust, the final poignant pages of Sarah's diary paint a forlorn picture: "Almost a constant pain in my side & pressure upon my lungs. . . . Have been bled & blister applied to my side . . ." (121). She ends her "little volume" with a very practical guide about what clothing to take should any other woman be so foolhardy as to repeat the overland journey and closes with a touching, "Till we meet in Heaven, Farewell, Farewell" (125). She clearly did not expect to see her family again.

Despite a hearty conviction in the legitimacy of their calling, the mission field was littered with disillusioned missionaries. The demands of the work, the lack of community support and provisions, and the slow progress of the Christian gospel proved wearying. Asa Smith summed up the problem in December of 1838, just months after arriving in Oregon Territory. He wrote home that "there is much novelty & romance in the missionary spirit, but with me this is all gone" (165). He had discovered that the missionary was "but a man & perhaps an ordinary man too" (165). If he found his coworkers "not in all aspects the most pleasant" (166), he found himself "but a man 'subject to like passions with others'" (165), and his piety in jeopardy. Although he blamed much of this on the necessary preoccupation with such "worldly" pursuits as farming and putting a roof over their heads in time for winter weather, his disappointments came of unrealized expectations and conflicted emotions. Though Sarah had hoped "to be instrumental in the saving of some souls," she was frustrated from reaching such goals by feeble health and an abundance of housekeeping chores (122).

The relationships between the missionaries and the Native Americans were even more complex than those among the missionaries themselves. A sense of cultural superiority often blinded the missionaries to the value of native ways and friendships. Intent on preparing them for heaven, the missionaries frequently stumbled over their earthly condition. Sarah's mix of appreciation for the fine figure a native wife made upon a white horse decked out in beads and "little gingles" (84) and her dismissive remark that "they are all unlovely, polluted in mind & body" (99), indicate her ambivalence toward those she had come to save. Asa Smith at first found the Indians "an interesting people & ready to receive instruction" (164), and no more "degraded" than those "we see in some measure at home" (165). Although he thought them "selfish in the extreme" (159), he believed they possessed only the same "wicked heart" that he believed all humankind possessed. In time, he became incensed that they seemed to want what the missionary offered only for the "hope of temporal gain" and to "appear wise & gain influence among the people" (174–75).

Missionary views of Indians were often one-dimensional. Indians were either good or bad, depending on how they responded to the Christian message. This made it difficult for the missionaries to understand the varying responses or the tribal politics involved in Native American interaction with them. Smith's language teacher, Lawyer, to whom Smith became "very much attached," and whose quick mind and eloquent speech he admired, encouraged the Smiths to settle in the Kamiah valley (170). While the move provided Smith a way to leave the cramped quarters of the Whitman mission station, he no doubt fell under the spell of Lawyer's persuasive argument that there would be more possible converts in the Kamiah valley. As Smith soon discovered when he undertook a census of the Nez Perces, that was not the case. Lawyer, however, gained the prestige of having his own missionary at a time when the Nez Perces still believed that there was great potential for material, if not spiritual, gain in having one among them.

In this early phase of missionary work in the Northwest, Native American responses were vital to the very security of the mission. Far outnumbered by the Indians, the missionaries remained in the field only by the good will of their hosts. When angered over what appeared the lack of a fair exchange for goods or services provided, the native hosts could be quite threatening to their guests. Missionaries had been pursued by the Northwest tribes in the hope of gaining the benefit of the white man's power. When that failed to materialize in tangible ways, acts of rebellion broke out. The Smiths and the Spaldings both experienced destruction of property, loss of livestock, and personal threats. The Whitmans ultimately lost their lives to the Cayuses whose own lives were threatened by the growing numbers of settlers moving in and the raging epidemics they brought with them. The mission survived the clash of personalities and an attempt of the American Board to shut it down after the embarrassment of the feuding missionaries reached its ears. But it came to a close in 1847 when their hosts turned on them and, in frustration and desperation, killed the Whitman party.

By the time the Oregon mission was closed, the Smiths had returned to the East Coast. Concern for Sarah's health and disillusionment with their coworkers and the Nez Perces prompted the Smiths' move to the Hawaiian mission. Although Sarah's health rallied somewhat in the warmer climate and the easier conditions of a more established mission station, her husband's contentious spirit continued to plague their relationships with both missionaries and Hawaiians. In less than four years they were on their way back to the States having been deemed by the Hawaiian missionaries to be more "useful among [their] own country-men than among Hawaiians" (224). While Asa Smith continued to have difficulties as a minister in various congregations in the States, Sarah finally found contentment as a mother to four orphaned children back home among her own kin. In 1855 she died of "consumption" at the early age of 41.

The story of the Oregon mission does not end, however, with the return of the missionaries or the closing of the mission stations. In one of the complex twists of history, Kamiah became the center of a Nez Perce Presbyterianism that, by the beginning of the twentieth century, had built six Presbyterian churches led by Nez Perce pastors. Lawyer's son, Archie Lawyer, was the second minister of sixteen Nez Perces to be ordained. Several went beyond the bounds of the reservation to begin Presbyterian churches among other tribes.

The diaries and letters carefully collected by Clifford Drury and re-printed here illustrate the complicated relationships among the Native Americans and the missionaries. They show the roots of a mixed legacy. Tribal divisions remain to this day between treaty and non-treaty, Chris-tian and non-Christian Nez Perces. But Nez Perce Presbyterianism con-tinues to be deeply embedded in the history and daily culture of several bands of the Nez Perces. The complex nature of missionary activity, to which Sarah and Asa Smith's writings provide a window, has left its mark upon this people. But as a people, the Nez Perces have taken what was offered and made it their own. If the messengers of the Christian gospel were beset by human frailties, the power of their message in the hands of the Nez Perces continues to have an impact on the tribe.

Contents

WILLIAM HENRY GRAY

ELKANAH WALKER

CORNELIUS ROGERS

MARCUS WHITMAN

CUSHING EELLS

THE OVERLAND TRIP FOR WOMEN — WAS IT WISE?

Illustrations

Sources and Acknowledgments

The recent discovery of the diary of Sarah White Smith and nearly one hundred letters of her husband, Asa Bowen Smith, has made possible the publication of this volume to complete the picture of the 1838 reenforcement of the Oregon Mission. The story of this discovery is given in the preface to this volume. The manuscripts, pictures, and other items consulted in the preparation of this volume, are located in several collections or libraries. Permission to publish all or part of the documents indicated in the text, has been received from the individual depositories concerned. The author wishes here to express his appreciation for such permission. Locations of the documents and pictures are as follows, with abbreviations indicated in parentheses which will be used in footnote citations:

The American Board of Commissioners for Foreign Missions [1] (Coll. A) has an extensive file of original correspondence with its Oregon missionaries. This is now on deposit in Houghton Library, Harvard University.

The Western History Department of the Denver Public Library owns the copy of Sarah White Smith's diary herein published, it is believed, for the first time.

The Henry E. Huntington Library and Art Gallery, San Marino, California (Coll. H), owns the diary kept by Elkanah Walker while enroute to Oregon in 1838.

The Hawaiian Mission Children's Society of Honolulu, Hawaii (Coll. Ha), has an extensive collection of the correspondence and other documents relating to the Hawaiian Mission of the American Board. Included is a collection of twenty letters written or received by Asa B. Smith during the years 1842-46, which the society recently secured from Richard W. Smith who is mentioned in the preface of this volume.

[1] Due to the union of the Congregational-Christian Church with the Evangelical and Reformed Church, the name of the American Board of Commissioners for Foreign Missions was changed on June 29, 1961, to the United Church Board for World Ministries. The old name of the American Board will be used, however, in this volume.

These supplement another file of about ninety letters of Asa Smith's correspondence for the same period.

Whitman College, Walla Walla, Washington (Coll. W), has a rich collection of diaries, letters, and other documents pertaining to the Oregon Mission of the American Board, including the unpublished reminiscences of Cushing Eells.

The Coe Collection in Yale University Library (Coll. Y) contains many letters written by members of the Oregon Mission. The Beinecke Rare Book and Manuscript Library, a part of the university library, recently acquired from Richard W. Smith a collection of sixty-seven letters written by A. B. Smith, largely to members of his family, and other relevant documents.

The author wishes to express his appreciation to the librarians of the institutions above mentioned, and especially to Mrs. E. C. Cluff, Jr., of the Hawaiian Mission Children's Society, for their invaluable cooperation.

First among individuals who have made this book possible and to whom deep appreciation is hereby expressed is Richard W. Smith, Chevy Chase, Maryland, who was the first to inform the author of the existence of a copy of Sarah Smith's diary and who subsequently made available for the author's use nearly one hundred letters of his grand-uncle, Asa B. Smith. Richard W. Smith has also helped with correcting both the original copy and the proof. Without his help, this book would never have been written.

Others who supplied important facts include the Rev. George S. Worcester, Dr. Louis E. Roy, and Mrs. Ruby Gilbert Merrill, all of West Brookfield, Massachusetts; the Rev. George E. Lawrence, Jr., and T. D. Seymour Bassett of Burlington, Vermont; and the Rev. and Mrs. Eric W. Bascom, Sr., of Buckland, Massachusetts.

To all who have so kindly granted permission to use source material; to all who have so patiently answered the author's numerous inquiries; and to all who helped in other ways in the preparation of this manuscript for publication, a most sincere Thank You.

CLIFFORD M. DRURY

Pasadena, California

ABBREVIATIONS: In addition to those indicated above for various collections, the following will also be used in the footnotes:

FWW — to refer to this author's *The First White Women over the Rockies*, with volume indicated by roman numeral.

SS — to refer to this author's *The Diaries and Letters of Henry H. Spalding and Asa B. Smith*.

T.O.P.A. — to refer to *Transactions of the Oregon Pioneer Association*.

Preface

I began my researches in the history of the Oregon Mission of the American Board of Commissioners for Foreign Missions [1] in 1934 when I was pastor of the First Presbyterian Church of Moscow, Idaho. Because of the proximity of Moscow to the Clearwater Valley of Northern Idaho, where most of the Nez Perces live, I had opportunity to become acquainted with many of them, especially with those who were members of the Presbyterian Church. In 1934 I began writing my biography of the Rev. Henry Harmon Spalding who, with his wife Eliza, settled among the Nez Perces in 1836. An amazing amount of original and unpublished source material came to light. The archives of the American Board in Boston, for instance, contain about a million words of the correspondence of the thirteen missionaries sent to Oregon by this Board in 1836 and 1838. Other important sources such as diaries and letters are located in various western libraries. Personal visits to the parental homes of these missionaries uncovered still more information in church and school records, published reminiscences of those who knew one or more of this mission band, and in a variety of other sources including tombstone inscriptions.

As a result of these researches, I first published a trilogy: *Henry Harmon Spalding, Pioneer of Old Oregon*, 1936; *Marcus Whitman, M.D., Pioneer and Martyr*, 1937; and *Elkanah and Mary Walker, Pioneers among the Spokanes*, 1940.[2] Each of these biographies centered in one of the three main stations of the Oregon Mission — Lapwai, Waiilatpu, and Tshimakain. *A Tepee in his Front Yard* appeared in 1949. This was a sequel to the Spalding biography as it told of Spald-

---

[1] This Board, also referred to as the American Board or the A.B.C.F.M., was established in 1812 by the Congregational churches of Massachusetts. This was the first foreign missionary board to be organized in the United States. The Presbyterian Church cooperated in supporting the Board from 1826 to 1837, at which time the Old School branch of that denomination withdrew. The New School branch did not withdraw until 1870. The Presbyterian members of the Oregon Mission, including the Spaldings, the Whitmans, and the Grays, were of the New School branch.

[2] See bibliography for name of publisher. The trilogy has long been out of print.

ing's old age and his part in the great revival that swept through the
Nez Perce and Spokane tribes in 1871-74 when Spalding reportedly
baptized about one thousand converts.

In 1958 The Arthur H. Clark Company of Glendale, California,
brought out *The Diaries and Letters of Henry H. Spalding and Asa
Bowen Smith relating to the Nez Perce Mission, 1838-1842.* One of the
most thrilling aspects of this epic story is the account of the six women
who accompanied their husbands on the long overland journey to
Oregon in 1836 and 1838. Mrs. Marcus Whitman and Mrs. Henry H.
Spalding crossed the Continental Divide on July 4, 1836, being the first
white American women to do so. They were followed two years later
by Mrs. Elkanah Walker, Mrs. Cushing Eells, Mrs. Asa B. Smith, and
Mrs. William H. Gray. I had the good fortune to find the diaries of five
of these courageous women which, with some additional material, made
up more than six hundred pages of my two-volume work, *The First
White Women over the Rockies,* published by The Arthur H. Clark
Company in 1963. This work did not include the diary of Mrs. Asa B.
Smith which I was then unable to locate, although I had evidence that
she had kept such a record. Thus, because of the scantiness of source
material, only eight pages of the six hundred were devoted to Sarah
Smith.

AN EXCITING DISCOVERY

But now the lost document has been found! Here is the sequence of
the discovery. The summer 1964 issue of the recently launched magazine, *The American West,* carried a review of *The First White Women
over the Rockies* by Bruce LeRoy of the Washington State Historical
Society. A copy of this issue came to the attention of Richard W. Smith
of Chevy Chase, Maryland, a grandson of John Curtis Smith who was
a brother of Asa B. Smith. After noting LeRoy's statement that Sarah
Smith had left no known diary, Richard W. Smith wrote on August
12th to the editor saying that a copy of her diary was in the Denver
Public Library. He also stated that a collection of twenty-eight letters
written by Asa B. Smith to his family in Vermont, describing his overland travel experiences and his life in the Oregon Mission, had been
sold to a collector who was intending to donate it to Yale University
Library.

"I feel," wrote Richard W. Smith, "that the Rev. A. B. Smith's letters
and his wife's diary should be published together if the two libraries
that own them would allow some historian to edit and publish them."
The editor sent this letter to my publishers who in turn forwarded it

to me. The exciting news of the existence of this primary source material reached me at my home in Pasadena, California, on August 26th.

I wrote at once to Richard W. Smith for further information. He replied on September 17th listing the twenty-eight Asa B. Smith letters with a brief summary of their contents. Included in this collection was a letter from Dr. Marcus Whitman to Asa Smith dated May 31, 1844, in which Whitman commented on his famous ride East in 1842-43 and gave some of his views regarding the future of Oregon. So far as is known, none of these letters has hitherto been published.

I then wrote to the Denver Public Library and to Yale University Library asking for microfilms of the documents each owned and permission to publish. Mrs. Alys Freeze, head of the Western History Department of the Denver Public Library, replied saying that the diary of Sarah Smith had been given to that library by Miss Lucretia Vaile, a grandniece of Sarah's, and that the document was not the original but a copy. This copy had been made by Miss Vaile's mother, Alice J. White, after which the original diary had been destroyed "because of its tattered condition." The copy in the Denver library fills 106 pages of a notebook 9½ by 7½ inches. Although the Library had been considering publishing the diary, permission was graciously granted to me to do so because of my extensive researches in this field.

The transcription of Sarah Smith's diary, made from a microfilm furnished by the Denver library, ran to about 15,200 words. Since the original document had been destroyed, there is no way to check to see if the niece made an accurate copy. In a few instances, I found that evident errors had been made in dates and names. These I have felt free to correct in my transcription.

My inquiry to Yale brought a response from Dr. Archibald Hanna, curator of the Western Americana Collection. He reported that the Smith letters had but shortly before been received by the library and that a microfilm would be sent to me with permission to publish. The transcription of these letters, including the one from Dr. Whitman, ran to about 16,000 words.

Because of an awakened interest in the story of Asa and Sarah Smith, Richard W. Smith then sent to me for examination and final disposal a collection of some eighty-five or more letters and other documents written by or to the Smiths. Thirty or more of these items, beginning with one dated October 27, 1832, covered the five and one-half years before Asa left for Oregon, including the time when he was a college and seminary student. Among the letters were a number written by

Asa to his brother John and to his sisters. Also included in this collection were six letters from the American Board, from November 2, 1836, to January 15, 1838, concerning his appointment as a missionary. Asa's letters to the Board during this period are on file in Houghton Library of Harvard University. Thus both sides of the correspondence were made available to me. From these letters we are able to know more about Asa Smith's early life and student days than we know about any other member of the Oregon Mission of the American Board. We see here revealed the motivation which led him to volunteer to go to a "heathen land" as a missionary, and we also see certain personality traits emerging which later contributed much to the difficulties which disturbed the life of the Oregon Mission.

Included in the collection of items sent to me by Richard W. Smith were some twenty letters and other documents dealing with Smith's experiences in the Hawaiian Mission where he served from 1842-45. A third part of the collection, consisting of ten items, deals with Smith's experiences after his return to New England in May 1846. That part of this collection which concerns Hawaii has been deposited in the library of the Hawaiian Mission Children's Society in Honolulu. The other items are now in the Yale University Library.

After consultation with my publishers, it was decided that Sarah Smith's diary, Asa Smith's letters dealing with their travel experiences en route to Oregon and their life at Kamiah, together with some related documents were of sufficient interest and importance to justify the publication of this third volume of *The First White Women over the Rockies*. The related documents include the journal of William Henry Gray, May 24 to July 10, 1838; the diary of Elkanah Walker, March 7 to May 15, 1838; a letter written by Cornelius Rogers at the Rendezvous, July 3, 1838; Marcus Whitman's hitherto unpublished letter of May 31, 1844; and the reminiscences of Cushing Eells covering his overland travel experiences of 1838. As can be noted, most of these documents refer to the experiences of the 1838 reenforcement to the Oregon Mission. A concluding chapter gives an appraisal of the American Board's experiment of sending six women over the Rocky Mountains.

This third volume of *The First White Women over the Rockies* brings the total number of my published works on the history of the Oregon Mission of the American Board to eight. And still the story is not completely told. Some important source documents remain unpublished and there is always the possibility of new material being discovered.

SIGNIFICANCE OF THE NEW MATERIAL

The publication of this volume makes available much new information regarding the travel experiences of the four newly-wedded couples of the 1838 reenforcement. The claim can justly be made that volumes II and III of this series give a much fuller documentation of the travel experiences of this party than that of any other Oregon-bound company of the pre-covered wagon era.

Mrs. Marcus Whitman and Mrs. Henry H. Spalding rode through the South Pass of the Rockies, in what is now west-central Wyoming, seven years before the first great covered wagon train rolled through that same gateway to Oregon. In those days riding horseback astride was considered highly improper for white women. The 1836 mission party did take a wagon with them part way for the convenience of the women, yet Mrs. Whitman and Mrs. Spalding rode most of the 1,900 miles from the Missouri frontier to Fort Walla Walla on side-saddles! Looking back on her experiences, Narcissa Whitman described it as "an unheard-of journey for females."

No other white women had crossed the Rockies after the Whitman-Spalding party until the American Board sent out its reenforcement for the Oregon Mission in 1838. Four newly-wedded couples were in this party, namely, Rev. and Mrs. Elkanah Walker, Rev. and Mrs. Cushing Eells, Rev. and Mrs. Asa B. Smith, and Mr. and Mrs. William H. Gray. With them was a single man, Cornelius Rogers, who joined the party in an unofficial capacity at Cincinnati. The women of this second party, like the two who preceded them, rode most of the 1,900 miles on horseback, side-saddle. This party also took a wagon for the first part of the journey but only a few references have been found of any of the women taking advantage of riding in it.

After leaving the western frontier, all members of the two mission parties had to endure the same kind of life common to the men of the fur company with which they traveled. They slept on the ground. After their first meager stock of provisions was exhausted, they lived on wild game, especially buffalo meat both fresh and dried. They were exposed to wind and rain storms, to extremes of temperature. They had to ford deep and dangerous rivers. They followed trails that clung precariously to the sides of deep canyons. They were obliged to travel with the caravan and were therefore rarely able to observe a day of rest on Sunday. Their route took them through the uncivilized Indian country, sometimes through areas occupied by hostile tribes. Listed among their trials were not only the physical hardships endured but also the petty and sometimes more irritating annoyances which arose out of fatigue and the clash of personalities. The fact that these people were missionaries, all devoted to the same great objective of evangelizing the Indians, did not negate the fact that they were very human in their reactions to one another. Sometimes they disagreed and sometimes some of the women wept.

The overland travel experiences of the four women who were in the 1838 party were similar to those endured by Narcissa Whitman and Eliza Spalding. For Mary Walker, Myra Eells, Mary Gray, and Sarah Smith, this too was "an unheard-of journey for females."

In a very real sense, this volume comes as the climax to the series already published, as it completes and rounds out certain aspects of the history previously told. More light is thrown upon the hardships endured in their overland travels. More detail is herein given regarding the difficulties and trials of their daily lives in their respective stations when surrounded by Indians who knew not the white man's law. New information is also given concerning the clash of personalities within the mission band which, through a series of events covering several years, led to Whitman's famous ride East in 1842-43. Although there was some basis of friction between Whitman and Spalding long before the 1838 reenforcement arrived in Oregon, the real trouble-makers were Smith and Gray. Such deep antipathies had developed between these two, even before they reached the Rendezvous of 1838, as to make effective cooperation impossible. This clash of personalities became the great misfortune of the Oregon Mission of the American Board.

None of my seven volumes on the history of the Oregon Mission previously published brings out so clearly the cleavage within the Mission as does this third volume of *The First White Women over the Rockies.*

Biographical Sketches

of

Asa Bowen Smith

and

Sarah Gilbert White

to March 1838

Biographical Sketches of
Asa Smith and Sarah White

On July 16, 1809, a son was born to Mr. and Mrs. Asa Smith, Jr., at Williamstown,[1] a small rural community nestled in a deep valley in north-central Vermont. He was named Asa after his father and given the middle name of Bowen, the surname of his maternal grandmother. On September 14, 1813, a little more than four years later and about two hundred miles south of Williamstown, a daughter arrived in the home of Deacon and Mrs. Alfred White of West Brookfield, Massachusetts, who was christened Sarah Gilbert.[2] These two, Asa Bowen Smith and Sarah Gilbert White, were married at West Brookfield on March 15, 1838, and left that same day for far-away Oregon.

ASA BOWEN SMITH'S EARLY LIFE

In his letter of application for an appointment under the American Board dated October 21, 1836, Asa summarized his early years by writing: "My parents were both pious [3] so that I was under a religious influence from my childhood. My father was a farmer in which business I was employed most of the time till the age of twenty one."

Thirteen children were born to Mr. and Mrs. Asa Smith, Jr., of whom only three sons and three daughters were alive during Asa Bowen's adulthood. An older brother by eight years, Oren, was off on his own before Asa left for college and does not figure in Asa's correspondence. John Curtis, fourteen months younger, was the recipient of many letters now in the Asa B. Smith Collection in Yale University Library. The three sisters, who are frequently mentioned in Asa's extant correspondence, were all younger than he. They were Laura and the twins, Marcia

---

[1] During Asa Smith's life, Williamstown was known as East Williamstown. To avoid confusion, the present day name is used.

[2] The tombstone marking the graves of Asa and Sarah Smith at Buckland, Massachusetts, states that Sarah was born on April 14, 1813, instead of September 14th. *The Memorial Sketches* by A. C. Hodge and correspondence from Miss Alice J. White, a niece of Sarah White Smith in Coll. Ha., support the latter date. The author, therefore, feels that the date given on the tombstone is in error.

[3] The word "pious" was then used as a synonym for the words devout or godly.

and Lucia. Asa's letters show that strong bonds of affection bound him closely to his younger brother and sisters.

There is abundant evidence to indicate that the Smith family was deeply religious. The parents maintained the family altar. Sunday, or Sabbath as the day was then called, was strictly observed by refraining from all unnecessary work and travel and of course by attending religious services in the meeting house when such were held. A Congregational church, the center of the life of the community, had been organized in Williamstown on August 13, 1795. The original building is still standing.

Asa Bowen's educational opportunities during his minority were strictly limited. His father was in very modest circumstances and so felt the necessity of keeping his sons on the farm until they became twenty-one. Regarding those early days, Asa wrote in his letter of application to the Board: "I had, however, during the three last years I spent on the farm, by spending a few weeks at a time in school & employing all my leisure time while on the farm, prepared myself for Coll. so that I entered Burlington Coll. at the age of twenty one." Following the death of Asa B. Smith in 1886, a twenty-seven page pamphlet by A. C. Hodge was published in Boston under the title *Memorial Sketches of Rev. Asa B. Smith, Sarah G. Smith, and Harriet E. Smith,*[4] which contains the following observations: "He was always studious and became very anxious to obtain an education. . . He prepared for college solely by studying at home and reciting to a lawyer in town. . . His anxiety to progress rapidly led him to take his Latin book to the sugar camp one season, with the view of combining work and study. The experiment was not deemed satisfactory by his father."

COLLEGE YEARS, 1830-34

Upon reaching his majority in July 1830, Asa was free to pursue his education but without any evident financial assistance from his home. The very fact that he was qualified to matriculate at Burlington College, now the University of Vermont, on August 31, 1830, without first being graduated from some academy, speaks highly of his ability to educate himself. Needing money, Asa taught school during the winter of 1830-31 at Washington, Vermont, within ten miles of his home.

[4] Much of the material from this *Memorial Sketches* appeared in an article by the Rev. Myron Eells, a son of Cushing Eells, entitled "Rev. Asa Bowen Smith, the biography of a missionary," *Washington Historian*, April 1901.

According to a report in *Memorial Sketches*, the locality was "a very godless place." There Asa learned to dance! When he returned home on a visit, he taught the art to his sisters and this shocked his mother. Dancing was not permitted in that Puritan-minded home. Greatly troubled over her son's spiritual condition, the mother "talked earnestly with him about it."

Shortly after Asa's return to college in the spring of 1831, a religious revival swept through the community. Of this Asa wrote in his letter of October 21, 1836, to the Board: "Nothing but ambition seemed to engage my attention during the hours of the holy Sabbath. Such was my condition when I entered Coll. & such it remained till the spring term of my freshman year, when it pleased the Lord to bring my stubborn heart to bow in submission to his will. I had been the subject of serious impressions repeatedly before that time, but I had resisted them all. At that time, I trust I made a full & hearty surrender of myself to the Savior & my inquiry was, 'Lord, what wilt thou have me to do?'"

Church records show that Asa joined the First Congregational Church of Burlington on June 23, 1831, and that he transferred his membership a few days later, or on June 29th, to his home church in Williamstown. In his letter of application to the Board, he wrote: "I immediately decided that it was my duty to preach the gospel." This was characteristic of Asa Smith. He had the zeal of a new convert. It was not enough just to be a church member. His commitment to Christ demanded that he take the next step: he would become a minister. Fired with an all-consuming religious zeal, Asa returned to his home and helped plan some "protracted meetings" for his community. These meetings resulted in the conversion of, among others, his two brothers and three sisters.

Asa's decision to enter the ministry and his evident religious zeal commended him to the American Education Society and they granted him a scholarship. This society, founded in 1815, was supported by the Congregationalists and Presbyterians for the purpose of assisting indigent students to prepare for the ministry. It is possible that the dubious orthodoxy of Burlington College led Asa to transfer to Middlebury College in the fall of 1832 or at the beginning of his junior year. This was a Congregational-sponsored institution of undoubted orthodoxy. "There," wrote Asa, "I was brought under a direct missionary influence. . . As I examined the subject, I became fully satisfied that a far greater number of our young men ought to go to the heathen & I could see no way of evading the command of Christ 'to preach the gospel to every creature'." Again, he was being consistent with his religious commitment by taking the next logical step. He would be a missionary.

In his letter of application to the Board, Asa explained: "I felt that I was unfit for such a work, but as others who were better fitted were unwilling to go, I felt that there was a still stronger obligation resting on me. I considered the perishing condition of the heathen & I could not content myself to stay at home & let them perish without an effort to save them. After careful examination of the subject with fasting & prayer, not being able to find any good reason why I should not be a missionary, I deliberately came to the decision to devote my life to the service of God among the heathen, should he see fit thus to use me. This decision was made Nov. 1832."

Here we see the religious motivation which led Asa to volunteer to go as a foreign missionary expressed in the terms and thought patterns common to ecclesiastical circles of that day. The words "heathen" and "pagan" were not then used in any derogatory sense. They were merely synonyms for "non-Christian."

The Asa B. Smith Collection at Yale includes fourteen letters written by Asa when he was a student at Middlebury College to his brother John who was attending an academy at Barre, Vermont. The first of this series, dated October 27, 1832, might on first reading be considered nothing more than an earnest exhortation for John to serve Christ by becoming a minister. The key sentence is: "You ought to do good in the world & thereby glorify God." This is more than an exhortation; this is an exposition of the central theme of the New England theology then current. This theology, the first indigenous theology to arise on American soil, found its best expression in the Second Great Awakening which began about 1800. The main emphasis was known as "disinterested benevolence." One should do good for the sake of goodness and without any thought or expectation of reward. This dynamic theological concept gave birth to a number of interdenominational movements such as the American Bible Society; the Colonization Society, dedicated to the idea of sending free Negroes back to Africa; abolition societies; and various missionary bodies including the American Board of Commissioners for Foreign Missions. Indeed it can truthfully be claimed that the so-called "social gospel" of a later generation began in this New England theology.

In this same letter of October 27th to John, Asa was not only urging his brother "to do good in the world & thereby glorify God," but he also indicated that he himself was being moved by the same principle. "I am almost persuaded it is my duty to become a missionary," he wrote. "I think if it be the Lord's will to go to heathen lands & spend my days in teaching the deluded pagans the way of salvation. The greatest obstacle in the way is I am not holy enough." Repeatedly in other letters Asa urged his brother to join him in the ministry and also to become a missionary. This John did and served as a missionary under the American Board in Ceylon from 1842 to 1872.

Asa's letters reveal student costs of those days. Middlebury College was then advertising the total expense per student for an academic term of forty weeks as $86.00. This included $20.00 for tuition; room rent for two in a room, $6.00; library and other fees, $8.00; and board for $42.00 or a little more than $1.00 a week. Asa was wearing home-spun and referred to the fact that his sisters were weaving the cloth from which his suits were being made. "I take pleasure in wearing homespun," he commented, "for I feel it is doing right & again I see it pleases my benefactors." The reference is to the Education Society which had granted him scholarship aid as a student for the ministry. Often when Asa visited his home in Vermont or when he found it necessary to go some other place, he walked. His letters contain a number of references to walking from twenty to one hundred miles.

Anticipating an appointment as a missionary to some foreign land, Asa felt during his senior year at college that some medical knowledge was essential. From a letter written to John on November 19, 1833, we learn that he was then reading medical books. "Besides my college studies," he wrote, "I have pursued the study of medicine as I have had opportunity & have finished anatomy & read about 150 pages in Physiology. . . I shall be able if Providence favors to accomplish a good years study in medicine by the time I get through college." This letter contains the following revealing self-diagnosis which should be remembered when we come to the story of Asa's difficulties with his associates in the Oregon Mission and, in fact, all through his life. Referring to his health, he wrote: "My health has been improving, rather than to the contrary. I have been vigorous in mind & body. Perfectly free from all distressing hypochondriac feelings." By his own admission, Asa was a pessimist and greatly concerned about his health.

Taking advantage of the spring vacation of 1834, Asa attended five weeks of lectures at Vermont Medical College at Woodstock. Medical education in the United States was still in its infancy. This college had been established in 1826. Friends contributed the cost including board, room, and tuition. In a letter to his brother dated April 30th, Asa told about arriving in Woodstock at 7:00 a.m. that morning "& at 8 went into the lecture room & was introduced to a dead body." He added: "Thus far the Lord has prospered me in my endeavors to prepare myself for the work of the Lord among the heathen." Asa returned to his college by walking the fifty miles from Woodstock, Vermont to Middlebury, Vermont.

Following his graduation from Middlebury College in the summer, Asa went to Pittsfield, Massachusetts, where he enrolled for a five- or six-weeks' course in the Berkshire Medical College. Here one of the members of the faculty, Dr. Childs, took a special interest in the young man, received Asa into his home, and gave him free board and room. Other friends contributed the cost of tuition. About one hundred miles northwest of Pittsfield was Fairfield, New York, in Herkimer County, where the College of Physicians and Surgeons of the Western District of New York was located. There Marcus Whitman had studied for two terms of sixteen weeks each in 1825-26 and in 1831-32, receiving his M.D. degree in January 1832. With the exception of Dr. Whitman, Asa B. Smith had more medical education than any other member of the Oregon Mission.

ANDOVER SEMINARY, 1834-35

On October 16, 1834, Asa enrolled in Andover Theological Semniary at Andover, Massachusetts. He was thrilled with his surroundings and with the opportunities opening up for an intensive study of theology. "This is a holy place," he wrote to his brother John on November 13th, "and we have holy men for instructors." He was good at languages and having previously studied Hebrew and Greek, found the language requirements rather easy.

In the first extant letter written from the seminary, Asa reveals to his brother his pathetic struggle to keep out of further debt. The aid received from the Education Society was not sufficient to meet all expenses and he was already about $50.00 in arrears, which by the standards of that day was considerable. Asa and a fellow student referred to as "Brother Clark" decided "to board ourselves this term, so as not to run in debt & have something to buy books. We have lived on crackers softened in water & molasses. Buy broken crackers for 5¢ per lb. & molasses for 2/ per gal. [i.e., two shillings or about 50¢ per gallon]. 5 lbs of crackers & 1 qt of molasses per week is sufficient, so it costs not more than 2/ per week. Thus far agrees with me very well."

Writing to his sisters a few days later, or on November 16th, Asa refers to the same spartan diet and explains that they soak the crackers in hot water, "add salt & molasses & it makes a very good dish." But from the following plea for a box of provisions to be sent from his home, it is evident that he soon felt the need for a more balanced diet. The list is interesting when we remember that these were the items a farm could supply before the days of tin cans and artificial refrigeration. Asa wrote:

"I have thought, as I suppose father will come this way to Boston in the winter, of writing to have you send me some things if convenient. If you would put up a box of provisions for me, it would be very acceptable. I could set it in the garret where it would keep frozen & it might be kept for weeks. . . A quantity of baked beans I think would go well enough to last 3 or 4 weeks. Bake with little meat in them, I don't care about any. I might eat a very little if I had it. If I were to have any meat, I should prefer a baked chicken or lean fresh pork." Here is evidence that Asa was inclined to be a vegetarian. Earlier that year, on July 11th, in a letter to his sisters he had stated: "I have tasted of no animal food & no butter but twice or three times when I have been away from home." Within four years Asa would be out on the great western prairies on his way to Oregon where the only available food would be fresh buffalo meat. A strange predicament for a vegetarian! We note many references to food in his letters written at that time.

Asa's list of needs continues: "Three or four loaves of brown bread, some plain nut-cakes & such things may be convenient. I should eat some cheese if I had it as I have no milk or any thing of the kind — butter I do not care about. Some dried apples or apple-sauce if convenient. If I had a peck of beans, I could boil them. I got one qt. & boiled them & they went well. You may make me, if you please, a bag of coarse cotton to carry my clothes in to wash & you may put in a few qts. of Indian meal to send me, if you please. If you can send these things without trouble, it would save me money & I should have the comfort of having something from home. If you would make some seabisquit, it would be kept ever so long. It is made of flour & cold water without yeast or any thing else & baked in thin cakes as thin as crackers so that they are perfectly dry. Soak them & they are as good as any bread."

Asa and his roommate did not stay on this meager diet of crackers and molasses for many weeks as in a letter to his brother dated January 25, 1835, he told of a doctor warning them about it. He then wrote: "I am satisfied it is not judicious to live as I did. . . A person may take too little nourishment as well as too much & I am inclined to think that either animal food or milk is necessary." As will be noticed in his letters, Asa remained somewhat fastidious about his food.

In order to help students earn some money, Andover Theological Seminary maintained a carpenter shop where the students could make furniture. Writing to his brother on November 13, 1834, Asa reported that he was making a bedstead but added: "We realize scarcely anything for work." Such little skill as he here gained with tools was to come in very handy a few years later when he found it necessary to erect and furnish his log cabin in the wilds of what is now northern Idaho.

On April 25, 1835, Asa, from Andover Seminary, writing to his brother John, then a student at Middlebury College, said: "As I have now finished my studying for this term . . . I expect to start late [Tuesday] afternoon to walk to Vermont." The distance was nearly one hundred miles. In this letter he also indicated his intention to return to the medical college at Woodstock that spring. He was back in the seminary for the summer months and on September 1st he left for Pittsfield, Massachusetts, to take part in a revival. Since Asa remained in Pittsfield for about six weeks, again it seems probable that he made good use of the time by attending more lectures in the medical college of that place.

In all probability while in Pittsfield on this visit, Asa met an attractive and vivacious red-haired girl, Miss Sarah Gilbert White, of West Brookfield, Massachusetts, who may have been a student at a female seminary in that city at that time. He learned that her father was a deacon in the Congregational Church of her home town, and that her sister, Adeline, had gone out as a missionary to Singapore. And more important still, he became aware of her deep and sincere interest in foreign missions. Like her elder sister, Sarah wanted to be a missionary. This common desire drew them together.

Writing to his brother John from Andover on October 19th, Asa told of returning to the seminary from Pittsfield via West Brookfield. Possibly Sarah accompanied him in the stagecoach for that first part of his travels and invited him to break his journey at her town and be a guest in her parents' home. In this letter to his brother, Asa wrote: "I spent a day in Brookfield, Ms. as I came from P. & passed the night at Dea. White's, the father of Mrs. Tracy, & such a family I never before found.

They are farmers in handsome circumstances & ready to part with every child to go among the heathen should the Lord call & rejoice to do it. O that every pious parent had the same feeling, then would the world soon be supplied with missionaries." Asa discreetly refrained from mentioning by name the second daughter of the White family who had already awakened his interest.

SARAH GILBERT WHITE'S EARLY LIFE

West Brookfield is an old town in south-central Massachusetts. The Congregational Church there was founded in 1717. In 1967 this church plans to celebrate its 250th anniversary. Among the oldest families in the town are the Whites and the Gilberts. Sarah's father, Deacon Alfred White, was a descendant of Sergeant John White, who was killed by the Indians at Brookfield on July 20, 1710. Sarah's mother was a Gilbert, which accounts for her middle name. Deacon and Mrs. White were parents of three daughters, Adeline, Sarah, and Roxana, and one son, Samuel. Deep ties of affection bound the family together. The original White homestead, built about 1707-08, is still standing. This with later additions is now known as Salem Cross Inn.

Sarah had a religious experience which left a life-long impression on her when she was fifteen, but for some unknown reason did not unite with the local church until 1835 when she was twenty-two. In 1834, Adeline, Sarah's older sister by four years, sailed for Singapore as a single woman missionary under the American Board. Shortly after her arrival, she was married to Ira Tracy, the pioneer missionary of the Board to that place. It is possible that the two were engaged before Adeline sailed. Adeline's decision to be a missionary had great influence on Sarah, who resolved, the Lord willing, to follow her example. In a day when the whole foreign missionary enterprise of American Protestantism was in its infancy, the fact that the White family of West Brookfield gave two of its daughters to this cause speaks eloquently of the religious devotion of the home. This was Sarah's heritage.

Little is known about Sarah's youth and early education. Hodge in his *Memorial Sketches* states: "Her early years were spent in quiet seclusion of her country home," and also that "she attended . . . a preparatory school in her own town, afterwards in the seminary at Pittsfield, Mass., and lastly at Murdock Place Seminary, New Haven, Conn. In these institutions she ranked high as an intelligent student."

Sarah was of small stature and at the time Asa first met her, she was of good but not rugged health. She seems to have had a cheerful disposition and her diary shows that she and her husband enjoyed playful banter. To the best of the author's recollections, Sarah Smith is the only one of the mission band who mentioned laughter in any diary or letter. In her diary for June 11, 1838, she referred to the incident of Mrs. Walker sitting on her baggage and weeping when she remembered how comfortable her father's hogs were back in the Maine barn. "This," wrote Sarah, "made us both laugh & cry together."

Evidently Sarah was attending the Pittsfield seminary in the early fall of 1835 when she first met Asa. We do not know just where she was during the academic year, 1835-36. Asa in his letter of March 3, 1837, to the Board, in which he wrote about his fiancée, mentioned the fact that she had been successful as a school teacher. We do know that during this year Asa was taking his second year's work at Andover Theological Seminary. This was the year in which they carried on their courtship, undoubtedly largely through correspondence. None of their love letters has been discovered.

In the fall of 1836 Sarah enrolled in Murdock Place Seminary in New Haven. All efforts to find further information about this school have failed. About the same time Asa transferred his theological studies from Andover to the Theological Seminary of Yale College, now known as Yale Divinity School. Thus during the academic year of 1836-37, both Sarah and Asa were in New Haven where they had opportunity to see each other frequently. Sometime, probably in October, 1836, Asa proposed marriage and Sarah accepted.

APPOINTED BY THE AMERICAN BOARD

For at least three years Asa had entertained the idea of becoming a foreign missionary. In his letter of October 19, 1835, to his brother John, he had written: "I long to be on heathen ground laboring for God. It is pleasant to labor for the salvation of souls & who can be idle when millions are perishing?" In his idealization of the role of a foreign missionary, Asa was unwittingly preparing himself for future trouble. After his arrival in Oregon and when confronted with the actual conditions of missionary work, he quickly discovered that his conception of "preaching the gospel to the heathen" did not harmonize with the harsh realities of life. Language difficulties, the self-interest of the natives, and honest differences of opinion regarding missionary methods held by his colleagues — all these and more took the romance and the anticipated joy out of his work. He became thoroughly disillusioned. But any thought of leaving brought further distress, as this would mean a repudiation of much that he had preached in New England before he left for Oregon. Any retreat would mean loss of face. This conflict of idealism with reality precipitated an emotional crisis which goes far towards explaining Asa Smith's difficulties while on the mission field.

In Asa's letter to his brother John, dated August 10, 1836, he referred to a trip he had taken when it was impossible to find opportunities for his "secret devotions." Without such opportunities for retirement, "one's piety must suffer." He emphasized his need for privacy when traveling by writing: "My religious feelings are in great danger of being impaired. Nothing is so necessary as retirement for reading the Scriptures, meditation & prayer. Without this we droop & die." This became an issue with Asa as he traveled with his colleagues across the prairies in the summer of 1838 with the fur company's caravan. He then found little time for private devotions and no privacy. As will be noted, he made frequent reference to the effect that this forced manner of life had upon their piety. The complaints made at that time can the better be appreciated when we remember his personality type.

Finding in Sarah complete agreement on the subject of being a foreign missionary, Asa in the summer of 1836 decided to submit his formal application to the American Board for an appointment. His file in the archives of the Board contains three letters of recommendation. The first was from one of his Andover professors, Dr. Leonard Woods, who on August 27th wrote: "Mr. Asa B. Smith . . . possesses very respectable talents & acquisitions & a good deal of manly energy & judgment, as I think. He is regarded as decidedly pious & as zealous in more than an ordinary degree, in the pursuit of great & good objects." Woods felt that he was well qualified for missionary service.

A second letter came from the Rev. Daniel Wild of Brookfield, Vermont, and was dated September 23rd. He wrote after a long acquaintance with Asa and testified that he "has always been a young man of steady habits," and that in college, "he was studious & stood above mediocrity in his class." The pastor of his home church, the Rev. A. Royce, praised his "fidelity, patience, fortitude and perseverance in the cause of Christ" and he too felt that Asa would be "a useful laborer in the vineyard of the Lord in foreign lands." Several of the officers of Royce's church added their signatures to his letter, endorsing his views.

Asa's letter of application was dated October 21, 1836, from "Yale Theol. Sem." in New Haven. He began by giving a brief resumé of his life, references to which have been previously made in this chapter. He explained his motivation and claimed that "for three years past I have had no doubts with regard to my duty." His exalted idea of the work of a missionary is found in his statement: "I ask no higher privilege on earth than to be engaged in the missionary work." In his discussion of a possible field of assignment, we find a reference to "the lady who is expecting to go out with me." This indicates that he and Sarah were already engaged.

Regarding his possible assignment, he wrote: "I have thought much of China, but it is my settled opinion that I am not the one to conquer that language. . . I have thought of Singapore & there is one reason for desiring to go there. The lady who is expecting to go out with me is a sister of Mrs. Tracy who is now at Singapore & it would be a gratification to her friends should we be sent to that place. . . Should it be thought best for me to labor among the Malays or Siamese in that region, I should be satisfied." There was no thought then of going to any tribe of American Indians. Rather he was thinking of some distant land across the seas.

Across the back of this letter of application is a notation in the handwriting of David Greene,[5] one of the secretaries of the American Board: "Appointed Nov. 1." Here is a good example of the way a candidate was appointed to be a foreign missionary back in 1836. Though it is possible that Asa previously had met one or more of the secretaries of the Board, we have no evidence of this. In all probability his appointment was made on the basis of three letters of recommendation and his own application. No physical examination was then required and of course a psychological analysis of the candidate's fitness was unthought of. Smith certainly had the necessary educational qualifications. He was apparently in good health and there was no doubt about his religious faith and missionary zeal. He seemed to be the ideal candidate. Moreover, the Board was faced with the fact that the number of young men offering to go to the foreign mission field was limited. And so Asa B. Smith was appointed without being assigned to any particular field at that time. As will be noted, when he was assigned, then he was commissioned.

---

[5] In addition to Greene, William J. Armstrong and Rufus Anderson were also serving as secretaries of the American Board. Each of these three had correspondence with Asa Smith and all three names appear on his commission, reproduced as an illustration in this book. Since Asa visited the offices of the Board in Boston several times, he no doubt had met each of these three secretaries. No other member of the Oregon Mission had such personal contacts with the secretaries as he.

SARAH SMITH'S GIRLHOOD HOME, WEST BROOKFIELD, MASSACHUSETTS

Originally built about 1708, and restored in 1960; now known as Salem Cross Inn. Surrounded by many comforts and some luxuries, Sarah was born and reared here. This she left to go with her husband to the wilderness of Oregon. See text page 33.

This is to Certify

That The Rev. Asa B. Smith

has been duly appointed, and is

hereby authorised to act as

a Missionary — of the

AMERICAN BOARD OF COMMISSIONERS FOR FOREIGN MISSIONS.

Boston, MASS. March 15th 1838 —

R. Anderson,
David Greene, } Secretaries.
Wm J Armstrong

ASA SMITH'S COMMISSION AS A MISSIONARY OF THE AMERICAN BOARD
The document bears the signatures of the three secretaries — Anderson, Greene, and Armstrong.
Text under the illustration is from Isaiah 9:2. Original in author's collection.

TWO PORTRAITS OF ASA BOWEN SMITH

Left: An unsigned miniature, at the age of 28 in 1837. See text pages 41-42. From
Missionary Album.

Right: A photograph probably taken when he was between 60 and 70 years of age.
From *Washington Historian,* April 1901; courtesy of Huntington Library.

The archives of the American Board contain eleven letters from Asa B. Smith from October 21, 1836, to January 11, 1838. The other half of the correspondence, including eight letters from the Board to Smith, are now in Yale University Library. From these letters we are able to gain a fairly clear picture as to what was happening to him during these fifteen months.

The main issue under discussion was the field to which Asa would go. In his letter of application he had suggested Singapore or Siam with the hope that he and Sarah could be somewhat near the Ira Tracys. Greene, in his reply of November 2nd, reported that the Board was not thinking of sending any workers to either place within the foreseeable future. Greene did suggest the possibility of the Board sending a reenforcement in the fall of 1837 to the Mahratta Mission in India and asked whether Smith might consider that location. In Asa's reply of November 14th, he said that he would not object to going to India. He wrote: "My desire is to go to that field where I can be of the most service to the cause of Christ." He also stated: "I have acquired considerable medical knowledge." During the academic year 1836-37, Asa was able to attend some of the lectures at the Yale Medical School. Whereas his medical studies were spread over several years and consisted of intermittent periods in three different medical schools, yet it seems evident that Asa probably had enough training by the limited standards of that day to have practiced medicine. After arriving in Oregon, we find no record of Asa ever consulting with Dr. Whitman regarding his own or his wife's health. It seems probable that Asa felt that he was just as competent a physician as Dr. Whitman even if he had not received the M.D. degree.

Asa and Sarah saw much of each other during the academic year, 1836-37, when both were living in New Haven. Asa was then a senior in the Theological Seminary at Yale and Sarah was attending a female seminary. The Board had informed Asa that it looked with disfavor upon any of its candidates for foreign service being married before being assigned to a definite mission and about to depart. Smith's studies at the Theological Seminary would end in August, after which he planned to be ordained. He was then ready to go to some foreign mission field. Asa and Sarah confidently looked forward to their marriage in the fall of 1837.

With the passing of the winter, the two felt that it was time to inform the Board about Sarah's qualifications and to get approval for her appointment. The Board did not then expect a personal application for appointment as a missionary from a woman who planned to marry someone who was commissioned. Of the six women in the Oregon Mission, only Narcissa Prentiss and Mary Richardson applied for an appointment and in each case this was before they were engaged and each was rejected because she was an "unmarried female." Each of the six was accepted as a missionary on the basis of her marriage and in no case was a physical examination required. In most instances, however, the Board did receive at least one letter of recommendation.

In line with this general policy, therefore, Asa and Sarah requested the Rev. F. Horton, pastor of Sarah's home church at West Brookfield, to send a testimonial to the Board. On March 3, 1837, he wrote:

DEAR BRETHREN. The object of this letter is to give you some information relative to the character & qualifications of Miss Sarah Gilbert White. She is a native of this place — daughter of Dea. Alfred White and sister of Mrs. Ira Tracy of Singapore.

Her training; from infancy there is reason to believe has been in some good measure in the way she should go. Her domestic advantages, temporal and spiritual, have been altogether more than usual. Nor has she failed to profit by the example & instruction of *industrious, prudent* and *pious* parents. I mean by this to express the opinion that in this respect her education is favorable to her being a worthy *wife*.

Miss White, I think, has a good degree of intellectual capacity (not a mind of *remarkable* strength), and is successful as a teacher within her sphere. Her literary acquirements are probably superior to that of Mrs. Tracy. She is to continue still at school, and I doubt not will be found qualified for missionary labor.

Her moral temperament is bland and equable — her disposition modest and peculiarly amiable — and yet I should think there is considerable energy. Few perhaps have so large a share of active benevolence with so small a measure of common faultness. Nay, I know not that she has any prominent faults.

Miss White has been a member of our church two years — and is supposed to have been a christian a longer period previous. Since making profession of her faith in Christ, her piety has appeared to be strengthening continually, and maturing for some generous purpose of well-being.

She is now 23 years of age. Her health, I believe, is uniformly good. Her reputation among her acquaintances is highly creditable, i.e., favorable to her contemplated connexion with a Foreign Missionary. Indeed no one I know doubts her fittness for such a station.

Her acquaintance with Mr. A. B. Smith, which has now been upwards of a year, has had in view from the first this great object, *the service of your Society as the way of serving her divine Master.*

The letter was signed also by two officers of the church with the notation, "We concur in the opinion above expressed." A notation on the back shows that the letter was not received until May 10th. In all probability Asa requested the letter be given to him for forwarding. On May 11th, a few days after putting the Horton letter in the mail, Asa also wrote to the Board regarding his fiancée's qualifications. He wrote in part:

According to the regulations of the Board, it becomes my duty to present to the Prudential Committee [6] the offer of service of Miss Sarah G. White . . . who has decided to go out as my companion in the missionary work. It is a year last Oct. since I became acquainted with Miss W. & I feel assured from the acquaintance I have had with her that she is one who will make a useful missionary & a valuable companion. . . Her father is a farmer & much of her life has been spent at home, where she has been trained to habits of industry & economy. Her opportunities for mental improvement have been very good. She has spent considerable time in teaching in which she has been very successful & her services are in good demand. . . She has always felt a deep interest in the cause of missions & indeed it may be said of her & the whole family, that it is *hereditary.* . . She looks upon it as a *privilege* to engage in the missionary work & it seems to be the desire of her heart to do good. The character of her piety is deep & ardent & she is eminently a person of prayer.

Sarah was not actually appointed by the American Board until it was definitely known that she and Asa were to be married and that they were going to Oregon. Then Secretary Greene took Horton's letter and wrote on the back: "Appointed March 13, 1838." That was two days before Asa and Sarah were married.

Among the letters in the Asa B. Smith Collection in Yale is one from Asa to his brother John dated from New Haven, August 4, 1837. After commenting on how much he and Sarah were enjoying each other's fellowship, he said: "We have had our miniatures taken for father White's people. Done very well $10. apiece. They will prize them very highly." A hundred years later, Miss Alice J. White, a grandniece of

---

[6] Today what was then called the Prudential Committee would probably be known as the Executive Committee. The name then used suggests the characteristic New England frugality in the stewardship of money.

Sarah's, lent those miniatures to the editor of the *Missionary Album* which was published in Honolulu in 1937. These pictures are reproduced in this volume. So far as is known, Asa and Sarah Smith were the only members of the Oregon Mission of the American Board to have had their portraits painted. The present location of the originals is unknown.

In order to supplement his income, Asa accepted a call as temporary pastor of a small church at Woodbridge, about five miles northwest of New Haven, sometime in the spring of 1837. This was in addition to his seminary work. Here his ministry was most successful, as is evidenced by the fact that forty united with the church in July of that year. Myron Eells, in his obituary notice of Asa Smith, reported that he was remembered with affection in that church some fifty years later.[7]

Asa attended the spring meeting of the American Board in Boston, held in May, and Sarah accompanied him. For this, as will be noted later, Asa was criticized by some who felt that it was improper for the two to travel together to Boston. The meeting undoubtedly made it necessary to spend one or more nights in the city, but there can be no question but that the two spent the night in separate homes or in different rooms at an inn. There Asa learned of the financial difficulties the Board was experiencing due to a general business recession. The Board was then facing the possibility of cancelling all sailings for the fall of 1837. This was most distressing news to Asa and Sarah.

After returning to New Haven, Asa on June 6th wrote to the Board proposing the rather drastic, and certainly unrealistic, idea of working his way to some foreign land as a common seaman:

> What course shall I take in order to awaken the churches to the greatest possible extent to their duty in giving the gospel to the heathen . . . that we must go whether the churches will furnish the means or not — go I say even if we must work our passage & support ourselves on the ground by the labor of our own hands. This appears to me to be the apostolic spirit. It was the spirit of the Moravian Brethren. . . Why, I ask, should not every missionary take this ground? Let us come before the churches & say to them, We *must* go to the heathen & if you will not furnish us the means, then we must go without means. Let us make the experiment if necessary, let us "go before the mast" & earn our bread with our own hands as Paul did, & will not this

---

[7] *Washington Historian*, April 1901, p. 66.

arouse the churches to their duty? . . . *I cannot, I dare not* give up the idea of preaching the gospel to the heathen even if the churches will not furnish the means. . . Shall the experiment of sustaining ourselves be tried? . . . For my part I am willing to make the experiment & if my life must be sacrificed to arouse the churches from their stupidity, then I say "Here am I, Lord, send me."

Secretary Rufus Anderson replied on June 9th and dismissed the proposal as utterly impractical. "In the panic which is now on the public mind," he wrote, "your working your way to the field of your mission would excite very little attention; it would pass for one of the *ultrainess* [8] of the day. Besides, in the paralized state of commerce, you might not find it so easy to work your way. The taking of a wife with you, would be out of the question." Anderson advised Smith to be "as patient as you can."

When the reenforcement of 1838 crossed the plains and the mountains on its way to Oregon, the men found it necessary to work exceedingly hard in packing and unpacking their animals and doing the other things necessary to remain with the caravan. As will be noted later, Asa then complained bitterly of the fact that they had to work their passage to Oregon.

The financial condition of the Board became so serious that it was necessary to inform all missionaries of the situation in a circular dated June 26, 1837. The Board then reported that even though the annual expenditures would be reduced to about $230,000, yet it faced an expected deficit of about $45,000 by September. In other words, the debt would amount to about 20% of the annual budget. Because of this situation, some of the missionaries whom the Board was planning to send out in the fall of 1837 could not leave. Asa learned of this situation with dismay as it meant that he and Sarah would not be able to go to some field. In turn this meant that their marriage would have to be postponed. There was also the question as to what he would do to earn a living in the meantime.

Asa notified the Board that he was ready to serve as an agent to raise funds for the missionary cause. Secretary William J. Armstrong, writing on July 26th, authorized Asa "to act as an Agent . . . in the vicinity where you now are. . . Whatever travelling expenses you may incur in this work, will be defrayed by the Board." Asa responded to this opportunity with enthusiasm. He hoped that by helping

---

[8] An unusual form of the word "ultraism," i.e., being an extremist.

to raise money for the Board, he would to that extent increase the possibility of being sent out that fall. Reporting to the Board on August 9th, Asa said: 'Thus far I am much encouraged in my labors, & I am satisfied that some of the churches of this region will do more than they have ever done before." Again he inquired as to the possibility of being sent out that fall. "I am ready to go at a few weeks notice any time," he wrote. "I have nothing to do but prepare my outfit & bid my friends farewell." He repeated his hope that he would be sent to Siam.

Following his graduation from the Theological Seminary in August, Asa found himself without steady employment and this meant without an assured income. The uncertainty of his position only increased his restlessness. Plans were made for his ordination in his home church at Williamstown, Vermont, on November 1st. In September, Asa visited the Whites in West Brookfield from which place he wrote to the Board on September 26th. "Is there any prospect that the state of the treasury will be such that I can be sent out before winter? . . . I need not say that I am very anxious to be sent this fall. . . The time has come when I expected to go. It is a time to which I have been looking forward for about 5 years with intense interest. All my calculations have been made in reference to it." Asa felt the urgency of getting on the field and preaching the gospel "to the perishing heathen." "I feel that I have no time to spare," he added, belaboring his point. "I shall have short time enough to labor among the heathen if I go immediately. . . I am willing to do any thing that is possible to sustain me even if it be to work with my hands as Paul did. . . In my present situation I know not what to do, or what calculations to make."

Secretary Anderson replied on October 13th and, as directed by Asa, addressed the letter to Asa's parental home in Vermont. The letter carried one welcomed bit of news. "The Committee have resolved upon designating you to Siam," Anderson wrote. Then came the discouraging report: "There is no probability that you can go this fall. How much there is that you can go next spring, I cannot tell. . . As the receipts now are, we are gaining no headway. . . The finances of the country are in a disordered state."

Asa had returned to his home in Williamstown to visit his relatives and friends and to await his ordination which was scheduled to be held in his home church on November 1st. Anderson's letter of October 13th plunged him into the depths of despair and frustration. He replied on October 25th saying in part: "The fact that I am detained here after having accomplished my course of preparation is in itself painful.

My field of labor has been designated & I look upon Siam as my home so long as I remain in this world. It is there I wish to spend my days & find my grave. . . The field to which I am designated is already white for the harvest, & the harvest is ready to perish for want of laborers. . . While I am detained here, souls are sinking into a wretched eternity beyond the reach of my influence."

Asa referred to his financial problem. "I must be settled down somewhere, where I can labor to advantage," he wrote. "To be in this unsettled state is very trying." Again he offered his services to the Board as an agent for the raising of funds.

Asa wanted to get married and in the following sentence he indicated that he knew about and was willing to practice some method of birth control.

If I am to be settled in any place while I am detained, it is my wish to be married. We both feel that we can be more happy & useful to be thus situated than we can to be separated. I know that there is a serious objection to this course & that the Board are wise in objecting for it might throw obstacles in the way of going out. But there is no necessity for this, & after thinking much on the subject & with some facts before me, I am inclined to think that there has been an error with many who have gone out in being in haste about having a family & much inconvenience & danger has been the result. Therefore I have made up my mind that whatever time I may be married, I will not take any step towards having a family till I have arrived at my field of labor. Taking this course, I can see no reason for deferring marriage till near the time of sailing. I know not why I do not need the assistance & sympathy of a wife as much while detained here as I shall hereafter. . . I should not however wish to take this step without your consent.

Asa's letter brought an immediate and stinging response from Secretary Anderson in a letter dated November 3rd. As has been noted, Asa kept his correspondence from the Board. This has been preserved by members of the Smith family to the present time, and is now in the archives of Yale University Library. But Asa did not keep this letter of November 3rd. We know in general its contents from Asa's humble reply of the 7th. He then wrote: "Yours of the 3rd inst. I rec'd yesterday & I thank you for your advice on the subject I proposed. I should be very unwilling to take any step which would hinder me from going among the heathen nor am I willing to act contrary to the wishes or advice of the Prudential Committee." Then Asa turned to some criticisms which Secretary Anderson had passed on about Asa taking Sarah with him on some of his trips: "Thank you, dear Sir, for your kindness in mentioning the report which has come to you concerning me. This was very unexpected to me for I was not aware that I had given any reasonable occasion for finding fault. I am grieved that any such report should have been made & it is very singular that I did not hear something about it while I was in the region where the report originated. . .

As to my riding in the manner mentioned, I can say that Miss W. was attending school in New Haven, & that at the urgent request of friends she did in one or two instances go out with me to spend the sabbath with them. I did not dream that any one would find fault with this. It was among my own friends & acquaintances. . . It was too at the soliticitation of ministers of the gospel. She went with me last spring to Boston & also to the meeting of the Board & I supposed this was perfectly right. I did not suppose that any one could find fault with it. Perhaps in order to avoid the appearance of evil, I ought not to have gone in company with her at all. In future I shall endeavor to be more cautious.

Asa was still undecided as to how or where he would spend the winter. He reported the fact that he had been ordained on November 1st. The Asa B. Smith Collection in Yale contains a manuscript giving the original minutes of an "ecclesiastical council" which convened in the home of the Rev. Andrew Royce in Williamstown on Tuesday, October 31st for the purpose of examining Asa's qualifications for ordination as a Congregational minister and if satisfactory to make plans for such a service. Five ministers of the vicinity, each with a deacon, were present. The testimonials submitted by Asa were found to be perfectly satisfactory. Recognition was made of the fact that he was under appointment by the American Board to go as a missionary to Siam. The ordination service was held the next morning in the Williamstown church. Asa was now the Reverend Asa B. Smith, both sensitive and proud of the rights and privileges bestowed upon him by his church through ordination.

Information is wanting as to just where Asa spent all of his time after his ordination and prior to his marriage on March 15, 1838. His keen interest in the study of medicine prompted him to turn to a cousin who was a doctor at Oxford, Massachusetts, a village about eleven miles south and a little to the west of Worcester. After not hearing from the Board for several months, he directed another letter of inquiry from Oxford on January 11, 1838. He had been reading the last numbers of the *Missionary Herald* and had learned of the return of William H. Gray from Oregon and of the intention of the Board to send out a reenforcement in 1838. Here for the first time Asa makes mention of the Nez Perces in his correspondence.

"I see . . . that 5 are to be sent early in the spring to the Nez Perces Indians. I should like to know what individuals are going there. But more particularly I should like to know how many have been designated to Siam, who they are & where they are at present. . . I should like to know also what is the present prospect of our going out in the spring." Asa was encouraged by the report that the financial condition of the Board had been improving. His letter shows his characteristic impatience:

I am at present with Dr. Paine, a cousin of mine in this place, studying medicine. I find no place to preach partly because there are but few destitute places in this part of the country & partly because I will not consent to settle. I should not care anything about it if I had the means to support myself for I can profitably spend my time in studying. . . The time of our detention is one of peculiar trial & it has been my earnest prayer that these days of affliction may be shortened. . . Orders to sail for Siam would be like *cold water to a thirsty soul*. I trust that before many weeks shall pass away I may receive such orders.

DESTINATION — OREGON

Other events were taking place in the meantime which were destined to change the lives of Asa and Sarah. The American Board in 1836 had sent a party of five missionaries overland to Oregon. They were Dr. and Mrs. Marcus Whitman, the Rev. and Mrs. Henry H. Spalding, and William Henry Gray, a mechanic. All were Presbyterians. These missionaries received such an enthusiastic welcome from the natives that Gray returned East in 1837 to induce the Board to send out reenforcements. The fact that Gray was engaged and wanted to be married was, no doubt, an important but unofficial reason for his return.

Gray wrote to the Rev. David Greene, the secretary of the American Board in charge of work among the American Indians, from Ithaca, New York, on October 19, 1837, giving a glowing account of the possibilities of mission work among the Cayuse and Nez Perce Indians. The appeal came at an opportune time as the Board's financial outlook had greatly improved that fall. The Prudential Committee of the Board met in Boston on December 5th and voted to send Elkanah Walker and Cushing Eells to the Oregon Mission should each be willing. These two had been designated for work among the Zulus of South Africa but tribal warfare had prevented their departure. Each was engaged and each had delayed marriage until he was ready to leave for his mission field.

Secretary Greene wrote to Elkanah Walker on December 6th asking whether or not he would be willing to go to Oregon in 1838 with Gray. Walker replied on December 23rd expressing his willingness but confessed that he had not consulted his fiancée, Miss Mary Richardson. "I am pretty confident," he wrote, "that she has always been in favor of going to some of the stations among the Indians." When informed of the change of destination, Mary made no objection. A similar inquiry was sent to Cushing Eells who also agreed to go to Oregon. His fiancée, Myra Fairbanks, also consented. Thus the board was assured of five including Gray for the reenforcement.

As an avid reader of the *Missionary Herald,* the official publication of the American Board, Asa was aware of the establishment of the Oregon Mission in 1836. The October 1837 number had carried about six thousand words of a letter written by Spalding on September 20, 1836, in which Spalding had described their overland travel experiences and the initial enthusiastic reception given the missionaries by the natives. Another optimistic letter from Spalding, dated February 17, 1837, occupied five pages of the December 1837 issue of the *Herald.* After learning that the financial condition of the Board had so improved that a reenforcement to the Oregon Mission was being planned, Asa took heart. As indicated in the quotation from his January 11th letter given above, he was sufficiently interested to ask who were the parties designated for Oregon. Greene replied on January 15th:

> Only two ordained missionaries are expected to go in the company for the Nez Perce Indians which is to set out early in the spring. They are Messrs Walker & Eells who had been previously designated to the Zulu Mission. The other three who are to go will be teachers of whom we have yet obtained but one. No person has yet been designated to the mission to Siam & it is not probable that we shall be able to send out any labourers beyond the sea before the next meeting of the Board. . . In the course of next Autumn, I hope we may be so far relieved from our pecuniary straits as to send reenforcements to Siam, etc."

Greene was not clear as to whether the three "teachers" included Gray or any of the wives. The statement regarding the inability of the

Board to send out any missionaries to Siam for almost another year was most disturbing to Smith who was fretting under the prolonged delay. Apparently it took Asa some time after he received Greene's letter of the 15th for him to grasp the idea that the closing of one door might mean that he could turn to another that was opening. If there were no possibility of going to Siam until the fall of 1838 and if the Board were looking for some teachers to go to Oregon, why not abandon the thought of going to Siam and apply for Oregon?

Harassed by financial worries, frustrated over the continued delay in being assigned to a field, and eager to be married, Asa was ready to seize any opportunity which promised a way out. Psychologically, he was prepared to make a quick, impulsive decision. No doubt he turned again to the *Missionary Herald* and read and reread the October and December issues which contained Spalding's glowing reports of the opportunities of that mission. After dreaming and talking so much about going to Siam, it could not have been easy for Asa to transfer his commitment on short notice to the Nez Perces. The fact that he made this transition within about six weeks is striking evidence of the intensity of his feelings. Anything was better than prolonged waiting.

Judging from statements made by Asa in a letter to his parents dated March 12, 1838, he made a trip to Boston sometime during the opening days of the month in order to have a personal interview with the Board secretaries. When Asa asked about the possibility of joining the 1838 reenforcement to the Oregon Mission instead of waiting to be sent to Siam, Secretary Anderson informed him that time was short for such a decision. Asa was told that William H. Gray had been married on February 25th to Mary Augusta Dix of Ithaca, New York, and that the two were already on their way to the Missouri frontier. Walker and Eells were each planning to be married on March 5th, which was just about the time Asa was in Boston. These two couples were to be present for a farewell service scheduled to be held in New York City on Sunday evening, March 18th. Asa was asked whether it would be possible for him to go to West Brookfield, be married, and then for him and his bride to be in New York for that same service.

The rush of events with the evident need for quick decisions was breathtaking. When Asa thought aloud and asked whether there would be opportunity for him to go to Williamstown, Vermont, to bid farewell to his parents, he was told that this would be impossible. He had less than two weeks to travel to West Brookfield, get married, make all preparations for travel to Oregon on what was then the possibility of a life-long assignment, and be in New York by March 18th.

In the archives of the American Board is the following letter from Asa to Secretary Anderson dated March 10, 1838, from West Brookfield:

> MY DEAR SIR: I arrived here yesterday & have proposed the subject of going to the Indians beyond the Rocky Mountains & find that so far as respects the field of labor, Miss White & the whole family are much pleased. The idea of laboring among these Indians is very pleasant, & the only objection in the minds of any is the hardship of the journey. We have but little time to think of the subject, but thus far it seems favorable. We hope that Miss White may be able to bear the journey & that it will result favorably in respect to her health. But we have some fears with regard to this point. Could we go by sea, we should not hesitate at all. As I must write something this morning, I will say that probably we shall go. The Board therefore may act on the probability that we shall go, & I will consult further on the subject, & write again by the next mail. Please to write to me as soon as you receive this & give me any information you may think necessary. In much haste.   Yours truly,   A. B. SMITH

Here is a reference to the fact that Sarah's health was not robust. This may have been the first time that the Board was informed of this. Evidently her parents were confident of their daughter's ability to endure a long sea voyage, but could she ride 1,900 miles horseback on a side-saddle? Would she be able to bear the privations of sleeping on the ground, living for weeks on buffalo meat, and traveling in all kinds of weather across the plains and the Rockies? Sarah had rarely if ever been on a horse. Judging by an entry in her diary for July 30 of that year, Deacon White borrowed a horse from a neighbor, placed his daughter on it, and led it about the yard. Looking back on that experience, Sarah wrote: "I have not felt as much fear today as when you put me on Rhoda Stone's horse and led it about the yard."

Not one of the other three couples of the 1838 reenforcement had been placed under such pressure for an immediate decision as were Asa and Sarah. And yet this was not of the Board's choosing but rather of theirs. Both had become impatient for an assignment. After being engaged for nearly eighteen months, both wanted to be married. Human nature is quick to rationalize what is emotionally desired. Asa showed Spalding's reports which had appeared in the *Missionary Herald* to Deacon and Mrs. White. This provided further encouragement and did much to break down their objections. Later, when cruel facts forced Asa to reexamine the factors which had precipitated him and Sarah into the distressing situation of being in an isolated station among the Nez Perces, he found it easy to blame Spalding. And so Spalding became the object of his bitter criticism. To him Spalding was the cause of all his troubles because Spalding had exaggerated and had misrepresented the facts.

Sarah's delicate health was an important factor to be considered and this evidently was the main reason why her parents hesitated to give their consent to the marriage at that time. There are indications that both Asa and Sarah laughed off such fears. Let it be said in all fairness, they did not know nor could they have imagined the hardships attendant upon such a long and difficult journey. The fact that Mrs. Whitman and Mrs. Spalding had crossed the Rockies seemingly without great difficulty was reassuring. Sarah's trial ride around the yard on a neighbor's horse was a pathetic gesture to support a decision both desperately wanted to make.

Another important factor which Asa failed to take into account was his temperament. Asa B. Smith was at his best in a study. He was not cut out to be a pioneer in the wilderness. He should have remained in an eastern parish rather than undertaking the rugged life of a missionary among the Indians of Oregon. By nature he was a perfectionist. What he demanded of himself, he expected to find in others and became critical and censorious when he did not find it.

Thus during the week-end of March 11, 1838, the disastrous combination of factors flowed together which would eventually bring great unhappiness to both Asa and Sarah, would undermine her health, and hasten her death.

Asa was careful in his letter of March 9th to the Board not to give a positive commitment about going to Oregon. ". . . thus far it seems favorable," he wrote, and again, "I will say that probably we shall go." After a thorough discussion of the subject over the week-end, Sarah's parents gave a reluctant consent. As will be noted later, Sarah's repeated assurances of being happy in her decision and her studied hesitancy to say anything in her diary about the hardships of the journey seem to indicate that she did not want to worry her parents. Months had to pass before either Asa or Sarah were willing to admit in their letters home that they had acted hastily or that they regretted their decision.

On Monday morning, March 12th, Asa reported to Greene:

After further consideration & consultation on the subject of going to the Indians beyond the Rocky Mountains, we have

decided to go, should the Board see fit to send us, & have begun
to make preparations for our departure.

Dea. White's family seem to be very pleased with that mission
as a field of labor & would rather have us go there than to go to
Siam, but they feel that the journey would be a very great undertaking & fear that Sarah would not have strength to endure it.
They feel willing to give her up to go there if it be the Lord's will,
believing that if he has a work for her to perform among those
Indians, he will give her strength to perform this journey. They
feel considerable solicitude respecting the effect which this long
& tedious journey may have upon her, yet they hope it may prove
beneficial to her health. Should the Board decide to send us to
that mission, we feel willing to undertake it & would do it cheerfully tho' we feel that it is a great undertaking to make so long a
journey on horseback. Our calculation is to put ourselves in readiness & to be in New York before next sabbath if the decision is
that we should take that course. We wish to be there before the
brethren leave so as to know what is necessary for us to purchase
for the journey & go on with them.

MARRIAGE AND DEPARTURE

Anticipating favorable word from the Board, Asa and Sarah began
to make plans for their wedding. When Asa called on Sarah's pastor,
the Rev. F. Horton, he learned somewhat to his dismay that under
the law of Massachusetts bans had to be published at least two Sundays preceding a marriage. Announcement of the intended marriage
had been made on Sunday, March 11th, but if the letter of the law
were observed the marriage could not take place until after the second
bans had been published on Sunday, March 18th. That date would
have made it impossible for Asa and Sarah to get to New York in time
to join the other members of the party. Asa found himself in another
quandary and of this he wrote in his letter of March 12th to Greene:
"I think that it will be the safe course for us to be married in Connecticut or New York. . . I have thought of going to New Haven
& being married there. We were published here yesterday which is all
the law in Connecticut requires. . . I have thought of writing to
Mr. Bacon respecting the matter, & call on him on our way to New
York. It would be more pleasant to be married in New Haven than in
New York, as we are acquainted there. It is a trial to us all to leave
here without being married, but I do not know as it can be otherwise."

The next day Asa wrote to Greene and gave news of later developments.

In respect to matrimonial matters, I find that it is not necessary to go out of the State. Since I wrote yesterday, I have called on Dr. Stone, the senior pastor of the church in the south parish of this town, & told him the circumstances in which we were placed & he said he would take the responsibility of marrying us. He said the spirit of the law was answered in this case tho' the letter was not, that the law was not made for such cases, but to prevent secret connections, that there was nothing morally wrong in the case, that he presumed no one would take advantage in this case of necessity & that he should not hesitate to do it. Dr. Stone is an excellent old man & a very judicious man. . . This has relieved the minds of the family very much & the way is thus opened for us to go forward. . . We expect to have things in readiness to leave here Thursday P.M."

Secretary Greene received Asa's letter of March 12th on the 13th, according to the following notation on the back of Asa's letter: "Recd. March 13th. Designation changed & Miss White appointed. . . Wrote to C. A. Harris, Com. of Ind. Affairs for a permit to reside in the Indian country." For a letter to be carried the sixty-five miles from West Brookfield, Massachusetts, to Boston within two days indicates a high degree of postal efficiency for that time. Greene at once wrote to Asa informing him of the Board's approval for the change of destination from Siam to Oregon and of the appointment of Sarah White. Asa received this letter on Wednesday, March 14th, and the Whites made immediate plans for the marriage to take place the next day.

Greene's notation about writing for "a permit to reside in the Indian country" calls for further comment. A letter of inquiry from the author to National Archives and Records Service brought a reply dated February 1, 1965, which stated: "The records of the Bureau of Indian Affairs show that the Secretary of War and the Indian agents issued passports to permit travellers to pass through the Indian country and to allow persons to trade with the tribes." Records of such passports being issued cover the years 1836 through 1844 inclusive. The passport of Asa Smith was dated March 19, 1838, and was forwarded to him at Cincinnati, Ohio. A reproduction of this document is included as an illustration in this volume. Curiously, the text of the passport makes no mention of Smith's wife, Sarah. The passport issued to Elkanah Walker on March 9th included the wording, "with his family." [9]

No record remains describing events in the White household during

[9] See Introduction to Gray's Journal, p. 237 of this volume. See also reproduction of Walker's passport, Drury, *Walker*, p. 69.

the days preceding the wedding. We can only imagine the turmoil of emotions which must have surged through every heart. The final packing had to be done. No doubt Smith had been informed while in the Board's offices that the baggage of each person going overland would have to be limited. Gray had instructed the Walkers to limit their baggage to what one horse could carry "say 140 pounds including your tent, bedding, etc." He recommended that each person be provided with one "large leather valice 24 inches long" for his or her personal effects. Mrs. Walker's valise, now in the museum of Washington State University, Pullman, Washington, measures 24 x 19 x 9½ inches. Asa and Sarah made arrangements for some of their goods including his books, to be sent by sea around South America. This shipment did not reach them at their isolated station at Kamiah in what is now northern Idaho until January 4, 1840, nearly two years after they had left for Oregon.

The facts that in those days a passport from the War Department was required of those going to Oregon, and that from one to two years were required to send letters or baggage by sea from their homes in the East to Oregon, give evidence of the remoteness of that land. The realization of these facts added poignancy to their farewells. All concerned felt that the separation would probably be for life.

On Monday, March 12th, Asa wrote to his family at East Williamstown, Vermont, and informed them of the sudden and unexpected developments. "It is necessary for us to go so soon, if we go," he wrote, "that it will be impossible for me to go to Vermont. I lament that I cannot see you again. . . Should we go we may perhaps meet again in this world, but if not, we hope to meet in a better world." Nothing was said in those days about furloughs for missionaries. An assignment to a mission field, especially overseas, was for an indefinite period, usually for life, without the expectation of a return visit home.

Asa received definite word about his commission on Wednesday, March 14th, and again wrote to his parents informing them of this. "And now my dear parents," he commented, "what shall I say? We probably shall never meet again till we meet in heaven. . . Be not grieved, my dear parents, in view of this separation, but rejoice that God has given you a son who may yet preach the gospel to those interesting tribes who are waiting for the law of God." Asa's fears of not seeing his parents again were partially realized, for his father died on December 14, 1844. His mother was still living when Asa and Sarah

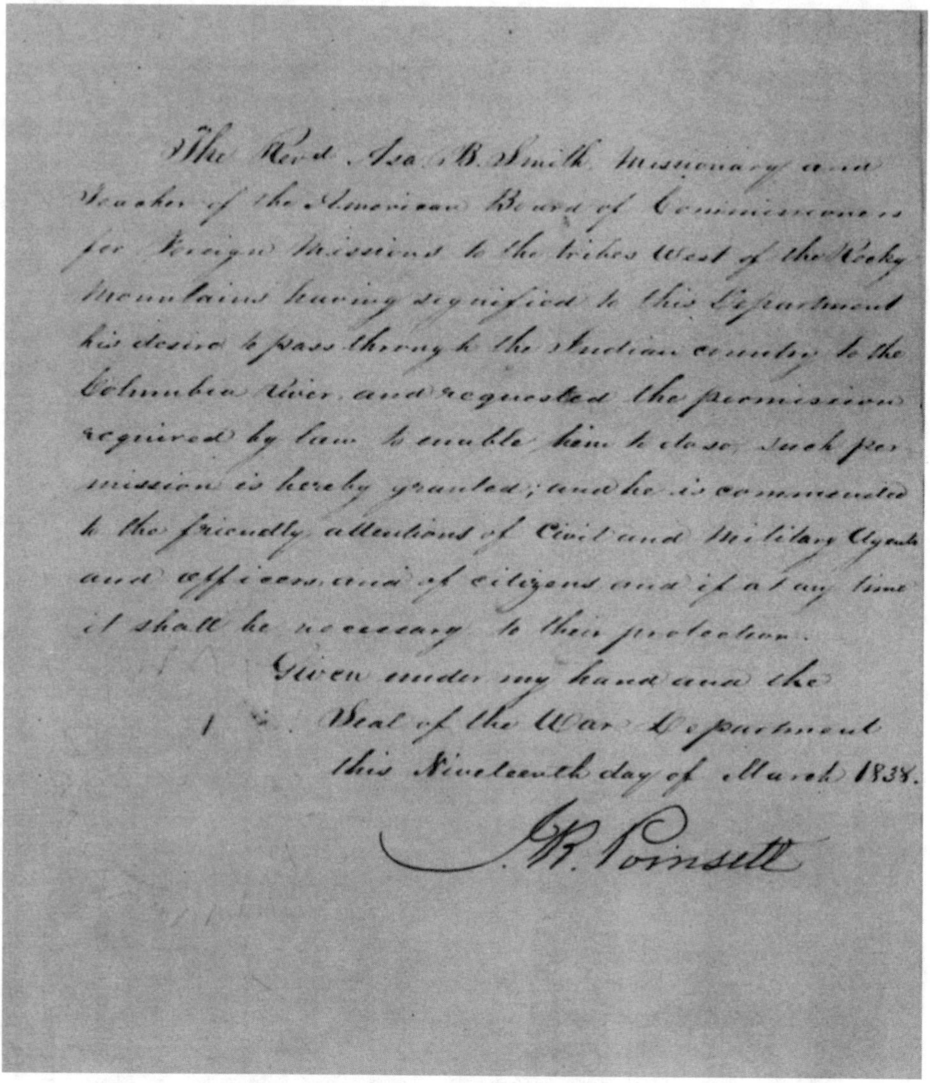
The Revd. Asa B. Smith missionary and teacher of the American Board of Commissioners for Foreign Missions to the tribes West of the Rocky Mountains having signified to this Department his desire to pass through the Indian country to the Columbia River and requested the permission required by law to enable him to do so, such permission is hereby granted; and he is commended to the friendly attentions of Civil and Military Agents and officers and of citizens and if at any time it shall be necessary to their protection.

Given under my hand and the
L. S. Seal of the War Department
this Nineteenth day of March 1838.

J R Poinsett

PASSPORT OF ASA B. SMITH

Issued by the War Department, granting permission to pass through the Indian Country, enroute to Oregon. See text page 53. Original in Coll. Y.

A LOCK OF SARAH'S DARK AUBURN HAIR
Fastened inside the cover of the copy of her diary.
Courtesy of Western History Collection, Denver Public Library.

(right) THE POSTSCRIPTS OF MARCH 15, 1838
Showing the handwriting of both Asa and Sarah; probably the first
signature by Sarah of her married name. Original in Coll. Y.

returned to the States in May 1846 after being away for more than eight years.

No account has been discovered of the ceremony which took place about noon on Thursday, March 15th. Following the wedding both Asa and Sarah added postscripts to Asa's letter of the day before to his parents. A reproduction of these postscripts is included as one of the illustrations of this volume. The text follows:

THURSDAY [March] 15th, 1838

MY DEAR PARENTS, BROTHERS & SISTERS. I am now to leave very soon for New York with Sarah who is now my wife. I hope you will be sustained in the trial of not seeing me again. The grace of God will I trust be sufficient to sustain me. Farewell till we meet again. I shall write again soon. Your earnest prayers, I trust, will follow us & may the blessing of God rest on us all. Your affectionate son & Br.   A. B. SMITH

MY DEAR PARENTS & SISTERS, for such I shall ever call you. I can now only say farewell. I am now to leave my dear home forever to dwell with a savage people not knowing the things that will befall me there. But I go trusting in God. I am happy, yes, very happy. I go joyfully. I trust your prayers will ever attend us.

Farewell dear Friends
from your affectionate daughter & sister
SARAH G[ILBERT] SMITH

Shortly after the wedding ceremony, and perhaps after a midday meal, the bridal couple took the stage for New Haven, one hundred miles distant. No record has been found describing the parting scene and we can only imagine the tearful farewells. For the second time Deacon and Mrs. White were giving a daughter to the foreign missionary cause.

Diary of Sarah White Smith
March 16, 1838 to September 14, 1838

Diary of Sarah White Smith

INTRODUCTION

Sarah Smith's diary is very personal. She was writing within the intimacies of a closely-knit family circle and, consequently, related many little incidents which never would have been mentioned were she writing for publication. Her diary should be read in a parallel chronological sequence with her husband's letters which follow, as they supplement each other.

The opening section of the diary contains an excellent description of the high religious idealism which induced her to be a missionary. This idealism reflects the training she had received in her home and in her church. She had become thoroughly imbued with the idea that there was no higher or holier calling than that of missionary and in this conviction she was wholeheartedly joined by her husband. Both had a strong sense of duty. Although some of Sarah's expressions seem to this generation to be empty clichés or too sanctimonious, yet for her they were very meaningful.

Counterbalancing the exhiliration of getting married and starting out on the great adventure of an overland journey to Oregon, was the pain of leaving her home and the members of her family. Conflicting emotions tore her apart. Once she had answered God's call to be a missionary, it was a sin to harbor any regrets. She had made a great decision which she thereafter felt necessary to defend. Notice her words in the postscript of Asa's letter of March 15th to his parents: "I am happy, yes very happy." This sentiment is repeated in the first part of her diary addressed to her family. Several times throughout her account of their overland travels, she reassures her folks that she is happy. Such expressions are evidences of her desire not to cause her parents to worry and at the same time, from a psychological viewpoint, reveal a continued inner conflict. She protests her happiness too much.

Nowhere else in the writings of the members of the 1838 mission party do we find a clearer exposition of the religious motivation which induced these nine to give themselves to be missionaries among the

"heathen." [1] *No other explanation accounts for their boldness to under-*
take this "unheard of journey for females" [2] *or their fortitude to endure*
the gruelling hardships, as this deep inner conviction — God had called
them. This was a holy cause. The diary begins:

SPRINGFIELD [MASS.] Mch. 16th, 1838

MY BELOVED PARENTS, BROTHER & SISTERS. However uninteresting this
narrative may seem to others, to you I doubt not it will be full of
interest. To you therefore it shall be cheerfully dedicated. Should it
afford you the least gratification or cheer you in a lonely hour, I shall
feel myself richly rewarded.

The long anticipated hour which was to sunder the tenderest ties &
remove me forever from the scenes of my childhood has come and
gone. I have torn myself forever from the fond embrace of my beloved
Parents, exchanged the last kiss with a beloved sister & with a dear
and only brother & going where I can no more meet their sympathies
or receive their kind attentions in the hour of affliction. But I am
happy. I feel there is an arm unseen that holds me up, an eye that
kindly watches all my path. Jesus my Savior, He for whom I make
these sacrifices is more than able to sustain me. I feel to lean on Him.
To brace myself on the precious promises & tho we meet no more on
earth we hope to meet in heaven where parting is unknown.

In taking a review of my past life, I am pained that I have made no
more effort to increase your happiness & lessen the trials of life. Instead
of doing much to increase the joy of my beloved Parents, who have
watched over me in infancy, childhood & in riper years, I fear that
your hearts have often been grieved at my unfaithfulness. I know I
have often spoken to you in a hasty manner, as I ought never to have
done, and now with tears I ask you to forgive me. I know you will do
it & will regard me with a parents love & often raise to heaven in my
behalf a parents prayer, & once more dear Father & Mother I wish
most gratefully to thank you for all your kindness and care of me. God
only can reward you. And of you dear brother and sister, who have
long been the sharer of my joy & sorrow, I cannot take a last farewell

---

[1] Today such words as "heathen" and "pagan" carry a derogatory connotation
but the missionaries used them back in the 1830s as synonyms for "non-Christian."
Until recently such words were used without apology and without giving offense
to the Nez Perce non-Christians.

[2] See FWW, I, p. 114ff for comment on this phrase twice used by Narcissa
Whitman to describe the experiences she and Eliza Spalding had undergone in
their crossing of the Rocky Mountains, the first such exploit by white American
women.

till I have sought your forgiveness, if at any time I may have injured your feelings.

Thus far our life has been spent in tranquility & ease, unruffled by the storms of time or the deep traces of sorrow. Our morning sun has thus far pursued its course without a cloud. But will our sky be always clear? May we expect no sorrow, no manhood's weary tract? Ah, let us not picture to ourselves a life of ease, it is not ours to choose.

Would we engage in the glorious cause of the world's conversion, we must welcome toil and suffering, welcome reproach & perhaps a martyr's crown. But it is only for a moment. It will only introduce us to a brighter world & happier home, where all sorrows end, all joys begin. And will not the happiness of introducing to the heavenly world some heathen souls, more than reward us for all our labor & suffering? I rejoice in the prospect of spending my life among the rude sons of the forest & though privation may be mine to share, I think I shall be happy in laboring for their conversion.

I will say again that I rejoice to go & should I never reach the field of labor, should I find a resting place upon the broad prairie, or among the Rocky Mountains, or the sandy plains of the far West, mourn not, nor regret that you gave me to this blessed cause.

I feel that God calls me & that it is His hand that has directed me & that it is [extended] to us in this undertaking & He will give me strength to endure it & will bring me in safety to my desired field, or remove me as will most glorify Him. Then why should we be anxious. God will do right! Infinite wisdom cannot err. O it is sweet to feel that my Heavenly Father rules & that I am in His hands & that nothing can remove me.

The bridal couple arrived at Springfield on Thursday night, March 15th, their wedding day. Because of the muddy roads, they did not reach Hartford until midnight on Friday. The Rev. and Mrs. Cushing Eells, also newly-wedded, were only one day in advance of the Smiths on the same road after leaving Hartford. The Rev. and Mrs. Elkanah Walker, another newly-wedded couple, had sailed from Boston for New York on March 15th. But at the time, Asa and Sarah Smith were unaware of the movements of their future associates.

The Smiths arrived in New Haven on Saturday afternoon too late to take passage on a ship bound for New York. They were obliged to spend Sunday in New Haven where they had many friends since each had lived there most of the preceding year. The pleasure of seeing

*old friends was lessened by their regrets at not being able to be present
for the farewell service for the departing missionaries scheduled for
Sunday evening in the Brick Presbyterian Church of New York.*

Yesterday after parting with you all, I felt that a burden of mountain size was removed. I found pleasant company on the stage. One warm missionary friend [was] acquainted with Mrs. Eells. Reached here [Springfield] late and much fatigued, feel somewhat rested today. Have called on Mr. Merriam.[3] He kindly gave me some books. We leave here at 4 this afternoon. Friday, the 16th, we left Springfield for Hartford, in company with Mr. Ladd, the peace agent. The road is bad and the coach crowded with passengers. Did not arrive at H. till midnight. But as Mr. L. amused us so well with his stories, the time past away very pleasantly.

Saturday morning after riding all day through mud and water, we arrived at New Haven. Were kindly received by Mr. & Mrs. Donoughe in whose family we found a home & who showed us every possible attention & provided for our wants. I shall long remember them.

Sab. 18.   On account of the badness of the roads we could not reach New York last night, so we shall fail of receiving our instructions.[4] But it is all right. It is so stormy, I do not go to church. Some friends have called to see me & we are to have a missionary meeting here this evening. Have received some presents from friends here.

Mon. Morn. 19.   We took the steamboat for New York. Arrived about two in the afternoon. Met the dear sisters who are going with me to the far West.[5] Find we have much to do. Friends kind. We must leave here tomorrow.

Tues. 20th.   Again on board the steamboat.[6] Have parted with many

---

[3] Unidentified, as is Mr. Ladd mentioned in the same paragraph.

[4] See Drury, *Elkanah and Mary Walker* for an account of the farewell service. Secretary David Greene in his speech said that the missionaries would be crossing mountains "25,000 feet above the ocean level, and thus surpassing all other mountains on the globe, except the highest points of the Himmalayah chain in Central Asia." Actually the highest elevation of South Pass in the Rockies, crossed by the missionaries, is only 7,550 feet. The ignorance of the best informed people in the East regarding the Far West at the time these missionaries were sent out to Oregon is astonishing. The Walkers and the Eells who heard Greene's speech did not know enough about mountains to be frightened by such a description. They did know that the Whitmans and the Spaldings had made a successful crossing and that was sufficient evidence to believe that it could be done again. See FWW, II, pp. 50-51.

[5] See FWW, II, p. 51 for reference to Mary Walker's comment in her diary after meeting Sarah for the first time, — "she is a little dear."

warm friends who have been very kind & done much for us. May God reward them. Must soon enter the cars, expect to ride most of the night.

26. MONDAY EVE.   We have had a hard fatiguing journey and have just arrived at Pittsburg. Expected to have arrived here Saturday night but could not. We have rode night & day & the roads bad enough. We have now crossed the Allegany Mountains. Witnessed their snow capped tops, been exposed to dangers seen & unseen but an Almighty arm has sustained us. Every variety of scenery has been presented to our view. Lofty mountains, steep declivities, extensive plains, cultivated fields, uncultivated forests, pleasant villages & villages composed of log huts, have alternately met our view, thus rendering our journey a pleasant & interesting one. I have not just the opinion of the West I formerly had, particularly those of the log hut villages & indeed most I have seen of Pensylvania. I think they can not be people of much enterprise. The soil I judge to be very fertile, but the people poor & indolent. The buildings look bad & the door yards converted into barn yards   I do not see what could induce any one to leave the refined society of New England for a residence among such a people, unless it be to do them good.

27. TUES.   We have had a pleasant time with the Rev. Mr. Riddle's [7] family & other Christian friends in Pittsburg. We leave this morning in the boat Norfolk for Wheeling. I love to ride in the boat, it does not make me sea sick at all.

28th. WEDNESDAY.   This morning we breakfasted in Wheeling, where I had the happiness to receive a letter from my dear Father & Brother Samuel. Although I had been absent from home but a short time, yet a letter from them was truly welcome. I could but shed some tears, but they were not tears of regret that I had parted from you: tho much I love you. No, I do rejoice that I have been permitted to show my love to Christ & his cause by making the sacrifice. *I am very happy.*[8]

[6] The three couples — the Eells, the Smiths, and the Walkers — left New York at 5 p.m. on this day. Since the railroad connecting New York with Philadelphia had not been completed, the party had to go by steamer to a point about thirty miles down the New Jersey coast where they landed in the night and took the "railroad cars" for Philadelphia. See Asa's letter for March 20th in a following section of this book. FWW, II, pp. 51ff, and SS, 40ff, give details of the gruelling five days' travel from Philadelphia to Pittsburgh.

[7] Rev. D. H. Riddle was pastor of the Third Presbyterian Church of Pittsburgh. He was the one who secured passage for the whole party on the "Norfolk" for St. Louis. The fare, including meals, was $25.00 each.

[8] Editorial italics.

I think I never enjoyed communion with God as since I left my dear home. Surely my Savior has been near to me — cheered my soul with His presence.

AFTERNOON. We have been riding most beautifully today and are now at Marietta. Brother & Sister Walker, Mr. Smith & myself [9] have taken a little walk in the city. It is as warm as summer & the grass green. Marietta is a pretty place. It looks some like a New England village. Ohio is not a wide river. I look on one side & see Virginia & on the other & see Ohio. The scene is rather mountainous. The houses are small & built of logs. The banks are skirted with hills, trees & plains.

29th. THURS. We have had a fine ride today. Called at noon at Maysville in Kentucky. Mr. Smith & myself with an Ohio lady took a walk in the city. Enjoyed it much. Maysville is a pretty place but small. Not as large as Boston near. The streets more regularly laid out and the houses much like New England.

30. FRIDAY. Cincinnatti.[10] Intelligence has been received from Mr. Gray that we do not leave Independence till the 1st of May. So we shall spend the rest of the week in the family of Doct. Peck. Lovely people. The ladies are assisting me about my sewing. We find friends everywhere. Even on the boat we find ladies ready to assist us (help me).

31st. SAT. Today Mr. & Mrs. Walker, Mr. & Mrs. Eells, Mr. Smith & myself have visited distant hills & Lane Seminary. Called on Dr. Beecher [11] at his own house. Saw Miss Catherine Beecher & the Dr's wife. Was introduced to many friends who love the cause of Christ. Had a pleasant time.

APRIL 1st. Have attended church today. Have once more cele-

---

[9] When the mission party crossed the plains and the mountains, they had only two tents. The Walkers and the Smiths occupied one, and the Grays and the Eells the other. Here is evidence that the Walkers and the Smiths were being friendly with each other shortly after they began their journey. Notice how Sarah refers to her husband as "Mr. Smith." The missionaries never referred to each other by their first names.

[10] In Cincinnati the missionaries met Cornelius Rogers, unmarried and in his twenty-third year, who decided to join the party on an unofficial basis. A disappointing characteristic of Sarah's diary is her failure to comment on others in the party. Since the missionaries decided to stay over the week-end, thus avoiding traveling on Sunday, they were entertained in the homes of some of the church people. Dr. and Mrs. George L. Weed entertained the Walkers; a Mrs. Bird received the Eells; and the Smiths went to Dr. Peck's. See SS, 43.

[11] Dr. Lyman Beecher, then president of Lane Theological Seminary where Henry and Eliza Spalding had studied 1833-35.

brated the Lord's Supper in a Christian land. If ever permitted the privilege again, it will be in a heathen land, where God is unknown. But no matter, the Savior will be present & communion with Him from a heathen land will be as sweet as from a Christian land. Heaven will be as near, God will be as near.

2nd. Mon.   Have been sewing all day. This evening attended a meeting.

3rd. Tues.   Again on board the boat. Have just received a letter from Mr. Gray saying we must be ready to move with the fur trading company the 15th of this month. Have had a pleasant time at Cincinnati. Friends exceeding kind. We go in the Knickerbocker. Pleasant stateroom, &c.

4th. Wed.   We find very pleasant company in the boat. One lady & daughter who saw Sister Adeline in Boston. Saw her sail, well acquainted with her room-mate. Some other very interesting company on board. The Captain is very kind & polite to us. He has given us the privilege of holding worship in the cabin every evening. The cabin is always full.

5. Thurs.   Still on board the Knickerbocker, Louisville Harbor. Mr. S. & myself have taken a pleasant walk in the city. Called on the Rev. Mr. Huber,[12] a Swiss gentlemen. His appearance is that of a devoted Christian & a whole Abolitionist, notwithstanding he is in the very heart of slavery. I have been walking on slavery ground & have seen many poor slaves. My heart pitied them, tho I saw no cruelty. I have conversed with one on board the boat who has been a slave but is now free. Her parents were torn from their family & sold to different masters & she has not seen them for a long time. Suppose they are still in slavery. She & her little brothers & sisters were carried to Virginia & sold. She was sold to a female who died years ago & who gave her her liberty at her death. She was 12 years old when her parents were sold. Is now 28. Says she remembers it distinctly. Oh, I think slavery is dreadful.

6. Friday.   We are riding upon the big waters of the Ohio. Have just passed the Wabash. Could not see its mouth because of an island. Here the river is about ¾ of a mile wide. It looks grand.

---

[12] Because of difficulty in transcribing Mrs. Walker's diary, Huber was identified as Sutter in SS, 45. Captain John Sutter, who crossed the country in 1838, evidently joined the caravan of the fur company on the Missouri frontier. Neither of the Smiths make any reference to him. See Asa's letter for April 5th in the following section.

7th. SAT. Spent the day sewing. Some of the ladies on board assisted me & this evening we have had a pleasant time singing. All our company sing & some others joined us.

SAB. 8. Still on the boat. The Holy Sabbath.[13] Expected to have reached St. Louis last night, but could not & there was no place where we could stop & if we had, we might not get another boat for a week, and consequently be detained perhaps a whole year from our field of labor. We have spent the day in our little rooms & tho separated from Christian civilization have enjoyed communion with God & I hope the day has been profitable to us.

9th. MON. We have now arrived at St. Louis where we shall spend the day. Afternoon, again on board the boat.[14] About 11 we called on Mrs. Doct. Jones.[15] Took dinner with her. In the afternoon several good ladies called upon me. Had a season of prayer together. I considered it one of the last meetings I should enjoy with Christian friends in a Christian land. Mrs. Jones purchased many things for us. Thus the Lord provides friends for us wherever we go. May we learn to trust Him for the future.

10. TUES. EVE. We are riding upon the Missouri. The Howard is a little distance behind us and the two boats are chasing. The Howard is endeavoring to pass us. It seems dreadful.

11. WED. We have had a little excitement by fire today. This afternoon as I sat in my stateroom, I smelt something like fire & saw some smoke. Immediately called the chamber maid and search was made but in vain. The smoke continued to thicken. The Capt. & others supposed it must come from the upper deck. Therefore cut through the ceiling & soon discovered where it was and were able to put it out.

---

13 All of the mission party were deeply troubled in conscience when they found it necessary to travel on Sunday or the Sabbath. Strictly speaking, the Sabbath is Saturday but to them the term always referred to Sunday. For the reactions of others in the party to this problem see SS, 45, and FWW, II, p. 56. Anticipating the necessity of traveling with the Fur Company's caravan on Sunday when crossing the plains, members of the party had asked Dr. Beecher what should be done. If they traveled on Sunday, they would be breaking one of the ten commandments. If they rested in camp and let the caravan go on without them, they might be killed by hostile Indians. "Well," replied Dr. Beecher, "if I were crossing the Atlantic, I certainly would not jump overboard when Saturday night came."

14 The mission party took passage on the "Glasgow" for Independence. On the 12th they were transferred to the "Howard." The boat fare was $15.00 each.

15 Unidentified. While in St. Louis, Walker wrote to Secretary Greene saying: "I think it was quite fortunate that Mr. Smith was enabled to join us. I do not know how we should have succeeded without him. I have much more confidence in him than in brother Eells." Of the three men, Smith was by far the most aggressive.

12. Thurs.   Today we were obliged to move from the Glasgow to the Howard. It was unexpected & occasioned some confusion.

13. Friday.   The Howard we find very inconvenient indeed. Instead of staterooms, there are berths with curtains very unpleasant.

15. The Holy Sabbath.   At this hour my dear parents are going to meeting, while I am far from Christian privileges & am obliged to travel, as we must be at Independence immediately. You can hardly realize the confusion of the hour. Children screaming, men hallowing & taking the name of God in vain. But I find some consolation in approaching the mercy seat. I find the throne of grace as near me here as when on Christian land.

16th. Mon.   At Independence. Arrived here last evening about 10 oclock, after taking a horseback ride of 3½ miles.[16] Our path lay over mountains, rocky & stony, but it was so dark I could not see the danger. Mr. S. led my pony. I felt quite safe. Have met Mr. & Mrs. Gray, find we have still much to do. Have been sewing all day.

17th. Tues.   Have been sick all day. Took an emetic. Thought some of dear Mother, but she is far away. I find my dear husband an excellent nurse.

18th. Wed.   Feel some better, have been sewing hard all day.[17] I find no rest. Have been making our tents, bags and other things for our journey.

19th. Thurs.   Spent another day at hard sewing. Have no rest.

April 20th. Friday.   I found myself much fatigued & almost sick. Feel unfit for reading, been on the bed some part of the day, but we must go to Westport 12 miles. Our horses are ready. I begin to feel

---

[16] The introduction to their long horseback ride across the prairies and the mountains came to the three women at night and under trying circumstances. See Asa's letter for April 10th. There at Independence the three couples met William and Mary Gray for the first time. During that first night at Independence, the nine members of the party were crowded into two rooms with but one double bed in each room. Mrs. Gray and Mrs. Eells took one bed; Mrs. Walker and Mrs. Smith, the other; and the five men slept on the floor. During this first night together, Gray and Smith, both individualists, ruffled each other's dispositions. Regarding this Mary Walker wrote in her diary: "Mr. Gray did not like Mr. Smith's movements, and considering it was the first time, we came very near having unpleasant feelings." This was a harbinger of greater unpleasantnesses to come. For further details about the days of final preparations for the long journey which lay before them, see FWW, ii, p. 58ff, and SS, 49ff.

[17] The mission party had only a week at Independence to complete their outfit before starting across the prairies with the Fur Company's caravan. While the men were buying their animals and provisions, the women were busy sewing on their two tents which were made out of blue, "thin duck" sailcloth.

this world is not the place of my rest, but it will soon be over. Eternity is near.

21st. WESTPORT.[18]   Arrived here last night late and much fatigued. Could hardly stand but feel better today than I expected. Good Mrs. McCoy has done my washing that I might rest. Hereafter we shall find no Christian friends till we reach our field of labor.

22nd. SAB.   The Holy Sabbath, but how profaned. Surely God is dishonored and his holy name blasphemed. The trading company have left here today for the mountains.[19] My dear husband is sick, taken an emetic. We know not what is before us. Our trust is in God.

WESTPORT TO FORT LARAMIE

The total distance from Westport, site of present day Kansas City, Kansas, to the 1838 Rendezvous, at the confluence of the Popo Agie and Wind Rivers near what is now Riverton, Wyoming, is about 1,100 miles. The fur company's caravan always stopped for several days at Fort Laramie on its way to the Rendezvous. The distance from Westport to Fort Laramie is about 775 miles. The caravan with the mission party reached the fort on May 30th after thirty-five days of traveling, thus averaging a little more than twenty miles a day. On two different days, the caravan traveled thirty miles each day, which meant about ten hours in the saddle. This must have been a grueling test for the women on their side-saddles. The mission party did take a light wagon with them as far as Fort Laramie but we find only a few references in any of the diaries or letters of the party to any of the women riding in the wagon.

The trail taken by the fur company followed the south bank of the Kansas River for about one hundred miles almost due west of

---

[18] Accommodations for the mission party were as hard to find in Westport as they had been in Independence. See Asa's letter of April 22nd. At Westport the missionaries met Dr. J. A. Chute, who was practicing medicine there. Being in full sympathy with the missionary project, Dr. Chute was able to render much help to the members of the reenforcement. Mrs. McCoy, whom Sarah mentions in her entry for this day, was the wife of a Baptist missionary, Rev. Isaac McCoy, who was ministering to the Indians of that area. See fn. 9 of Eells reminiscences, herein p. 296.

[19] Since the prairie country bordering the western boundary of Missouri was considered safe, the missionaries decided to remain at Westport over Sunday rather than to travel on that day. They left on Monday and caught up with the caravan five days later. They paid dearly for their scruples because marauding Indians stole three of their best horses which had cost them $200.00. For a parallel account of these days, see Sarah's postscript of April 10th and 23rd to Asa's letter of April 5th, herein, pp. 136-137.

Westport to the site of present day Manhattan, Kansas. After crossing the Kansas River just above the mouth of the Big Blue River, the trail followed the west bank of the Big Blue to the Little Blue, then along its southwest bank into what is now Nebraska. After going over a low divide, the trail came to the broad and shallow Platte River. After crossing the South Platte, the trail continued along the southwest bank of the North Platte to Fort Laramie located near where the Laramie River joins the North Platte. Since the mission party tarried one day at Westport after the departure of the caravan, they did not catch up with the fur company until it had reached the crossing of the Kansas River.

Sarah in her entry for Sunday, April 22nd, reflected her haunting fear of the future when she wrote: "We know not what is before us." Her diary entries for this period show a remarkable restraint in her comments on the hardships endured. She does mention the two severe rain storms which drenched them during the nights of April 30th and May 16th. She also wrote of the cold bitter winds and the short food supplies. But for the most part, as though she would not give undue concern to her parents who were to receive her diary, Sarah wrote about the scenery, the Indians, and the novelties of their method of travel. Asa's letters for this period, dated April 22nd, 28th, May 15th, and June 1st, should be consulted in parallel sequence.

[APRIL] 23rd.   We are about leaving. A few hours more & we shall be upon the broad prairie. The earth our bed & the little tent our shelter.[20] Privations and trials will be mine to share, but I go cheerfully, yes gladly, joyfully. Evening — Have travelled today 13 miles over a beautiful prairie, frequent spots of timber were to be seen but most of it was level green as far as the eye could see, rising in gentle undulations, presenting a fine appearance.[21] The soil rich. Have taken

---

[20] Mary Walker in a letter to her family begun on April 23rd, but with later notations, wrote on the 24th: "We are now travelling on the dry sea. . . We have two tents eight feet by twelve. Have a curtain to separate the families." Thus each couple had a space of only four by ten feet for bed and baggage. The experience of having two newly-wedded couples share such limited sleeping accommodations did not prove satisfactory. Cornelius Rogers slept out-of-doors as did the men of the caravan. It is doubtful if any of the mission party had any experience in camping, before this rugged manner of life was so suddenly thrust upon them.

[21] There is much verbatim duplication of material in the diaries and letters of Asa and Sarah. Asa in his entry for this day wrote: "Often as far as the eye could reach nothing was to be seen but the beautiful grass land, rising in gentle undulations." SS, 52. It is the author's opinion that Asa copied from his wife's notes more often than did Sarah from her husband's.

our supper of fried ham, bread & a cup of tea, sitting upon the ground in the open air. Our table is a cloth spread on the ground. We are happy, find our little tent very comfortable. Think we shall sleep well.

24th. Tues. Rose early this morning & after taking a breakfast of ham, started off. Stopped a short time at noon, took some more ham, broiled on a stick, to refresh us for the afternoon ride. Encamped about 5. Have travelled 23 miles. The prairie has presented the appearance of a garden, less woodsy than we passed yesterday.

25th. Wed. This has been a cold windy day. The cold winds from the southwest are occasioned by the snow capped mountains of Mexico.[22] Have forded a river where the water was so deep I was obliged to hold up my feet to keep them from being wet. Rode up the river about 100 yds. Have taken tea, washed our dishes, & are ready to retire to rest when we have committed ourselves to the care of our Father in Heaven. The country through which we have passed today has been more uneven than formerly and more wooded.

26th. Thurs. Passed over rolling prairies today, more uneven, yet often as far as the eye could see nothing but an extensive plain was visible, not a tree or a bush nor even a twig on which a bird could light. It has the appearance of an ocean, the gentle undulations resembling the motion of water.[23] Few stones are found. Travelled 20 miles. Very warm & pleasant today.

27th. Friday. The prairie today more uneven than any we have passed before. Crossed several streams. Found limestone upon the summit of a hill which had the appearance of having been acted upon by water. This has been common wherever we have found stones. This gives reason to suppose that the whole country has at some time been covered with water.[24]

28th. Sat. Have travelled 5 miles this morning and overtaken the fur company. Received a call from Capt. Dripps & Stewart.[25] They treated us kindly. Received a present of a piece of fresh pork from

----

[22] Sarah's references to the "snow capped mountains of Mexico" refers to the Rockies of Colorado. She was writing before the Mexican War of 1846 transferred to the United States the great Southwest.

[23] Comparing the rolling prairies to the waves of the sea frequently occurs in the writings of the members of this mission party and especially in the diaries and letters of Asa and Sarah. See footnote 20 above. Asa, looking back on his overland journey, wrote to Greene on April 29, 1839: "I have not indeed worked my passage on board a vessel to a foreign port [which he once proposed doing], but I can say in truth I worked my passage across the Rocky Mountains." SS, 96.

[24] Sarah writing for her parents refrained from making mention of the fact that marauding Indians had stolen three of their horses the night before. Inexperienced in the ways of the Indians, the missionaries had not posted a guard.

Major Harris.[26] We are encamped in the woods with the fur company & they are not a little noisy. Also some Indians with us in their savage costume, half naked. The men wear leggins and blankets. Their ears are pierced in many places and strings of beads & other ornaments strung in. Their hair is shaved off, a small tuft on the top of the head which is left long.[27]

29th. SAB. We have been under the necessity of crossing the Kansas river today & the gentlemen have labored hard lifting the baggage to & from the boat. Never did I pass such a Sabbath in my life.[28] No Sabbath bell invites us to a place of worship & we are prevented from Sabbath duties even in a private manner. O, I long for the Christian Sabbath where we can enjoy its privileges again.

30th. MON. Encamped on the bank of a little creek. Travelled 16 miles, been followed by the Kansas Indians. They were not a little troublesome, frightened our horses & cattle.[29] Stopped at noon on the bank of the Kansas. Took dinner of ham & corn sitting in a wagon.[30]

---

[25] The mission party arose at 4 a.m. this morning and caught up with the caravan of the American Fur Company at 9 o'clock. The caravan was then making preparations to cross the Kansas River. Capt. Andrew Drips was in charge of the caravan and Sir (sometimes called Captain) William Drummond Stewart, a Scottish nobleman, was with the caravan just for the love of adventure. He had also been with the caravan of 1836 when the Whitmans and the Spaldings crossed the prairies. See fn. 13 in Eells reminiscences, herein p. 297.

[26] Moses Harris, also called Black Harris or Major Harris, was one of the trappers of the Gen. W. H. Ashley party which entered the Rockies in 1823. See FWW, I, p. 52.

[27] These last two sentences of Sarah's entry appear verbatim in Asa's diary for the same day. See SS, 54.

[28] Working or traveling on Sunday was a painful experience for the missionaries with their puritanical reverence for the day. See index, "Sunday observance" and "Sunday travel" in SS and FWW, II, for many references to this subject.

[29] The missionaries started their overland journey with twenty-five horses and mules and twelve head of cattle including two fresh milch cows. The Whitman-Spalding party had twenty horses and mules and seventeen head of cattle including four fresh cows. Thus the second party with almost twice as many had fewer horses or mules per person and only one-half as many fresh milch cows. Moreover the 1838 party lost three of their best horses the first week.

[30] There is much evidence that Gray, as leader of the 1838 party, was far too economical in his expenditures for food supplies. According to a letter written from the Rendezvous by Myra Eells, the missionaries took with them when they left the frontier "a hundred and sixty pounds of flour, fifty-seven pounds of rice, twenty or twenty-five pounds of sugar, a little pepper and salt." FWW, II, p. 58. Altogether these supplies, weighing about 230 pounds, could have been loaded on one horse. Such supplies were supposed to carry the party of nine through four months and over 1,900 miles! Of course, it was expected that the party would have buffalo meat and other wild game and also they had the milk from their two cows. Nevertheless, the supply fell short of actual needs and caused considerable suffering. Myra

It was rainy & we did not spread our table. Most of us ate from one dish & with our fingers. Could not open the cases for dishes.

MAY 1st. TUES.   A cloudy day, rode 12 miles. Last night we had a heavy shower. The water came through our tent so that our bed & clothing were quite wet. The waist of my dress I could almost wring & my other clothing was wet. I felt afraid to dress me, feeling that my health was exposed but I put them on as they were & I do not feel that I have taken cold. The rain came through on to my head so that my pillow was wet. I thought a little of home & of what dear mother, if she should know it [would think].

2nd. WED.   Last night we had a heavy thunder shower. It rained most of the night. It beat hard upon our tent & we were in danger of being thoroughly wet. We took the water from the oil cloth which is on our floor with a sponge. Dr. Chute [31] was with us & without a tent, so he took lodging with us. After getting up the water as well as we could, we spread our blankets. Mrs. Walker & myself with all our clothing loose, Indian rubber coats & shoes on, lay down & the gentlemen covered us. Then they spread their blankets & lay down beside us. We had a good nights rest & feel well this morning. Mr. and Mrs. Walker, Mr. S & myself occupy one tent.

3rd. THURSDAY.   Have had a pleasant day. Encamped early in the afternoon. The ladies went to washing [32] & I prepared some dinner, & did some baking. Some of the company found some wild honey & a

---

in her diary of April 30, reports that they bought some "dried green corn" from the Indians that day. FWW, II, p. 76. This corn with the ham given by Major Harris provided the dinner for the party that evening.

[31] Dr. Chute joined the party this day bringing word that he had been unable to locate the three missing horses. Since the party had started with only the minimum number of animals, the loss was serious. A mule was purchased from the Indians on April 30th. Now Dr. Chute offered to sell his horse and his offer was accepted. This gave the mission party a total of twenty-four horses and mules. After deducting nine for riding, one for drawing the wagon, this left only fourteen animals to carry all of the necessary baggage which was not in the wagon.

[32] For the first time for nearly two weeks, the women found an opportunity to wash their clothes. While Sarah remained in camp to prepare dinner, the other three women retired to a secluded spot on a nearby creek where they heated water in a kettle over a camp fire and did their washing. Myra Eells wrote of the three being dressed "in our night dresses" for the occasion. FWW, II, p. 76. Mary Walker in her entry for this day commented: "Our company do nothing but jaw all the time. I never saw such a cross company before." The difficulties under which the missionaries were traveling and camping were beginning to corrode ordinary politeness and mutual respect. Since Mary Walker was the only one in the party who was writing a diary just for herself and for no one else to read, we find that she is much more frank and revealing in her comments than any one else, regarding the petty bickerings which were beginning to arise.

portion was sent to us. Here I will remark that most all the cooking is done by the gentlemen. Travelled 14 miles.

4th. FRIDAY. This has been a cold windy day and we have travelled 21 miles without stopping. When we encamped for the night, we are much fatigued. Have travelled over an elevated tract of country. Our hunters have killed some venison, and we are glad having had nothing but salt fat bacon to eat for a long time.[33] We have almost a constant wind upon the prairie, which is very unpleasant.

5th. SAT. Travelled 14 miles without stopping when we encamped for the night.[34] The company's burning the prairie. It looks fine, particularly in the night. We have passed through a beautiful country today. Some places would almost surpass New Haven for beauty. Have forded another river, the Big Blue, a branch of the Kansas. A windy day but not as cold as yesterday.

6th. SAB. This has been a cold windy day.[35] The wind sometimes so strong we could hardly hold on our horses. After riding 24 miles without stopping, we have encamped on a ravine where there is no wood & no water except a little pond of still water. It is so cold we suffered much before a fire could be made for us, the gentlemen having to take the mules to go to get wood. But we have now taken supper & a cup of tea made from standing water & very thankful for that. We have made our beds as comfortable as possible and when we have sought the protection of our Heavenly Father shall retire to rest.

7th. MON. Travelled 20 miles, another cold rainy day. Mr. Walker is sick, taken an emetic.[36]

33 Asa was by this time becoming more and more critical of their daily fare. See his letter for April 28th in which he wrote: "The principal part of our living has been bread & bacon." Now Sarah comments on the same fact and refers to the joy they felt in having fresh venison.

34 This day Asa wrote: "Felt quite unwell, having taken cold but there is no release in this warfare." His weariness added, no doubt, to his crustiness. Mary noted that evening in her diary: "Mr. Smith undertook to help Mr. W. [her husband] correct me for dictating to Mr. Gray. I think the reproof quite unmerited." Mary is also critical of her husband. "He seems to think more of Mrs. Smith than of me. Spends a great deal more time in her society than in mine. . . I feel that I am cruelly neglected."

35 Mary Walker reported that ice had formed in their water pail during the night. She also stated: "Some of our company expressed regret that they have undertaken the journey." Without a doubt, Mary was referring to Asa Smith. Thus within two weeks after leaving the Missouri frontier, Asa was beginning to regret that he had ever started. He wrote that day in his diary: "I fear we shall lose all our piety before we get across the mountains unless we can spend the Sab. in a different manner."

36 The mission party took a great risk in venturing to cross the prairies in com-

8th. Tues. Travelled 16 miles, another cold rainy day. Travelled over high prairies. Saw some wood. Mr. Walker assisted Mr. Smith to drive the cattle.

9th. Wed. This has been a beautiful day. We have travelled 21 miles without stopping, expected to have stopped at noon on a small creek. When we reached it we found no water. Wood, water & grass are the three important requisites for an encampment. We have passed today over high level prairie. It had the appearance of an ocean. For 21 miles we saw no tree or shrub or brook or pond of water, no hill but some gentle undulations. Passed some dry prairie to which the company set fire & this moment it is a wide extent of burning prairie. It looks grand in the night. I have had a pain in my side today so that I have got off my horse and walked some. Mr. & Mrs. W. have again drove the cattle with us. This is to be our work I expect the remainder of the way. It is no small work but easier now Mr. W. assists. Mr. S. has drove them alone most of the way thus far & the other gentlemen have led the mules.

10th. Thurs.[37] We have passed today over level prairie along the Blue river. 20 miles. Stopped at noon. I would like to give you an idea how we looked moving along today. On our right hand lay an extensive plain rising in gentle undulations. On our left the waters of the Blue river. Its banks skirted with trees. Before us a train of 30 black covered carts with two ladies. Mr. Gray & Eells behind them. Next 12 cattle with their few drivers. Then 10 packed mules, following in regular

---

pany with the fur company's caravan knowing that once on their way there was no turning back and there was no possibility of tarrying in case of serious accident or illness. No matter how miserable one might feel, he had to mount his horse and keep up with the company.

[37] From Asa's diary for this day: "Our appetite is good & provision short & most of it fat meat. Could we take a meal at our father's table, it would do our souls good." Neither Asa nor Sarah refer to an incident which occurred this day and which is mentioned by both of the Walkers and Myra Eells in their diaries. On the night before, "a small suckling calf was torn some by a wolf," according to Elkanah Walker. Walker and Smith, without consulting Gray and Eells decided that it was best to kill the calf and eat it. The calf was killed and this greatly displeased Gray. Mary wrote that the other two couples, the Grays and the Eells, refused to eat the veal. On the 11th, Mary wrote: "I think Mr. S[mith] is stubborn & have about as lief things would go on & our family [i.e., the Smiths and the Walkers] devour the whole calf." Finally after some discussion that evening, according to Mary, "a treaty of peace was negotiated" and all joined in enjoying fresh veal. "Several resolves were passed," wrote Mary in her private journal, "but the peace so far as it related to Mr. Smith, I fear was a forced point." No reference to this troublesome incident appears in the diaries of either Asa or Sarah Smith. See FWW, II, p. 78.

file. Next a company of loose horses accompanied by the brave moun-
taineers with their equipment for war & hunting make up the train.
This is something the style, dear Parents, we pursue our journey, except
as we are often interrupted by the deep ravines & creeks over which
we pass.

11th. FRIDAY.   Travelled 23 miles & encamped on the banks of the
Blue river.

12th. SAT.   Travelled about 28 miles. This afternoon it has rained.

13th. SAB.   Have again travelled 28 miles without stopping. We
find no rest even on this Holy Day. I hope we are the last missionaries
that will ever attempt to cross the mountains. I should advise to go
round [the Horn] unless they are willing to lose all their piety.[38]

14th. MON.   Travelled 25 miles up the Platte river. It has been a
windy day & we are all fatigued. Have seen some war Indians. We
are now among the Pawnees. Some where near us fell the brave [Dr.]
Satterlee.[39] Supposed to have been murdered by the Pawnees. We have
been looking for his bones today. They probably lie bleaching somewhere. We know not what is before us. May God prepare us for His
holy will.

15th. TUES.[40]   A very fine day, have travelled 25 miles. Are encamped on the Platte river, which we have been following up for 3
days. Our hunter has killed a goose & an (reindeer) antelope. Thus
the Lord has provided for us. O that we might be thankful for His
goodness.

16th. WED.[41]   Have travelled 10 miles. Did not ride this morning on

---

[38] In words reminiscent of what Asa had written in his diary a few days earlier,
Sarah now pens her feelings regarding the wisdom of sending missionaries overland to Oregon. No doubt she and her husband had spent hours discussing this
subject as they together herded the small herd of cattle at the tail end of the long
caravan. Thus within about three weeks after starting their land travels, the two
had come to the conclusion that the whole thing was a mistake. Now Sarah was
ready to admit this in the diary which was to be sent back to her parents.

[39] Dr. Benedict Satterlee and his bride, missionaries under the American Board
to the Pawnees, had gone out to the frontier with the Whitman-Spalding party in
1836. Mrs. Satterlee died just before she reached her field on April 30th. About a
year later Dr. Satterlee was murdered on the prairie. Although an effort was made
to place the blame on Indians, evidence clearly implicated a white man. See undated newspaper clipping, John Dunbar file, Coll. A.

[40] Mary Walker noted in her diary that on this day she enjoyed the company of
a Swiss gentleman who regaled her with stories of "Swiss dogs digging men out
who are buried in snow." Undoubtedly the reference is to Captain John Sutter who
was on his way to California and who travelled with the caravan to the Rendezvous
and then with the mission party to Waiilatpu.

[41] Mary Walker: "Mr. Smith short as pie crust." FWW, II, p. 81. That day Asa

account of the rain. Had a little time to rest.

17th. THURS.   Past night it rained very much and the water came through our tent & had it not been for our Indian rubber clothing, we should have been very wet. The water came in at the sides & foot of our tent very much, so that in putting our feet down, we put them in cold water. When I dressed in the morning my clothes were wet but I do not know that I have taken cold. As I lay in bed & the rain falling on us, I could not help thinking of dear sister Roxana in our little bedroom, sweetly sleeping & quietly. I did not wish to return nor did I feel that my lot was a hard one.[42] I share more of the comforts of life than I may deserve. O that I might ever consider this. I cannot endure as much as my Savior endured for me & I will endure patiently every trial with Christian meekness. Dear Parents pray for me.

18th. FRIDAY.   Travelled 27 miles. This morning received a visit from some of the Pawnee Indians. Curiosity I suppose prompted their visit. They love to look at us & examine all we have about us & would gladly steal a little if they could. They encamped at noon with us. I sat a little distance from the company watching my saddle &c. when a company of them came around me. They would look at me & laugh & talk to each other.[43] One came & looked under my umbrella as I was sitting on the ground. I looked up to him & smiled & said ha, ha. He was pleased with the attention & quickly said ha, ha, shook hands with me & passed off. The Pawnees like the Kansas wear very little clothing, most of those I saw were naked except a piece of cloth around the middle of their bodies. Their limbs were painted with vermillion & black lead. Their ears were pierced in many places & strings of beads & other ornaments strung in. Their countenances expressive, tho I

wrote in his diary: "Often I have no time to read the Bible from morning till night. At night I find myself so fatigued usually that I do not feel able to stir." The caravan was then on the south bank of the big bend of the Platte in what is now south-central Nebraska. That day Gray traded for some dried buffalo meat with the Pawnees. Fresh buffalo meat was secured two days later, some four weeks after the missionaries had left the frontier.

[42] Mary Walker: "Our bed was utterly flooded & almost everything wet." And yet after such a night, Sarah could reassure her parents that she had no regrets in going!

[43] All of the wives of the missionaries were a wonderment to the Indians, but especially Sarah Smith because of her red hair. A Smith family tradition tells of an Indian chief going to Asa and offering to buy his wife in order to get a red scalp. Such an offer may reflect the chief's sense of humor. According to the tradition, the Smiths compromised by giving the chief a clipping of her hair. (From letter to author, Mar. 17, 1965, from Ruby Gilbert Merrill of West Brookfield, Mass.) Asa noted in his diary: "They stood & gazed at her till our horses were saddled & we were on our way."

thought not as much as Kansas. Their foreheads were not as high &
they are not as large a people. The Kansas are said to be the largest
framed of any tribe. The females are very muscular & perform most of
the labor.

19th. SAT. Travelled 25 miles up the Platte river. Buffalo many.
Our hunter has killed 5 & brought us the meat of 3. We have had a
fine supper. Have travelled on low prairie along the Platte. On the
north of it, at the distance of some miles, rose numerous bluffs with
lofty bluff peaks. Their irregular situation, huge form & ragged sides
gave them an appearance of grandeur rather than beauty. We have
been troubled with gnats along this river. A little insect of the fly kind,
the bite is much worse than the musquito & we are all handsomely
bitten. I assure you, my health is good.

20th. SAB. This is the Holy Sabbath, but how desecrated. We are
in the country of hostile Indians & deem it unsafe to pursue our journey alone. Therefore we must move with the company & they do not
regard the Sabbath or God of Sabbaths. We have today forded the
south fork of the Platte, more than a quarter of a mile wide. The
water came to the body of the horses & the wind was high, but we
all crossed in safety. Travelled 18 miles.

FORT LARAMIE TO THE RENDEZVOUS

*Fort Laramie in the Black Hills of Wyoming was about two-thirds
of the way from Westport to the 1838 Rendezvous. The caravan arrived at the fort on May 30th and remained there for three days. This
gave the women another opportunity to wash their clothes and to rest.
Sarah failed to write anything in her diary from May 20th to the 30th.
In a long entry made on the 30th, she summarized the experiences of
the previous ten days. For a detailed description of these days we
must turn to the diaries of other members of the party.*

*Mary Walker's diary for this period, May 20-30, is especially reveal-
ing. The hardships attendant upon their method of travel — including
lack of proper food, extreme fatigue, the cramped camping conditions
when two couples shared one small tent, and the inevitable personality conflicts — created tensions which increased with the passing of
the days. On May 21st, Mary wrote: "Mrs. Smith very much out with
Dr. Gray, in a fret all the time." Notice the title, "Dr. Gray," Because
of his few weeks at a medical school, Gray had encouraged the other
members of the reenforcement to call him "Doctor." After the arrival
of the reenforcement at Waiilatpu, Dr. Whitman quickly corrected the*

*situation and wrote to the Board asking for a correction in their
records. After being listed as "Doctor" for one year in the American
Board's annual report, a correction was made and thereafter Gray was
called "Mechanic & Teacher." On May 27th, Mary wrote again: "Mr.
Walker & Gray agree pretty well now & Mr. Smith & Walker apart.
We have a strange company of Missionaries. Scarcely one who is not
intolerable on some account."*

*The missionaries left their light wagon at the fort and four of their
cattle which were unable to travel further because of poor feet. Two
more horses were purchased. Some 325 miles remained to be traveled
before they would reach the Rendezvous. This took another three
weeks or from June 2nd to the 21st. After leaving the fort, the trail
continued along the north bank of the North Fork of the Platte until
June 8th when this stream was crossed. The caravan then cut across
country to the north bank of the Sweetwater, a tributary of the North
Fork. The company arrived at Independence Rock, one of the most
noted landmarks along the Oregon Trail, on June 14th. Four days west
of Independence Rock, the caravan turned to the right and crossed the
divide into the valley of the Big Horn River, a tributary of the Yellowstone River. The Rendezvous of that year was held at the junction of
the Popo Agie and Wind Rivers, about forty-five miles north of the
Sweetwater. This part of the journey proved to be one of the most
strenuous for the women because of the mountainous terrain.*

30th. WED.   Since I last wrote we have travelled 250 miles over an
uninhabited wilderness. Have been following the Platte & have today
crossed Laramie fork & are encamped near the fort. There are no
Indians here, they have all gone to fight with the Pawnees. We are
among the Sioux. We see some females probably the wives of white
men. Last eve we received a call from one of the wives of some trader.
Her attendant said she had never seen a white woman & had come 3
miles to see us. She was dressed in fine style. Perhaps her dress cost
100 dollars. It was trimmed in beads & other ornaments throughout &
beads of a costly kind about her neck. Her dress was mountain sheepskin, white & soft as kid. I wish you could have seen her. I certainly
never saw so much ornament but it all showed the barrenness of her
mind. It is said these trappers take great pleasure in dressing their
Indian brides but care not for their minds. Some of our company will
take wives from here to go with them to the mountains. Capt. Dripps
has two. The country over which we have passed since the 20th is very
interesting.

After crossing the south branch of the Platte, we travelled about 40 miles up the river, when we crossed over to the north fork. As we approached the north fork, we found deep ravines and high bluffs among which we wound our way. Also the country along the north fork is very interesting. The soil is usually good. We have often found beds of salt, not pure but a combination of salts as Epsom or Glauber salts together with the common salt. The Platte river is shallow with a sandy bottom & the water like the Missouri is medicinal & very turbid. Have found but little wood & for a substitute have used buffalo manure to boil our tea or cook our meat. A description of some of the numerous bluffs & deep ravines would not be interesting perhaps. I think we found no water in any of the ravines but an appearance of their having been much water at certain seasons of the year & channels of several feet deep were cut by these torrents.

Some of the bluffs were very remarkable, rising almost perpendicular & of peculiar shape, some nearly square, others conical resembling a work of art rather than nature. One perhaps more remarkable we saw called the chimney presents a very irregular appearance. Its form is pyramidal & at the top it rises perpendicular to the height of several hundred feet which gives it the appearance of a chimney.[44] From its appearance we suppose it must be composed of earth or clay & that the earth must have been washed away leaving these various shapes, but how it could be done is very singular. We have travelled with great rapidity & have often been much fatigued, but the prospect of soon reaching our field of labor & engaging in our Master's work has inspired us to press on.

One thing I greatly desire of which I must be deprived, that is retirement.[45] In the morning as soon as it is light & even while yet the moon & stars are shining, we must rise & hasten to our labor. The tent with two families is the only place for prayers. If we seek the prairie it is an open plain, without a shade or rock or even a hill to hide us from the gaze of a noisy company. At noon the umbrella is our only shelter. When possible Mr. Smith & myself have gone to some ravine or tree & there prayed, but even there have often been disturbed. Yet I hope my Savior has not forsaken me, but has often been near to cheer & comfort me.

---

[44] All of the missionaries commented on the spectacular scenery along this part of the Platte River and especially Chimney Rock.

[45] Here Sarah mentions one of the most grievous trials of their overland travels, that of the lack of privacy. In Asa's letter of August 10, 1838, to his brother, John, he had stressed the importance of retirement for the cultivation of "personal piety."

31st. Thursday.   Have been much engaged today, washing & repairing my clothes, found it very pleasant to rest a day or rather change exercise for I have labored as hard today as on any day. We prepared a dinner & invited some of the company to dine with us.[46] We shall remain here some days.

June 1st.   Much engaged repairing our clothing. Received a call from some Indian females, wives of Capt. Dripps & Fontenelle, also a son of Fontenelle, a fine lad of 12 years. They wished to have us sing, & so we sang, Yes, my Native Land, I love thee.[47] It is interesting to converse with these people & also to learn some of their superstitious notions. In passing through the buffalo country, we have often seen buffalo heads lying with the faces toward the east. The Indians believe if they face the sun's rising, buffalo will rise, if toward the sun's going down, buffalo will go down. We often see several placed in a circle, around these the Indians meet, sing, smoke the pipe & pray to the great Spirit that buffalo may increase. One thing is interesting. When they have been on a hunting expedition & been successful, they will build a fire & bake the best pieces of meat they have & offer it as a sacrifice to the great Spirit.

June 2nd. Sat.   Moved camp today & were very glad. Had remained quiet as long as we could enjoy it. Travelled 15 miles. We can judge of distance only by the supposed miles we move in an hour & then count the hours.[48] The scenery today has been very interesting, bluffs & mountains with their snow capped tops, beautiful streams of water, lofty trees, plains & ravines have met our view. We are among the Black Hills between Laramie's fork & north fork. Are encamped at the foot of some beautiful bluffs with a deep ravine passing through them. We have now a heavy thunder shower but with the oil cloth over the tent the water does not come through.

June 3. Sab.   Again travelled 25 miles. O, when shall I again enjoy the privileges of this Holy Day. My dear Parents you know not the privileges you enjoy of going to the house of God & attending on the means of grace. I sometimes doubt with regard to our duty. Often feel

---

[46] Myra Eells mentions having Captains Andrew Dripps and Lucien Fontanelle for tea. Mary Walker wrote: "To dine with us had Mr. Clark, son of the Clark who accompanied Lewis."

[47] This hymn, "Yes, my native land! I love thee," was sung at the wedding of Narcissa Prentiss and Marcus Whitman, February 18, 1836. See Drury, *Marcus Whitman, M.D.*, p. 123. The author of the hymn was the Rev. Samuel F. Smith who also wrote "My country, 'tis of thee."

[48] See FWW, II, p. 63ff and 96, fn. 5, for a discussion of the possible ways by which distances were estimated.

that we should be more safe to leave the company & go forward trusting in God to protect us than we are to violate his commands & break his Sabbath. I hope no other missionaries will be obliged to do as we do. Are encamped among the Black Hills. Large trees all around us so that we can have a little retirement. Mrs. Eells & myself have sought a seclusion where we could pour out our full hearts in prayer to God. Found it good to pray together.

4th. Mon.[49] Yesterday we witnessed one of the most beautiful prospects I ever saw & some truly grand. We followed around among the bluffs. Saw their ragged sides & the deep indentations made by falling water. Passed among beautiful groves of pine trees, foliage of the deepest green. We crossed some beds of sand, where some beautiful river had once flowed & where now is only left a rill to tell us what has been. Passed some delightful plains studded with beautiful pines & some lofty bluffs whose towering tops & ragged sides presented an appearance of grandeur rather than beauty. Today the scene has been indeed grand. Our course has been more mountainous than yesterday. Have rode where it was so steep I was obliged to hold to my saddle lest I should fall over my horses head and again ascended where I must hold by her mane to keep from slipping off backward but I enjoyed it much. Of course we went where the waggons could not. Travelled 25 miles, 10½ hours.

June 5th. Tuesday. Travelled today about 15 miles over mountains & ravines. The scenery grand. Many of the bluffs appeared to be composed of red sandstone. The hills which we see on every side of us are I think rightly named Black Hills for they indeed present a very dark appearance, most of them being covered with pines of a heavy green.

6th. Wed. Move at 4 this morning as usual. Took breakfast of buffalo & again commenced travelling. Our leader told us if we would leave the company and follow him, he would lead us 4 miles, where the wagons would go to. So Mr. & Mrs. Eells, Mr. S. & myself with the pack animals concluded to follow him. He took us over awful places, mountains & deep ravines where in many places we dare not ride the horses, & then he did not know where the company would camp for

---

[49] Another incident took place this day which disturbed the peace of the mission band and which is not mentioned by Sarah. Mary Walker wrote: "Mrs. Smith & Eells being unwilling to give away milk, we divide & give away part of ours. Think we shall enjoy what we have left as well as they." And on the 7th, she wrote again: "In the evening gave Mrs. Smith a small piece of my mind about milk, mothers, &c." Just what was the need for sharing some fresh milk with some one not in the mission party is not stated.

noon but guessed at it & the company did not come there but so near that we could see them. We had a fine time, had all the food with us. Cooked our dinner & ate it alone. Then started to meet the company. Came to them about 2. Soon left them again, witnessed some most romantic scenery. Crossed deep ravines, rode along the side of one high bluff that overhung the water. Encamped about 4 on the Platte. Travelled at least 20 miles, 9½ hours.

7th. Thurs. Have been travelling near the Platte today of course more level. This afternoon we had a prairie gale of wind, thunder & rain. It has been windy all day & about 3 the sky grew dark, the rain began to fall & our horses refused to advance but instantly whirled about & stood still till the gale was over. Travelled 12 miles and encamped in the woods near the Platte.

8th. Friday. Have been travelling near the Platte 20 miles, the scene monotonous. The Black Hills on one side of us & the Platte on the other. The soil among these hills usually poor. Much red sandstone. Whole bluffs appear to be composed of it. Find very much of the prickly pear. Are still encamped on the Platte.[50]

9th. The company are making boats to cross the river. I have been much engaged doing some sewing. I find little rest but this world is not the place of rest. We have in company with us, the wife & 4 little children of Eneus, one of the 3 men who were murdered last autumn in company with Mr. Gray.[51] Eneus, it is said, was a noble Indian, a Flathead. He had some property which the trappers were owing him, was intending to go with his family somewhere to have his children educated. What will become of them now, we know not. Several female Indians are journeying with us. The two wives of Captain Dripps. They are trimmed off in high style, I assure you. The oldest wife rides a beautiful white horse, her saddle ornamented with beads and many little gingles. A beautiful white sheepskin covering for the horse, cut

---

[50] The caravan was then in the vicinity of what is now Casper, Wyoming. Sarah's reference to the "prickly pear" is to the pear-shaped and prickly fruit of a flat-stemmed cactus.

[51] Gray, who went out to Oregon with the Whitmans and Spaldings in 1836, returned for reenforcements in 1837. He decided to drive a band of horses to the Missouri frontier with the hope of making a good profit in their sale. He had with him three Nez Perce or Flathead Indians. Being impulsive and acting contrary to the advice of such experienced mountain men as Jim Bridger, Gray and his party left the Rendezvous of 1837 in advance of the returning caravan. They were attacked by the Sioux at Ash Hollow in what is now western Nebraska on August 7th. Gray's Indian companions were killed and his horses were stolen. He barely escaped with his life. This incident accounts for much of the hostility shown to Gray by the mountain men at the Rendezvous of 1838.

in fringes ½ a yd. deep, ornamented with collars & a great number of
thimbles pierced in the top & hung to the fringe like little balls, making
a fine gingle as she rides along. Then comes the rider with her scarlet
blanket, painted face & hankerchief on her head, sitting astride. This
is the fashion of the country. The second wife acts as an attendant.
This is a rainy day.

JUNE 10th. SAB.[52]   On account of the rain we have not moved camp,
so we have had an opportunity to rest & give ourselves a little reflec-
tion. Have spent the day in our little tent reading the Bible. Have not
had religious exercises publicly, as the only way we could possibly
keep ourselves comfortable has been to cover ourselves with our
blanket, it has been so cold & wet, but we are glad to have a rainy
Sabbath for the sake of not laboring. Soon I hope the time will come
when we can spend the Sabbath according to the dictates of our consciences, even if we be separated from Christian friends, society &
privileges. The rain continues & it is beginning to come in under our
tent & wet our bed. The oilcloth which we use as a floor in a dry day is
now spread upon the top of the tent to keep the rain from coming
through & it shields us very well.[53] But now the ground is becoming
very wet but I will not complain. I have more of the comforts of life
than my Savior had, for he had not where to lay his head.

It is sunset. My dear parents may be thinking of Sarah & perhaps
offering a prayer for her. O, I know you pray for me at the family altar.
I often think of that hour & I feel I meet you there although separated
in person, we can meet in spirit at the throne of grace. I love to meet
you there. I love to pray for you. I love to feel that my God & father
is your God & Father & that hereafter when these bodies are worn out

---

[52] Mary Walker again with caustic frankness wrote in her diary for this day:
"The uneasy, fretful disposition of Mrs. Smith, together with her persistent whispering are very unpleasant to me." The caravan was encamped that day while making
preparations to cross the Platte. Since it was raining the missionaries stayed in
their tents as much as possible. The whispering of the Smiths on one side of the
dividing sheet in the tent became annoying to Mary. Her account continues: "Her
husband is much of a hog at table as I have seen. He frequently treats me with
what I deem rudeness. There is about them what looks a good deal like pure
selfishness." Mary was critical of others as well. "Mr. Eells is very uninteresting
and unsocial, and in his character the 'I' eclipses the whole horizon. Dr. Gray is
exceedingly fractious. It is rather difficult getting along with him." FWW, II, p. 91.

[53] The "thin duck" sailcloth out of which the women had made their tents at
Independence, Missouri, was not heavy enough to keep out the rain. Perhaps this
is another instance of where Gray, wishing to economize in order to cut down
costs for the board, had purchased inferior material. The Smiths had to choose
between putting their oilcloth over the top of the tent to keep out the rain or putting it under their blankets to give them a dry bed.

in the cause of our Master we shall meet in Heaven no more to part. My dear Parents, brother & sister, let us reverently consecrate ourselves to God, let us live devoted to His service & strive to glorify him. What is this life worth if not spent in the service of God. Then may we meet in Heaven.

11th. Mon. Dear Mother, I would like to give you an idea how we look in our little tent this rainy morning. Being encamped on low clay soil, there is mud & water all around us & some water within. Our tent is 10 feet long & 8 wide on the ground. Sometimes have a curtain to separate the families that we may be more retired as yesterday & today. Also put up the curtain when we sleep. In our part we have this morning our two saddles & blankets, my work basket, our India rubber valise, Mr. Smith's gun & shaving apparatus, a long box that holds the dishes, my cloak, bonnet &c. Not having chairs, we are sitting on the blankets writing on our laps. All our things are very damp. The ground soaked with water. We have a buffalo hide spread down but that is now wet & I have been taking the water off it with the sponge & the water is now dripping through upon us & we can't help it. We sit with our India rubber shoes, shawls & hoods on, it is so cold. Mrs. Walker has been crying. I asked her why she cried. She said to think how comfortable her father's hogs were. This made us both laugh & cry together.[54]

AFTERNOON — The rain has ceased & we have crossed the river. We crossed in the company's boats which were wagon bodies covered with green buffalo hides. At one oclock we were all safely landed. Our ride upon the water was about one fourth of a mile. Have just taken our supper of buffalo.[55] We love it very much when it is cooked good as it was tonight. Mr. Gray & Mr. Smith are cooks. They sometimes make nice soups of it, sometimes boil & fry, sometimes chop it & make it appear like sausage. After it is fried, make a milk gravy & it is very

---

[54] May 10th and 11th were two of the most trying days endured by the missionaries on their long trek to Oregon. The weather was miserable being both cold and rainy. The missionaries found it a constant struggle to stay warm and dry. On the morning of the 11th, Mary Walker sat on her baggage in her soggy tent and wept. Of this she wrote in her diary: "In the forenoon I cried to think how comfortable father's hogs were." This incident seems to have become the best remembered anecdote of their overland travels. Sarah's comment as to how she and Mary laughed and cried together shows that even in their misery they retained a sense of humor. See Eells reminiscences, pp. 299-300.

[55] An exclusively meat diet often caused diarrhea. See Mary's entry for May 11th, FWW, II, p. 92 and Smith, SS, 64. How ironical that Asa who was at one time a vegetarian should now be forced to subsist on an almost exclusively meat diet.

fine. Such was our supper tonight. We eat no bread at all, are saving the flour, fearing we shall need it more when on the sandy plain where there is no game.

JUNE 12th. TUESDAY. Rose this morning at 4. Moved camp at 6½ [o'clock], travelled till two without stopping, then encamped for the night, moved slow, travelled about 12 miles. Have seen but little timber, built our fire of mountain sedge which grew in abundance. The scenery less romantic than much we have passed, more level. Have witnessed the distant snow capped mountains of the Wind river. These are the first we have seen of the Rocky mountains.

We have seen snow upon many of the mountains of the Black Hills. It has been cold today. It is now raining. Encamped on a small creek in the open plain.

13th. WED. Travelled 8 hours, supposed to go about 15 miles. Are encamped among the hills near a little spring of water, no wood, our fuel mountain sedge. This is a rough barren region, sandy & stony. Our course today less mountainous. Soon we shall reach the Rocky Mountains. I long to be there, for I long to be at my journey's end. I long to be telling the dying heathen the story of the cross. O, how happy I shall be in my laboring for the good of those dear Indians. May God prepare me to do them good. I feel that I need to possess more of the spirit of heaven & more of that wisdom which is from above ere I shall be prepared to engage in the holy work before me. But there is one to whom I can go for needed grace. I need not fear if I will put my trust in him. He is able to sustain me.

14th. THURS. Have been travelling over high prairie today, with the Rocky Mts. full in view & white with snow. We have mounted some hills, crossed some ravines, but most of the way has been level. The soil has no grass, no timber, fuel buffalo manure. Are encamped on Sweetwater, a branch of the Platte, at the foot of Independence rock,[56] so called because here the Fur Company once celebrated Independence. It is very large, covers several acres of ground & rises to the height of perhaps 120 feet. It looks as if thrown up by some volcanic power. At its foot is a salt lake. Have passed several today. Have travelled 9 hours. Supposed to go 25 miles.

JUNE 15th. FRIDAY. This morning Mr. and Mrs. Gray & Mrs. Walker

---

[56] The turtle-shaped rock which arises abruptly out of the plain on the bank of the Sweetwater River, is about one-eighth of a mile long, 110 feet wide, and from sixty to seventy feet high. So many of the passing travelers carved their names on its gray granite sides that it became known as the great register of the desert.

ascended the height of Independence rock. Invited me to go but I felt I must spare my strength for the duties of the day. At 7 mounted our horses, followed along the Sweetwater a little distance till we came to a fording place. In attempting to cross Mrs. Eells' horse plunged upon quick sands & sank. Mrs. E. extricated herself as soon as possible without injury except to be much wet & muddied.[57] The horse was soon got out.

16th. SAT.   Travelled about 16 miles up the Sweetwater, most of the way level with high granite mountains near us. These mountains rise back from the river to the height of some hundred feet. Our supper is ready, it consists of roasted buffalo. I think father would love to take supper with us. I am sure he would enjoy the buffalo. It is very fine. I sometimes feel I would like to sit once more at dear mother's table with father, mother, brother & sister, but I fear it is wrong. I would not send one wicked, sinful glance to my dear home. I would not abandon the glorious work before [us], if by so doing I might return to the loved mansion or be situated in any situation of ease or comfort New England could afford. Rather would I wear myself out in the cause of my Master if I might be counted worthy to labor for him who died for me.[58]

17th. SAB.   Travelled about 15 miles & encamped on the Sweet Water. A beautiful day but no Sabbath of rest.

18th. MON.   Rose this morning at 3½, breakfast at 4½, travelled about 12 miles when we encamped for the day on the Sweetwater. It is very warm & our animals are tired & we are all tired, have been very busy this afternoon mending my booties &c. Mr. Smith is nearly sick.[59]

19th. TUES.   Have had a long day's ride & gone but a little distance, started at 7 & travelled till 4 without stopping. Are encamped on a creek. We left the Sweetwater & passed over a creek that enters into the Yellowstone. The scenery was beautiful. When we reached the height of land between Sweetwater & Yellow Stone, the prospect was fine. A deep valley of considerable extent spread before us. In this valley were numerous hills here & there, rough & broken. On one side of this valley, the Wind river mountains, white with snow stretched along for a great distance. In some places the descent into the valley

---

[57] See comment on this incident in Eells reminiscences, p. 303. Yet Myra Eells made no mention of her frightening experience in her diary entry for that day.

[58] Mixed emotions were still surging through the heart and mind of homesick Sarah. Her sense of Christian duty was clashing with the hard facts of their manner of life from which there was no escape. Still, any regrets were sinful.

[59] Asa was still afflicted with diarrhea because of the buffalo meat diet.

was almost perpendicular. We descended into the valley & after riding a long distance reached the encampment.

20th. Wed.   Travelled about 15 miles over a rough & barren country, followed down the creek on which we encamped last night, stopped at noon where I refreshed myself with a dinner of buffalo & a pleasant sleep on the ground. This I usually do and can sleep as sweetly as on the best bed in my father's house. Are encamped on the same stream that we did last night.

21st. Thurs.   Travelled today over mountains and awful ravines, so steep that the horse could hardly carry me. It seemed many times as if I should fall over his head. Many places were frightful. We ascended one mountain & rode along on its summit some distance where we had an extensive view of the surrounding landscape, which was most splendid. What fartherest met our view were the lofty snow capped mountains of the Wind river stretching along from north to south, a great distance below them numerous bluffs & plains. Here & there clusters of beautiful trees clothed with green the Popesia [river] flowing in beautiful meanderings through the valley. We encamped at noon on the river, expecting there to rendezvous but again took our horses & rode about a mile. Are now encamped on the Popesia. Expect to cross soon & rendezvous on the other side where is better feed for our animals. We may remain here a month before we can get company to go with us to the Columbia. This company will go no further with us. Travelled 12 miles.

AT THE 1838 RENDEZVOUS

During the heyday of the Rocky Mountain beaver trade, i.e., 1825-39, an annual gathering of trappers and traders, sponsored by various American fur companies, was held at some convenient site in the Rockies and called the Rendezvous. Here supplies from civilization would arrive, usually during the latter part of June or the first part of July, which would be traded for furs. Hundreds of trappers and sometimes thousands of Indians from several tribes would gather for the great Rocky Mountain emporium. This was also the greatest annual social event in the lives of the trappers who were making their living by trapping beaver. Most of the Rendezvous were held west of the Continental Divide. The extensive and well-watered meadows on Green River in the vicinity of what is now Daniel, Wyoming, was a favorite meeting place. Only three — 1829, 1830, and 1838 — were held east of the Divide. The last of the three met where the Pope Agie (more commonly called the Popeasia) and the Wind Rivers join to make the Big Horn. Here the American Fur Company's caravan of 1838, with its party of nine missionaries, arrived on Thursday, June 21st.

By 1838 the beaver trade was on the decline. The proximity of the Hudson's Bay Company's post at Fort Hall, near what is now Pocatello, Idaho, presented a continuing competition to the Americans. Records show that representatives of the Hudson's Bay Company were often at the Rendezvous, no doubt to the great displeasure of the Americans. Writing to Secretary Greene from Waiilatpu on October 15, 1838, Walker explained that the Rendezvous of that year was held east of the Divide because "its place being kept a secret, it was expected that the H.B.C. would not find it." Eells, writing his reminiscences many years later, makes a similar statement. According to Eells, Gray had made an arrangement with Francis Ermantinger, who was in charge of Fort Hall in 1838, to meet the missionary reenforcement at the 1838 Rendezvous and escort them as far west as Fort Hall. When Ermantinger with a small party of about fourteen men arrived at the Green River site during the first week of July, he found it deserted. According to Mrs. Walker's diary, he found a notice Jim Bridger had posted on the door of an old storehouse there which read: "Come to Popeasia; plenty of whiskey and white women." The reference to white women was clearly to the missionary ladies. Ermantinger then hastened across the Divide to Wind River where he arrived on Sunday, July 8th. Walker informed Greene: "He came a long distance out of his way for the sake of meeting us & conducting us to his place, Fort Hall."

With Ermatinger was the Rev. Jason Lee, head of the Methodist Mission in the Willamette Valley, then on his way East with the three sons of Tom McKay, a Hudson's Bay employee, and two Indian boys. The youths were being taken East in order to be educated. Since the mission party had arrived at the Rendezvous seventeen days before Ermatinger arrived, they were becoming greatly concerned about the remaining part of their journey. They were facing the possibility of traveling through some hostile Indian country without an escort. The arrival of Ermatinger at the Rendezvous was, therefore, a source of great relief to the Oregon-bound missionaries.

The diaries and letters of the members of the 1838 reenforcement written while at the Rendezvous are filled with interesting comments about the mountain men, their native wives, and the "multitude of half breed children." The excessive drinking, the carousing, the blas-

phemies, and the scalp-dances were shocking and offensive to the missionaries. Yet, according to Smith, with the exception of some hostility shown to Gray because of the Ash Hollow incident of the previous summer, the mission party was treated with "much kindness and attention." The presence of white women at a Rocky Mountain Rendezvous was a novelty. This had happened only once before and that was when Mrs. Whitman and Mrs. Spalding were present in 1836. Now for four to appear was indeed an historic occasion.

Sarah's diary contains some charming descriptions of their experiences at the Rendezvous. She writes of using the inside of some peeled bark as a bread board and a peeled branch of a tree for a rolling pin. Her several references to her home back East suggest her homesickness. Mary Walker wrote that Sarah was often weeping. Yet Sarah was careful not to permit her writing to betray any heaviness of heart. This she kept secret from her parents. When Jason Lee continued his eastward travels with the returning caravan, he carried with him a number of letters from various members of the mission party.

22nd. [JUNE] FRIDAY. Find it very pleasant to rest today. Have been sewing this afternoon. Mr. S. & myself took a short walk in the grove [60] & it being very cold, Mr. S. built a fire & we sat by it some time, read our Bible & held a season of prayer together. We find it good to get away alone & pray. Retirement is what we most need & for that we have little opportunity. O I long for some little spot we can call our home & can live as we please. We still love Mr. and Mrs. Walker & are happy in their society. Still we love retirement. But that in our present situation we can not have. We shall know how to prize it when we can enjoy it.

JUNE 23. SAT. Spent part of the day washing clothes. In the afternoon crossed the Popesia by fording. Crossed in two places, the river being separated by an island. Are encamped on the bank of the Big Horn. Mr. S. has built a little house by putting down poles & fastening the oilcloth & blankets to them.[61] It is a little larger than the tent

---

[60] Myra Eells in her diary tells of the mission party camping in a grove of cottonwood. Mary Walker wrote about picking gooseberries and currants. The author visited the site on July 15, 1960, and found that the cottonwood trees were still growing there and that the gooseberries and currants were still to be found. See FWW, II, p. 95 and for picture of junction of the streams, *ibid.*, p. 85.

[61] For the first time since they left the Missouri frontier, the Smiths found an opportunity to have their own separate shelter. Mary wrote in her diary: "Mr. S. has gone to living by himself. Query, does not the course he is pursuing cost him some misgiving? It will be pleasant not to hear so much fault finding." FWW, II, p. 97.

because it is the same size at the top as at the bottom or on the ground. Here we keep all our baggage & have things convenient & pretty. Mr. & Mrs. Walker are also more comfortable.

24. SAB.   Have had worship today in the open air, under the shade of some large trees. Some of the company met with us.[62] Brother Walker led the services this morning, Brother Eells this afternoon. Were happy to enjoy such a privilege in this wilderness.

25th. MON.   Have been sewing today. It is very warm & we are much troubled with mosquitoes. Saturday night we had a rice pudding, except for that we have had nothing but buffalo for a long time and I should love a crust of brown bread even if it was very poor. It being so warm, we feel the need of vegetable food more than we did. We did not take a sufficient supply of flour & rice & what we have we dare not eat. For Mr. Gray is often telling us we shall starve & starve to death unless we use the most rigid economy. Dear friends when you sit at your table loaded with the good bread, vegetables & other luxuries, will you not think of those who are deprived of them? Will you not think of the missionary who has left them all for the cause of Christ & who is looking to your charity for a bare support?

JUNE 26. TUES.   Am quite alone today. Mr. S. with some others have gone after the cows which have strayed away.[63] Have been reading & writing this morning. The other ladies are washing. No gentleman at home but Mr. Gray. We are camped a little distance from the company to be freed from their noise. I have been thinking of home this morning & how you look there. I can see every one of you. Mother is flying about preparing something good for dinner. Father & brother are making hay. Dear little Roxanna is in school & all things going on pleasantly. Perhaps some one may be thinking of Sarah & wishing to hear where & how she is. Little Charlie is in school too. I hope he is a good boy & will make a missionary.[64]

27th. WED.   Spent the day sewing. Am making a gingham sunbonnet which I had not time to make before I left the States. This afternoon

---

[62] Evidently only a few of the mountain men knew of a religious service to be held that day, as only a few attended. Between fifty and sixty were present the following Sunday. Hearing women's voices raised in sacred song must have been a stirring experience for these men who had been so long removed from their eastern homes.

[63] On this morning the missionaries discovered to their dismay that their small herd of cattle had taken to the trail of their own accord. Walker and Smith set out to find them and caught up with them twelve miles distant. According to Mary, they were "walking on as regularly as though they were driven." This had been the daily routine and the cattle had accepted it as a matter of habit.

Mr. S. & I have been berrying, picked more than a quart of wild currants. They are green, but may be good cooked.

28th. THURS.   Spent the day writing & sewing. To prevent our being idle, we have taken in a little sewing for the company. Have four calico dresses to make for some hunters & it is some work to make one being much ruffled.[65] We feel under obligation to the company for their kindness to us & are happy to confer a favor on them. Mr. S. has had some opportunity to furnish a little medicine for them and has also given them some Bibles which were kindly received. Have had a visit this afternoon from 6 Indian females.

29th. FRIDAY.   This morning spent several hours washing flannels. Was not near as tired as I used to be at home. Think the journey has increased my strength much. This afternoon ventured to make a rice pudding, thought it very nice without eggs & very little sugar.

30th. SAT.   Spent the morning sewing on the hunter's dress & this afternoon made a couple of pies, chopped the meat with a butcher knife on the back of a cottonwood tree which Mr. S. pealed off. Rolled the crust with a crooked stick in a hollow bark, baked them in the tin baker out of doors in the wind but they were good & we have had a good supper.

JULY 1st. SAB.   This is communion Sabbath in Brookfield but not in the mountains. Mr. S. preached this morning, Brother Walker this afternoon.

JULY 2nd. MON.   This is monthly concert day. I trust the Christians in Brookfield will not forget those who have gone out from them & to whom they have pledged their prayers. Surely they cannot if they love the cause of Christ as they ought. Have today finished the hunter's dress.

3rd. TUES.   Been assisting Mrs. Walker finish her dress today. Been feasting on dry buffalo. It is very good, better than you would expect. This is what we shall use upon the plains where there is no game.

4th. WED.   Independence day.[66] I suppose you are having some

---

[64] "Little Charlie" remains unidentified. Sarah's entry breathes a certain spirit of homesickness. In her imagination she pictures what each member of her family was probably doing. We have to turn to Mary Walker's diary to fathom the full depth of Sarah's unhappiness. Referring to Sarah, Mary wrote that "she has seemed to cry half of the time." FWW, II, p. 97.

[65] Evidently the white women were making dresses for the native wives of the mountain men.

[66] For that generation of New Englanders, Fourth-of-July was the great holiday of the year. The observance of Thanksgiving was not an established national custom. Because of their Puritan inheritance, Christmas and Easter were not regarded as anything special. New Year's Day was observed.

celebrations in New England. I spent the morning washing & made a biscuit pudding for dinner. Received a call from an Indian with nothing on but a buffalo hide. It is very warm and I am sitting under a tree.

5th. THURS.   Mr. S. & myself have taken a pleasure ride this morning of some miles, breakfasted at 10. Received a salute from some of Bridger's [67] party who have just arrived. This company consists of about 100 men & perhaps 60 Indian females & a great number of half breed children. Their arrival was attended with firing of guns & noisy shouts. Thought perhaps that we would be interested, therefore came & saluted us with firing, drumming, singing & dancing. Their appearance was rude & savage, were painted in a most hideous manner. One carried a scalp of the Black Foot in his hand. It is dreadful to hear how the whites treat the Indians. Bridger's party have just been among the Black Foot tribe. This tribe have long been a terror to neighboring tribes & to the whites, but now their number is much reduced by the smallpox & it is still raging. The Indians made no attack on B's party but this party attacked them & shot 15 of them dead without excuse but to please their wicked passions. Thus sending 15 souls to eternity & to the bar of God unprepared. A man told me of it who had a part in the horrid scene. Said that one they shot and wounded but not killed. Said that this Indian grasped the limb of a white man who stood near & made signs begging that his life might be spared while others dragged him away & cut his body in pieces regardless of his groans & entreaties. This fellow seemed to exult in it.

6th. FRIDAY.[68]   Received a call this morning from a company of Indian females, half-breeds & children, who gave us a salute of music accompanied with the scalp dance. This is a favorite amusement with them. Their singing is little more than a yell & their dance a hop.

7th. SAT.   Have been writing most of the day. Nothing of interest has taken place. Very windy & our little house suffers some.

8th. SUNDAY.   Today a company from Fort Hall has arrived with

---

[67] Jim Bridger was one of the most famous of the mountain men. Dr. Whitman had cut an arrowhead out of his back at the 1835 Rendezvous. Bridger had become involved in a battle with the Blackfeet Indians in 1832 at which time a three-inch arrowhead had lodged under his shoulder blade which could not be extracted. This Bridger carried until relieved by Dr. Whitman. Incidentally, we note which way Bridger was going when he was wounded. No doubt in the Bridger party was a three-year old daughter, Mary Ann, who in the summer of 1841 was taken to the Whitman station at Waiilatpu. Mary Ann escaped death at the Whitman massacre but died in March, 1848.

[68] Asa wrote a long letter to his family on this day in which he gave some caustic criticisms of Gray.

Mr. Ermatinger at their head. Rev. Mr. Lee is in company with them on his way to the States. He is one of the Methodist missionaries from West of the Mountains. This arrival fills our hearts with joy. This company will go with us through the most dangerous part of the country. We were intending to move camp on Tuesday next, but were feeling anxious for our safety. Supplies have been sent us from Mr. Spalding of flour, rice, Indian meal &c.[69]

9th. Mon.   Have done quite a washing & baked a rice pudding for dinner. Mr. Lee dined with us.

10th. Tues.   Had a call from a poor drunken creature who professes great attachment to Mr. Smith. Presented me with a butcher knife & a large red feather. Must receive them or offend him.

11th. Wed.   Been making preparations to leave here tomorrow. Had a rice pudding for dinner.

12th. Thurs.   Travelled 20 miles & encamped on the Popeasia. Forded the Great & Little Popeasia where the water was deep. Wet my feet.

13th. Friday.   Travelled 16 miles, moved camp about noon. Travelled over mountains & ravines, steep & rugged.[70] Many of the bluffs appear to be composed of red sandstone which abounds in this region. For considerable distance we followed along the side of a mountain where flowed the Popeasia below & a lofty steep [bluff] above us. Had anything started our horses, we most probably would have been killed as we should have gone to the bottom. We are often obliged to descend a mountain by following along upon its side. One of the mules feeling desirous of taking a shorter course than the rest leaped down a ledge of rock about 5 feet in height, displaced his pack &c. We are encamped in a garden of gooseberries, but a nest of mosquitoes.

14th. Sat.   Left the encampment at an early hour, & have had a hard day's ride. Travelled not less than 30 miles over the height of land between the Popeasia to the Sweet Water. Have passed over frightful places of which you have no idea. I was told before I left the

---

[69] Actually the supplies sent by Whitman and Spalding met the mission party at Fort Hall. This was good news to the reenforcement for they felt free to ration out their meager supply of provisions to cover the intervening three weeks. Notice how Sarah mentioned the fact that twice in the next three days they enjoyed rice pudding. Ermatinger tarried at the Rendezvous for only four days and then with the mission party started his return trip to Fort Hall.

[70] Mary Walker in her diary mentions the fact that on this day the party had to abandon their dog, King, because "having his feet blistered," he was unable to keep up with them. This part of their journey was one of the most rugged of the whole distance traveled. See FWW, ii, p. 103.

States that the ascent was so gradual that we should hardly know we had reached the mountain before we were over them, or that we should hardly know we were rising. For my part I thought we were rising today. We ascended & again descended strong mountains where I could hardly sit upon my horse. I walked down one mountain where I had to catch by the stones to keep me from falling. All this I enjoy much compared to a ride upon the prairie. I am not at all afraid. Are encamped upon a pretty brook where the water is like New England.

15th. Sab. Travelled 18 miles, encamped early on account of a party of Snake Indians who have followed us, wishing to sell skins. They are all around our tent & some almost in it. They look at my [red] hair with great interest. They are talking & laughing, greatly pleased to see a white squaw as they call me. I suspect they would like my scalp.

16th. Mon. Have had a hard day's ride, travelled 45 miles.[71] Stopped at noon on the river Sandy. This afternoon travelled 35 miles before we could find water. Are now encamped on Green river. Have crossed the dividing ridge between the eastern and western water, encamped on the eastern water for the last time last night. This is the hardest day's ride we have ever had, & I am much fatigued. Shall probably feel the effects of it many days, can hardly walk or stand for travelling.

17th. Tues. Have had a short ride of about 12 miles. Forded the

---

[71] This was the longest distance covered in one day on the entire trip from Westport to Walla Walla. See mileage chart in FWW, ii, p. 65. Forty-five miles in one day meant, according to Mary's diary, about thirteen hours in the saddle. The missionaries rode through South Pass this day, thus crossing the backbone of the Rocky Mountains. Mrs. F. F. Victor in her *River of the West* tells of how Joseph Meek, one of the mountain men travelling with the party, found the Smiths alone on the desert. According to Mrs. Victor: "Meek found the woman to be one of the missionary ladies, a Mrs. Smith, and that her husband was lying on the ground, dying, as the poor sufferer believed himself, for water." In answer to Sarah's "weeping appeal" for water, Meek, who had no water, offered alcohol. The story according to Mrs. Victor continues: "Seeing that death really awaited the unlucky missionary unless something could be done to cause him to exert himself, Meek commenced at once, with unction, to abuse the man for his unmanliness. You're a ——— pretty fellow to be lying on the ground here, lolling your tongue out of your mouth, and trying to die. Die, if you want to, you're of no account and will never be missed. Here's your wife, who you keep standing here in the hot sun; why don't she die? She's got more pluck than a white-livered chap like you." Drury, *Elkanah and Mary Walker*, p. 90. According to this story, Meek lifted Sarah to her saddle and took her into camp. Asa aroused himself and followed. Neither Mary Walker or Myra Eells mentions this incident, but it is possible that neither knew anything about it. Eells in his reminiscences branded Meek's story as "outrageously false."

Green river where the water comes nearly to the necks of the horses but the most shallow place we could find. Have encamped on a small creek emptying into Green river.

18th. WED. Travelled about 20 miles among the Rocky Mountains. Witnessed much that was grand & awful. The first part of the day we followed along a creek into the mountains. Have been travelling the high lands between Green & Bear rivers. Passed some awful places but passed in safety. In one place we rode along the side of a mountain where below us at the distance of 50 or 60 feet flowed the river & above us a lofty peak towering proudly in the air. Our road was only a narrow path where we could move only in file. Such places we often pass. The mountain was red sandstone. Are encamped in a beautiful place on Grand Creek surrounded by hills. It is quite cold. We are in the region of perpetual snow. A good fire is comfortable.

19th. THURS. Have had a most interesting ride today. The mountains we have crossed have some of them been covered with beautiful pine trees. Some times we found it almost difficult to get along without tearing our clothes or breaking our heads. Some of them are very high but we wound our way along their sides & gained their summits & from their awful height looked off on the surrounding country or landscape when every variety of scenery would present to our view lofty mountains white with snow, others clothed in deepest green & flowers of different hue, the deep valleys & less elevated bluffs. All this variety of scenery could but tend to fill my heart with wonder & adore the hand who formed them. Travelled 20 miles.

20th. FRI. Again been travelling the Rocky Mountains. This forenoon crossed two very high mountains in going from Smith's fork to Salt river, where we would ascend & descend only in zigzag direction as we often do making the distance near a mile from the top to the bottom. This afternoon we rode over frightful places where has been the greatest danger. We rode along the side of a lofty mountain where there was only a narrow path for our animals to walk overhanging the river. This mountain or bank was exceeding steep having the appearance of having been cut away by the river. The mountain was full of stone & the path full of small rolling stones & flat slate stones & almost every step the stones would slip away. In one place a rock projected out leaving not more [than an] 8 inches path & we perhaps a hundred feet from the base of the mountain. Our situation was really dangerous. Had anything frightened our horses or they taken a misstep, we must have plunged to the bottom. Mrs. Walker rode just behind me on a horse that wished to go faster, therefore she often spoke to me, saying go faster, go faster or my horse will fall, so I urged mine along as fast as I could. Mr. S. just before me. Perhaps, dear mother will ask why I rode. I answer because I dare not walk. I could not walk. Had I attempted it, I should probably found myself at the bottom. We had other precipices to pass in file, where below us flowed the river & lofty heights above us with overhanging rocks, as if threatening to fall upon us. I felt if you could see our situation you would at least pray for our safety. But a kind Providence has preserved us, notwithstanding the danger. I have enjoyed it. I cannot say that I felt at all afraid tho I was glad when we had crossed them. We have passed some salt lakes today, collected some for our own use, found it crushed upon the ground to the thickness of from ¼ to ½ an inch. The company have killed two bears, the flesh resembles pork. Travelled 25 miles, encamped on a creek that flows into Bear river. Father, I have not felt as much fear today as when you put me on Rhoda Stone's horse & led it about the yard. So you see I have not suffered much.[72]

21st. Sat.[73]   Today about noon we ascertained that a company of Indians were within a short distance of us. Not knowing who they were or their intentions, the men immediately picketed their animals & put their firearms in order, ready to meet them if necessary. One of our company went out to them, found them friendly. Soon they came to our encampment to trade. Are clothed in skins.

22nd. Sab.   The Bannock Indians have again visited us. They are all about our tent. Mr. S. gave them some roasted meat, they were pleased. Said they loved the whites, that their hearts were good to us. I suspect their chief called on us this morning. He was dressed very pretty with a gingham skirt, skin pantaloons, trimmed with beads. Had various ornaments about his neck. Shook hands with us. Afternoon — have had worship. The Indians assembled with us. Much interested in the singing & attentive to the other exercises. In prayer they fixed their eyes on the ground, & looked devotional.[74] When the sermon was about half done, some of them left & came again when singing commenced. One old squaw was very busy hunting & eating lice from her child's head.

---

[72] Because of the mountainous terrain, this day's ride was one of the most difficult of the entire journey and yet Sarah seemed to have endured it very well.

[73] Since they were in the vicinity of a large herd of buffalo, many had been killed for food. The party remained in camp over Saturday and Sunday in order to dry buffalo meat for the remaining part of their journey.

[74] Sarah's curiosity was greater than her spirit of devotion for she looked around during prayer.

This is a common practice. When they just came they would talk to each other. But Mr. Gray motioned to them to be still & there was little more disturbance. O when will these deluded souls be brought to a knowledge of God & the way of salvation through Christ? In their present situation, they are all unlovely, polluted in mind & body, but the Spirit of the gospel alone can purify their hearts & prepare them for heaven, but how shall they hear without a preacher.

23rd. MONDAY. Travelled today about 28 miles. Have encamped on Big Bear river valley on a small creek that empties into the river. Am much fatigued & feel almost sick. My bed is a little softer than the ground. But I am satisfied. It is good enough & I never slept better in my life. Soon after we left the encampment, we passed the Bannock villages. They live in skin lodges, poor protection against the wintry winds & storms of this cold mountainous region. We this morning crossed the last ridge of the Rocky mountains & our hearts are glad, though they form almost an impassable barrier between us & our dear home. Yet we are glad to look back & see them stretching behind us. Our home is among the savage tribes of the far West & we long to be there. This afternoon our course has been level & we have travelled fast, were obliged to on account of the many large flies that troubled our horses. Each of us took a brush & brushed fast all the time & this was all the way we could ride. Our horses were much blooded on account of the bites.

24th. TUES. Travelled about 22 miles along the bank of Bear river & are encamped at Soda Springs.[75] This is indeed a curiosity. The water tastes like soda water, especially artificially prepared. The water is bubbling & foaming like boiling water. I drank of it. It produced a little sickness. We find it excellent for making bread, no preparation of the water is necessary, take it from the fountain & the bread is as light as any prepared with yeast. Seen much lava. A rainy day.

25th. WED. Have today visited another soda fountain, to me a greater curiosity than that we saw yesterday. The water as warm as blood & issued forth from a rock on the bank of the river. At intervals of about half a minute, the water would spurt out with considerable

---

[75] Gray in his *Oregon,* p. 178, commented: "The day the party arrived, notwithstanding they had made a long day's drive to reach the camp, the four ladies — Walker, Eells, Smith, and Gray — wished to go round and see the springs and drink of the water, and look at the Steamboat Spring, a place where water and gas issue at intervals of about a minute, like the blowing of steam. These places the ladies, tired as they were, must look at and admire. . . Next morning . . . nothing would satisfy the ladies but another look at the Steamboat."

force, throwing the water several feet in the air with considerable noise, something like a steam-boat, consequently the name steam-boat has been given it. We are encamped on Portsmouth [Portneuf River], a branch of the Columbia. This region bears the appearance of once having been volcanic. Have seen much that looked like lava.

26th. THURS.   Travelled over high land between Portsmouth & Ross Fork. Nothing particularly interesting has transpired, travelled 28 miles. Encamped on Ross Fork.

27th. FRIDAY.   Rose this morning as soon as it was light & set off for Fort Hall. Arrived about nine. Took breakfast at the fort. Were politely treated by the company. Found here 6 Nez Perces Indians direct from the Spaldings. They have brought melancholy intelligence of the death of Mrs. Lee, wife of the missionary we met at rendezvous.

FORT HALL TO WAIILATPU

The mission party was up and on its way by 4:30 a.m. Friday morning, July 27th. After riding eighteen miles in five hours, they arrived at Fort Hall in time for a hearty breakfast of boiled ham from Fort Colville, bread, and salted buffalo tongues. For the first time since leaving the Missouri frontier, they sat on stools at a table. A party of six Nez Perces, who had been sent by Whitman and Spalding with fresh horses and supplies, was waiting for them at Fort Hall.

The Nez Perces brought a letter, perhaps from Dr. Whitman, which carried the news of the death of Mrs. Jason Lee in childbirth on June 26th, together with the infant. The missionaries decided to send an express at once to Jason Lee to inform him of the sad news. Paul Richardson, who had been hired to assist the mission party on May 18th before it left the frontier, was asked to carry the message together with other letters which the missionaries hastened to write. Richardson caught up with Jason Lee at the Shawnee Mission near Westport on September 8th. James Conner, a mountain man who had a Nez Perce wife, was hired at Fort Hall to take Richardson's place.

Sarah in her diary entry for August 16th commented on the fact that the missionaries left their small herd of cattle at Fort Hall. It seems that they were told that it would be difficult to find forage for them while crossing the desert along the southern bank of the Snake River in what is now southern Idaho. It may be also that the cattle's feet were in no proper shape to continue the march. Ermatinger pledged the Hudson's Bay Company to supply them with a like number after they reached their destination. No doubt he was delighted to get some

American stock. After arriving on their field, the missionaries dis-
covered that Oregon cattle were inferior to their American stock.

After tarrying four days at Fort Hall, the missionaries continued
their journey on July 31st, now without escort save for the Nez Perce
Indians. They still had about five hundred miles to cover before reach-
ing Whitman's station at Waiilatpu. The restless Grays left the mission
party on August 13th and pushed on ahead of the others. They arrived
at Waiilatpu on the 21st, a week or more in advance of the others. The
main party arrived at Fort Boise, a little more than half-way to Waii-
latpu, on August 15th. Here they were warmly received by Francis
Payette, the Hudson's Bay official in charge of the Fort. The mis-
sionaries spent the week-end at the Fort and continued their travels
on Monday, the 20th.

The Smiths were the last to arrive at Waiilatpu. James Conner's
native wife gave birth to a baby on Saturday, August 25th, and on the
Monday following, Rogers was thrown from his horse and seriously
injured. The Smiths volunteered to tarry with the Conners and Rogers
and this delayed them one day. On Thursday, August 30th, Asa and
Sarah arrived at the Whitman station. The long, fatiguing, and some-
times dangerous journey was over.

28th. [JULY] SAT. Have done some washing, am quite fatigued.
Mr. Ermatinger very kindly gave us the privilege of washing at the
Fort & let his servants bring wood, water, &c. The Fort is built of
dobie, a kind of clay made into brick & dried in the sun, cool in the
summer & warm in the winter. We receive many calls from the Indian
ladies, wives of the gentlemen who own the Fort. They are very pretty
but their minds uncultivated. The Nez Perces are very fond of visiting
us & learning us their language.

29th. SAB. This morning the Nez Perces came to our tent, knew it
was the Sabbath, said it was wicked to work & wicked to talk bad.
Wished to have the Bible read. They could readily find the name of
God, Holy Spirit, Jesus Christ, John & many could tell the story of the
cross stretching out their arms, pointing to their hands & side telling
us he was nailed & pierced. They had also the story of Abraham offering Isaac, of Cain killing his brother & many others. Surely truth is
finding its way to the minds of this people. O that the Spirit would
make it effective to their conversion.

30th. MON. Spent the day in our little tent. It has been very warm
& the tent not very comfortable. Are preparing to leave here tomorrow.
Have now about 500 miles to travel. We feel that we are near home.

We begin to see the end of our journey & our hearts are glad. I hope the trials we have experienced will be blessed to us & we be prepared for great usefulness among the heathen.

31st. TUES.   Left Fort Hall at 1 o'c this afternoon with the kind wishes of all at the Fort. Several men & women rode with us to our encampment on Portsmouth river about 10 miles. We have been treated with the greatest kindness by this company for which we would be thankful.

AUG. 1st. WED.   Travelled about 18 miles. Are encamped at the falls of the Snake river. Mr. S. has gone fishing, so I have made an Indian pudding for supper.[76] It appears to me that the flies of Egypt could not surpass the multitude of mosquitoes here.[77]

2nd. THURS.   Travelled about 15 miles, encamped on Snake river. In many places the banks of the river are very high with much basaltic rock. Had this morning a breakfast of fish & Indian pudding, dinner of dry buffalo & pudding, supper do [i.e. ditto] with tea.

3rd. FRIDAY.   We have today fallen in company with a large village of Indians. More than 100 men, women & children going for buffalo. Our company is small, only 18 men.[78] Had this been a hostile tribe, they might easily cut us all in pieces, but they are the friendly Snakes. Their chief is called one of the best Indians in the mountains. We felt no alarm when we were told he was their leader. Had they been the Blackfoot or the Bannocks, our situation would have been alarming. But a kind Providence has protected us from these hostile tribes. Have travelled about 12 miles. Are encamped on the Casia [79] river where we have found a little spot of grass for our animals. We are now travelling the sandy plains of which I have heard so much. It is dreary, nothing but sedge can grow here, but it is not half as unpleasant as I expected. It is warm but I have not suffered much with my wool dress on. In

---

[76] Indian pudding was made with molasses, cornmeal, and milk. No doubt the missionaries were able to get further supplies at Fort Hall. Since they did not drive any cattle west of Fort Hall, perhaps some milk was taken along for the first few days of their journey.

[77] Myra Eells in her diary noted: "Mosquitoes so troublesome that we can not go out of our tent without everything but our eyes covered; horses nearly black with them, and they cannot eat for them."

[78] In addition to the five missionary men, the two hired men — Stevens and Conner — the Nez Perces, and Captain John Sutter, there were a few others who were traveling with the mission party in order to have company while crossing what is now southern Idaho.

[79] The present Raft River. There is a Cassia creek which flows into Raft River above where the Oregon trail crossed. Sometimes in early days Raft River was known as Cassia River.

passing a small stream where the water was quite rapid, one of the mules that carried the bread, flour meal &c. plunged over into the water & got everything finely wet. So we have the pleasure of drying them tonight. It is nothing uncommon for a mule to get into the water, throw their packs, &c., but no serious harm has happened.

4th. SAT.   Travelled about 32 miles. Encamped on the Snake river. The country through which we have passed is very barren, producing nothing but sedge of a dead appearance except on the stream. At noon we stopped at a spring where the grass was beautiful & it is good here. The basaltic rock is very abundant, a proof that it has been a volcanic region. This morning we had a thunder shower. I rode with a blue blanket on native fashion.[80] Shall remain here till after the Sabbath.

5th. SABBATH.[81]   This morning we held a prayer meeting & this afternoon Mr. S. preached. Was very happy that we were not obliged to travel as formerly. We very much need the Sabbath to prepare for the duties & trials of the week.

6th. MON.   Feel almost sick today, having taken cold. Last night was uncomfortably cold. I believe it is dog days yet.[82] I expect I came as near freezing to death as sister Roxanna ever heard of one. I recollect when she was a very little girl, she had often known people to freeze to death in dog days. Have travelled 35 miles, the country rough, barren & sandy.

7th. TUESDAY.   Travelled about 25 miles & encamped for the night on the river. The descent into the valley of the Snake river is very steep, perhaps two hundred feet & at the top several feet of perpendicular trap rock. On the opposite side of the river are large quantities of salt white as snow & on the bank several feet from the river a huge fountain of water bursts forth, foaming & roaring & forms a stream of considerable magnitude.[83]

---

[80] Sarah was referring to the custom of the native women riding with a blanket wrapped around them. The nights and mornings along the Snake River can be rather cold even in the summer.

[81] Since the missionaries were in command of the party, they were able to decide to stay in camp over Sunday. Sarah noted that her husband preached; Myra Eells read a sermon, possibly out of a book; and Mary Walker wrote in her diary: "Mr. S. preached in his old patched pantaloons. Sermon rather flat." FWW, II, p. 111.

[82] The *Shorter Oxford English Dictionary* defines dog-days as: "The days about the time of the heliacal rising of the Dog-star; noted as the hottest and most unwholesome period of the year." The contrast between what was supposed to be and what actually existed was surprising to Sarah.

[83] The volcanic soil of this part of Idaho is such that often streams disappear only to gush forth as springs along the north bank of the Snake River.

8th. WED. Travelled about 14 miles over a barren waste & are encamped on a creek near Salmon falls. Nothing of particular interest has taken place. We find here some Indians who are fishing.[84] They are extremely poor, are called diggers because they get their subsistance from the roots which they dig. During salmon season they fish, but in the winter many of them die from actual starvation. They have nothing to shield them from storms & wintry winds. They are entirely naked except a very small bit of skin about the middle of their bodies & many of them not even that. I pity them but it is out of my power to help them. They have nothing here & nothing future to hope for. We have purchased salmon of these Indians, find it beautiful & we are feasting on it.

9th. THURS. Travelled about 21 miles, encamped on the Snake river. At noon we stopped on a dry & barren place where was no feed. Therefore obliged to move again about two miles. On arriving there we found that Mr. and Mrs. Gray had gone on to another encampment 12 or 14 miles distant. As we had travelled far & our animals tired, our company thought they would not go after them, but let them come back & encamp with us if they chose not to encamp alone. This noon we again saw the poor diggers, one having no piece of skin to tie about him & still feeling some delicacy like Adam & Eve he sought to cover himself with leaves, had broken some little willow bushes & held them before him for an apron. His appearance was very novel, but he really manifested more modesty than I have often seen in civilized society. The same feeling appears to be manifested by all.

10th. FRIDAY. Travelled about 20 miles along Snake river. The bank very high. We have rode up & down & have passed some very deep ravines & low places. At noon we found Mr. and Mrs. Gray anxiously awaiting our arrial. As they had had nothing to eat since yesterday noon, I think now they will be satisfied to move with the company & not urge to go faster & further than they ride.

11th. SATURDAY. Travelled about 35 miles. This afternoon passed a company of Indians. It is very warm & we are much fatigued. Are encamped on the river in a poor place for the animals. Will remain until Monday.[85]

---

[84] These belonged to a branch of the Shoshone Indian tribe. They were among the most abject of all of the western Indians.

[85] Sunday was so uncomfortably hot that, according to Mary Walker, they had no worship service. Although they might have been more comfortable traveling, their consciences impelled them to stay in camp with no other shelter from the blistering sun than their tents.

13th. MONDAY. Rose this morning at an early hour. Took our horses from the picket & again pursued our journey wishing to improve the cool of the day, as it is extremely warm. Could find no suitable place to stop till we had travelled 10 hours, perhaps 40 miles without our breakfast. We are all extremely tired, some of our animals gave out & we left them behind. Could not get them along. Mr. Gray has left us, wishing to go faster than we & get to Dr. Whitman's.

14th. TUESDAY. Have been looking for Fort Boise all day & have not seen it yet. Travelled 25 miles. Are encamped on the river. The country is exceeding barren. See very little that is green. The sedge is abundant of dead appearance. Have seen some drifts of sand but most of the soil appears gravelly, like the roads in New England, very rocky & stony. We find some green places for our animals at distances of 12, 20, & 25 miles, good water from the river & little willows for fuel & are well supplied with food. We have abundant reason to speak of mercies.

15th. WED. Have at last arrived at Boise.[86] Travelled hard all day. We are all tired, yes, very tired. We often ride miles over the barren plains & under the scorching sun when I feel that I can hardly ride on my horse & feel if I were at home I should immediately go to bed. When we come to camp, we pitch our tents, spread our blankets & there rest our weary frames. Thus the days & weeks wear away, but we are now almost at our journey's end, only 200 miles further to go. Probably accomplish it in 10 days if prospered. We shall remain here till after the Sabbath to rest ourselves & animals. Travelled today 25 miles.

16th. THURSDAY. Find it good to rest. Have baked a pie & biscuits today. The good people at the Fort kindly supplied us with milk, pumpkins & turnips. It is good to get hold of vegetables once more. Mr. Payette [87] has the charge of the Fort. Has showed us many favors. I often think this company outdo the Americans in kindness & hospitality. Left our cattle at Fort Hall & will receive as many at the Columbia in return.

---

[86] Fort Boise was established by Thomas McKay in the summer of 1834 on the Boise River, about ten miles above its mouth. In 1838 the fort was moved to a location on the east bank of the Snake near the mouth of Boise River. This was the place visited by the mission party of 1838.

[87] Myra Eells in her entry for this day reported that Francis Payette and Captain John Sutter took tea that afternoon with the mission party. Although both Mary Walker and Myra Eells mention Captain Sutter as traveling with them, neither of the Smiths do so. The missionaries spent the week-end at the Fort with Asa again giving the sermon at the Sunday service.

20th. MONDAY.   Left Fort Boise this morning with the kind wishes of Mr. Payette who has charge of the Fort. Travelled 28 miles, stopped at noon on a stream Malheur. Here we found hot springs, for several rods along the bank the water issued boiling hot with much vapor & the stones were as hot as I could hold in my hand. We find many hot springs in this region indicating that it is volcanic at the Malheur. There is a sulphuric odor & the stones are covered with a salt. Are encamped on a small spring in the prairie. I have today rode a mule for the first time. It carries me very pretty but is hard to manage. This afternoon it stumbled into a deep hole in the road & fell. I was holding the umbrella in one hand, therefore I fell off. My foot somehow caught in the bridle & the mule ran with me dragging [me] on the ground a little distance before I could extricate my foot.[88] I was not hurt & but little frightened. Immediately mounted her again & rode to camp.

21st. TUESDAY.   Travelled about 28 miles, encamped on Burnt river. Again rode the mule. Have been wandering over the hills after choke-cherries, find them beautiful.

22nd. WED.   Have travelled only 10 miles, obliged to stop at 10 o'clock on account of the sickness of one of the company. Encamped on Burnt river.

23rd. THURS.   Mrs. Connor is no better, unable to ride.[89] The company are going on, but Mr. S. & myself feel that it is unchristian to leave them alone, perhaps to suffer, have decided to stop with them & let the company go on without us, tho still surrounded by Indians. God is our protector. Last night the company lost several horses, one from our band. Evening — Mrs. Connor has been able to ride this afternoon. Made a camp of 10 miles, found our company had encamped there. Hope we shall be able to go on together tomorrow.

24th. FRIDAY.   Travelled about 25 miles. Are encamped at the lone tree, a single pine tree standing far from any other tree in the midst of the prairie.[90] Here we find a Kyuse [Cayuse] Indian direct from Doct. Whitman's with letter from him & Mr. Spalding wishing us to come with all possible speed as Mr. S. is there awaiting our arrival.[91] The

---

[88] Eliza Spalding suffered a like experience during her ride over the mountains.

[89] Conner's wife was about to give birth to a child. A baby girl was born two days later and her mother was able to ride the same day. Seemingly giving birth to a child was not the same ordeal to native women that it was to white women.

[90] A lone pine tree stood here for years as a landmark on the Oregon Trail until it was cut down by some needy emigrant in 1843.

[91] Anticipating the arrival of reenforcements with Gray's return in the latter part of August or the first part of September, Henry and Eliza Spalding with their

Kyuse will pilot us over the mountain in the nearest possible way. We hope to be there soon, Providence favoring us.

25th. SATURDAY. Left our encampment this morning at an early hour & travelled with speed along Powder river. Travelled 15 miles before we stopped at noon. In the afternoon travelled about 18 miles, when Mr. S. & myself were obliged to stop by a little spring of water in a little grove of timber with Mr. and Mrs. Connor. Before sunset we had the happiness of welcoming to our number a little half breed. Fine little girl. In a few hours its mother was at the brook washing, well & happy as ever.

26th. SABBATH. This morning we travelled 5 miles to meet the company encamped in the borders of Grand Round. This afternoon religious exercises. Mr. Eells preached. Our native woman appears well as ever.

27th. MONDAY. Set out early this morning, but had not left the encampment when an accident happened to one of our company. Brother Rogers was thrown from his horse & so badly hurt that he was unable to move with the company. Mr. S. bled [92] him & we moved ten miles & overtook the company. Here we found Mr. Rogers too ill to proceed further. Mr. S. & myself, with one of the hired men remained behind with him while the company went on. We are encamped in a beautiful place on the creek where the soil is good for cultivation.

28th. TUESDAY. This morning I washed & after three this afternoon we moved about 10 miles over a beautiful plain. Encamped on a creek. Indian boy's mother with us. Mr. R. some better.

29th. WEDNESDAY. Left the encampment early. Travelled 10 miles & reached the Blue Mountains. Passed a village of Kyuses. Stopped at noon at the foot of the mountains where we met a man & some horses from Dr. Whitman's to hasten our arrival. The others have arrived & were anxious to see us. This afternoon we travelled the Blue Moun-

---

eight-month old daughter, went to Waiilatpu where they arrived on August 12th. A series of "protracted meetings" were held for the Cayuse Indians. On August 18th, the Whitmans and the Spaldings organized the First Presbyterian Church of Oregon, which has the distinction of being the first Protestant church to be established on the Pacific Coast. The Grays arrived at Waiilatpu on August 21st with the glad news about the three couples and a single man who were following them. Spalding was eager to return to Lapwai but decided to wait until the reenforcement arrived and a mission meeting could be held to decide their locations. Hence this letter from Dr. Whitman which met the mission party at the lone tree urging them to hasten with all possible speed.

[92] Bloodletting was then common practice for many ills and diseases. Here it seems to have been drastic treatment for an accident. The practice of bleeding continued until after the Civil War.

tains covered with beautiful pines & spruce trees, 20 miles. Encamped on the summit of the mountains where we found beautiful grass for our animals. Br. Rogers is better.

30th. THURSDAY.   This morning Mr. S., Br. Rogers & myself with an Indian to guide us started off for Dr. Whitman's, traveled 10 or 12 miles down the mountain covered with thick timber, then over a plain 10 or 12 miles to Dr. Whitman's, arrived about three in the afternoon. Were most cordially welcomed by our missionary brethren & sisters. I can hardly describe my feelings on reaching here. The place so long desired to see. I could hardly believe that the long journey & trying journey was accomplished & I had found a home. I could but shed tears in view of what God had done for us. That he had spared our lives amidst dangers & privations. We have been led as it were by a pillar of cloud by day & fire by night. He hath made good his promise, "Lo I am with you." [93] In passing through the waters God was with us & through the rivers & they did not overflow us, neither have our bones been broken & now we are standing on heathen ground where we have long desired to be & now my prayer is that I may be faithful in my Master's service. This afternoon we have held a meeting with the Indians. Mr. Spalding addressed them & Doctor Whitman interpreted. Then each of the brethren spoke & Mr. Spalding interpreted to the Indians. After that many Indians arose & expressed their gratitude that we had come to teach them. Said they had long been in ignorance but expected to be ignorant no longer. We had a very interesting time. We find Doctor Whitman provided with many of the comforts & even the luxuries of life. He has a fine garden of melons, abundance of corn, some wheat &c. We are glad to eat once more some nice potatoes, milk & vegetables. We all feel very happy & I trust thankful.

31st. FRIDAY.[94]   The brethren have today been consulting where to locate. Have not yet decided. May God direct. This afternoon & again this evening had a season of prayer together. Found it good to call on God. Doct. Whitman & Mr. Spalding have recently held a protracted meeting & many appear to understand their duty. O that God would make the truth effective to their salvation.

SEPT. 1st. SAT.   After much consultation & prayer, the brethren have decided that Mr. Walker & Mr. Eells form a new station some-

---

[93] Matt. 28:20: ". . . and lo, I am with you always, even unto the end of the world."

[94] For the only time in the history of the Oregon Mission of the American Board, all members were present.

where near Colvile among the Spokans & Flat-heads. Mr. Gray with Mr. Spalding [95] and Mr. S[mith] remain with Doct. Whitman. Have today formed a temperance society. Also the ladies formed a maternal Society.[96] Have had a female prayer meeting this p.m.

2nd. SABBATH. This has been an interesting day. We have united ourselves with the little mission church & have celebrated the Lord's Supper.[97] Sure I had no certificate from the church at home but was received on the testimony of the American Board as an assistant missionary. I ought to have taken a certificate from the church in B[rookfield] but the hasty manner in which we were called away, it was forgotten. It has been an interesting & I trust profitable season to our souls.

3rd. MONDAY. This is the monthly concert.[98] We have observed it together. Had an interesting time.

4th. TUESDAY. Mr. and Mrs. Spalding, Mr. and Mrs. Gray have left us today & we are arranging our things, begin to feel a little at home. The Doctor's house would be considered in the States a very rough one.[99] Part of it is log & part dobie or dried clay. One side of it has partly fallen down & [is] propped up with large poles. Some of the floors are nailed & some of them loose boards & all unplaned. But we are glad to find a home in so comfortable a place. Our room is the Indians meeting house, school room, wash room & store room, so you may well suppose [how] it is furnished. But we are happy & glad to get a room so good & with such conveniences even. Soon Mr. W. & E. will leave to visit their station & make provision for the winter. Their ladies will remain here. Soon I hope to engage in the duties of a missionary life, *instructing the ignorant, relieving the distressed & leading to virtue the degraded host.*[100] First of all the language must

---

[95] None of the reenforcement wanted to live with Gray, so for the time being he was assigned to Lapwai.

[96] Called the Columbia [River] Maternal Association. See FWW, I, p. 209ff. This has the distinction of being the first women's club formed by white American women west of the Rockies. Myra Eells and Sarah Smith were the only two of the six women not elected to an office.

[97] The original record book of this church is in the archives of the Presbyterian Historical Society in Philadelphia.

[98] The word "concert" was then used to indicate a prayer meeting, i.e., a concert of prayer. Sarah's entry for this day is exactly the same as her husband's.

[99] Sarah here gives more detailed information about the Whitman home than is found in any of the other writings of the missionaries, with the possible exception of Myra Eells. See FWW, II, p. 116.

[100] Editorial italics. Here succinctly expressed is Sarah's conception of her missionary duties.

be acquired which will require much time & labor. The natives appear interested & are anxious to receive instruction.

CROWDED WAIILATPU

The safe arrival of the reenforcement of 1838 at Waiilatpu brought great joy to all concerned. The Whitmans and the Spaldings were delighted to have associates in the work which was then so encouraging. The weary travelers were equally delighted to know that the hardships of their overland journey were over; that they had arrived at their destination in safety; and that now they could begin the missionary work to which they had given their lives. And the natives, who were at Waiilatpu at the time the new missionaries arrived, also expressed their joy and gratification. There was indeed much reason for general rejoicing.

The Whitmans, not knowing how many would be in Gray's party or even whether he would return with any assistants, were wholly unprepared to receive so many. They were embarrassed by lack of room. When Whitman first settled at Waiilatpu in the fall of 1836, he and Gray began building an adobe house which measured 30 x 36 feet. Realizing, however, that they could not complete such an ambitious structure before winter, they compromised by erecting a lean-to along one wall which measured 12 x 36 feet. The two ends were partioned off for bedrooms. The central room had a fireplace and was used as a kitchen and dining room. In 1837 the house as originally planned was erected and divided into two compartments. One room was used for instruction and worship for the natives and was called the Indian room. The other room was no doubt used to provide sleeping quarters for the Hawaiians and others in Whitman's employ. During the winter of 1837-38, the flood waters of the Walla Walla River, which flowed within twenty feet or so of the house, flooded the small basement of the house and undermined a part of the adobe wall. Sarah noted that one side of the house was still propped up by large poles. Whitman was planning to erect another house on higher ground but was so engaged with other duties that he had no opportunity to do so before the reenforcement arrived.

By the first of September 1838, there were at least thirteen people living in the Whitman home. In addition to Marcus and Narcissa and their eighteen-month-old daughter, Alice Clarrisa, there was a Frenchman, Charles Compo, his native wife, and their eighteen-month-old son; Margaret McKay, the daughter of Thomas McKay, perhaps in her early teens; Mungo Mevway, a twelve-year-old half-Hawaiian and half-native boy; a sick boy, Havier Foier, who had been taken to the mission perhaps by some Hudson's Bay man for medical treatment; Joseph and Maria Maki, Christian Hawaiians from Honolulu who were hired by the Whitmans to assist them and who were charter members of the First Presbyterian Church of Oregon; and two Hawaiian men who were also hired to work at the mission, one of whom was Jack. In addition to this number, the Spaldings and their six-months-old daughter, Eliza, were being entertained when suddenly the mission reenforcement of nine arrived together with James Conner, his native wife, and infant daughter. This brought the total to be housed and fed to twenty-eight. The total square footage of the Whitman home, including the lean-to, was about 1,500 square feet. It seems probable that during this crowded period some had to sleep in tents outside.

Immediate steps had to be taken to prepare for the coming winter. The six men, not including Rogers who was not an appointed missionary, began their business sessions on Saturday, September 1st, and continued them on the following Monday. The women were not given voting privileges and were rarely invited to attend such meetings. It was agreed to open a third station among the Spokane Indians who spoke the Flathead language. Thus this station was sometimes referred to as the Flathead Mission. None of the reenforcement wanted to be in the same station with Gray. Therefore, Walker and Eells were assigned to the Spokane field; Smith was to remain with Whitman at Waiilatpu; and Gray was to be associated with Spalding at Lapwai. Rogers was also assigned to Lapwai. Dr. Whitman was authorized to go to Fort Vancouver for supplies. It was also agreed that the construction of another house at Waiilatpu was to proceed with all possible dispatch. Actually work did not begin on the new building until after Whitman returned from Vancouver on October 17th.

Some matters of missionary policy were discussed and some fundamental principles adopted. Both Whitman and Spalding, on the basis of their two years' experience, were united in urging the necessity of settling the Indians before effective educational and evangelistic work could be accomplished. It was not enough just to preach the gospel. The natives had to be taught how to farm. This implied changing the basic social structure of whole tribes of Indians. It is possible that the missionaries themselves did not fully appreciate the radical and far-reaching issues involved in their decisions. The decision to settle the Indians meant that corn and flour mills had to be built. A blacksmith shop had to be erected so that hoes could be made for the Indians. The Mission voted to accept the offer of the Sandwich Island Mission to send a printing press to Oregon. This meant that the Indian languages had to be reduced to writing so that books could be printed in the native tongue.

The members of the Oregon Mission of the American Board had the good fortune to be on their field at the beginning of a transition period. The great tide of white emigration began rolling over the Rockies into the Oregon country in 1842, just four years after the arrival of the reenforcement. Inevitably the Indians of Oregon would be involved in a conflict of their age-old customs with the civilization of the white man. The time for the missionaries to help the Indians get ready for that conflict was short, so very short. The basic question which the missionaries were discussing was whether or not one could Christianize the Indians without first civilizing them. Later, when Smith appreciated the full significance of the issues involved, he became critical of the decision of the Mission to spend so much time, energy, and money on this policy of trying to civilize the natives before they were Christianized. Asa's views were echoed in his wife's entry for January 1, 1839, which follows.

On April 29, 1839, in a letter to Secretary Greene, Smith expressed himself on this subject: "Much has been said about furnishing the Indians with cattle, ploughs, sending out farmers, mechanics &c. With regard to this I must say that it appears to me to be departing from the object which the Board has in view. A few cows are important for our comfort & support but to think of furnishing a nation with them, it would I believe defeat our object in coming. I feel that there is a very great danger of introducing the habits of civilized life faster than the natives are capable of appreciating them."

Another question debated at the September 1838 mission meeting concerned the language that was to be used in instructing the natives. Whitman and Spalding had already learned that it was practically impossible to give any consistent teaching of the English language when the natives were so irregular in their attendance at school. This irregularity arose out of the roving habits of the Indians made necessary by their constant search for food. Although both Whitman and Spalding agreed that some instruction in the English language was desirable, yet they realized that most of the teaching would have to be in the native tongue. This meant that the missionaries would have to learn the language of the tribe with which they worked. Asa applied *himself diligently to the study of Nez Perce and within two years be-came the best linguist in the Mission.*

The Spaldings, the Grays, the Conners, and Rogers left for Lapwai on Tuesday, September 4th, the day after the business sessions closed. The departure of these nine people relieved somewhat the congestion in the Whitman home. Walker and Eells left on their exploring tour of the Spokane country the following Monday. They returned on October 13th after having selected a site about seventy miles south of Fort Colville on the main trail leading to Fort Walla Walla. The place was known as Tshimakain. Here a beginning was made on the erection of two cabins but the men soon realized that it would be impossible to build comfortable dwellings and move their wives there before winter. So, leaving the unfinished cabins, they returned to Waiilatpu arriving there on October 13th. This made it certain that these two couples would have to winter with the Whitmans. Dr. Whitman left for Fort Vancouver on September 17th, leaving Smith as the only male member of the Mission to supervise the harvesting of the crops at Waiilatpu. Thus at the very beginning of his missionary experience, Asa Smith was plunged into secular activity.

The fleeting glimpses that we catch into the life of the mission family at Waiilatpu during the fall of 1838 and the following winter, from the letters written by the various missionaries and especially from Mary Walker's diary, reveal growing tensions and personality conflicts. How could it have been otherwise when we remember the primitive conditions under which they were living and their crowded quarters? These people were human beings before being missionaries and the very fact that they were missionaries is evidence that each and every one was a strong-minded individual.

A multitude of little things arose to corrode the original good feel-ing. Nowhere do we find more intimate revelations of what was happening than in Mary's diary which she was writing for no other eyes but her own. On Tuesday, September 18th, Mary wrote: "Mr. Smith came to the pantry & found nothing but milk & melons. Didn't like it. Mrs. W.[hitman] [made] cut[ting] remarks about milk, sugar &c. At supper Mr. S. said he was very hungry, had had no dinner. In forenoon Mr. Smith sent out to give a melon to some boys for pounding, [i.e., pounding clothes while washing them], Mrs. W[hitman] counter-manded." Just why Asa had missed his noon meal is not clear. Evidently Narcissa did not approve his raiding the pantry without her permission or paying out melons to Indian boys for work performed. Yet a few days later, on September 29th, Narcissa in a letter to "Brother Judson" wrote: "We find Mr. and Mrs. Smith excellent helpers. Their hearts appear to be very much on their work."

But little points of irritation continued to arise as the following entries from Mary's diary so clearly indicate:

"Oct. 3.   Mrs. W[hitman] has said and done many things that do not suit Mrs. S[mith] to-day."

"Oct. 13.   Mrs. Whitman quite out with Mr. Smith because he was unwilling to let her have Jack [a Hawaiian] help her."

"Nov. 17.   After breakfast Mrs. W. went to her room & there remained through the day without concerning at all how or what was done. I know not, I am sure, what she wishes or thinks. But I think her a strange house-keeper. It is hard to please when one cannot know what would please."

"Nov. 30.   Dr. W. quite out of patience with Mr. Smith. Mrs. W. Washing. Think she has less help from the other ladies than she ought."

"Dec. 3.   Monthly concert in the evening after which Dr., his wife & Mr. E[ells] & wife, husband & self sit up till midnight talking about Mr. S[mith] & G[ray]. Mrs. W[hitman] gets to feeling very bad, goes to bed crying." By this time matters were taking a more serious turn. Evidently after the Smiths had retired for the night, the other three couples withdrew perhaps to the privacy of the kitchen where the Walkers and the Eells poured into the ears of the Whitmans a long recital of their grievances and criticisms of Smith and Gray arising out of their cross-country travels. The Whitmans were already aware of some of Gray's difficult characteristics and also had had some minor difficulties with Smith. But now they heard more, much more, about the two. Narcissa was greatly upset. The next day Mary noted: "Mrs. W. in a sad mood all day, did not present herself at the breakfast table. Went out doors, down by the river to cry."

On Tuesday, December 4th, Asa and Sarah Smith moved their belongings into one of the rooms of the new house which was sufficiently finished to receive occupants. There is good reason to believe that the Smiths wanted to relinquish the space they were occupying in the Indian room so that a private bedroom could be partitioned off for Mary Walker who was about to give birth to her child. Asa was highly critical of the fact that Mary had become pregnant so soon after her marriage. As will be noted in his letter of December 18th to his brother John, which follows, he commented: "Mr. Walker has a son born the 7th of this month which was just 2 days over 9 months from the time

they were married, the 5th of March. What I think about such things,
you know already. I feel thankful that I am not in such an embarrased
situation & at present there is no prospect of it."

But Asa was not content just to be out of the old Whitman house
during the time the baby was being born: he decided to leave on an
exploring tour of a possible site for a new station on the trail leading
to Lapwai in the vicinity of what is now Dayton, Washington. So with
Sarah comfortably settled in the new room, Asa left on Wednesday,
December 5th and returned on the 8th. The Walker baby, named
Cyrus Hamlin, arrived on the 7th. He was the second boy born of
white American parents on the whole Pacific coast who lived to ma-
turity. First honors go to a son of Mr. and Mrs. Thomas Larkin,
American consul at Monterey, California. On Friday, December 7th,
Mary wrote in her diary: "Mrs. Smith stayed with me thru the night,
her husband being gone from home."

During the long and sometimes cold winter days, the men and
women of the Mission often crowded into Narcissa's kitchen in order
to get warm. Much to her disgust, Elkanah Walker chewed tobacco.
In a letter to her sister Jane dated May 17, 1839, Narcissa asked:
". . . now how do you think I have lived with such folks right in
my kitchen for the whole winter?"

Sarah Smith's overland diary closes with the entry for September 4th.
She wrote a postscript dated October 1st to her husband's letter of
September 30th (which is found in the next section of this volume) in
which she told of her endeavors to teach English to some thirty Indian
boys and girls. But this school did not continue long as the natives
moved away taking their children with them. In January she added
three entries in her diary which are given below. In her comments for
January 1st she reflects her husband's views about the dangers of
civilizing the Indians before they are Christianized. Between the end
of Sarah's overland diary and the entries made in January, we have
four letters from her husband written to his home folks from Waiilatpu
on September 15, 30th, October 29th, and December 18th. These
should be read before continuing with Sarah's observations.

JAN. 1, 1839.   Another year of my short existence has gone forever
& my situation — O how altered & how unexpectedly changed. One
year ago I numbered one of that happy family I shall meet no more on
earth & then looked forward to Siam's sultry clime as my home, expecting there to wear out a short life in the cause of him who had sacrificed his own for a world's redemption. But God in his providence

directed otherwise & with an unseen & powerful hand brought us safely through an extensive wilderness inhabited only by savage tribes of Indians. All the way through those dangerous deserts, God was with us. As with a pillar of fire & cloud, he guarded us & daily we witnessed his signal mercies. Not one of his promises failed. He who long ago commanded his disciples to carry the Gospel to every creature with the precious assurance "Lo I am with you alway" stood ever near to sustain & comfort us. Tho we often departed from him, He forsook us not, but with a father's tender care watched over us every step of the way & brought us after a weary & trying journey to our long desired home. With these benighted tribes we hope to live & when life's toils are over, with them we hope to find a grave. And when we enter heaven, should we meet some heathen souls brought there through our instrumentality, shall be more than paid for all our toils & suffering here. This life will soon be over. A few more revolving years at fartherest & we shall have done with the scenes of earth. Yea this year may prove my last. O may it be spent to the glory of my God & Savior.

Soon after my arrival here by the advice of those long upon the ground, I commenced teaching in English & continued the school till but five scholars attended having all gone to their winter quarters. Very few people are with us now. In this situation we feel that we are performing little missionary labor. The wandering habits of the natives, we feel, will prevent the speedy introduction of Christianity among them. In some respects it is favorable, as when they are with us they are all encamped very near us & can be assembled almost any time of the day for instruction or religious worship. Whereas if they were settled, they must necessarily be scattered some miles from us. Of course instruction [would then be] much more difficult. We have no desire that the people advance in civilization unless more advanced in Christianization. We [do not] believe the saying, Civilize the heathen first & then make them Christians if you can. Fruitless indeed would be the attempt to reclaim these savage tribes to habits of industry, virtue, or to heaven, unless the truths of the Gospel are brought to bear upon their hearts, making them feel in some measure the dignity of their nature & the relation they sustain to God & eternity. Great indeed is the responsibility resting on those who are called to aid in the great work of Christianizing these heathen tribes. God alone can give us wisdom.

JAN. 7. Yesterday we observed the annual concert of prayer. Trust our Christian friends were engaged with us. The prayers of faith will meet with acceptance above. Heathen nations are perishing for the Gospel. But the Gospel alone will never save them. The Holy Spirit must accompany it to their hearts & this is granted in answer to prayer. Let me but know that Christian friends are praying for me, that they are wrestling with God for his blessing to descend & I shall be more strengthened than to hear of their liberal donations. But when the Christian sincerely offers the prayer "Thy kingdom come" he will not with-hold his treasures. But with a willing heart give them to the Lord for the advancement of this kingdom.

Brother Walker & Eells with their wives are still with us making a very large family, much of the time twenty-one in number. Mr. S. & myself are now living alone in the new house, one room having been made comfortable, find it much pleasanter. Some sick in the family. One boy from Vancouver brought here for medical aid we fear will die. The winter thus far has been very mild & pleasant, very little snow, quite unlike New England. I have not mounted my horse since our arrival. Intend going this week to Walla Walla to visit Mr. Pambrun [101] who has been long inviting us. A ride & visit will surely be very agreeable to my feelings. Perhaps shall do some good. His wife is a half-breed.

THURSDAY, JAN. 9th. was one of the finest mornings that ever dawned upon the Columbia. With high hopes & pleasant anticipations, husband & I with an Indian to guide us set forth on our contemplated visit to W.W., distance 25 miles. Unfortunately the Indian, at the request of Mr. Pambrun, took Eneus [102] who died before we had gone half way. Soon some flying clouds appeared with a little rain. Thinking it but for a moment, we ventured on till the sky grew more dark & the wind began to blow & the rain fell thicker & faster. The Indian evidently fearing to carry the corpse alone, urged us on saying it was but a little way, that we had come more than half the distance &c. Therefore we proceded on, the rain falling in torrents & the wind violent. We were obliged to move slow on account of the corpse & it proved we were not half the distance there. When we arrived I had nearly perished, my clothes wet through & my strength nearly gone. I could hardly hold myself upon the horse for the wind, which was

---

[101] Pierre C. Pambrun was in charge of the Hudson's Bay post at Fort Walla Walla about twenty-five miles from Waiilatpu. He was a Roman Catholic but friendly to the missionaries. He died on May 15, 1841, as the result of injuries suffered when thrown from a horse.

[102] Evidently this Eneus was a very sick Indian who was being taken to Fort Walla Walla.

nearly in our face. In all our journey across the continent, we never experienced any thing like this & perhaps never [in] our life so much exposed. But through the goodness of God, we were preserved & received no serious injury. On Saturday returned home, having had a good visit & contented that it should last some time.

THE MOVE TO KAMIAH FOR LANGUAGE STUDY

Asa Smith was temperamentally prone to become involved in controversy with his associates. He lacked patience and tolerance. He was a perfectionist and this made him critical of the shortcomings of others. He quarreled with his brother missionaries in the Oregon Mission and later in Hawaii. And after he returned to New England in 1846, he became the center of a controversy in his church at Buckland, Massachusetts.

Smith had been at Waiilatpu for less than two months before he was telling his parents: "The probability is that we shall remain at this place only till next spring. We think it best to form another station in this field from 25 to 50 miles from this place." Here he was speaking for himself and Sarah and not for the Mission. There is no evidence that the other members of the Mission ever dreamed of opening a second station among the Cayuses or the adjoining tribes. For one thing the total number of natives in the vicinity of Waiilatpu was only a few hundreds. After Smith's exploring tour of the region to the northeast of Waiilatpu during the first part of December 1838, he realized the impracticability of such a move and said no more about it.

During the winter of 1838-39, Smith had a prominent Nez Perce for his teacher who came from the Kamiah region, about sixty miles up the Clearwater from Lapwai. This native had been nicknamed "Lawyer" by the whites because of his sharp mind and eloquence. No doubt Lawyer was eager to have a mission station established in his native place and found his pupil most receptive to the idea. There was no place, argued Lawyer, where a person could better learn pure Nez Perce than in Kamiah. This was exactly what Smith was prepared to hear. Moreover, the Nez Perces were estimated to number between three and four thousands. Did this not justify the opening of a second station among these people? Smith told Whitman and others that he wanted to move to Kamiah.

A special meeting of the Mission was held in Lapwai on February 22, 1839, to consider Smith's request and some other questions which had arisen. In order to strengthen his case, Smith made a special trip to Kamiah before the Mission meeting. He was highly pleased with the prospect and was more determined than ever to settle there. By this time he was openly saying that he could not live in the same station with the Whitmans. The other members of the Mission were not in favor of the Smiths moving to Kamiah. There was a long debate on the subject. A substitute proposal was made to have the Whitmans open a new station somewhat central to all three of the points already established and turn Waiilatpu over to the Smiths. This idea appealed to the Walkers and the Eells in distant Tshimakain and to the Spaldings and the Grays at Lapwai. Neither Smith nor Whitman seemed to welcome the suggestion but consented to think about it. Later Mrs. Whitman strongly objected and by April 1st, the proposal was definitely rejected. Whitman then notified his colleagues that he would not move.

Smith's despondency over the situation is revealed in a letter he wrote to Walker on March 28th: "The prospects of this mission I assure you look dark to me. What is before us I know not. Should this mission be broken up, I should not be disappointed. At any rate I doubt whether I shall have any connection with it for a long time to come." [103] The process of disillusionment was continuing. Unhappy in his personal relationships with his associates, he became increasingly critical of them in his letters to the Board and especially in his more personal letters to his parents, sisters, and brother.

Finally the Smiths decided to move to Kamiah even without the consent of the Mission. He told his brethren that he would go there temporarily for the purpose of learning the language. Sarah in the entry given below states that they left Waiilatpu on April 30th and after tarrying a few days at Lapwai reached Kamiah on May 10th. Gray accompanied them from Lapwai and assisted in the erection of a rude shelter on the north bank of the Clearwater River. Sarah gives a vivid description of the cabin and of their experiences while it was being built. Notice her statement: "The many cracks furnish us with sufficient light." [104] In the corresponding section of Asa's letters, which follows, a fuller description will be given of this cabin and of their living conditions during this first part of their stay in Kamiah.

By deliberately leaving Waiilatpu with its plentiful gardens, the Smiths were cutting themselves off from their food supply. None of

---

[103] Coll. Y.

[104] Smith in his diary for Nov. 11, 1839, wrote: "The summer we spent in this place in a rude hut hastily built." SS, 121. Writing to Levi Chamberlain of the Hawaiian Mission on Jan. 17, 1840, Smith called it "a mere hovel."

the missionaries lived in such an isolated place and under such primitive conditions as did the Smiths at Kamiah in the summer of 1839. Little sympathy, however, was extended to them on the part of their colleagues. Asa had defied the judgment of the whole Mission. His bed was of his own making, let him lie in it. In the meantime, however, Sarah's health began to decline. In the author's opinion, there is no writing of any of the members of the Oregon Mission so charged with pathos as the latter part of her diary entry which follows.

JULY 18, 1839. Mr. Smith feeling it is of the first importance that a perfect knowledge of the language be obtained as soon as possible & there being no good teacher at Wailatpoo, we have taken summer quarters with the upper Nez Perces among a most interesting & intelligent people, unquestionably the most intelligent & influential of all the Nez Perce tribe, perhaps the most eligible situation for a station of any size in this country. It will probably embrace as large a number as can be gathered at any station & what is still more favorable, they will be here the greater part of the year. Here is their rooting ground. The females go continually to their work as soon as it is light & return in the evening laden with their roots & then collect together at any time we desire for worship in the evening & are also present on the Sabbath. Here also is their salmon fishery. With their fish weir, they may catch hundreds every night & here also is their hunting ground. In the winter particularly, they can have an abundance for several years to come. Some will probably go to buffalo river [*sic*] this summer, excepting that they will be here all the time. Again this is the finest country we have seen anywhere in the country. Many acres of excellent land, sufficient to settle an immense number of people. This place is about 60 miles east or northeast of Mr. Spalding's [station at Lapwai] & nearly 200 miles from Wieletpoo.

On the 30th of April we left our home, packed our bed which is husk & all we use, a few dishes, clothing & what food we thought we should need, upon the backs of animals & started for this place. Arrived the 10th of May, having spent 3 days at Mr. Spalding's. After arriving, husband with a little assistance from the natives prepared us a little house of three rooms, kitchen, buttery & bedroom, without floor or window, having no tool but an axe & grooving axe. It was made by grooving posts & setting them in the ground & filling up the sides with split cedar. The many cracks furnish us with sufficient light. The chimney is made of green pine, mud & stones. The roof of the house is the cedar covered with dirt. Our furniture costs but little, our bedstand is made by putting sticks in the ground & covering it with sticks instead of cording. Our table a split log with legs put in, our chairs pieces of logs & stools, not very comfortable for a sick person. During warm & pleasant weather, we have been quite comfortable but not so in storms. In one we were completely drowned out & obliged to seek protection in an Indian lodge amidst flees and lice. It rained most powerfully & the roof became soaked so that it rained equally as hard in the house as out of doors. The first night when we retired, our bed was dry & we nailed up a blanket over us to protect us, but it proved worse than nothing & the water came upon us & soaked our clothing & half filled our bed. I cannot explain just how it was but at any rate we were very wet. The next night the rain ceased & we did what we could to dry our things & make us comfortable for the night. We found our bed wet thru. That we could not dry but dried our blankets [so] that we could spread them upon the bed & retired. We could not spread them upon the ground or any thing else for all was wet. We could not stay comfortably at the lodge for that was very small & piled full. Mr. & Mrs. Gray who were unfortunate enough to be with us slept at the lodge & we thought to make as comfortable as possible at home. We put on all the bed clothing we had with us, tho wet, so that we slept warm, but oh, how damp it seemed. I was not sensible at the time of taking cold but how far it has tended to fix disease upon me, I know not. At present my health is very poor. Almost a constant pain in my side & pressure upon my lungs. My physician [105] calls it the liver complaint & hopes to relieve me. Am taking medicine every day. Have been bled & blister applied to my side twice, which is very reducing. I fear that when my Dear Parents read this, they will say Sarah is complaining & thinking more & saying more of little trials than Adeline. Perhaps with her this would have passed unnoticed & I believe that were I in health none of these things would move me. I think, however, I have in all my writing endeavored to represent my situation as favorable as I could. When I decided upon a missionary life, I did it in full expectation of trials & hardships. I have found them no greater than I expected & in them all I think I have found my strength equal to my day. Dear sister Adeline doubtless finds trials of which we are strangers & we have others of which she by experience knows nothing of. But if we improve them rightly, they will work for us, a far more exceeding & eternal weight of glory. I do not regret the life I have

---

[105] Her physician was her husband. There is no evidence that Asa ever consulted Dr. Whitman regarding his wife's feeble health.

chosen. I hope to be instrumental in the salvation of some souls. This will more than reward me for all my toil & suffering.

In the Coe Collection of Yale University Library is an undated letter from Sarah Smith to Mary Walker from "Nez Perce Country." The letter was evidently written some time in the summer of 1839 and reveals much not only of the primitive conditions under which the Smiths were living but also something of Sarah's poor health. Sarah wrote:

DEAR SISTER. Was much gratified on receiving your kind letter. It was as unexpected as it was welcomed. It being unexpected might render it the more precious. We are very pleasantly situated this summer in a little grove of pines, & in a little cedar house of three rooms, kitchen, buttery, and bed room. The whole costs about one weeks labor, no floors or windows. But very comfortable & pleasant for us.

Mrs. Gray will tell you that it is not very convenient or pleasant for company, as she had a trial of it. But it was worse then than in good weather. I think it will not be consistent for us to see you at Clear Water as Mr. S. is so much engaged in his studies that he can hardly afford time for any thing else. We shall be happy to receive a visit from you here before you leave & will endeavor to make you as comfortable as circumstances will admit.

When we get into a good house if within (———) I shall enjoy receiving company much better than we can now. As Mr. S. has only his axe & auger you may judge what furniture we have. I write this that you may know how to excuse things if you should come. My health is not very good. The pain in my side is evidently increasing, together with a pressure upon my lungs. What is before us we know not. I sometimes feel that my labor here is nearly done. Mr. S. feels very anxious about me. Intends immediately to apply blisters to my side. Love to the Sisters. Yours truly,   S. G. SMITH

THE CLOSING ENTRY OF SARAH'S DIARY

The 1839 annual meeting of the Oregon Mission was held at Lapwai beginning Monday, September 2nd. Even though Sarah was in poor health and Asa was inclined to absent himself because of his language studies, they finally decided that it was best for both to attend. The journey to Lapwai was made in an Indian canoe which had been fashioned by digging out the central part of a long tree trunk. They probably returned by the same method, as Sarah's health might not

*have permitted her to ride horseback. The Smiths reached Lapwai on
August 30th. Among the items of business transacted was the approval
of Smith's transfer from Waiilatpu to Kamiah. There was nothing else
the Mission could do in view of his determination to remain in Kamiah.
Rogers was asked to go to Kamiah to assist Smith.*

*Believing that the goods shipped from their New England home at
the time of their departure for Oregon in March 1838 had arrived at
Fort Walla Walla, Smith traveled there after the Mission meeting to
get them. He found to his disappointment that he had been misin-
formed. The baggage did not reach Kamiah until the following January
4th, thus taking almost two years to make the long voyage around
South America to Honolulu, thence to Fort Vancouver, from there up
the Columbia to Fort Walla Walla, and then on horseback to Kamiah.*

*During the time Asa was on his errand to Fort Walla Walla, Sarah
remained at Lapwai. With plenty of time at her disposal, she filled out
the remaining blank pages of the notebook containing her diary. Looking back in review, she wrote about the dangers and hardships of their
overland travels and added an interesting observation on the nature of
the wardrobe anyone undertaking such a journey should have. This
section of her diary comes as a welcome addition to her three extant
letters written in 1839. These letters will be referred to in a later
chapter. Notice the last sentence of the diary: "Till we meet in Heaven,
Farewell, Farewell." Sarah still had no expectation of ever returning
to New England and seeing her loved ones again.*

SEPT. 14, 1839.   Clear Water, Nez Perce Mission. Last week we
observed our annual meeting of the Mission. Had an interesting time.
Closed exercises on Wednesday when we observed the communion.
Had with us Mr. and Mrs. Hall [106] from the Sandwich Islands & two
of their native converts who had come to assist & do them good. It
was decided that Mr. Smith to be of greater service to the mission by
way of writing & translating, remove to the Kamiah where we have
passed the summer. He has now gone to Weiletpoo for our goods.
Expect to go home next week as it is now voted that we remain
there.[107] Husband will immediately prepare us a house so that my

---

[106] Edwin Oscar Hall, printer from the Hawaiian Mission, took a press to the
Oregon Mission arriving at Fort Walla Walla on April 29, 1839. The press was
later taken to Lapwai. The Halls remained in Oregon until the spring of 1840.
Mrs. Hall, although an invalid, accompanied her husband. The press is now on
display in the Oregon Historical Society, Portland, Oregon.

[107] Smith returned on September 21st bringing with him an Hawaiian by the
name of Jack who had been hired to assist him at Kamiah. The Smiths started back

friends may not think me suffering any longer. As my health is poor & unable to ride horseback, we came down the river in a little Indian canoe, or hollow log. Had a fine time. The rowers were very merry & our half breed girl furnished sport enough for us. In passing over some rapids, a wave dashed upon me & wet me finely. We made to shore where I took off my clothing & hung them on bushes to dry. The distance down the river perhaps 100 miles.

I find I have still some blank paper & I don't know how I can better fill it than by telling you what clothing I consider necessary for a journey across the Rocky Mountains. I think I have never fully informed you in any letter. I almost hope that none will ever cross them again, for I think it a tremendous journey, still I do not know but one would be better prepared for the duties necessarily devolving on them than they would be after a voyage at sea. They surely would be inured to hardships & in that respect be prepared for future trials. But oh! the journey & the necessary suffering attending it. The constant exposure of life. It does seem to me that it is improper for a female to undertake it. We are ever exposed to the mercy of savage men. When we retired at night we knew not what would be our situation in the morning. We might be in eternity or what we considered more dreadful still, our husbands might be slain & we be left to wear out a miserable existence. I do not say that we always considered this our situation, but O! how many times have I retired laying every article of my clothing in just such a position that I might dress in a moment, should an attack be made & perhaps the other ladies fearing to undress at all & this is not all the danger. Our animals were ever liable to throw their packs, become frightened, run & thus perhaps set the whole caravan in commotion, & we in the midst of them liable to be thrown & our limbs broken or our lives taken. When I look back upon it, I tremble at what we have passed through. But I will say no more. I leave you to form your own opinions with regard to the propriety or duty of ladies engaging in such an enterprise. I will therefore proceed with the outfit necessary in case it should be attempted again.

It is best that they take as little as possible & send their outfit by water. First the ladies dress simply for the journey should be 1st one pair of thick booties; 1 pr. of gaiter boots & one pr. of thin shoes; 2 pr. of dark woolen stockings & 2 pr. of dark cotton or linen; 3 pr. of soft

---

to their home on the 24th. Now that they had been regularly assigned to Kamiah, they could begin the erection of a better house. This is described in Asa's correspondence which follows.

dark colored flannel drawers; 4 changes of dark gingham. This is indispensably necessary, white is not only inconvenient as it respects washing, but I consider it *altogether improper;* 2 pr. of woolen under jackets; 3 pr. of brown corsets; 2 good colored flannel skirts; 1 good new cambric quilt; a good broadcloth or camlet riding dress. It should be made with two waists or rather a jacket to put on over & one good pongee dress made in the same manner for the last part of the journey when the broadcloth may be too heavy, & one good calico or gingham dress also; long full apron of perhaps 3 breadths to wear when encamped to wash dishes in &c. She should have one large wool shawl & one small cotton one. Good cloth cloak lined with flannel. A straw bonnet with dark lining & dark trimming; an Indian rubber cape that will come down over the saddle. What other clothing she feels she will need after arriving before she can get her outfit should be taken.[108] A gentleman should have deer skin drawers; 1 pr. good strong wool pantaloons; 1 thick strong frock coat; 2 or 3 linen spencers; one thick warm vest, one thin vest; 6 good calico shirts (such as will not fade, should be fine figure true colors or they may suit their own taste); a good wide brimmed hat, thick gloves. Each should have a long flannel night dress, colored. I will also add that on the Platte, we were extremely annoyed by the gnats. Some of the company were bitten & their heads and faces were swollen to blindness. Thick veils are necessary & if anything could be taken to wash the face and kill the poison, it would be a comfort. None should come without taking little articles of comfort, a few bottles of preserves, loaf sugar, some raisins, medicines &c.

Now I have done. If this little volume be any amusement to my dear Parents, Br. & Sister for whom it has been particularly written, I shall consider myself richly rewarded. I give it to you. I have prepared it for you. I wish you to be its protector. Think not that the stranger will read it with the same interest as yourself. No they will not & I had rather you would expose it but little & with regard to the last [section], if you think it improper to be inserted here, please cut it out. And now Dear Parents, what more shall I say but to bid you a last & silent *farewell.* Forgive wherein I have ever grieved you & again accept my thanks for your love & care of me. Till we meet in Heaven, Farewell, Farewell.

---

[108] Compare Sarah's list of items with that given by Myra Eells in a letter she wrote on October 4, 1838. FWW, II, p. 119. Both women recommended colored clothes, including their undergarments. Myra wrote that white garments were harder to keep clean and also that she considered them "altogether improper." Sarah was more specific than Myra. She also noted what a man should take.

Home Letters of Asa Bowen Smith
March 20, 1838 to February 3, 1842

Home Letters of Asa Smith

INTRODUCTION

*Asa Smith's letters to his parents, to his brother John, and to his
sisters, tell of the difficulties and internal dissensions which disturbed
the life of the Oregon Mission during the years 1838-42. Here lie revealed the chief reasons why Spalding, Gray, and Smith were dismissed.
It was the receipt of this order at Waiilatpu in September 1842 which
prompted Whitman to undertake his famous ride East during the following winter. Since both Gray and Smith were already out of the
Mission, the order actually applied only to Spalding. The author, in
his biographies of Spalding and Whitman, has developed the thesis
that Whitman rode to save Spalding and the mission stations at Lapwai
and Waiilatpu and not to save Oregon as legend would have it. Here
in these twenty-five letters to his home folks, Asa Smith pulls the curtain aside and we see in his free and penetrating comments the basic
reasons for the difficulties.*

*Few fiction writers could have imagined a more diverse assortment
of personality types than were gathered in this Mission. Three of the
six men — Whitman, Walker, and Eells — were of a peaceable disposition. They worked well with others. The other three — Spalding, Gray,
and Smith — had personality traits which often irritated others. Three
of the men — Whitman, Spalding, and Gray — were, as Smith described
them in his letter of December 18, 1838, "western men." They came
from the new regions of western New York and were accustomed to
frontier life. The other three were New Englanders, or Yankees, from
older communities. These differences in background colored much of
each individual's outlook.*

*The Smiths, the Walkers, and the Eells met each other for the first
time in New York on Monday, March 19, 1838. Before they arrived in
St. Louis on April 9th, Smith was the accepted leader of the party. He
was by far the most assured and aggressive of the three men. It was
he who made the decisions for the group, as Walker indicated in his
letter to Secretary Greene written from St. Louis: "I do not know how
we should have succeeded without him."*

The first five of Asa's home letters were written after the three couples left New York but before they started west from the Missouri frontier. They include the dates March 20 to April 22, 1838. Here we see Asa at his best. He is supremely happy, but in a different way from his bride Sarah. As has been noted, Sarah's emotions were torn asunder by the sadness of leaving her home and the feeling that she ought to be happy because she was now a missionary on her way to a heathen land. The repeated assurances found in her diary, which was kept especially for her parents, that she was happy give us the feeling that she was desperately trying to be what she felt she ought to be. With Asa it was different. He was really happy because at last, after eighteen months of frustrating delays, he was married and on his way as an appointee of the American Board to his mission field in Oregon. His highest ambitions had been realized.

The outline of contemporary events as previously given in the introduction and notations of Sarah's diary will present the background necessary for the understanding of Asa's home letters. Footnotes in this section will deal with items arising out of his letters which have not been discussed previously.

The author's The Diaries and Letters of Spalding and Smith *contains Smith's diary written for the American Board, April 23, 1838-December 5, 1840, and his letters to Secretary Greene, July 10, 1838-April 29, 1841.*

STEAM BOAT FROM NEW YORK TO PHILADELPHIA
March 20, 1838

MY DEAR PARENTS.   I feel that I must take a few moments to write to you tho I am some fatigued & have only steam boat accommodations for writing. I would gladly write you a long letter but it does not seem possible just now & I shall probably have not time for 2 or 3 days to come. You will doubtless wish to know how I feel now on my way to my missionary field. I can say, my dear Parents, that I feel *happy*, yes, *happy*, tho I must be denied the privilege of seeing you again, yet I feel that this is for the best. T'is thus the Lord has ordered it & doubtless it is right. Grieve not, my dear parents, that we meet no more perhaps in this world but rejoice that God has given you a son for this blessed work. O it is a blessed work & should I be spent to engage in this work, I feel that you are indeed highly honoured. Rejoice then that God has thus dealt with us. This separation may cause us pain but O how much reason there is to rejoice. We feel very happy & contented & enjoy each others society very much. We feel to commit our way unto the Lord & we feel that the Lord will sustain us.

We left Brookfield on Thursday, the 15th, but on account of the bad travelling only got to New Haven before Sabbath. We had a very pleasant interview with our friends & yesterday morning took the boat for New York. Arrived a little after noon & immediately put ourselves in readiness to start on our journey. Spent only one night in New York in the family of S.V.S. Wilder where we were very kindly treated & this afternoon at 5 o'clock we got into the boat for Philadelphia. Thus we are riding on our way & feel happy that we are permitted to go towards our field of labor. I can write but little now for I feel fatigued with the cares & labors of the day, but I will write again as soon as I have an opportunity. When you think of us, remember that we are happy. Your daughter Sarah sends her love. She feels happy in view of the work. It cost some tears to leave her friends, but when it was over, she felt very happy. The family shed some tears, but Mother W. said 'We weep not because we regret to have you go." It cost a struggle, but I trust it was done cheerfully. Pray for us. Remember us every day at the family altar. Farewell, Your affectionate Son.   A. B. SMITH

MY DEAR SISTERS. Grieve not that we must part perhaps to meet no more till we meet in heaven. I can write no more now, but I will write you again as soon as I can. Dear Sisters, Farewell. Sister Sarah sends her love.

                    Your affectionate brother.   A. B. SMITH

                                    CINCINNATI,   April 4, 1838
MY DEAR FATHER. I did not receive your letter before I left New York & it was forwarded to this place so that I rec'd it as soon as I arrived here. The money you wished to let me have, I did not of course receive. If I had it I might make use of it tho there is no particular necessity for it, as I am furnished with what is necessary for the journey. If I had it I should make use of it to buy a cow to take over the mountains. We shall take some, how many I know not. We shall lay out all the money we have, except a little specie we take, before we leave the states in purchasing cows, so we can have milk on the way & when we get there. Cows are worth $100 beyond the Rocky Mountains so it is important that we should take our cows on this side. There are some things to be purchased for me & sent out, books &c & the money you wish me to have, you had better send to Boston with express directions to have it used in purchasing articles which are to be sent to me. It can

be sent to the Miss. Rooms to Henry Hill, Esq., Treasurer, in your name, to be expended for my particular benefit. They will know how to dispose of it if it is thus sent. Tell Br. Fann (?) that I thank him for his kindness & that I regret that I had not the pleasure of receiving his offering as from his hand. If he wishes, he can send his also to Boston for me.

I was very happy, my dear father, to receive a letter from you & to know that you are glad to have me in the field of [missionary] labor & rejoice that the Providence of God has opened the way before me. You regret that you could not see me again; & so do I. It would have given me much pleasure could I have seen my dear parents, brothers & sisters once more, but the providence of God has ordered it otherwise & we must submit. The thought that I am now away & probably shall never meet my friends again in this world, sometimes causes me pain but when I think that this separation is short & that we shall soon meet again where there will be no sorrow & no more parting, I find it a pleasing thought. Yes, it is a happy thought that we shall meet again, no more to be separated. Let us keep our mind on that & labor to do the work which the Lord has for us to do & this separation instead of being painful will be rather pleasant.

We arrived here last Thursday evening & we are now on the boat very soon to start for St. Louis. We have had a pleasant time in Cincinnati, went to the Seminary, saw Dr. Beecher at his own home, met several old acquaintances, &c. I can write but little more now for the boat is soon to leave & the man who is to put this in the office is waiting. I will write again soon on a double sized sheet & when I get it full, I will send it probably not before I get to Independence, Missouri. Give my love to all. Sarah is much better than when we started. She endures the journey better than I expected. Rec'd the girls letter here & will answer it next time.

Your affectionate son.   A. B. SMITH

Tell Mother to cast her care on the Lord & feel that her children are safe in his hand. We are happy.

MY DEAR SISTERS. I will this morning commence a letter to you on a larger sheet & when I get it full I will send it to you. I have given you something of an account of our journey to Cincinnati when I wrote last. I have said nothing about the weather since we arrived in this region. We find the weather much warmer & the season much farther advanced. Last Saturday was a very warm day. We went to Walnut

Hills to the [Lane Theological] Sem. The grass was green & the trees were putting forth their leaves. It was the last day of March. We felt as tho we had jumped out of winter into summer. But a few days before we were crossing the Allegany Mountains where there was a plenty of snow, & the weather rather cold.

We left Cincinnati yesterday about noon & arrived some time in the night at Louisville where we remained till near noon to day. At Louisville I had a letter of introduction to Rev. Mr. Huber & an order on him for $70. Called & found him this morning at the Sabbath School depository & rec'd the money. I found him to be an interesting man. Sarah & I went & sat with him an hour & conversed with him & were very much instructed. He is a Swiss from Basle & is full of the free spirit of Switzerland, an abolitionist, tho' in a slave state. Said he, I never knew a Swiss slave holder. He manifested much interest in our undertaking & went with me to obtain some vaccine matter.[1] Dr. Jarvis who is a Mass. man kindly gave me some, & refused to take any compensation. Thus we find some good people even in wicked places, for Louisville has the reputation of being a wicked place. Population from 25 to 30,000. We are now on our way again & have passed the rapids just below Louisville. The river is quite angry & can be passed only when the water is high. There was just water enough to carry us down safely. We are pushing on as fast as the boat will carry us towards the west — away from our New England home: but we do not regret that we have undertaken it & I trust we never shall. The Lord has been our helper hitherto & has brought us along in safety & will trust in him for the future. We are safe in his hands wherever we may be & we are safe no where else. I think I never felt that confidence in God which I have since we set out on this undertaking. I have felt to commit all my ways to the Lord & let him direct all my steps & with this feeling I have been happy.

FRIDAY 6th.   We are now below the mouth of the Wabash River along the bank of Illinois. The river is now noble in size & presents a very fine appearance. We are riding along finely on the broad sheet of water at the rate of about 15 miles an hour. This is taking us rapidly away from our home & from the friends we have. I often think about you, my dear sisters, & wish I could see you once more, but God has ordered it otherwise & he knows for what reason & we must submit to

---

[1] No doubt smallpox vaccine, first introduced by the English physician, Edward Jenner. The fact that Smith wished to obtain such vaccine speaks well for his acceptance of the latest approved methods of his day.

it, tho' it causes us pain. Perhaps some of you may yet come out to teach the Indians. I should like very much to have you with me or near to me.

We have some very pleasant company on board. Some from New England which I assure you makes it quite pleasant. There is a Mrs. Griggs & her daughter from Roxbury, Mass. She saw Sister Adeline before she went out & was much interested to find that Sarah was her sister. We find some difference between Yankees & western people. The ladies here at the west who think themselves something are very fond of puting on jewelry & making a show. There is not so much solidity as there is among our good solid Yankee ladies. I find some wickedness at the west, but not so much as I expected from what I had heard. There has been some gambling & drinking on the boat, but less than I had anticipated. The Capt. is very kind & gentlemanly but not a Christian. He gave us permission to attend prayers in the ladies cabin. So every night we have had family worship. We have been very kindly treated & I think have commanded the respect of those with whom we have been associated. There are several pious persons on the boat.

SAT. 7th. We are now going up the Mississippi. We entered it sometime during the night, so that we did not have an opportunity of seeing it after its junction with the Ohio. It presents a fine body of water. It is commonly about one mile in width. The water is very muddy, just like the streams after a violent shower. It is impossible to see any thing in the water, it is so thick with mud. This muddy water is all we have to wash with & all we have to drink.[2] After standing awhile it settles some & does not look quite so bad. It tastes better than it looks. We have had nothing but river water since we came on board the boat. The water of the Ohio river was not so dirty as this but the taste was scarcely better than that of the Mississippi. We have generally to have [?] weak tea or coffee on board the boat, sometimes we have milk & sometimes not. We had nothing but river water while in Cincinnati, except when we went to Walnut Hills, there the water was very fine. But these are privations scarcely worth naming. I have scarcely thought of them as inconveniences. It is nothing compared with what it would be to cross the ocean. The privations are yet to come. We have as yet had good living — too good for our health — but soon we expect to be put on a different fare. Our principal diet will be

---

[2] Asa is the only one of the mission party who made any extended comment on the river water which they had to drink. Narcissa Whitman, in her diary for April 7, 1836, commented on the ill effects from drinking the river water. FWW, I, p. 46.

buffalo meat with some bread, but we must be very temperate in the use of bread, for we cannot take a very large quantity of flour. We shall have milk & that will be a very great comfort. Tho' there will be hardships & privations, yet I think we shall enjoy the journey & find much that is pleasant.

We have now a slave state on one side & a free state on the other. We stopped to take in wood on the Missouri side today & black boys came with eggs & hickory nuts. They were slaves & we learned that the owner of the place had about 100. We have not as yet had an opportunity to see much of slavery. There are coloured people on the boat, but they are all free & some of them are gentlemen. We treat them kindly & take notice of them & they are very kind & attentive to us. It is very easy to gain their esteem. It gives me a great deal of pleasure to notice them. They seem to be so much gratified.

10th.   We are now on our way up the Missouri, fast getting out of the regions of civilization. We had to ride all day on the Sab. wh. we did not like at all, but there was no other way to do. There was no place for us to stop to spend the Sab. & we were under the necessity of sticking to the boat. It was about the same as tho we were on the ocean. We spent the Sab. in our staterooms reading the Bible &c. Perhaps it would not be best to say any thing about our riding on the Sab. for others might not know the circumstances & would make a noise about it. But I feel satisfied because I saw no other way for us to do. Arrived at St. Louis sometime during Sab. night, found ourselves at St. Louis when we awoke in the morning. Soon found a boat going up the Missouri & moved our baggage on board. Did not know till just at night. Called on Mrs. Jones, formerly Miss Bacon, the teacher at Brookfield of whom we had heard while there. Found her a very pleasant woman, heartily glad to see us & we enjoyed ourselves very well. It was good to get on shore & be welcomed by a Yankee & sit down to a Yankee cooked dinner for I am heartily sick of negro cooking on the boat — so much grease & molasses.[3]

We saw several New England ladies at St. Louis & they were glad to see us, I will assure you. They presented us with several small articles wh. we needed. Thus we find friends everywhere. Last night we rode all night & now we are a good distance up the Missouri — shall see Jefferson City probably before night. We have gone thus far more rapid than is usual on this river. The motion of the boat is such

---

[3] The lack of proper food while crossing the plains and the mountains became for Asa a point of major concern.

that we cannot write while it is going. They have now stopped to take on wood. I went on shore a few moments, saw the log-huts of the natives a little distance from the river, ground hard [?] & the soil seemed to be of the first quality — timber principally white ash & button wood. The trees are green — the wild plum in blossom. We had a very interesting time on the boat from Cincinnati. We liked our company very much & left them with some regret. The Capt. tho' not a Christian became exceedingly interested in us & treated us with every possible attention. He went on board with us to find a new boat & see that we had good accommodations & treated us with the utmost kindness. We were told by one of the company after we left that at the dinner table he said he had never had any passengers on board that he felt such an interest in as he did in us. He came on board just before our boat started to bid us farewell. We expressed our gratitude for his kindness. He shook hands with us all & bid us farewell & it was with much emotion. He could scarcely keep from tears. It was interesting. It was affecting to see a man destitute of religion manifesting such feeling. My own feeling was affected. We had treated him very kindly & with respect & taken some pains to interest him. I think we were enabled to gain the respect & confidence of the whole company. Truly the Lord seems to give us favor in the sight of those who care not for his cause.

Rec'd your letter at St. Louis & was very glad to hear from home once more. It would give me much pleasure could I see you once more, but we must not think too much about it. I know you feel very anxious to see me again & when I read your letters it causes me to think about it. I see from your letter you feel deeply on the subject & I can but enter into your sympathies. It touches my feelings to read your letters, but we must be careful & not indulge our feelings too far. I love you much, my dear sisters, & know not that we shall meet again. But let us not grieve. Let us rather rejoice & think of the time when we shall meet again. It will soon come & it will be a happy meeting. Sarah wishes to fill the next page, so I must close. Shall write you often so long as I have opportunities for sending. Your affectionate brother,

A. B. Smith

Sarah's letter occupies page seven of A. B. Smith's long letter of April 5, 1838 to his sisters.

Steam boat   April 10, 1838

My very dear Sisters.   Mr. S. has given me the privilege of writing a letter in his letter which I am very happy to do. I trust you will be happy to hear from me & learn how I feel now on my way to a heathen land. I think I can say that I never was so happy as since I left my home & all my dear friends for the sake of telling the dying heathen of a Savior. It was trying indeed to bid farewell to my dear Parents, brother & sister but I was enabled to do it calmly. Sure I shed some tears but they were not tears of regret that I was going to leave them for I felt that I was doing it in obedience to the commands of my Savior & I felt that He sustained me in making this sacrifice.

[APRIL] 23.   My dear Laura, this is the first moment I could get to finish this letter & now am in great haste as we are leaving Westport. We arrived at Independence Sabbath eve, rode into town horseback 3½ [miles] in the evening, with Mr. Smith to lead my pony. I felt quite free from danger & enjoyed the ride much. Friday we left Ind. for this place, 12 miles, rode horseback. I should like to give you a description of our ride but have not time. The horse I am to ride is a pony. Our horses are all young & spirited, but I expect we can manage them. Our burdens are carried by mules. We shall take one waggon so that if we are sick & unable to ride horseback, we can ride in that. The trading company left here yesterday. We hope to overtake them soon as we shall immediately come into an enemy's country. I suppose we know but little yet of the trials & dangers of our journey but I trust we go relying on an Almighty arm for protection. If he has a work for us to do among that people, He can carry us there. We feel to commit our way to God. Our tents are very comfortable ones, two families will occupy one but with a curtain in between. We find our missionary friends very kind, trust we shall be happy with them. Give my best love to dear Mother, do all you can to comfort her. Tell her we are happy & that ere long we hope to meet her in heaven. Tell her I have a kind husband, one I love & one I shall endeavor to render happy. Tell her that nothing shall be wanting on my part to make him comfortable & happy both in sickness & in health. Farewell dear Parents & sisters, farewell till we meet in heaven.

Yours truly,   SARAH

INDEPENDENCE, Mo.   April 16, 1838

DEAR BRO.   We have at length come to land & to the end of our steam boat navigation. I have almost forgotten when I wrote you last & do not know where to begin to give you particulars. And I think I need not go back far in giving particulars respecting the journey as I have written home respecting it & you will have an opportunity of seeing that at some future time. The last I wrote home was on the passage up the Missouri River. We remained in St. Louis only one day — had to be on the boat over the Sab. before we arrived there, which was not at all pleasant; but there was no other way for us. It was about like being on the ocean, there was no place for us to stop if we wished. Arrived in St. Louis Sab. night & Monday evening started up the Missouri for Independence. We had good accommodations on the boat we started on but when we arrived within 150 miles of Independence, we were put off upon another boat in rather an ungentlemanly manner because there was not freight enough to make it profitable. We had poor accommodations the rest of the way & were detained so that we were under the necessity of spending the Sab. on the boat again. Arrived last evening which was Sab. Came to the landing late in the afternoon & we got upon the shore & went into a log hut with the ladies & dispatched Br. Rogers to town to find Br. Gray & obtain some conveyance for the ladies. It was 3½ miles. They returned with horses for the ladies to ride & we started off about 9 to go to the town. We had to go up a very steep hill & then stretch across a plain. It was some dark & occasionally some mud. We put our ladies upon the horses & then started on walking by their side & leading them as we found necessary. It was rather amusing [4] but it was rather a hard walk. The ladies seemed to enjoy it very well & in an hour & a half we arrived at Br. Gray's lodging & here we found only two beds for 9. At that those who had no bed had to put down upon the floor. This was not quite so pleasant but we made the best of it. It is difficult to get any accommodations here & we have to put up with such as we can get.

WESTPORT [SUNDAY]   April 22nd, 1838

MY DEAR BRO.   From this date you will see that it is the Sab. & I can assure you that Sab. in this region means something different from what it does in New England. The place where we now are is 12 miles from Independence. We came here on Friday afternoon & it was a hard afternoon's work, I will assure you. We had 10 mules to carry our

---

[4] One of the very few references in the writings of any of the missionaries to amusement or laughter. While such references are few, still we can believe that since these were normal young people, they must have found many occasions for good-natured banter and laughter. This was such an occasion with the men walking in the mud leading the horses through the darkness. It was a novel experience for all of the party.

baggage & about a dozen cows & young cattle. This made work enough
for us to do. We had one river to cross. Ferried some over & some
forded. We had to lead the mules. The last part of the way, they were
in two strings, one tied on after the other & the forward one led. My
business was to lead one string. We were all on horseback, except Br.
Rogers, a young man from Cincinnati who is going with us. Bro's Gray,
Walker, Eells & myself & wives, in all 9 persons. Br. Gray & Eells
thought we could get along without a man to help us, but I think they
were both very thoroughly convinced that it was best to have help &
accordingly a man is hired.[5] We did not arrive here till after 9 in the
evening, much fatigued I will assure you. Sarah endured it much better
than I expected, She was rather unwell last week & on Tuesday took
an emetic. She was very much fatigued but seems to be quite as well
now as usual. I am writing you today for the cause I have no other
time. We leave tomorrow. The company with whom we are to go
started today. They care not for the Sabbath. Bro. Gray said something
to us yesterday about going on with them today, but we were very
unwilling to move on the Sab.[6] When we get into the Indian country,
we shall be under the necessity of travelling if the company do & this
is what they generally do. Br. Gray asked Dr. [J.A.] Chute's opinion.
Dr. C. is a New England man [7] & is doing all he can to make us comfortable. He was utterly opposed to our leaving & said he would rather
sacrifice $100 than do it. He offered to go with us & conduct us till we
overtake the fur company. This decided it at once & we remain till
Monday & glad enough I assure you we were to remain for some of
us are about sick. So much hardship & change of climate affects our
health somewhat. Today I have been taking medicine & have not been
out. I have taken an emetic & cathartic & have not got through with it

---

[5] Gray, who had given the American Board certain assurances regarding the
maximum cost of conducting a party overland, was looking for every possible means
to economize. Eells was inexperienced and for a time agreed with Gray. The short
ride from Independence to Westport had demonstrated the necessity of hiring a
man to help. A fellow by the name of Stevens was hired who remained with the
party until it reached Waiilatpu.

[6] The caravan of the American Fur Company traveled seven days a week as
occasion demanded. Gray had had enough experience with the Indians to feel
that it was best to travel with the caravan even if it meant violating their consciences. But the others decided to remain. Later events proved that Gray was
right.

[7] With great provincial pride, Smith considered the New Englanders or the
"Yankees" to be among the elite of American citizens. The New Englanders had
more culture and refinement than those from areas farther west. Gray was not a
New Englander.

yet. I am now on the bed sitting up against the logs of the house while writing & my dear wife is with me to take care of me. I enjoy myself very much with her & feel that she is truly the one from the Lord.

I feel much better since the operation of my medicine & think I shall be able to go on tomorrow. Dr. Chute says he will take my place & relieve me from all the care of the mules, so that I shall have nothing to do but to ride along with my wife. Had I nothing to do but this, I could get along very well. Our journey must of necessity be a very hard one, but I am confident that if the Lord has any thing for us to do among those Indians he will carry us through — if not, he will dispose of us in some other way.

There are two things which cause me pain & of them I will speak to you freely. One is travelling on the Sab. & this I suppose we must do when the Fur Company say for we are dependent on them. But it is painful to think of it because we shall need the rest of the Sab. & our animals also need it & more than this, it is violating God's holy day. When I think of this it pains me. The other thing is we are under the necessity of taking guns.[8] The Fur Company will not allow us their aid unless we do this. This you know is painful to me for I am a peace man. O how does it look for a missionary of the Prince of Peace to go forth to preach the gospel carrying with him the weapons of war? I shudder at the thought. The Savior says 'He that taketh the sword shall perish by the sword." But if I perish, others I think must bear the responsibility. I should feel far more safe to go without any weapon. We need these weapons, they say, to hunt with on our way, but the real purpose is I suppose to defend ourselves from the attacks of the Indians. All that I can do is to commit my way to the Lord & leave the event with him. There will doubtless be many things to try us on this journey from the company with whom we go, being wicked men who care for nothing good. Trials doubtless we shall have with our own company,[9] — fatigue, hunger & thirst — but the Lord is able to carry us through them all. I feel to commit my way to him & my desire is that he would place me in that situation where I shall most glorify him. I would not choose for myself but pray that the Lord would choose for me.

I expected to have found a letter from you at St. Louis, but was

---

[8] The author has found no instance in which Asa ever used his gun even for hunting game.

[9] Here is the first hint that all was not well between Smith and Gray. Thus within a week after the two first met at Independence, a clash of personalities had begun.

disappointed. Have not heard from you at all since we started. Have rec'd 3 letters from home. Shall not hear from you probably till I get to my field. I shall have but few more opportunities to write to you on this side of the mountains.

SAB. EVENING. [APRIL 22]   I find myself quite comfortable after taking medicine. Last night & all day yesterday I had an unquenchable thirst so that I could not be satisfied, even by drinking almost the whole time. Now I feel relieved from the difficulty & think I shall feel quite well tomorrow. I should like very much to see you & the rest of our family. We begin to know how to prize our friends when we have left them. When we are fairly away and never expect to see them again, we begin to find that it is a serious matter. However I scarcely feel the loss of friends compared with what I should were I alone. I find that one dear bosom friend does much towards compensating for the loss of all others. Those who go unmarried, I fear, will not be very contented, certainly if they are possessed of social feelings. Could I see you I would talk much with you but I must be brief when I write. I might say much to you about what I have seen but I cannot say much now.

Wickedness abounds in this region, but I find there is a desire to receive instruction. I was pressed very hard to remain at Independence & teach. There I think would be an opportunity of doing much good. This western region is a barren waste & every place is full of iniquity. Here we find slavery & tho' I have not witnessed any unkind treatment of slaves, yet I have witnessed enough of the system to render it odious. Every slave that I have found out any thing about is anxious to be free. Sarah was very fond of conversing with the chambermaids on the boat & invariably she won their affections & fared well. But we were cautioned by some not to say anything to slaves lest it should do mischief. Slaveholders are afraid to have anything said to their slaves or to have them instructed at all, lest they should learn to value their liberty & takes measures to obtain their freedom. This feeling is very plain to be seen & it is one of the horrors of slavery. It is an accursed system, look at it in whatever light you may. But I must close. I shall send back letters when I can. This I have written in haste & perhaps it will be best to be cautious about some things which I have written. Pray for me for I feel much the need of prayer & have not so good an opportunity for devotions as formerly.

Very affect. your br.   A. B. SMITH

WESTPORT TO FORT HALL

The next five of Asa's home letters include the dates April 28th to July 27th and describe travel experiences from Westport to Fort Hall. After meeting the Grays at Independence, the leadership of the party naturally passed to Gray because he alone of the group had been to Oregon and back and it was he who had induced the Board to send out the reenforcement. Smith found himself demoted.

Difficulties arose between Smith and Gray from the very beginning of their association. They were opposites in many respects. Smith was a "New Englander" and proud of it; Gray was a "western man." Smith was the best educated man in the mission party; Gray, the least. Smith was a scholar who was at his best in the study with his books; Gray, a mechanic, worked with his hands. Smith was an introvert; Gray, an extrovert. Both were opinionated and critical of the shortcomings of others. With such a combination of personality traits thrown together under the trying circumstances of overland travel, trouble was inevitable.

The following five of Asa's letters trace out his growing resentment against Gray. On April 28th, Asa told his parents: "We have not been altogether satisfied with Br. Gray's management. . . He is rather petulant & sometimes acts rather ungentlemanly." On May 15th, he complained: "Dr. Gray has been so anxious to get along cheap that he subjects us to more hard labor than we have been really able to bear." By June 1st, Asa's resentment had been so aroused that he wrote: "He is actually the most uncomfortable man I have had to deal with. He is commonly cross and crabbed & has no regard for the feelings of others & we have to endure much of his snapping & scolding." And by the time the reenforcement reached the Rendezvous, Asa was avoiding Gray as much as possible. On July 6th, he wrote: "He has treated us like servants. . . His conduct has been such that he is hated by all who have been with us."

In addition to the light these letters throw upon the growing disaffections within the mission party, Asa's descriptions add many colorful pieces to the mosaic of this epic story of the Oregon-bound reenforcement of 1838.

ON THE BANK OF THE KANSAS RIVER NEAR
KANSAS VILLAGE — April 28, 1838

MY DEAR PARENTS. As I now have an opportunity of sending back a letter to you, I will improve it. I am now beyond the place where I can

send letters by mail as I am in the Indian country & have not seen a
house since I left Westport last Monday. We set out about noon on
Monday & this morning about 10 we overtook the fur company which
started the day before we did, encamped on the bank of the [Kansas]
river & now are waiting for their boat to come up the river. We have
come about 100 miles this week & have had some hardships to endure.
We have 10 mules to carry our baggage on their backs [10] & it is no
small job to pack & unpack them — tho' I have not had that part to do
much. My business has been to drive a dozen head of cattle — most of
the time I have had one to assist. Yesterday & today I have driven
them alone. We have one cow that gives milk so that we have enough
to use with tea & coffee, & I drink some because we dont always have
good water. When night comes we find a place for encampment where
there is wood, water & grass & pitch our tents, get our supper & lie
down on the ground. The principal part of our living has been bread
& bacon. We have a tin baker [11] so that we can bake bread before the
fire. You would think I suppose that sleeping on the ground would be
very hard & uncomfortable but I can assure you that I never slept
better in my life than I have this week. Our tent keeps out the wind &
then we have a buffalo skin to lay down, then oil cloth to keep away
the moisture — then five or six thick heavy blankets. We have two
blankets to each horse, one under the saddle & one over & fastened by
a [——] cinch — two or three of these I double & lay on the oil cloth
& then spread on the ones on which we sleep & then put two on over
this, with the long flannel night dress which we have has kept us
sufficiently warm. Our tent is about 8 feet by 10 feet on the ground.
This is occupied by two families. Br. Walker & wife are with us. At
night we have a curtain in the middle to separate one family from the
other. Here we sleep & our table is at morning & night in one of the
tents. We have no table of course, but spread the table cloth on the oil
cloth & then put on our dishes as comfortably as people in New Eng-

[10] The total baggage for nine people for an overland journey of some 1,900 miles
extending over a period of over four months, was so limited that it could be
loaded on ten mules. This included tents, bedding, cooking equipment, food supplies, and personal belongings. The work involved in packing and unpacking,
setting up and tearing down camp, caring for the animals, and cooking their meals
out-of-doors, proved to be burdensome. Once started there was no turning back or
escape.

[11] This tin baker is mentioned several times in the writings of the missionaries.
After reaching Waiilatpu, the Walkers inherited the item. It is difficult to understand why the missionaries did not take a greater quantity of food with them for
the first three weeks of their travel or until they reached the buffalo country.

land. We have no seats to sit on but put ourselves down on our knees or any way we can. I can eat as well as I sleep & eat meat too, for I must eat it or go without. Never did food taste better than it has today. We have a little bread now but some of the way we may have nothing but meat. We expect to be in the buffalo country in about 20 days. Thus far we have endured the journey well. Sarah has now rode about 100 miles on horseback & has endured it far beyond my expectations. Her health is decidedly better than when we started. I hope that the Lord will give us strength to go through with the hardships before us.

The journey is a long & tedious one but I trust it will be the means of improving our health. The climate is fine & healthy. You would suppose it very dangerous to sleep out as we do, but in this region there is no danger at all. None of our company have had a cold since we started. The air is very dry & we have had no dew except one night since we set out. The ground is very dry so that there is no injury from lying on the ground. We have three with us who sleep without any tent in the open air. One is our hunter, another the man who assists in packing our animals.[12] Many who go on this route wrap themselves in blankets & lie down in the open air & enjoy excellent health.

We have been now the whole week travelling through the prairie & it is one of the grandest sights I ever witnessed. New England people would stare to see such immense fields — often as far as the eye can reach nothing is to be seen but green meadow, hundreds of acres. It is not level, but gently undulating, sometimes cut by water courses, occasionally a strip of woodland to be seen in the small streams. It has been very windy since we have been on the prairie & sometimes it has been so hard as to be quite unpleasant. We have thus far passed along tolerably pleasantly. We have not been altogether satisfied with Br. Gray's management.[13] He has seemed a little too much like driving [?] & wishes to have every thing go as he says. He is rather petulant & sometimes acts rather ungentlemanly. This is rather unpleasant, but we don't mean to have any difficulty. Saw some Indians today. They were dressed with leggins & a blanket over their shoulders. Their brawney shoulders were bare some of the time & they looked savage. We have a good deal that is amusing on the way & enjoy it quite well. Sarah rides with me most of the time after the cattle & we enjoy it quite well.

---

[12] The reference is to Cornelius Rogers, Stevens, and a second man who was hired to assist, Paul Richardson.

[13] For the first time in his letters to his parents, Asa criticizes Gray by name.

When you think of us, think of us as happy for we do enjoy much tho deprived of much. Yet we feel that the Lord is our helper & he will lay no more upon us than we are able to hear. Pray for us that we may be sustained. Sarah sends her love to all.

Very affectionately yours,   A. B. SMITH

The letter was so folded as to permit part of an outside page to carry the following address: "Mr. Asa Smith, East Williamstown, Vermont." It also bore the inscription in writing: "West Port, Mo. May 1st. 25¢."

ON THE BANK OF THE PLATTE RIVER
ABOUT 400 MILES FROM WESTPORT
May 15th, 1838

MY DEAR PARENTS. As I have opportunity of sending you a letter by some Indians whom we have met, I will spend the few moments I can snatch this noon in writing to you. You doubtless have been very anxious to hear from me & know how I get along &c. I wish I had time to write more, but I must be short. We have endured the journey thus far beyond our expectations. Our health is much better than when we started, tho our labor has been very hard & we have been extremely fatigued. Dr. Gray has been so anxious to get along cheap that he subjects us to more hard labor than we have been really able to bear.[14] My business has been to drive a dozen head of cattle, some of the time I have had help, some of the time alone. It has been very hard & at night I have been so fatigued that it seemed as tho I could not move. Yet my appetite is excellent, sleep sweet, & when rested feel well.

Sarah has endured altogether beyond my expectations. She rides horseback very well now. We travel now about 25 miles per day. Generally it has been less — one day 28. One of the greatest difficulties is about getting enough to eat. We have not really suffered but I presume you would think it very hard to live as we do. We have eaten no bread for a few days past. We have about 120 lbs of flour & nearly 40 lbs of hard bread but we expect the time will come when we shall need it more. We bought some corn of the Kansas Indians when we were in their country. This we boil and eat with our meat. We have smoked hog — not ham. It is all fat & some fresh meat, some venison. Last week we killed a calf we took with us.[15] This corn & meat is all

14 Here was a justifiable point of criticism. In his eagerness to save money, Gray was forcing his three clergymen associates to endure more physical labor than should have been expected. Gray was a mechanic and used to outdoor work. The other three men were accustomed to a more sedentary life.

15 See fn. 37 of Sarah's diary regarding this incident involving a wounded calf.

we use at present & that rather sparingly. Very soon we expect to be where we can get a plenty of buffalo meat & then I think we shall have enough to eat. Often have I thought it would be a pleasure to sit down at your table & satisfy my hunger & I know it would be a pleasure to you to have me. I cannot have time now to write all I wish to. The country through which we have travelled has been very beautiful. It has been prairie — some level, some undulating, some still more uneven, but all smooth & destitute of timber except on the streams, covered with grass. The soil is rich & as far as the eye can reach after, it has the appearance of the smoothest meadows that can be found in New England.

The company with whom we travel is a company of wicked men who regard not the Sab. & we are obliged to travel with them or be left unprotected in this Indian country. They have however treated us very kindly. We are now in the Pawnee country. A war party of 20 encamped near us night before last. They seem very friendly to us. There are many things very interesting in this route. It is very hard & fatiguing. Every fourth night we must stand on guard. The night is divided into 3 watches. This I do not like very well for I need the night to sleep & I think I shall hire some of the men of the company to stand on guard for me. If I had $20 you wished me to have, it would do something towards relieving my hardships. You might send it to the Board to be applied to my own private use. My travelling expenses from Brookfield to New York, I paid myself, but I have the right to charge that to the Board & I think I shall & apply it to my own use.

If I had less labor, I could get along quite comfortably. But this fatigue is good I suppose to fit us for future labors.[16] We have some trials & some joys. Some trials among ourselves for Dr. Gray is not in all respects such a man as I could wish & this has made things rather unpleasant. But I hope things will go more pleasantly in future. He has not treated us as we wish to be treated but I think he will do differently in future. Remember us in your prayers & believe me your affectionate son.

A. B. SMITH

MAY 19th. Today we have an opportunity of sending letters as we did not have them ready to send by the Indians. We are still going up the Platte, generally 25 miles per day. Had some rain which was not

---

[16] As is evident from other writings, Gray was telling his associates that the hard work attendant upon traveling to Oregon was the best possible preparation for their future life on the mission field.

quite so pleasant. So far we are all in good health. Sarah sends her love. Her health continues to improve & she endures well. Yours

A. B. SMITH

Letter bears the address: "Mr. Asa Smith, East Williamstown, Vermont" and was mailed from Westport on June 6th. Postage 25¢.

LARAMY'S FORT OR FORT WILLIAM [17]

ON LARAMY'S FORK, A BRANCH OF THE PLATTE RIVER,

750 MILES FROM WESTPORT.   June 1st, 1838

MY DEAR SISTERS. Could I make you one more visit & enjoy your society once more, it would be very gratifying to me; but I am now far removed from my father's house & probably shall never see it again. Could you see me as I am now situated you would doubtless be amused. I am sitting on the ground in our tent with nothing but a buffalo skin under me & the wind is blowing strongly & the dirt flies not a little. You would find me rather dirty & ragged for it is impossible to keep clean here & I wear out my clothes very badly.[18] I calculate to get some leather clothes soon. They are better for riding on horseback & the labor we have to perform. We arrived here day before yesterday in the morning, having only 5 miles to travel from the place where we encamped the night before. It was the 39th day since we left Westport & not a day passed, even a sabbath, without moving camp.

We found it very hard to travel so without having any time to rest & we were very glad of having [here] a little rest from our labors. Our journey thus far has been exceedingly hard & trying. The worst trial of all which we have experienced *(I say it to you)* is that which is from our own number, Mr. Gray.[19] He is actually the most uncomfortable man I have had to deal with. He is commonly cross and crabbed & has no regard for the feelings of others & we have had to endure much of his snapping & scolding. This has been far more uncomfortable than any thing else we have experienced.

---

[17] Fort Laramie was first called Fort William and was named after William Sublette. William and his brother Milton were with the William Henry Ashley party which visited the Rockies in 1822. Both of the Sublettes were subsequently very active in the fur trade.

[18] The author has not found a single reference to the men shaving while on their overland journey. Their manner of travel and lack of conveniences must certainly have made all look and feel unkempt and dirty.

[19] What Asa was now saying privately to his home folks, he was not as yet telling the board. But as will be noted, by the time the party had reached the Rendezvous, all such reserve had melted away.

But the Lord has thus far sustained us & given us strength to perform the labors incumbent on us. We are now more than one third of our way from Westport to the place of our destination. In 20 days we expect to be in the mountains at the Rendezvous when most of the company with us stop. We shall then have about 800 miles more to travel to reach Walla Walla which will take from 40 to 50 days more. Our fare for two weeks past has been buffalo meat for breakfast, dinner & supper.[20] We have had bread only twice during that time. I have experienced less inconvenience from living on animal food than I expected. I do not feel very much the need of vegetable food, that is, I do not materially suffer from want of it. I should be very glad I assure you to get some potatoes & bread &c., but nothing but meat must be my fare for the present. We use flour to make gravy for the meat & shall have enough to use in this way. Our milk is a very great comfort to us & I have used coffee & tea because we did not find good water, & this made weak, & a good supply of milk added, I have found [to be] the best of any thing to quench the burning thirst which I have much of the time. Our health is much improved. Sarah is more rugged than she has ever been before & I am doing well. Today I have felt rather unwell but it was in consequence of eating too freely yesterday, as we had not much to do but to cook & eat. I might mention many things of interest but cannot for want to time. Sarah sends much love. Pray for us that the Lord will still be with us & bless. We enjoy much in each other's society & this is almost all the society a missionary can have.

Very Affectly. your brother.   A. B. SMITH

Addressed to "Misses Marcia & Lucia Smith, East Williamstown, Vermont" and postmarked "St. Louis, Mo. Jul. 8."

RENDEZVOUS OF THE AMERICAN FUR COMPANY ON WIND
RIVER, ONE OF THE BRANCHES OF THE YELLOWSTONE

July 6th, 1838

MY DEAR PARENTS. BROTHERS & SISTERS.   You will of course wish to hear from me every opportunity I have to write you & I with pleasure improve the opportunity of sending back a letter by the Fur Company on their return to the States. It is now about two weeks since we arrived at this place after a long & tedious journey of more than 1100 miles.

---

[20] No other member of the party made as many or as detailed references to their food as Asa. This reminds us of similar references to food found in some of his letters written while a student at Andover Theological Seminary.

We were very glad I will assure you to come to a stopping place where we might have some rest, but we begin to feel desirous to be on the move again for we have about 800 miles to travel yet before we reach the place of our destination. Our journey has been extremely hard & trying, but the Lord has thus far sustained us & given us strength to perform these arduous labors. We have become thoroughly accustomed to horseback riding so that we look upon a ride of 10 or 12 miles with pleasure & find it pleasant amusement. The last part of our journey has been through a rough country when we have had to ascend & descend rugged steeps, so that it was difficult to keep on horse back. We have had many rivers & small streams to ford, but as yet these have not been at all dangerous. Many of them were so deep that it was necessary to hold up my feet to keep them out of the water. One river that we forded, the Platte, was more than half a mile in width. This was a good long pull through the water. As we approach the mountains the streams are more rapid & at this season very high in consequence of the melting snow on the mountains. The Wind River mountains are quite near to us & they are covered with snow which now melts very fast & the river is constantly rising. This gives us good cool water. The water from these rivers I think is very fine & palatable.

The usual distance that we have travelled has been from 20 to 25 miles per day — sometimes less than this when not good travelling. We have usually found ourselves much fatigued at night, tho not so much the last part of the way as the first. We have had to rise very early, as soon as it was light & started usually between 6 & 7. Our living has been very uniform, buffalo meat for breakfast, dinner & supper. This is very good meat, especially the fat cow, but the bulls are strong. We had nothing but bull meat for a while at first & it went hard. But I think the fat cow is equal to beef tho we have not the means of cooking & seasoning it as beef is with you. It has not agreed with me very well to live entirely on meat. I have been very much troubled with a diarrhea which has left me very weak.[21] I am now relieved from this & feel stronger, tho it is a fact which I have learned from my own experience & from the testimony of others, that no one is as strong living on this diet as on the usual diet in the States.

I have often longed for bread & potatoes & could I have got to your

21 Several of the party suffered from the same complaint, which must have been a most unpleasant experience while riding. None of the party commented on what provisions were made to give privacy to the ladies when the caravan was in open country.

table, I don't know but I should have killed myself with eating. I have often thought how glad you would be to share your portion with me did you know how I had to live. Many a time would I have been glad to get into your barn or even into the pig pen to sleep but we had nothing but a tent to cover us.[22] When we were on the Platte River it rained almost constantly for 3 days so that we did not move. It was a very cold storm & our floor which was nothing but a buffalo hide was thoroughly wet through. We kept ourselves however from getting very wet. These you see are some of the pleasures of mountain life. Notwithstanding all this we have been preserved in safety & no disease has been permitted to visit us. We have a thousand things to be thankful for. We have had a thousand times more than we deserve & the trials which we have been called to pass through were designed for our good & I hope may have the desired effect. The privations we have experienced, tho' grievous to be borne, will not I trust prove any injury to us. Our health is good. Sarah has endured far beyond my expectations [23] & has not suffered in consequence of the dirt so much as I have. Her health is very much improved & I trust that this journey will prove a great benefit to her.

Our journey has in some respects been very interesting & many things pleasant. We have had too some unpleasant things. I have hinted at this in previous letters. Our leader, Mr. G[ray] is unfit altogether for the place he is in & has caused us much difficulty. Were I to relate particulars I could fill this whole sheet but perhaps it would not be best. This much I can say in truth — I never rec'd so much personal abuse in all my life as I have from this man since we set out on this journey. He has been cross & crabbed & scolds & frets & has talked to us as tho' he had not the least regard for feelings. I manage to have as little to do with him as possible for this is the only way I can get along with him. He has treated us like servants & "Lorded it over God's heritage." [Perhaps reference to the ordained ministers.] His conduct has been such that he is hated by all who have been with us. His conduct is suspect by the loss of those Indians last fall, is very much censured by the Fur Company. He was strongly advised not to go on as he did but to wait till the Company went down which was in about

---

[22] See fn. 54 of Sarah's diary where reference is made to the time that Mary Walker remembered the pigs in her father's barn in Maine and envied them for their warm, dry, and protected situation. The use of such similes paint vivid word pictures of their hardships.

[23] It is doubtful if Asa's home folks were aware of Sarah's frail health. Later Asa wrote of this in more detail.

10 days after he left. Mr. Bridger told him that he would certainly be defeated if he went on. But notwithstanding all this, he rushed on rashly & all his men were killed & he barely escaped.[24] This is the character of the man. You can judge how unfit he would be for the station he is now in. This part of the letter had better not be exposed for it might do harm.

About 3 weeks travel from this place will bring us to Fort Hall where we shall fall in with the Hudson's Bay Company & have their protection the rest of the way. If we can get safe to that place, I apprehend no further difficulty. Then we shall be able to get supplies of flour &c & have safe protection to Wallawalla. I long to be at our journey's end. The last part will be the worst. It is a rough country to pass through & the weather will be very warm. But I trust the Lord will carry us through. We are safe only in his hand. If he has work for us to do in that field, he will bring us there. O that I may have unbroken confidence in him.

THURSDAY, the 5th.   Capt. Bridger came in with his party of men, about 100 in number, about 60 squaws & a multitude of half breed children, for it is the custom with men who live here in the Indian country to take unto themselves the women of the land. Bridger has been in the country 17 years & understands well the country & the character of the Indians. Only a few Indians have come to the Rendezvous this year. There are some half breeds. We have rec'd some visits from them. Two or three times they have come to our camp & danced to us. They sing & have a drum to accompany the voice & then they dance in a fantastic manner, jumping & turning themselves into all manner of shapes. Some squaws came with their children on their backs. This looked rather ridiculous. I have seen more drunkenness since we have been here than I have seen for a long time before. It has been a continual scene of dissipation. Alcohol in considerable quantities is brought up here & sold for $4 a pint, & tho' so dear, gallon after gallon is bought & used here.

MONDAY 9th.   Yesterday morning an Indian came to our camp & soon we learned that he was a Kayuse from Wallawalla who had come

---

[24] See the journal of William Henry Gray which follows for a brief reference to the Ash Hollow incident. In Smith's letter to the Board written from the Rendezvous on July 10th, he said: "We have not found Mr. Gray such a man as we hoped to find . . . he is not judicious in all his movements. He is rash & inconsiderate & not at all calculated properly to fill the station he now does. . . It is nothing uncommon when I go out among the men to hear some one express their dislike of Mr. Gray." SS, 72.

on to meet us. We learned from him that a party were on the other side of the river & that a gentleman of the Hudson's Bay Company wished to see Mr. Gray. He went over & found Rev. Mr. Lee, a Methodist missionary on his way to the United States & Mr. Ermatinger [25] of the Hudson's Bay Company with a number of men come on to meet us. This [was] very joyful news. Five of his men will return in company with us. We learned that provisions were sent up for us to Fort Hall which is about 3 weeks travel from this place & also a quantity was left at another place between that & Wallawalla, so we are kindly provided for. We expect to start about the middle of this week & proceed on our way. By the last of August or the first of Sept. at fartherest, we hope to be to the end of our journey. The rest of the way I hope we shall have an easier time than we have had thus far,[26] tho' the weather will be oppressive after we get thru the mountains. However, I trust that he who has kindly preserved us thus far will carry us through the remainder of the way in safety.

We learn from Mr. Lee that Mr. Spaulding & Dr. Whitman are prospering in their work, but much is undone for want of help. Pray for us that God would make us eminently useful among those whom we go to teach. I hope you will improve every opportunity of sending letters to us. Send them to Boston & the Secretaries will know when to send them. Whatever articles you may wish to send to us should be put up in something very tight so that it would not get wet if it should get into the water. Any thing that you may feel disposed to send which would be for food or raiment would be acceptable. No articles should be sent but such as would keep. A barrel or keg is the best to send things in. Dried apple is an article that might be sent, if well dried & it would be a great comfort.[27] I shall send this by Mr. Lee. You can write me by him next spring. Send letters to Boston the latter part of winter & the Secretaries will send them. Best to direct them to send by Rev. Mr. Lee.[28]

---

[25] Francis Ermatinger was a jovial person and later frequently visited the Walkers and the Eells at their homes at Tshimakain. He was always friendly to the missionaries.

[26] Actually the Blue Mountains in what is now eastern Oregon, which had to be crossed before reaching Waiilatpu, were much more rugged than anything the missionaries had yet encountered.

[27] In Asa's letter to his father of August 27, 1840, which follows, he acknowledged receipt of a half-barrel of dried apples.

[28] While in the East, Jason Lee was married to Miss Lucy Thompson on July 28, 1839. The Methodist Church chartered the "Lausanne" which sailed from New York for Oregon on October 9th with a company of fifty-one missionaries, includ-

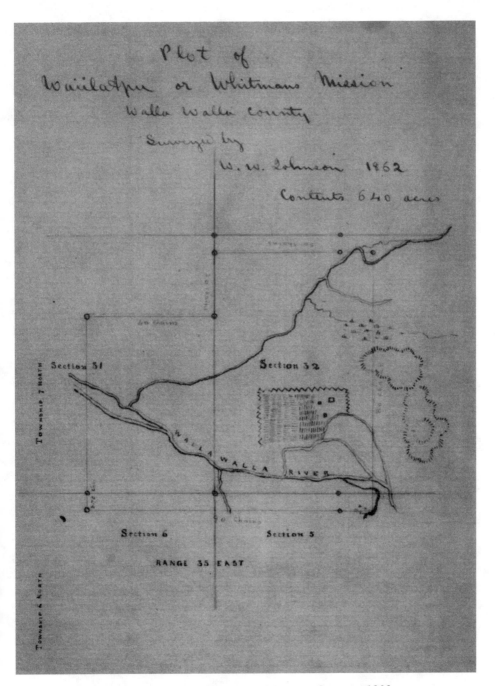

Plot of
Wailatpu or Whitmans Mission
Walla Walla County
Surveyed by
W. W. Johnson   1862
Contents 640 acres

Section 31   Section 32

TOWNSHIP 7 NORTH

WALLA WALLA RIVER

Section 6   Section 5

RANGE 35 EAST

TOWNSHIP 6 NORTH

SURVEY MAP OF WHITMAN MISSION SITE IN 1862

Showing confluence of Mill Creek and Walla Walla River. Most of the area
shown here is now part of the Whitman Mission National Historic Site.
Rev. and Mrs. Cushing Eells lived here from 1860 to 1872. Shown are their
buildings and garden, enclosed by a rail fence. See text page 153.
Original in Coll. A.

Remember me to all my friends. Sarah sends love to all. The next time I write, I suppose will be from the other side of the mountains. I often think of home & think I should like to be there ever more, but we shall soon meet to part no more.

Very affct. yours,   A. B. SMITH

[Across side of outside page] Remember when you write letters, I shall want information. I want you to write every thing you think will be interesting to us. News papers would be very acceptable. Father White's offer of sending the Vt. Chronicle. I should like the Evangelist. If they could be put up regular in a bundle after you have used them & sent at the end of the year, they would answer my purposes as well as any.

This letter was addressed to "Mr. Asa Smith" at Williamstown, Vermont. The following inscription is in the lower left-hand corner "By Rev. Mr. Lee, Missionary beyond the Rocky Mts." The letter was postmarked "New York, Oct. 31."

FORT HALL,   July 27th, 1838

MY DEAR PARENTS.   We arrived here today, 16 days from the Rendezvous, a distance of 400 miles & over the most rugged & mountainous part of the way. We have travelled very safely, but it has not been so fatiguing here as on lower ground where it is warmer. We have had a cool bracing air, as we have been some of the time in the region of snow. We have an unexpected opportunity of sending letters from this place as an express arrived here last night from Walla Walla with the intelligence that Mrs. Lee, the wife of the missionary we met at the Rendezvous, was dead & an express will go on to inform him of this mournful event. We are all well, tho some fatigued with our labor. We can endure it better however now than the first part of the route before we became accustomed to it. We have now 500 miles to go to reach Wallawalla which makes 900 from the Rendezvous instead of 800 as I mentioned in my last. Six Nez Perces are here, came to meet us here with fresh horses. They are very glad to see us & are very ready to tell us the names of things in their language. I have already learned several words so that by these & signs I can make them understand very well. I like the appearance of the Nez Perces better than

---

ing the children. Lee returned to Oregon with this party. The "Lausanne" dropped anchor at Fort Vancouver on June 1, 1840. Spalding noted in his diary for June 27th: "Letters arrive from Mr. Lee's ship." SS, 293. Undoubtedly mail for all members of the Mission came on this ship.

any Indians I have seen as yet. They are all, however, filthy in their appearance & practice. Last Sabbath we were with a party of Bannocks. They were friendly and troubled us some with their company. Several sat around while we had a sermon preached. One squaw caught lice & eat them most of the time. This is common among the Indians to eat lice.

We shall doubtless find many things trying in our labors among them, but I trust we shall have some delight in the work.[29] The Lord has truly been our helper thus far & I trust we shall come through in safety. Sarah sends much love. Pray for us much that the grace of God shall dwell richly in us.

Very affectionally yours,   A. B. SMITH

ASA MEETS FURTHER FRUSTRATIONS

Without a doubt, one of the greatest thrills Asa Bowen Smith ever experienced in his twenty-seven years was when he and Sarah arrived at Waiilatpu on Thursday, August 30, 1838. Their long, arduous, and at times dangerous, journey was over. The dream of years was now realized. He was on heathen ground and ready to begin his evangelistic labors. The warm welcome extended by the Whitmans and the Spaldings and the enthusiastic reception given by the natives heightened his ecstasy. And yet, within only four months, he confessed in a letter to his brother John that all of the "romance in the missionary spirit" had vanished.

The story of this disillusionment gradually unfolds in four of Asa's letters to his family dated September 15th to December 18, 1838. No longer is Asa writing about Gray for he had moved to Lapwai to assist Spalding. Now three new factors had arisen which brought frustration and disappointment to him. First there was the language barrier. Although Asa began to acquire a vocabulary of the Nez Perce tongue from the six Nez Perces that Whitman and Spalding had sent to Fort Hall, and although he had a special gift for languages, yet he quickly realized the futility of trying to preach or teach in a language which he felt was "barren and destitute of terms to convey religious truth." This was frustrating to one who was as impatient as Asa Smith.

---

[29] By the time the reenforcement reached Fort Hall, there was considerable speculation as to where each couple would be located within the enlarged Mission. Mary Walker in a long letter to her parents wrote: "Mr. Walker is expecting to settle with Dr. Whitman. Mr. Gray among the Flatheads [i.e., the Spokanes]. Mr. Smith & Eells, I know not where, but unless some one should like Mr. S. better than at present, he will have to settle alone. He is as successful in gaining universal ill will as Mr. Walker good." FWW, II, p. 109.

Secondly, the unending physical labor needed to supply their daily requirements evidently came as a surprise to him. The lack of proper equipment and the unreliability of native help only added to the responsibilities of the men. The Board expected their Oregon missionaries to raise their own food supplies. "You may think," wrote Asa to his parents on October 29th, "that I think more about farming than I do of any thing else." He confessed that this was so but he was "under the necessity of thinking much about such things." He had been too idealistic.

And finally, there was the crowded condition within the Whitman home where eating and sleeping accommodations had to be provided for twenty or more people in a house planned for one family and its hired help. Here many little irritating incidents arose which annoyed Asa exceedingly. Usually Asa was able to work with Dr. Whitman who was gifted with a kindly disposition. Narcissa Whitman, however, had a quick temper and sometimes spoke sharply to Asa. Moreover, Mary Walker was soon to give birth to a baby. So the unhappy Asa redoubled his efforts in the construction of the new mission house so that he and Sarah could move as soon as possible into the first room that would be ready for occupancy. This goal was achieved on December 4th just three days before the Walker baby arrived. The room in the new house afforded the Smiths much appreciated privacy during the winter of 1838-39.

These were some of the factors which took the romance out of Asa's idealistic conceptions regarding the life of a missionary.

WIELETPOO,[30]   Sept. 15, 1838

MY DEAR PARENTS. Through the goodness & tender mercies of God, we are at length at the place which we expect will be our home for life. Arrived here the 30th of August & were rec'd with rejoicing by those who were in the field before us. This is the place where Dr. Whitman is stationed & is called Wieletpoo, which was originally the name of the Kayuse people. It is situated on a beautiful stream, a branch of the Columbia 25 miles from Fort Wallawalla. The place

[30] The Cayuse name for "the place of the rye grass," a coarse grass that grows six or more feet high. According to a statement made to the author by the late Dr. Stephen B. L. Penrose, once president of Whitman College, the two sons of the Rev. Cushing Eells, Myron and Edwin, differed as to the correct pronunciation of Wai-i-lat-pu. One put the accent on the second syllable, the other on the third. The Whitman National Monument was formally established in 1940 and in 1962 Congress changed the name to Whitman Mission National Historic Site. The area now contains almost one hundred acres.

occupied is on a point of land formed by the junction of two streams. The point is amply sufficient for a large farm, much more than we can ever occupy ourselves. The land is level, of good quality. Dr. Whitman's house is perhaps ¾ of a mile above the junction of the two streams, on the bank of the largest one. There is a hill of considerable height just above the house overlooking the plain.[31] The soil here contains a considerable proportion of clay mixed with good earth which is a wise provision for the region as there is but little rain here except in the spring & autumn. This soil retains its moisture & the crops thrive well without rain. The climate here is very fine, possibly one of the finest in the world. It is mild & the winters are very short & but little snow. It is not necessary to cut any hay for winter. Animals find grass the whole year. This is an immense saving of labor.

Thousands of horses are raised here in these plains. Some individuals of the Kayuses, I have been told, have a thousand horses apiece. As we came to this place, we saw large bands of horses here & there grazing on the plains. Horses constitute the principal wealth of the people.

In making a disposition of ourselves after we arrived, it fell to my lot to remain with Dr. Whitman at this place. Mr. Gray is associated with Mr. Spaulding.[32] Messrs. Walker & Eells have gone to select a new station in the region of Colville. I am well pleased with my situation & was glad to find myself at home almost as soon as I arrived. My first business here has been to assist in securing the crops. For two weeks I have been engaged in this work. Dr. W. has about 17 acres in all under cultivation. His crop of wheat was very fine. It is not threshed but he thinks there will be from 75 to 100 bushels from 2½ acres. Nicer wheat I never saw. His crop of corn was good. No frost touched it. There has not as yet been frost enough to injure any thing. The leaves have been slightly nipped. The corn is all gathered & put up in big cribs — near 300 bushels of it. Potatoes do well here. Dr. has about 6 [?] acres, all in the field yet — thinks there will not be less than 1000 bushels. He has about 2 acres of turnips, & garden vegetables in abundance. We have had an abundance of melons all the time since we have been here.

The labor of gleaning the crops is done considerably by the natives. The women do most of the work. They have harvested the corn almost

---

[31] A thirty-foot obelisk crowns this hill as a memorial to Dr. and Mrs. Whitman. The monument can be seen for many miles in all directions. See illustration of mission site included in this volume at page 153.

[32] Spalding spelled his name without the "u". Later Smith adopted the correct spelling.

entirely. Some of it was brought from the field to the house in bags on the backs of the women. We have no vehicle of any kind for the transportation of articles. No cart, sled, or corn dray. Much of the corn was cut up & drawn to the house by the oxen on brush. This was very hard dragging.

We labor to great disadvantage in many respects. We are in great want of tools of most every kind. Dr. has two ploughs but neither of them very good. If I could have a good cast iron plough sent to me, it would be very acceptable indeed. The irons might be boxed up & sent out from Boston very safely. Here I would remark once for all that every thing that is sent out should be put up in kegs or boxes water tight & never weighing over 100 lbs. In coming up the Columbia, there are portages around the falls. Everything has to be carried on men's shoulders & 100 lbs. is load enough.

We labor under disadvantage in respect to building. There is no good building timber nearer than 20 miles.[33] On the mountains there is a great abundance of excellent pine & spruce but at present it is very difficult getting it. There is a limited supply of cottonwood (a kind of poplar) on the streams near us & scarcely any other timber. By careful management this will probably be sufficient for firewood but we are in great want of stoves. We build our houses here with *dobies,* or clay dried in the sun in the form of brick 20 inches long, 10 wide & 5 in thickness. This is the best of anything we can use. We are soon to commence building another house & intend to complete it before winter. Dr. W. will go to Fort Vancouver next week & leave me alone to take care of the business.

I have already got started in the language, so that I can get along with the Indians tolerably well about the work. We find the Indians in a very interesting state. But still they are heathen & we find them selfish in the extreme. They have some external forms of Christianity, are regular in their prayers & never eat without asking a blessing, but still they are strangers to vital piety. They are selfish in their desire for missionaries. This is true with but very few exceptions. There is much of the Pharisee among them & they need searching truth to show them their true condition. Still they seem to be groping after the truth. This is truly an interesting field of labor, but you need not receive all that Mr. Spaulding has written. He wrote from first appearance — wrote

---

[33] Whitman built a sawmill in the Blue Mountains about twenty miles from Waiilatpu during the winter of 1844-45. Prior to that time, the only way to manufacture lumber was by the laborious whipsaw method.

too soon & was thus deceived. He would write different now. He finds
the same wicked heart in those Indians that others possess. They hope
however that some few souls have been converted at both of the
stations. No Indians however at this station, but some in the family,
one Frenchman, one Sandwich Islander & one half-breed. This Frenchman is married to a native woman & is settled here & will doubtless be
a valuable helper to us. A man & his wife from the Sandwich Islands
came here this season from Mr. Bingham's church & he has been
instrumental in the conversion of some in the family.[34] He came with
the spirit of a missionary. But I must close.

Yours very affectionately.   A. B. SMITH

Postmarked "Ship" and "Boston May 30."

WIELETPOO   Sept. 30, 1838

MY DEAR SISTERS. This Sabbath evening I will spend a few moments
in writing to you for I know you will always be glad to hear from me.
I often think of you & feel anxious to hear from you. I should rejoice
to see you but this will probably never be unless you should come to
this part of the world. It often gives me pain to think that you may be
sick & die & for a long time I may not hear of it, & perhaps may not
know it till I meet you in another world. But it matters little if we are
prepared for heaven, if we do not meet nor hear from each other till
we meet in heaven.

Since I have been here I have been very contented & happy, tho'
sometimes I feel a little sad when I think that I am so far away from
my friends. I find some trials here, but no more than I expected. The
Indians are a little troublesome sometimes, tho' not so much so as in
some other places. We have their company sometimes when we do not
wish it, & they are very fond of looking into the windows. This is the
way the heathen act every where.

I have been very much engaged in business since I have been here
as Dr. Whitman has gone to Vancouver & has not yet returned. I have
had all the care of the business, making dobies for the house,[35] getting
in crops &c. Today I have attempted for the first time to preach to
these Indians in their own language. I have as yet acquired but little

---

[34] The Frenchman was Charles Compo; the single Sandwich Islander was Jack
who later was hired to assist Smith at Kamiah; the half-breed was Margaret McKay,
the daughter of Thomas McKay of the Hudson's Bay Company who was himself
a half-breed. Therefore Margaret was really only one quarter white as her mother
was a native. The Sandwich Islands couple was Joseph and Maria Maki who were
charter members of the First Presbyterian Church of Oregon.

language & it is quite difficult to communicate religious truth to their minds, & if I had the whole of their language it would be a very poor vehicle for conveying the truth of the bible to their minds. The language is barren & destitute of terms to convey religious truth. At the best there must be much circumlocution & then the idea is but poorly expressed. The subjects I took today were the prodigal son & the rich man & Lazarus. What I could I expressed in the Indian language & the rest by signs & one of the Indians rehearsed [36] for me & filled out the language himself. So that the Indians had it from him tolerably correct. A story may be told in this way tolerably correct, with sometimes a drawing to assist; but I find it more difficult to make an application of the subject. I attempted to make an application of the subject today in both cases & succeeded in conveying some truth to their minds which made them appear quite solemn.

It will be some time before I shall be able to preach with ease in the Indian language but I find I am making some progress in acquiring it. The Indians are very ready to assist me in learning the language & some to be much interested in what I say to them. Many of them I find quite interesting & some to be possessed of fine minds. The children generally look as intelligent as the children in New England & seemed much interested in receiving instruction. I should like very much to have some of you here to assist in instructing these children, but this I suppose will not be. Where God will cast your lot, I know not. I feel anxious to know what is to be your situation in life & I want you to write me often & let me know every thing. I have not time to write to Br. J[ohn] this time. He will want a letter I suppose, but you must write him & let him know what I have written if he is not at home & give him my love. I suppose he is now commencing his Theological course. I want to know where he is & how he is getting along & where he expects to go when his studies are completed. Sarah sends love. Give my love to all & believe me as ever.

Your affectionate brother,   A. B. Smith

[35] Whitman, in a letter to Greene dated May 10, 1839, said that the "T" shaped house was to measure "nineteen by forty feet front & an ell of twenty-two by thirty." The building had a wooden frame with walls of adobe bricks and a roof made of poles, straw or rye grass, and earth. The top of the "T" was a story-and-a-half. Government archaeologists have determined that the foundations of the "T" actually measured 60'10" by 19'3" and the ell, 80' by 22'. Thus the completed building was considerably larger than Whitman had originally planned. The new house was not ready for occupancy until June 1840, except for the one room which Smith succeeded in finishing by December 4, 1838.

[36] The missionaries used the expression "to rehearse" to mean "to interpret." It is possible that Smith's interpreter was Lawyer, who knew some English.

*The following postscript was closely written on the outside page
which bore the address.*

OCTOBER 1. Monday morning.   Dear Sisters.   I am happy to fill out
your dear brother's letter as he has given me the privilege. It is not
often I can converse with you even by letter & therefore I will improve
every opportunity & trust you will do the same. We are all well &
happy & I hope doing some good. Mr. S. can talk considerably [in the
Indian language]. Yesterday preached or told some scripture stories
with one to rehearse for him. The Indians were interested. My school
is increasing in interest, have now 30 scholars. How long they will continue to feel interested, I know not. Fathers, mothers, & old grand-
mothers come & look on to see & hear their children read with more
interest shown than is often manifested in New England, & I often find
them reading from the black board in concert with them.

I love to teach & when I can talk better I hope to do them much
good. I have never regretted the life I have chosen but rejoice that I
am permitted to engage in this work. I am happy in the hope of doing
something to save this perishing people. This morning a poor old man
& woman came to receive medicine. She is sick & looks as if she would
die. She was poorly clad with skins, no shoes or stockings on & looking
very sick. I am going out to see her now. I have closed [?] writing &
see what I can do for her. Probably she has nothing but some roots or
corn to eat. Her husband works some for the Doct. & receives corn for
pay & this they often eat raw. I can write no more for the man is waiting to take this to Walla Walla. Please write every opportunity.
Your sister SARAH.   Love to Brothers.

MY DEAR PARENTS.   I suppose you will be happy to hear from me as
often as I can find time to write. This is not very often for since I have
been here I have been very much engaged in business & have worked
almost the whole time. Dr. W. went to Vancouver soon after I came
here & was [gone] about 4 weeks so that I was under the necessity of
having the charge of all the business. He has returned & Mr. Walker
& Eells have returned from their exploring tour & have concluded to
spend the winter here. This makes a house full. There are 4 families of
us besides an Owihee & his wife & a Frenchman & his wife who work
for the Dr. & has become a Christian man since he has been here. This
makes six families in one small house consisting of 3 rooms & 2 bedrooms. Besides these six families there are 2 Owihee men, 4 boys & one
girl. Dr. W. has one child & Compo, the Frenchman, has one. The

room where we stay is the one where the Indians come for morning & evening worship & we have a sick boy [37] that came here to receive medical attention sleeping on the floor nights & is there much of the time during the day.

All of us who are missionaries eat at the same table. You can judge how comfortable it is to have such a house full. The house in which we are is a poor one, but Dr. W. is now putting up another. The walls are now up, nearly to the chamber floor. All last week I spent in laying up these walls. They are made of dobies, brick dried in the sun. We hope to have a place soon where some of us can live. We calculate to go to keeping house for ourselves as soon as we have any place so that we can. The probability is that we shall remain at this place only till next spring. We think it best to form another station in this field from 25 to 50 miles from this place where we can bring in a large number of Indians who would not come to this place to settle. We shall probably leave here & go to form this new station in the spring.[38] There is a beautiful place, I am told, 25 miles from this place, where is a plenty of good land & timber but it may be thought too near this station & a place may be selected beyond this. This place is on the road towards Mr. Spaulding's. It will cost some labor to commence a new station having every thing to make as we do here but soon we can be in a situation to raise a good supply of grain & vegetables. The land here is generally very hard to break, especially at this station. It is covered with a large kind of grass,[39] 5 or 6 feet high with very strong roots so that it requires a strong plough & a strong team to break the soil. In one letter that I have written since I have been here, I mentioned that I should be very glad to have a cast iron plough sent out to me. I should like the largest size & more than one if I could get it for we wish to have the Indians use ploughs as soon as possible. I would like to have one set of the wood parts come out if I could for a pattern to

---

[37] Narcissa in a letter dated September 29, 1838, identifies the patient as "Havier Fovier, the sick boy from Vancouver." Hulbert, *Marcus Whitman*, I, p. 323. Nothing further is known about the lad.

[38] Within two months of the Mission meeting of September 1-3, Smith is openly informing his parents that he expected to leave Waiilatpu "next spring." This, no doubt, would have been a startling announcement if made at that time to the other members of the Mission. The statement shows that Smith was already unhappy in his associations with Dr. Whitman and yearned for a station of his own. Already he had a site in mind on the Tucannon River which he explored during the following December. See SS, 92.

[39] This is the rye grass, Waiilatpu, which is still growing on the site of the Whitman mission.

make others by. I suppose the plough might be taken apart & the whole put into a box & sent. If one should be sent, I should of course want several spare noses sent with it. There is nothing that you could send me which would be of more service.

We have no hoes in this country, except a kind of hoe 4 inches wide made for the purpose of digging up hard ground. Thus you see that we labor under a great disadvantage in many respects.

You may think from the manner I have written that I think more about farming than I do of any thing else. It is true. I am under the necessity of thinking much about such things but I hope I shall not forget the spiritual good of these perishing souls around us. I have advanced considerable in the language so that I am able to give some instruction. Have morning & evening worship with the Indians & generally talk to them some. I find them an interesting people & ready to receive instruction. If we are faithful I have no doubts but that we may see many here brought into the fold of Christ. Pray for us that we may be kept from becoming worldly minded & that we may be the instruments of great good among this people. Our health is good. Sarah sends love to all.

Very affectionately yours.   A. B. SMITH

Addressed to "Mr. Asa Smith, East Williamstown, Vermont, U.S.A." Postmarked "Ship" and "Boston. May."

WIELETPOO, OREGON TERRITORY
Dec. 18th, 1838

MY DEAR BROTHER: It is now a long time since I have written to you & you may begin to think that distance causes me to forget my dearest friends. But be assured you are not forgotten tho' I have neglected to write you. One reason why I have not written you is that I did not know where to direct letters to you & another I know that you would hear of me from the letters I have written home. I know of no other way but to direct your letters to Wmstown & from there they can be directed to you.

I suppose you will now be anxious to know what are my feelings since being on missionary ground &c. And here let me say, tho' it is no new idea, that the transplantation of a man from one part of the world to another produces no essential change in his character, habits, or feelings, tho' there may be circumstances attending this change which will tend to develope character. I find myself the same individual here that I was when at home, possessing substantially the same character, disposition & feelings which I did before I left home — tho' I fear that the labors, cares, trials & perplexities of our tedious journey have tended to damp the ardor of piety I once felt & give me the feeling of a worldling. And indeed my business since I have been here has had the same tendency; for my whole time has been occupied in taking care of crops & preparing a place for winter. All this of course has a tendency to divert our minds from the great object of saving the souls of those around us & it is a temptation against which we need to be on our guard.

I find nothing in the thought that I am on heathen ground that causes any unusual excitement to keep up a spirit of piety. Neither does the sight of perishing souls awaken a deeper interest that it did at home. We see those around us degraded & some of them peculiarly objects of pity, but all this we see in some measure at home & it produces the same feeling here that it does there. At home there is *much novelty & romance in the missionary spirit, but with me this is all gone* [40] & I now find every thing reality & I am in the same world & breathe the same atmosphere that I did when at home. I often heard it said in the States that missionaries were but men & I believed it & now I find it fully true. I find myself but a man "subject to like passions with others" & I find my associates the same. When we hear from a missionary from a distant land, it comes to us like the voice of an angel but come to the spot where he is we find him nothing but a man & perhaps an ordinary man too. We generally form our opinion of missionaries & missionary matters at home but when we reach the ground & see for ourselves, I imagine that all find things not entirely as they expected. The notions we have when at home are very vague & indefinite. I have not made these remarks because I am disappointed & discontented. It is true that I do not find every thing as I expected, yet I feel satisfied with this field & shall be contented & happy here. In many respects this is one of the most desirable locations in the world. As to climate, we can find no better probably in the world. It is mild & temperate free from sudden changes, tho' further north than our own home in Vermont. As yet we have had no severe weather. No snow at present. Had a little one two or 3 weeks ago which went off immediately. The weather is now comfortably cool & has been for some time past.

---

[40] Editorial italics. Asa's highly idealized conception of the life of a missionary had by now been somewhat deflated by the harsh realities forced upon him. He was now writing more frankly to his brother than he ventured in his letters to the Board.

I feel that it was a wise Providence which directed us to this field for I imagine that neither of us should have endured a hot climate well. Sarah especially I think would have sunk under it, but here she enjoys better health than she did at home. She is able to do here what she never was able to do at home. As to a field for usefulness, this is an interesting field. We are not surrounded by thousands & millions as we should have been in Asia but still there are more here than we are able to instruct ourselves. As to the land here, there is but a limited supply that is good. There is no land fit for cultivation except on the streams. The land back is good for grazing & thousands of cattle & horses can be raised here without any difficulty.

Since we have been here we have boarded in Dr. Whitman's family till within a short time. Now we have a room fitted up in a house which we have just built & are living by ourselves. This we find very pleasant & are very happy. We feel very contented with each others' society & care but little about any other. We began to feel rather homesick before we began to keep house, but now time passes away very pleasantly.

Br. Walker & Eells are both in Dr. W's family which make a very large family. Mr. Walker has a son born the 7th of this month which was just *2 days* over 9 months from the time they were married, the 5th of March. What I think about such things, you know already. I feel thankful that I am not in such an embarrassed situation & at present there is no prospect of it.

I am beginning now to find a little leisure for study & am beginning to devote some study to the grammar of the language. This has been neglected by those who were here before me. They are not men who do much in the study. Dr. W. & Mr. Spaulding are both western men & partake of the peculiarities of western men.[41] This I find not in all aspects the most pleasant. Half of our number however are eastern men. I often feel anxious to know to what part of the earth you will direct your steps but suppose it will be some time yet before I can know. If you could be in the same field with me, it would be pleasant but I suppose that no man will be sent here at present as there are far greater demands in other parts of the world.

I feel anxious to hear from you & know what you are doing & what

---

[41] Here is a key to one of Asa's prejudices. Whitman, Spalding, and Gray were all "western" men and each in turn became the object of his animus. From all evidence, Asa was never in serious difficulty with Walker or Eells who, like himself, were New Englanders or "Yankees."

are your future prospects. The thought that I shall probably never see you again nor our dear sisters, often causes a sigh, but still this is a small consideration. We shall soon meet, we hope, in a better world. Pray for me that I may be eminently useful.

Very affectionately yours,   A. B. SMITH

Letter addressed to: "Mr. John C. Smith" at East Williamstown, Vermont. Postmarked "New [———?] May 2."

A RESTLESS YEAR — 1839 — WAIILATPU TO KAMIAH

The story of Asa's growing unhappiness with his lot as a missionary to the Oregon Indians unfolds in the following three letters to his home folks dated March 11, September 8, and November 29, 1839. These letters supplement the few entries Sarah made in her diary for this year which have already been considered. Also, we have two letters which Asa wrote the Board, dated April 29th and August 27th, and a few short entries made in his diary after November 11th. These documents have been published in the author's The Diaries and Letters of Spalding and Smith.

A brief review of the major developments which took place within the Oregon Mission during 1839 will aid in the understanding of Smith's attitudes. During January 1839, Spalding held "protracted meetings" for the Indians at Lapwai when, according to his optimistic estimates, as many as two thousand were in attendance. Spalding wrote to his brethren for help. Smith responded from Waiilatpu and Walker from Tshimakain. Since Gray and Rogers were already with Spalding at Lapwai, this meant that five of the seven men of the Mission were there. Seemingly it was then that Smith let his feelings be known. He threatened to resign and leave the Mission "rather than be connected with Dr. Whitman." [42] Just exactly what was the cause of trouble is not explained. It was therefore decided that a special meeting of the Mission was necessary to settle the problem.

Messengers were sent to Whitman and Eells asking them to come to Lapwai. All seven men were present on February 29th when they began their two-day special session. Smith repeated his determination to withdraw from Waiilatpu. He asked for permission to open a new station. A long debate followed. A compromise was suggested. Let the Whitmans move to some new location central to the other three established stations and let the Smiths take over Waiilatpu. This idea ap-

---

[42] Spalding to Greene, Oct. 15, 1842. Coll. A.

*pealed to the Spaldings, the Walkers, and the Eells, who were some-
what unhappy about being so far removed from the only doctor in the
Mission. Neither Whitman nor Smith seemed to welcome the idea but
consented to consider it. It later developed that Narcissa Whitman
was opposed to the idea, so before the end of April, Whitman informed his brethren that he did not care to move.*

*Writing to Walker from Waiilatpu on March 28, 1839, Smith said:
"It is very evident that the Dr. & his wife were not so willing to leave
this place as was pretended at the meeting. He told me that he did not
expect that such a decision would have been made. So it seems that
neither of us have been suited by the arrangement. I lament that I
ever consented to remain here. Indeed my heart never has consented
to it & I do not expect ever to be satisfied or contented with my present
situation. I lament the day that connected me with this mission. Why
it is that I am here, I know not." [43]*

*When Marcus and Narcissa decided not to leave Waiilatpu, Marcus
began to encourage Asa to go to Kamiah which lay in the heart of the
Nez Perce country. This was Lawyer's home and no doubt he too had
made the same suggestion. The advantages of studying the pure Nez
Perce tongue there were stressed. The Smiths responded favorably to
the idea. Although the Mission had not approved the idea of Smith
opening a new station, yet there could be no objection if he spent some
months at Kamiah in language study.*

*The story of the Smiths camping out in Kamiah during the summer
of 1839 has already been told by Sarah and in the annotations and
footnotes for her diary. Smith has little to add to this part of the story.*

*The next important event was the annual Mission meeting held at
Lapwai, September 2-5, 1839. Sharp differences of opinion were expressed regarding the best way to evangelize the natives. Even before
the arrival of the reenforcement, Whitman and Spalding had concluded that the best way to Christianize the natives was to settle them
on the land. They had to be civilized. Thus both Whitman and Spalding were eager to get the natives to farm and to raise cattle, sheep,
and pigs. They also favored the building of mills and a blacksmith
shop. Smith opposed such a program. Spalding noted in his diary for
September 1st: "Rev. Mr. Smith preaches against all efforts to settle
the poor Indians, thinks they should be kept upon the chase to prevent
their becoming worldly minded." [44] Time has proved that Whitman and
Spalding were right and that Smith was wrong.*

---

[43] Editorial italics. Original in Coll. Y.   [44] SS, 274.

The other members of the Mission, faced with Smith's uncompromis-
ing attitude, voted to approve his request to open a new station in
Kamiah. Smith's letter of November 29th gives an excellent descrip-
tion of the way his house was constructed. This letter contains a rude
drawing of the floor plan which is reproduced in this volume as an
illustration. His letters to his family written during 1839 speak much
of the selfishness and wickedness of the Indians. Even as Asa found it
difficult to get along with his white colleagues, he now finds it equally
hard to work with the Indians. He insisted that this was because they
were so selfish and wicked. He was also repelled by what he con-
sidered to be their dirty, filthy habits.

WIELETPOO, OREGON TER'Y
March 11, 1839

MY DEAR PARENTS, BROTHERS & SISTERS. As we now have an opportunity of sending you letters by the express [over] the mountains to
Canada, we gladly improve it & probably this will reach you as soon &
perhaps before the letters which we have already sent by sea. We dare
not send much by this express as every thing has to be carried for some
days on foot across the mountains on snow shoes. So we limit ourselves to a single letter to our friends. Letters in this way reach you
much sooner than by sea.

As this may be the first intelligence you will receive of our arrival
here, I will say that after much fatigue & many trials we arrived here
in safety the last of August. Thus far we have remained at this station
which was occupied by Dr. Whitman before we came. Whether we
shall continue here or not is uncertain. One of us will have to form a
new station. Perhaps the Dr. may in order to have a more central
location as physician.

As to climate, health &c. I have written you already. Our health continues good & if we could enjoy health any where we have the prospect
of it here. No place probably is better calculated for the improvement of health than here. With regard to our prospects for usefulness
here, I know not what to write. The Kayuses I find rather a difficult
people to manage & at present my fear is that many of them will be
drawn away by the Catholics. Two priests came into the country last
fall.[45] One of them is now on his way to this region & will probably
see many of this people at Walla Walla this week. What the result
will be I know not. The Nez Perces are indeed an interesting people.

---

45 They were Fathers Francois Norbert Blanchet and Modeste Demers.

During the winter there has been an interesting state of feeling among them at the Spaulding station & some few we hope are truly the children of God.

One of the chiefs named Joseph I think gives very satisfactory evidence of piety.[46] The Nez Perces have of late manifested a great anxiety to hear the gospel. Last month I visited Mr. Spaulding, was much pleased with the appearance of the people then. There is however much of the Pharisee among them & they are full of selfishness. This is their general character. There are some few exceptions. I think it will not be so easy for the Catholics to draw away the Nez Perces. Some of them already know something of the character of the Catholics & they are ready to talk to the people & set them on their guard. Some of them are very shrewd in arguing against the Catholics. One in particular who has spent the winter here & been my principal teacher in the language is very expert in bringing arguments. He is called the Lawyer from the fact of his being such a speaker. He heard that the priests said we were bad because we had wives. They had none &c. Week ago last Sabbath, he talked to the people on the subject & told how Abraham & the people of old had wives. Peter had a wife &c. & wanted to know how there would be any children if there were no wives &c. One shrewdly asked me a few days ago if the Catholic priests were not eunuchs. This shows something of their minds. I have become very much attached to some of the Indians, the Lawyer especially. He is a man of mind & will speak with the eloquence of an orator.

What is before us we know not. Our fairest prospects may all be blasted in a moment. Our hope is only in God. The present is certainly a critical time with this mission. We need especially the prayers of the church.

With regard to our experience as missionaries, we find it as we expected, a life of toil but generally our trials are such as we did not expect. This is generally the case. The thought sometimes comes over me with weight that I am separated for life from my friends & I often feel that it would be pleasant to see you again but this thought does not make me unhappy for I enjoy the society of one who compensates for the loss of all other friends. Were I deprived of this one, I fear I should sink under it. This is a trial which comes upon others & doubt-

---

[46] The reference is to Old Joseph, father of Chief Joseph of the Nez Perce uprising of 1877. The first natives to become members of the Mission church were Joseph and Timothy who were received by Spalding on Nov. 17, 1839. This reference of Smith's to Joseph is one of the few favorable comments to be found in his letters to any progress being made in evangelizing the natives.

KAMIAH, IDAHO, SHOWING LOCATION OF THE SMITH MISSION

Smith wrote to Greene, February 25, 1840 (SS, p. 146), "Our house . . . is situated on the bank of the Koos-koos-kee . . . , adjoining which is a small circular plain of about 30 acres," Some older Nez Perce Indians locate the site as being near the railroad bridge shown in this view. See text page 176. The site will be included in the recently established Nez Perce

ASA SMITH'S FLOOR PLAN OF THE HOME AT KAMIAH

From his letter of November 29, 1839. Sarah also described the house and drew a floor plan. (See SS, pp. 113, 118.) Asa's drawing locates the outdoor oven and leach tub for obtaining lye for soap. See text page 176. This home, which Asa once termed a "hovel," contrasts with the beautiful and comfortable home Sarah left in West Brookfield.

less it will some time come upon me. For such a trial I fear I should not be prepared. Pray much for us. Sarah sends love.

Very affectionately yours.   A. B. SMITH

No envelope with this letter so it is impossible to learn through postal cancellations when it was received.

WAIILETPU.[47]   Sept. 8th, 1839

MY DEAR SISTER M[ARCIA]. I have just finished a letter to my other sisters & now I will spend a few moments this evening in writing to you. I have as yet rec'd no letter from you, tho' Sarah has one. Yours, I presume, are coming round by ship as Mr. Greene wrote that a part of our letters were sent across the mountains & the rest would be sent round [the Horn]. Our outfit we have not yet rec'd. It arrived in April at the Sandwich Islands & we expect it at Vancouver by a vessel about to come in. Our letters came from the Islands by a British man of war, but no goods were brought. The invoice of the articles sent from Boston was forwarded to us by Mr. Chamberlain from wh. I learn there are on the way for us 2 Barrels, one half barrell, 2 Boxes & three trunks. My Woodstock friends were unwise enough to prize their articles which makes it the same to me as paying for them out of my stipend from the Board.[48] Friends ought never to prize articles which they propose for a particular one. It may prove a favor wh. costs him a great price.

We feel ourselves near neighbors to our brethren at the Sandwich Islands & we hear encouraging intelligence from them from time to time. Many thousands there are now gathered into the church. Mr. Coan's [49] church now numbers, I think, about 6,000 & Mr. Lyons about

---

[47] Following the Mission meeting, Smith went to Fort Walla Walla hoping to get his goods which had been shipped from New England nearly eighteen months earlier. In this he was disappointed, for they had not yet arrived. A major reason for the long delay was the lack of any regular communication between Honolulu and Fort Vancouver.

[48] See p. 29 for reference to the Vermont Medical College located at Woodstock, Vt. Evidently the Board deducted the value of the goods sent out in missionary barrels from the modest sum allowed to individual missionaries for expenses. Thus the kindness and charity of friends back home could actually work a hardship on the missionaries in the field.

[49] Smith in this paragraph refers to a number of missionaries of the American Board then serving in the Hawaiian Islands. Edwin O. Hall and his wife took the printing press to Oregon arriving at Walla Walla on April 29, 1842. Mrs. Hall was an invalid. They returned to the Islands in the spring of 1840. When the Smiths arrived in Honolulu in January 1842, they lived for several months in the Hall home.

5,000. For two or three years past the Lord has been doing a great
work there. Mr. Hall & wife are now here spending a year on account
of Mrs. H's health. She has for some time been feeble in consequence
of a spinal difficulty. Mr. Hall brought a printing press &c. which was
presented by the members of Mr. Bingham's church, amounting in all
to near 400 dollars. They have learned the benevolence of the gospel
& are beginning to exercise it towards others. A small book of 20 pages
has been printed — prepared by Mr. Spalding. The work is very incorrect & needs to be revised & reprinted immediately. This language is
much more difficult than was at first supposed. It is no easy matter to
prepare a book in it. By hard study however we hope to be able to
master it.

The people are a heathen people.[50] I have remarked in one of my
sister's letters — They are immodest like all other heathens. The men
often go almost naked in the summer, young boys often entirely.
Females always have their nakedness covered. Their language is often
immodest & outrageous in the extreme. Men & women talk together in
a manner wh. we should think vulgar in the extreme, without a blush.
Adultery is a common crime among them. Even [?] this year wicked-
[ness] of this character has been carried on to a high degree. In the
buffalo country, they carry on their wickedness to a high degree. Many
this year have thrown away their wives & taken new ones & almost all
the young people have come together without any regard to marriage.
So much for the goodness of this people.

The more I see of this people, the more I see of their wickedness
their deeprooted selfishness & their hatred to the gospel. Their desire
for missionaries seems to be with many of them only a hope of temporal gain. Their desire for instruction is often only to appear wise &

---

[50] Smith in his letter to Greene of August 27, 1839, goes into detail regarding
the selfishness and wickedness of the natives. He is critical of the over-enthusiastic
reports which Spalding had sent East regarding the eagerness of the Nez Perces
for Christianity. Smith wrote: "Every thing that has been written or that was
published before I left the States was in praise of this people so that the impression in the States seemed to be that the people were already christians or certainly
almost christians." Such accounts, he said, were false and misleading. More and
more Smith felt inclined to blame Spalding. If Spalding had not written such
glowing accounts, then he, Smith, would not have volunteered for the Oregon
Mission. Increasingly after this date, Spalding became the special object of Smith's
animosity. This letter of August 27th had much to say about the construction of
the Nez Perce language. About a year later, Smith sent to the Board a complete
paradigm of the active transitive verb, "hakisa" — "to see." This is now in Coll. A,
18.5.3. No member of the Oregon mission had such a fine mastery of the Nez
Perce language as Smith.

gain influence among the people. True they are not so degraded as the heathen in some parts of the world, yet they have the same wicked hearts which lies at the foundation of heathenism.

We are able now, some of us, to present the truth with some degree of clearness to the people but they do not love it. During this year we may expect to see the truth taking some effect on the hearts of the people. Already some of them begin to find fault with the truth & some [are] uneasy. Evidently they cannot remain long as they are. They will either oppose the truth, or we may expect to see them brought under its influence. I do not expect that their self-righteousness can be easily torn away from them. Nothing but the Spirit of God can do it. Satan is now holding them in strong bonds. He will not give them up without a struggle. We are placed in a responsible situation. Pray for us that we may be fitted for our work.

Your affct. br.   A. B. SMITH

KAMIAH,[51]   Nov. 29th, 1839

MY DEAR PARENTS, BROTHERS & SISTERS. I will now begin a letter to you which I design to fill up during the winter & send you in the spring by the express through Canada. You will I presume wish to know how things go with us from time to time, somewhat in a connected form more so than I have heretofore written you. I have written you heretofore when in much haste & have perhaps not written so particular as I ought.

When I wrote you last, we had just moved our effects to this place, which was about two months ago, & was about commencing building a house. Then not a stick of timber was cut, nor a board made. Now we have a very neat comfortable house. It is built entirely of cedar, excepting sticks [perhaps supporting beams] of timber, some of the window frames & window sashes. Our first work was to cut the timber. This we obtained on the bank of the river some 3 or 4 miles above where it had been logged [?] when brought down by high water. This we cut up. The Indians assisted in getting it into the water, rafted it, & took it out of the water on to the bank where we have built. In the first place we hewed posts, then grooved them & set them in the ground. Then split the cedar logs, first in the middle, then split the two halves, thus making 4 pieces of each log wide like planks. Eight

---

51 Kamiah is from the Nez Perce word, "kamo", the name of a plant growing in that locality which furnished fibers from which the natives made rope. Drury, *A Tepee in His Front Yard*, p. 49.

feet was the usual length. These we hewed on the inside, straightened the edges, fitted the ends to the grooving of the posts & this filled up the body of the house. Then we put on the plates & upon these laid the beams crosswise, & upon the beams laid the ridgepole, making a low roof. Upon the plates & ridgepole we laid the roof pieces of split cedar, straightened & placed close together. This we covered with a thick coat of grass & upon this a covering of dirt to the depth of 8 or 10 inches. In the meantime we made a saw pit & set Jack, our Owyhee,[52] & Thomas our Indian boy to sawing boards. They have sawed several for present use. Our floors, partitions, doors, table, &c. are all of cedar. Our floor boards were smooth so we have a very neat floor. I have a set of planes, so that I can make things somewhat comfortable.

The walls of our house are tolerably neat in the inside. The cracks are calked with moss & the outside plastered or daubed over the cracks with mud or clay mortar. Fireplaces & chimneys are made of dobies, i.e. unburnt brick. Our house is 28 ft. by 14, this contains a kitchen 14½ by 15, pantry 5 x 7, bedroom 9½ by 13, with a nook 5 by 6 at the end of the pantry where the bed stands. The roof is low so we have no chamber [above] nor chamber floor.

We have another building standing at right angles to this 22 ft. by 9 containing a room for Mr. Rogers, 14 by 9 & one 8 by 9 for Jack & Thomas. The plan of the house I will give you as follows.[53] This will give you some idea of our situation. I design to make other additions to these buildings. The corner I design to fill up for a wood house. One or two rooms will probably be added to the other end joining the kitchen & a room at the end of the building for a storeroom. The sides opposite I design to fence & thus enclose a small yard. The piece of land which I intend to inclose & cultivate lies directly back of the house from the river.[54] It is a very handsome little plain, sufficiently large for cultivation & for a cow pasture. It can be watered by a little stream coming into the plain from the hills. The house will be in one corner of the inclosure & the field & pasture both coming close to the house & all in plain view. Thus you see it is a very convenient situa-

---

[52] Owyhee was another way of spelling Hawaii. There is an Owyhee County in southwestern Idaho. Many Hawaiians were brought to the Pacific Northwest by the Hudson's Bay Company as laborers since they were willing to work and the American Indians of the Northwest were not.

[53] See accompanying illustration, text p. 172. See SS, 114 for a picture of Sarah's drawing of the same floor plan.

[54] A picture of the site is given in SS, 131. The First Presbyterian (Indian) Church of Kamiah now stands near this place. See also illustration of this site at page 171.

tion. The Indians have had their camp on the bank of the river above the house, but are now camped for the winter about 40 or 50 rods below on the bank. I must close this evening & will write more at another time.

Dec. 3d.   This evening I will write you a little more respecting our common temporal concerns as I suppose you will be interested to know how we live & what we have to eat &c. I will begin by telling you that last Saturday an Indian came from beyond Salmon River, two days travel from this & brought me a horse load of deer meat, 8 gammons [55] & 8 shoulders, weighting in all about 200 pounds. Yesterday 4 legs more of venison came in. We begin now to have plenty of meat. Hitherto we have not had as much as we have needed for our family consisting of six. Mr. Roger, McKee, a man from Illinois who works for me this winter for 8 dollars pr. month, Jack the Owyhee & Thomas, our Indian boy. For meat I pay powder & balls, 4 balls & powder for a gammon & 3 for a shoulder. We usually boil our deer meat, break the bones so that the marrow boils out & it makes a very fine soup. It is the most simple & healthy meat that can be eaten. I find it not so comfortable living without meat as I did before I crossed the mountains. This is all the meat we have except a little dry buffalo meat now & then which the Indians let us have. Deer meat can be obtained tolerably plenty during the winter season but little at other seasons. I intend to salt & dry a supply this winter for the rest of the year. I have already put down one keg. We have all the bread we want this winter. It is made of coarse wheat flour, ground in an iron mill & sifted. (By the way we have no sieve & none are to be obtained in the country. Dr. Whitman has the only one in the mission. A good wire sieve would be very valuable to us.) We sometimes mix corn meal with our wheat. We have obtained some potatoes at Mr. Spalding's. In addition to this we have boiled peas & corn. This forms our living. We have a little butter. We made out to save a two gallon kegfull for winter. We have but two cows, one of them a two year old heifer of the poor breed of this country, the other an American cow from the States, dry for several weeks & the heifer much longer. The cow will have a calf probably one month more when we hope to have milk again. All that we have in the shape of a dessert is dried pumpkin stewed, which in the absence of other things I have become very fond of. We have sugar & molasses which was sent to us by our good friends, the native Christians at the Sandwich Islands.

---

[55] A ham, or a hindquarter. Asa never mentions going hunting or fishing himself.

TWO LETTERS FROM SARAH SMITH TO MARY WALKER

Very few of the original writings of Sarah Smith are extant. Her diary exists in a copy made by her niece. Several of the letters of Asa to his relatives carry postscripts in her handwriting. Only three of the original letters written by Sarah during their residence in Oregon have been discovered. One, written in the summer of 1839, has already been given in a previous section of this book. The other two written in December of that year to Mrs. Walker and Mrs. Eells, and to Mrs. Walker follow.[56] *There is a fourth letter dated in October 1840 which described the terrifying events of October 13th when the Smiths were ordered by two of the chiefs at Kamiah to leave. The text of this is to be found in a later chapter. The original letter has been lost but Gray made a copy.*

Sarah Smith had not seen Mary Walker or Myra Eells since March 5, 1839, when they left Waiilatpu with their husbands for Tshimakain. After the Smiths left for Kamiah in April of that year, Sarah had not seen another white woman except Mrs. Spalding and Mrs. Gray for a few days at the Mission meeting held in Lapwai in September and Mrs. J. S. Griffin who, with her husband, may have visited Kamiah for a week or so following the Mission meeting.[57] *The Griffins were independent missionaries who had arrived in Oregon in the fall of 1839 and who spent the following winter with the Spaldings at Lapwai. Sarah's brief reference to Mrs. Griffin reveals the foolhardiness of the independent missionaries who ventured into the Oregon wilderness without the support of a church board and with meager resources.*

KAMIAH, Dec. 18, '39

DEAR SISTERS: [Mrs. Walker and Mrs. Eells] This morning Mr. S. has put a blister on my spine as he says, to keep me still, & threatens to continue it till I will become obedient, so you see what is before me. It is not very pleasant but if I can be benefited by it in any way I shall be glad. O, I want to see you more than words can express. Somehow or other I feel very differently towards you two than to either of the other sisters. If I could see you what a good long talk we would have. But that cannot be for a long time yet. In Mrs. Walker's letters some time ago, I received a piece of riband for which accept by thanks. I think you are getting me quite in debt. But I am waiting for my ship to come in when I shall remember it.[58]

---

[56] Originals in library, Coll. Y.

[57] The Rev. and Mrs. John S. Griffin went out to Oregon in 1839 as independent missionaries. For a listing of the five independent missionary couples who migrated to Oregon in 1839 and 1840, see SS, 19ff.

What is best for us to do about giving to Mrs. Griffin? What they can do I know not, or how they can get things to make them[selves] comfortable I know not, unless some one gives them. I would give her with all my heart if it is right. Mr. Smith, Mr. Hall & others say they have come in opposition to the Amr. Board & ought not to be assisted. But the poor woman has come without a sheet or pillow case, & how they will get them I don't know. Mrs. Spalding while I was there gave her three *broken plates* for her to [. . . ?] & enough wide striped cotton to make a pair of sheets. If husband will consent I shall give her some things. She has plenty of clothing, probably more dresses than I shall have after mine get here. She has two pretty silk dresses, several muslin & fine calico, & two or three pieces unmade. She has more neck dresses than she will ever need & all *very pretty.* Mr. G. has enough. But *sheets, pillow cases, paper & crockery* they need. Would you give them: Shall you do it?

I fear I shall not hear from you for a long time. *Do write every opportunity,* & I will do the same. Yours with much affection.

Sarah G. Smith

The next letter, also dated from Kamiah, was addressed to Mrs. Walker on December 22, 1839. In this she writes first about the house her husband had erected that fall.

I said we had now a little house to live in of which I would give the plan. It is small but we intend to enlarge it sometime. I know well how to prize it, I'll assure you having lived in a mere shed for so many months & without a floor or window.[59] Our bed. I am going to have a curtain which will entirely conceal the bed, not yet a clothes press, we hang some clothes within the curtain. . . Our windows are small only 9 lights.[60] In the bedroom Mr. S. has made a pretty book case. . . We have a nice large table & a working table. We left our little one at Wielatpu. These with our two chairs are all the furniture we have. Our boxes cushioned makes a good settee for our present use in the bedroom, & I find it very comfortable to lie down on. I have

---

[58] Sarah was not just repeating an old saying. She was referring to their belongings which had been shipped from New England in the spring of 1838 and which as yet had not arrived.

[59] See fn. 53. Full text of this letter is in SS, 118-19. In general this was the same as the outline Asa drew in his letter to his parents of November 29th.

[60] A "light" is the old word for a pane of glass. The missionaries were able to get some thin (1 mm.) window glass from the Hudson's Bay Company which measured 7 x 9 inches. Many fragments of such glass have been found in the archaeological diggings at Waiilatpu.

commenced a carpet for our little parlor, when it will be done I know not, at present I am able to sew but little. Mr. Smith seems much trouble about it, sometimes says he will burn it, says it will be selling his wife too cheap to exchange her for a carpet.

I am making a feather bed. It is now half full. Tis already quite a comfort. I have made me a good black bombazine dress to wear this winter & a cape lined with flannel, so I shall be warm. Mr. Rogers is now making Mr. S. a suit of blue broad cloth clothes . . . we have a nice oven out doors & yesterday I baked some first rate *yankee* bread of corn & wheat. I should like to send you a loaf. If you have not made any, I am sure you would like it.

We are troubled about potatoes. Hired Indians to go to Weilatpu & for some reason the Dr. sent us poor little things, not fit to eat. I presume to say that not one half of them were much bigger than a walnut. Being tired of that sport, on Mr. Gray's authority & Mr. S[palding's] invitation, we sent to Clear Water & those were worse yet, 9/10 of them not as big as your thumb & half of them not biger than a birds egg. This is a specimen of their good feeling & desire to oblige us I suppose. . .

Mr. Smith wishes me to say that he & Rogers are counting the people, that is, how many Nez Perces there are in all, both those that are here & those that are at buffalo. They go to the principal man in each little band & he can after a little study give the numbers of men, women & children, also to know in particular the number of boys & girls, that we may judge what the people will be hereafter. He is also wishing to know whether the people are now on the decrease or not & therefore is taking the numbers of births & deaths, that have occured since we came here. Something of this kind he intends to send to the Board feeling that they have long enough been deceived with regard to this people.

The culls of Spalding's potato crop! Taking a census of the Nez Perce tribe! Was there any connection between the two? Let us look at the evidence.

The Smiths first moved to Kamiah in the spring of 1839 on a temporary basis. He was to study the language. He did not, therefore, feel it necessary to plant an extensive garden. He did have a small garden and he did have a fresh milch cow. Although it is possible that the natives supplied some incidental items of food as wild game and fish, yet for the most part the Smiths were dependent on the labors of

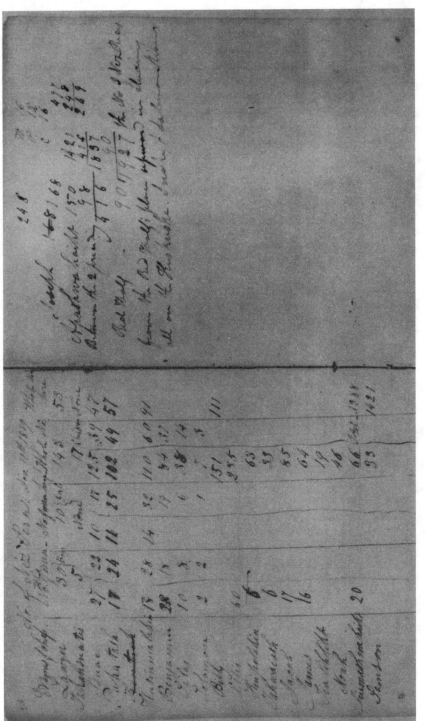

CENSUS OF THE NEZ PERCE TRIBAL BANDS

Made by Asa Smith and Cornelius Rogers in the fall of 1839. (See SS, p. 136; and text herein, p. 185.) The census included all bands along the "Kuskuski," i.e., the Clearwater, Snake, and Salmon Rivers. The figures on the left apply to the Clearwater area, and those on the right to the region south and west of the Snake River.

Whitman and Spalding for the major part of their supplies. When Spalding visited the Smiths in July 1839, he observed in his diary: "Mr. Smith's little garden will produce nothing from drought, but he can irrigate. . ." This, evidently, Smith was not doing. Spalding also referred to the "very open house without floor or windows" in which Asa and Sarah were living, "much to the injury, I think, of Mrs. Smith's health." [61] *This was the open house which Sarah called a "shed" and Asa later referred to as a "mere hovel." In Asa's letter to Secretary Greene of February 6, 1840, we may read: "Many a time should we have been thankful for such accommodations as we could have found in our father's barn among the cattle." This is reminiscent of the comment Mary wrote in her diary just before the reenforcement reached the rendezvous after a most uncomfortable experience in crossing the North Platte: "In the forenoon I cried to think how comfortable father's hogs were."*

After the September Mission meeting, having received permission to remain in Kamiah, Asa built a better home. But due to the lateness of the season, he had no time then to plant a garden. Again he was obliged to look to Whitman and Spalding for supplies. Spalding made an entry in his diary for November 1, 1839: "Send Mr. Smith 10 bushels potatoes." These were the potatoes about which Sarah complained in her letter to Mary Walker. It should be noted that the potatoes received from Dr. Whitman were also small and that Spalding commented in his diary on September 24th, when he harvested his crop, that the potatoes "very good but small." This was due to the drought of that year.

After Spalding had heard the distressing news of being dismissed by the Board, he wrote a letter to Greene in which he referred to the small potatoes sent to the Smiths. He explained that when the Indians came to get them, he showed them his supply and told them: "Don't pick out the largest." Evidently the Indians then deliberately selected the smallest. Spalding was at fault in not personally seeing that the Smiths got the same mixture of potatoes of all sizes which he had reserved for himself. It is reasonable to believe that Sarah overstated her point when she reported that "9/10" of the ten bushels sent by Spalding were "not as big as your thumb & half of them not bigger than a birds egg." But these are the petty things which sour friendships even among missionaries.

Both Asa and Sarah had reason to be offended. The sending of the

---

[61] SS, 267-68.

*potato culls by Spalding to meet their winter's needs seemed to be
inexcusable. If mild-mannered and soft-spoken Sarah could have written as she did to Mary Walker, we can only imagine what the more
outspoken Asa was saying. Even before the potato incident, Smith had
become very unhappy with his lot in the Oregon Mission. The move
from Waiilatpu to Kamiah did not change his mental attitude. Again
and again he had reviewed in his mind the series of events which had
brought him and Sarah to that lonely and isolated station at Kamiah.
He attributed much of his misfortune to the misleading information
about the Nez Perces which had appeared in the* Missionary Herald
*in several of its 1837 issues. These numbers had quoted at length from
Spalding's glowing accounts of the eagerness of the Nez Perces for the
gospel and had also given the impression that the tribe numbered
many more thousands than was actually the case.*

*On August 27, 1839, Smith had made the following observation
about the number of Nez Perces in a letter to Greene: "The highest
estimate has been 5,000. All are now convinced that this is much too
high an estimate. There are probably from 3000 to 4000 speaking this
language. . . The thought of spending one's life in translating [the
Bible] for such a little handful of people while millions speaking the
same language are sitting in darkness, is truly heart sickening. Had I
known what I now do before I left the States, I can not say that I
should have been here." [62] It should be remembered that the small
tribes, such as the Cayuses, Umatillas, and Walla Wallas, also spoke
the Nez Perce tongue and that their numbers were included in Smith's
revised estimate of "3000 to 4000."*

*The potato incident intensified Smith's feeling of resentment against
Spalding. The chronological sequence of events, following the receipt
of the ten bushels of small potatoes during the first part of November
1839, suggests that this was the reason which inspired Smith to make
an accurate count of the Nez Perces and report to the Board. Notice
the last sentence in Sarah's letter of December 22nd to Mary Walker:
"Something of this kind he intends to send to the Board feeling that
they have long enough been deceived with regard to this people."*

*In taking a census of the Nez Perces, Smith had the sympathetic
assistance of Rogers. The two adopted the simple expedient of collect-
ing a bundle of sticks from each band, one stick to stand for each
individual. These were then counted after the collections had been
made. In his letter of February 6, 1840,[63] to Greene, Smith wrote: "We*

---

[62] Editorial italics. For full text of this letter, see SS, 102ff.

*have thus far numbered 1,421, & we think that certainly one half &
perhaps more are already numbered. All the large bands are numbered."* [64] *After including the Nez Perces in the buffalo country, in areas
other than along the Clearwater and Snake Rivers, and also including
the Nez Perce speaking tribes in the vicinity of the Whitman station,
Smith calculated that the total number would not exceed 3,000. Smith
laid such statistics before the Board as a part of his argument to show
that Spalding had exaggerated and misrepresented the facts.*

*Thus the first census to be taken of the Nez Perces, which figures are
of such interest to us today, seemingly arose out of the unhappy incident of Spalding sending his cull potatoes to Smith. An indirect result,
which should not be overlooked, is that later Smith used those same
figures to justify his action in leaving the Mission. The Nez Perces
were too small in numbers to warrant his remaining among them.*

1840 — DISCOURAGEMENT, DISCORD, AND DANGER

*February 3, 1840 began as a day of great beauty for Asa and Sarah.
A winter storm had gently laid a four-inch mantle of snow over the
hills and valley that surrounded their lonely home at Kamiah. The
branches of the pine trees bent earthward with their burdens. But
before the day ended, Asa and Sarah were plunged into deepest grief
for their one American cow, which had given birth to a calf a little
more than a month previous, had eaten a poisonous weed and had
died. "The loss to us," lamented Smith in a letter to Greene dated the
6th, "is beyond calculation."*

*Asa had no barn to shelter his cow nor was there any storage of hay
to provide forage for wintry weather. All of the livestock of the missionaries, such as horses and cattle, had to stay out-of-doors throughout
the year and fend for themselves when snow covered the ground by
pawing through it to find the grass underneath. Ordinarily cattle will
not eat the poisonous weed that grows to this day in the Kamiah
Valley, but in this case Asa's cow seemingly was unable to distinguish
it as she pawed for food through the snow. An autopsy revealed the
cause of her sudden death.*

*No more poignant passage is found in any of Asa's letters to his
eastern relatives than that which appears in his postscript of February
5th to his letter begun the previous November. The loss of a fresh
milch cow was indeed a tragic experience, especially when one remem-*

---

[63] See Drury, *Spalding,* 177. For full text of Smith's letter of February 6, 1840,
see SS, 124ff.

[64] See illustration, p. 181.

bers the meagerness of the Smiths' diet and how much they depended on fresh milk. The intensity of Asa's grief is revealed in the passage where he repeats the words so often used in the commital service at a funeral: "The Lord gave & the Lord hath taken away & blessed be the name of the Lord."

On February 4th, the day after the cow died, Smith sent a letter to Spalding asking for one of his fresh milch cows to replace the one that had died. Spalding in his diary acknowledged receipt of the letter and then wrote to Smith on the 7th saying that the only available cow had been sold to Conner, the mountain man who assisted him. Gray later asked Conner when he had bought the cow and was told that he did so on the 7th. When Smith learned of this from Gray, he was incensed, for it appeared that Spalding had sold the cow to Conner just after receiving Smith's request. Strange to say, it was Gray who came to Smith's relief and provided the needed milch cow.

On February 6th, Smith began a letter to Greene which ran to 9,500 words or more.[65] He first told of the death of his cow. It may be that he received Spalding's letter of the 7th before he had written more than a few pages as he then launched into a blistering criticism of Spalding. He dealt especially with Spalding's exaggerated reports of his early successes among the Nez Perces which had been published in various issues of the Missionary Herald for 1837. Asa raised point after point, documenting them by quoting page numbers from the Herald and showing how misleading the reports had been. Although he did not so indicate it in this letter, Asa on other occasions did say that these misleading and exaggerated reports of Spalding's were largely responsible for the sudden decision he had made in March 1838 to join the Oregon Mission.

Sometime during the first part of March 1840, Gray visited Smith at Kamiah. These two, who had been almost on a non-speaking basis while crossing the Rockies in the summer of 1838, now became most friendly as they shared with each other their opinions of Spalding. This prompted Gray to send in a letter of criticism of Spalding to the Board. Altogether Smith wrote four such letters to the Board in 1840; Gray sent three; Whitman wrote twice making some minor criticisms; and Rogers and Hall each wrote once. It was this accumulation of letters, piled up on the desk of Secretary Greene, which prompted the American Board to issue its fateful order of February 24, 1842, dismissing Spalding; recalling Smith and Gray; and closing the Lapwai and

---

[65] For full text of these letters, see SS, 124ff.

Waiilatpu stations. And it was the arrival of this order at Waiilatpu in September of that year which prompted Whitman to mount his horse and start on his famous ride over the Rockies to Boston.

It is interesting to speculate as to what might have been the history of the Mission if Smith's cow had not died or if Spalding out of sympathy and brotherly love had provided a substitute.

Asa's letters to his loved ones in Vermont written during 1840 tell of other difficulties and discouragements. He had servant problems. Jack, the Hawaiian, left Kamiah in June and did not return until October. This means that the Smiths were alone during the summer with only a few Indians in the valley.[66] *It also meant that he had no reliable assistance to aid him with his farming activities. A more serious problem arose with Sarah's declining health. She suffered from a spinal affliction which steadily grew worse so that by the spring of 1841 she was unable to ride horseback and could walk only with difficulty. A generation later she was remembered by the Nez Perces of Kamiah as "the weeping one."* [67]

To cap a long series of discouragements and difficulties, a grave danger visited the Smiths on October 13th of that year when two sub-chiefs of Kamiah — Insinmalakin and his brother, Inmtamlaiakin [68] *— ordered the Smiths to leave Kamiah and even threatened physical violence. This incident seems to have been related to similar events taking place elsewhere. A few weeks earlier, Pierre Pambrun, who was in charge of Fort Walla Walla, had been tied and beaten by some Indians. A Nez Perce by the name of Meiway or Blue Cap* [69] *seems to*

---

[66] Smith in his letter of February 6, 1840, describes the way the Nez Perces were obliged to scatter over a wide territory in search of food. "Out of 497 people who belong within 15 miles of this place," he wrote, "249 are now in the buffalo country & only 248 in this vicinity." In the summer the number remaining in Kamiah became even fewer. This made it very difficult for him to conduct any regular school work or Sunday worship services. Smith argued that the Board would be well advised to close its missions with small tribes of natives and concentrate on areas where more people were available.

[67] McBeth, *The Nez Perces Since Lewis and Clark*, p. 60.

[68] According to Narcissa Whitman's letter of October 10, 1840, to her father, Insinmalakin and Inmtamlaiakin were brothers "to the Indian who went to the United States for some one to come and teach them." *T.O.P.A.*, 1893, p. 131. The reference is to the Nez Perce "delegation" of 1831 to St. Louis. Two of the four who arrived in St. Louis died there. One of these was Keepellele, or Speaking Eagle. This is the one to whom Narcissa was referring. See also Drury, *Spalding*, 79ff.

[69] Alvin Josephy, who is on the editorial staff of *American Heritage* and author of the recent book on the Nez Perces, has identified this Meiway or Blue Cap as the father of Looking Glass, one of the leaders in the Chief Joseph 1877 uprising.

*have been the ringleader of this outrage. Spalding in his diary for
October 9th described an unpleasant incident which had taken place
at his school when two young fellows, hideously painted, had insulted
Mrs. Spalding and had carried on "savage talk" with him. In his diary
entry for October 14th, Spalding noted the receipt of a letter from
Smith and added: "The Blue Cap has ordered Mr. S. to leave the
country."*

*Thus it appears that Blue Cap, after harrassing Pambrun, had gone
to Kamiah and had induced the two subchiefs to threaten the Smiths.
Only the presence of Jack, the Hawaiian, who had returned to Kamiah
a couple of days before the incident, seems to have saved the Smiths
from harm at that particular time. The attitude of the Indians was so
alarming that Asa sent a frantic message to Spalding and Whitman
begging them to come at once to Kamiah. The last extant letter that
we have of Sarah's is the following note addressed to Mrs. Whitman
and Mrs. Spalding, which she enclosed in her husband's letter to
Spalding, and this exists not in the original but in a copy that Gray
made for Greene:*

DEAR SISTERS — I did not anticipate when I commenced this that I
should have to tell you what has this day transpired. We have again in
the most absolute manner been ordered to leave this place immediately
even tomorrow. Never did I see such a day as this. Never did I before
feel that our lives were in danger. *But I feel so now.* The talk was in
the house and though Mr. Smith was calm, he was as white as a piece
of cloth. The Indians became so insolent and so warm with anger that
I thought it time to call Jack.

I with difficulty got him within the house. One of them held the
door to prevent his coming in. But Mr. S. opened the door himself &
let him in. I fear to stay another day as we were ordered to leave
tomorrow. I do not know what they will do with us if we do not. Mr.
S. is forbidden to speak to the people again. We hope that some one
will come to our help as soon as possible. We shall send to Mr. Spalding to come up tomorrow.

                    Yours in great haste.   S. G. SMITH [70]
P.S.   Feel extremely tired to night, excitement has over come me.

*The Smiths spent a sleepless night. Jack slept in the kitchen. The
two subchiefs returned the next day and repeated their demands that*

---

[70] Gray to Greene, October 16, 1840. Coll. A. See also FWW, ɪ, p. 277.

the Smiths leave but they were less belligerent.[71] *Spalding arrived in Kamiah on the 15th and Whitman a few days later. By this time the better elements within the tribe began to assert themselves so that the trouble died down. Spalding and Whitman found the Smiths to be thoroughly discouraged. Sarah was in poor health and very lonely. Both Asa and Sarah were ready to leave and go to the Hawaiian Mission. In reporting on his trip to Secretary Greene, Whitman commented that Smith felt he had brought his unfortunate predicament upon himself "for being in so much haste to be sent out (or in other words to get married)."* [72] *The trouble-makers were induced to drop their demands. The majority of the Nez Perces at Kamiah did not want the Smiths to leave and denounced the action taken by the two subchiefs. The Smiths, even though they had promised to leave, consented to remain.*

After his return to Waiilatpu, Whitman made arrangements for the independent missionaries, the Rev. and Mrs. Harvey Clark, who had arrived at Waiilatpu that fall, to go to Kamiah and spend the winter with the Smiths. Three missionary couples, all independent of any missionary board, had made the overland journey to Oregon in 1840, among whom were the Clarks. Spalding in his diary for November 21st noted the arrival of the Clarks on their way to Kamiah. They remained with the Smiths until the following March.

Even though the Smiths' loneliness was relieved by having another couple live with them, Asa continued to be disheartened. On December 5th, he made a long list in his diary of his problems and the insurmountable difficulties which beset him. Then in utter despondency, he wrote: ". . . in view of these things I must say that I feel discouraged & disheartened & know not what to do." This was the last entry in his diary.

JAN. 7th, 1840. Our outfit arrived here on the 4th inst, almost in time to be a New Year's present & since that time we have been much

---

[71] For Smith's report to Greene of this incident, see SS, 194 and 200.

[72] Drury, *Whitman*, 244. Whitman was still at Kamiah when Smith wrote his letter of October 21st to Greene but, evidently, Spalding had returned to Lapwai. In this letter Smith continued his detailed criticism of Spalding and included this comment: "The above remarks I have just read to Doct. W. & he concurs in what I have written & says moreover that Mr. Spalding has a disease in his head which may result in derangement especially if excited by external circumstances." Whitman was not a co-signer of this letter so Smith's remark should not be taken as a professional diagnosis. Smith's judgment should be tempered with the knowledge of his own choleric disposition. On the other hand, it is known that Spalding was excitable and at times most difficult in his relationships with others.

engaged in looking over our things, &c. Rec'd letters from Father, Br. J.C., Sisters Laura, M. & S. Tho' we had rec'd many letters of a later date, still I read these with as much interest as tho they had been the last. We found our things in a much better state than we expected after so long a voyage. We found them some damp but very few mildewed. They have suffered much less injury than I expected. My books & every thing came in very good order, without any injury of any consequence. I was much gratified at the pleasure you manifested in preparing the things you did for me & I feel thankful that I have parents & sisters who are so ready to provide not only for my necessities but for my comforts. The articles you sent were all valuable. If the shirts had been of coarser cloth they would have been quite as good for this country. The cloth for pantaloons was very acceptable. The cotton cloth too is valuable here. Give my thanks to the merchants for providing the materials for the bedquilt & also to all who assisted you. The maple sugar we find very nice indeed, so much refined that the peculiar taste of the maple is rather indistinct. All the sugar we get of the H.H.B.C. is white loaf sugar. They have no other. We have had a present of 50 lb. from the Islands of brown sugar.[73] Probably we shall have more [?] from them every year. The articles we have rec'd are abundant to make us comfortable in respect to clothing &c. We have even more than we need at present, but should we live we shall need them all probably. We have them all to store in our bed room & it fills it quite full. I rec'd quite a quantity of clothing from Woodstock, Vt. There were only two shirts among it. But I have shirts enough to last for certainly 5 years I should think. Had some bedticking come with our things, it would have been very acceptable, as it is not to be obtained here. I am happy to see your readiness to supply my wants, but you need not be in haste to send me more clothing. Should I live I may need hereafter more shirts, stockings, &c. You might send me some coarse shirts, such as are good to work in, as I am under the necessity of working some here, & besides it is not often that we see white people here & coarse ones will do just as well.

---

[73] The native Christians of the Hawaiian Islands were making contributions of their products to the Oregon Mission at this time. Several of Smith's letters to Levi Chamberlain, secular agent of the Hawaiian Mission, are in Coll. Ha. In Smith's letter of January 17, 1840, to Chamberlain, we may read: "The stories which have been told of the religious character of this people, I can assure you, are but poetry and romance. . . When I think of the millions in other parts of the world who are sitting in darkness, I can hardly content myself to remain here expending my energies in attempting to give the gospel to such a small number."

Should you feel disposed to send any thing, I will tell you what would be a great comfort to us. It is dried apple. We have no fruit here & I feel greatly the loss of apples. Dried apple needs to be put up with great care. It should be thoroughly dried, perhaps in the oven after drying before it is put up & then put up in a water tight cask. Half barrel is as large as can reach us. Barrels would be of great value to us if we could get them here. Father White sent two barrels & one half barrel. The barrels were unpacked at the Islands & did not reach us. The half barrel came without unpacking. I have sawed it in the middle & made two wash tubs of it. Good tight boxes answer very well for packing most things in, yet tight casks are not so likely to admit moisture. No box should weigh over 100 lbs. & should be of good proportion so that it can be packed on a horse. The one you sent was either too high or too broad. It made it too clumsy to pack. Mr. Rogers therefore opened it when he went for our things & cut off 3 or 4 inches from the top of the box & packed all the things in [it] still. You would be amused to see two of these great boxes on a horse, one on each side to balance the other, or two half barrels. But this is the way we have to bring every thing about 200 miles. The next time you send, I would like to have a few seeds sent viz, Red Clover & White Clover. Say one pint of each if convenient. Seeds should be put in bottles & corked tight to come across the ocean or it will spoil. Put it in pint bottles that are strong & will not easily break. The bottles will be valuable to us.

FEB. 5th [1840]   In the previous part of this letter, I have spoken of our cows, &c. About a month ago one cow had a calf, which I took away from the cow before it sucked at all & the cow gave me no trouble, but has furnished us well with milk & added much to our comfort & we were flattering ourselves that we should in future not want for milk & butter. But alas! Our hopes have been blasted. Day before yesterday the cow went out in the morning as well as ever & at evening the boy that hunts the cows for me came & said the cow was dying. We ran to the place where she was & only arrived in time to see her die. We found upon examination of the stomach that she had eaten during the day a poisonous root which I suppose to be the wild parsnip which was the occasion of her death. There was about 4 inches of snow on the ground on account of which probably the cow did not distinguish what she ate, tho' it is a very offensive plant. It grows in wet ground & it seems that the root or part of it come up with the top.

The loss to us is incalculable. It is what money cannot replace here. The one we have left is one of the breed of this country & we can place but little dependence on her. This was a good American cow. Had you lost every cow you have, were it 10, your loss would not equal ours, for they could be easily replaced. But now our means of support & comfort are taken away & we know not hardly how to live without our cow. Our hearts are made sad indeed by this loss, but it is the Lord that has done it, & it is all right. I loved the cow too well. I now find I was placing too much dependence on it, & the Lord has shown me that it was not mine, & has taken only that which was his own. The cow has left me a nice calf but it is a male. I am raising it on porridge which it learned to eat well before the cow died. I hope to be able to raise it tho' I have no milk for it except what the cow gave before she died which I am giving by little & little with water porridge. A few days ago we lost our only sow pig which we obtained but a month ago, kicked by our remaining cow on the head so that it died. The skull was cracked.

Thus the Lord is taking away our earthly dependencies in order to lead us to place our entire dependence on him. We deserve the chastisement & it is far ligher than we deserved. He might as easily have taken one of us but yet we are spared. He came as near to us as he could without touching our own persons. Had our house been consumed, we could not have felt it more, for soon we could have built another. I presume you cannot in your situation realize our feelings. Separated as we are from the comforts of civilized life in a great measure, when our cow is taken we feel that our only comfort as respects our living is taken away.

But I hope we do not feel to murmur, but to say "The Lord gave & the Lord hath taken away & blessed be the name of the Lord." I hope we have profited already by this affliction. It has shown us the vanity of every earthly dependence & I trust that in future we shall place our dependence more on the giver of all our gifts. I know you will sympathize with us in this loss & would gladly make it up to us, but it is beyond your power. But the Lord is able to provide. He has taken care of us thus far, protected our goods on the ocean, & this is the first time that he has seen fit to remove anything from us. He has indeed been merciful to us & why should we not trust him for the future.

Feb. 24th.   Since writing the above, Mr. Gray has kindly offered us one of his cows to supply the loss of ours.[74] We have not rec'd it yet &

---

[74] The following action was taken at the Mission meeting held at Lapwai, July

it will not give milk for two months yet. We are getting along with preparations for cultivating the coming season. We are now making fence around a piece of land, perhaps 25 acres or 30, a part of which will be divided for a cow pasture. I intend to cultivate 6 or 7 acres, not 100 as Mr. Spalding stated as was published in the Herald. That was cultivated only in the air. He always comes short of his calculations & you must think of this when you read his accounts.

Sarah's health is poor & she is able to do but little.[75] Since I wrote last we have discovered that she has a spinal affection for which I am now blistering her, & requires several months of constant blistering to affect much in this disease & many times it is never cured. She is about the house & sees for [?] things but she can do but little. I hope she will be relieved by blistering.

We are now expecting a vessel in from the States by which we expect letters. We are glad to get letters here, I can assure you. I must now close this long letter to you & I will soon write again to go by way of the Sandwich Islands. Do not cease to pray for us. Very affectionately yours.   A. B. SMITH

[Across the page bearing the address] You may if you please when you send any thing, send a little stocking yarn, coloured. [Across first page on margin] Sisters letter through Canada came safe. Rec'd it in Oct.

Addressed to Mr. Asa Smith, East Williamstown, Vermont, U.S.A. via Canada. Stamped "Highgate Sept. 11." Also bearing penned inscription "15th Sept. 1840."

4-9, 1840: "Resolved: That no member of the mission be at liberty to dispose of the cattle belonging to the mission, except by vote of the mission." This was a rebuke to Spalding.

[75] In his letter to Greene of August 31, 1840, Asa is more specific: "Our situation has been the more trying on account of Mrs. Smith's health. The case has become rather critical & gives me no little anxiety. The hardships & exposures she has passed through have been too great for her constitution to bear up under. Last autumn it became evident that she had a spinal affection. During most of the winter & spring she was kept under a course of blistering from which I have no doubt she would have rec'd material benefit, could she have been during the summer relieved from the care & labor of the family & kept in a recumbent posture. As it has been, we have had no one to relieve us & she has performed the labors of the kitchen, tho often with much pain & fatigue & in great danger of aggravating the disease & rendering her ultimately a confirmed invalid. During the summer we have worn our clothes without ironing & when we have not been able to get native assistance, I have been under the necessity of doing most of the washing myself." Since Sarah is reported to have died of "consumption" in 1855, it is possible that she was suffering at Kamiah from tuberculosis of the spine.

KAMIAH, OREGON TERRITORY,   April 21st, 1840

MY DEAR SISTERS M. & L.   Five letters were rec'd from you on the 17th inst. dated as follows, one from each Nov. 17 /38; one from M. Jan. 26 /39, & one from each April 19 /39. I have not time now to write much to you but will endeavor to write each of you again soon, when I may have more leisure. We expect more letters very soon as Mr. Lee's vessel is not in yet.[76]

I have not time to look over carefully your letters & answer them particularly. Many questions you have asked me are already answered in other letters. But one thing appears in your letters. You suffer your imagination to paint scenes which are far from reality. The heathen are far different from what you imagine & they do not listen to the truth as you suppose with so much attention, tho' they appear attentive for heathens, yet they understand but little and often pervert what they do. The natural heart reigns in them & they are truly under the dominion of Satan, led captive at his will just as all other heathen are. They often make us much trouble by their insolence. Usually when they are hungry, they are tolerably kind in order that they may get favors of us. But when they have enough & are not in want, they are usually very insolent indeed.

All they want of us is to supply their temporal wants. This is manifest both from their conduct & what they sometimes say to us. They are indeed a selfish wicked people, but to do them good requires much self-denial & patience. Missionary labor viewed from our native land is all poetry, but here it is stern, severe reality. Your letters show that you have altogether a wrong idea of it. Should you ever become missionaries you would write very different from what you do now.

We have trials here which you know not of & cannot know till placed in like circumstances. We have trials from the heathen. They are deceitful & no dependence is to be placed on their word. Twice has the land been solemnly given to me on which we live by the principal man here & as often has he taken it back because his wicked selfish notions were not gratified. He is a great villain & all he wants is to have his temporal wants gratified.[77] But I have learned to pay but

---

[76] The "Lausanne," with the large Methodist reenforcement, dropped anchor at Fort Vancouver on June 1, 1840.

[77] The reference is to Insinmalakin who was the leader in the October 13, 1840, incident. Four Nez Perce chiefs made a trip to Washington, D.C., in 1868 with Indian Agent Robert Newell to present their grievances and claims to the U.S. government. One of the four was "Utes-sa-ma-le-kin", believed to be Insinmalakin. This individual died in Washington on May 25th "of typhoid fever" and was

little attention to his threats. He has not a great number of friends among the Indians.

We have trials too from unfaithful servants, who need looking to almost continually. Indeed it is a life of trial & perplexity & much grace is necessary to prepare one for such a trying work. My health is good, Sarah's is improving, I think. Your Afft. br.   A. B. SMITH

Addressed to Misses Marcia & Lucia Smith and postmarked "New York, Ship," Feb. 5.

KAMIAH, OREGON TERRITORY,   Aug. 27, 1840

MY DEAR FATHER. Last evening the half barrel arrived containing dried apple, a pr. of boots & shoes, some papers & other things. Also a plough has come to me sent with others to the mission, so that there is no need of your sending a plough to me. This is enough, I wish no more. The barrel is still at Vancouver & will not come up till Oct. probably, when boats again will come up the river.

I think you are very kind in thinking so much about our wants & in being so ready to supply them. You have even done more than I should have asked or ever desired. The boots & shoes I did not need as I have a good pair of boots which were given me in New York & have worn them but little, & the shoes you sent me before I have not worn at all. I wear moccasins when it is not wet, which I find very comfortable, but in so doing my foot has enlarged considerable so that all you have sent are quite too small to be comfortable. The shoes I shall probably be able to wear, but I fear I shall not be able to wear the boots. We can also get all the shoes we need at Vancouver, so that you will not need to send them. I used to wear No. 9 at home but I find it necessary to send for No. 10 here. Perhaps the No's here do not agree exactly with those at home. Shoes here are better calculated for this country having some nails at the toes & sides to preserve the soles: for we have no shoemaker to run to & get new soles, so that when one is gone, the shoe is done.

The apple we shall find very good here. We fear however it is somewhat injured. It is a long voyage for it & we may find that it is not best to have it sent in future. But after trying it I will write more.

---

buried in the Congressional Cemetery. The other three chiefs who made this trip were Lawyer, Timothy, and Jason or Eagle. See article by Drury, "I, the Lawyer," in New York *Westerners,* May 1960. The author has visited this cemetery in Washington and has confirmed the report of the burial of the Nez Perce chief there.

And now about sending things in future. I will say do not be in haste. Should we live many years, we may want many things hereafter; but for the present we have enough of every thing that you could help us to. We have an abundance of clothing & bedding for a considerable time & we have not house room to store any more, even now we are crowded with boxes, having no clothes press. In some few particulars we might desire some things a little different for this region & climate. But about this I have already written something.

I would say then, as a general thing, do not send us in future any thing except we write expressly for it, so that you can know just what we want, lest you make yourself trouble & expense to no purpose. Your readiness to do all you can for us is very gratifying to us & makes us feel a stronger attachment for you & we do not wish to have you make yourselves needless trouble. Since you have shown this readiness of yourselves, I will in future endeavor to let you know frankly what we need, when if it be convenient for you, you can supply our wants. If you have designed any thing more for us at present, let brother John have it for he will need it more than we do now. So far as you are able, I hope you will keep him from pecuniary embarrassments.

The opportunity for obtaining articles in this country is improving, so that we shall not in future be under the necessity of sending home for many articles. Bedticking I understand can now be had at Vancouver. I wrote you for a sieve sometime since, but now find it is not necessary for I have obtained wire cloth of which I have made one myself. Clothing is the principal article to which you can help us & of this we have at present a good supply.

This summer we have been very much alone. Jack, our Hawaiian man, left us in June & since then we have had no one to assist us in the house or out of doors which has rendered our situation rather unpleasant, on account of Sarah's feeble health. But we are able to take care of ourselves & we find but little time to do any thing more. Indeed I have been this summer a mere farmer for it is by "the sweat of our own brows we eat bread" here. No markets where we can get our supplies, but must raise them from the ground. This takes much time & Indian help is such as you would consider at home worse than none. You can form no idea of our situation here & of the difficulties we have to encounter here. In cultivating what we need, we have not every thing at hand as at home nor faithful help to depend upon, but labor under great inconvenience for want of conveniences to do with, & if we have help, it is nothing but the most awkward kind & often is more trouble than to do it yourself. But we can expect nothing more of a rude savage people & they will be such till the gospel savingly affects their hearts. Sarah sends much love. With much affection, I remain, your son,   A. B. SMITH

[Postscript] If you could send me the Vt. Chronicle regularly, I should value it more than almost any thing else that you could send. They might be put up in a bundle & directed & sent to the Miss'y House 3 or 4 times a year. I want all the No's regularly.

Addressed to Asa Smith and postmarked "Ship" and "Philadelphia, Sep. 30."

KAMIAH, OREGON TERY.   August 28th, 1840

MY DEAR SISTER M[ARCIA].   Yours of June 27 /39 rec'd in due time & was happy again to hear from you. I hope you will continue to write me often, even if I should not answer every one. You must remember that I have many to whom I must write & to give them all a letter, it requires considerable time. You must not be discouraged then from writing even if I do not write as much as you do to me.

I have one remark to make respecting your writing which I wish you all to remember. It is this. I wish you to remember that we are far away where we have little opportunity of knowing what is passing in the world. We have no weekly publications to go to & get news. No, scarcely a newspaper has come to us & we are getting very ignorant. The Herald & Hawaiian Spectator, a quarterly paper, are all that we get, except the very few you have sent us. We wish therefore that you should make your letters rich in *facts*. Tell the news.

I fear you neglect to remember many things because you think it will not interest. Tell me about Wmstown, about the people, our old neighbors, anything that can be [of] any kind of interest. Mention over the names of those I know & tell me something about them. Tell me too things of a public character. Who is the Governor of Vt? I would like to see the Mr. Walton's Register. What about politics? What is the bone of contention? Is it antislavery or Van Burenism or what is it? I hardly know how to think of home or any thing relating to it for want of information. We are certainly far out of the world. What about the war with Great Britain? [78] A little is said here & there about it in some papers, but I cannot know any thing definite.

---

[78] Rumors had reached Oregon of a possible clash between the United States and Great Britain over the disputed northeastern boundary between New Brunswick and Maine. This is sometimes referred to as the "Aroostook War." A truce was signed in March 1839.

You see from what I have said something of what I would like to have you write about. Not that I wish your letters all a collection of mere dry facts without any expression of feeling towards us. No, it is gratifying to see in your letters expressions of feeling for us & sympathy with us in our trials. Such expressions bind you more strongly to our hearts & make us feel more tenderly towards you. All we wish is to have your letters contain more important information. But every thing is changing at home with awful rapidity & soon an entire new generation will be upon the stage with whom I am not acquainted. And I should love once more, before so great a change shall have taken place, to see New England again. New England is dear to me & always will be. It is a favored spot. There is not another like it in all the world. New England institutions too are the ones to train up young men for usefulness. They furnish more substantial men than those of the West. I become more & more partial to New England the more I learn of the world. I should love again to see my old home, my parents, brothers & sisters. I could hardly contain my feelings were I permitted again to visit that dear place. But whether this will ever be is known only to him who knows the end from the beginning.

Perhaps you think that because we are on heathen ground we must of course be more spiritual & heavenly minded than if at home. But I can assure you that it is not so easy to keep up a high tone of piety here as at home. What are the influences that are constantly operating upon us? Only such as to degrade instead of elevating & inspiring. The means of promoting piety which are enjoyed at home, we have not here. All the means we have are the bible & other religious books & the influence of each other. No Christian society, no preaching, no prayer meetings & conferences. Take away all these influences & can you wonder that we should sink. People at home often think, O if I were a missionary, how holy I should live, but alas! they know not what it is to be a missionary. They consider not that these opportunities for living a holy life will be far less than at home. The novelty is soon gone & then it is up hill work without the influences which are enjoyed at home to push one onward. Pray much for us that we may be kept from religious declension.

Your afft. br.   A. B. SMITH

Addressed to Miss Marcia Smith and postmarked "Ship" and "Philadelphia Sep. 30."

KAMIAH, OREGON TERY. August 29th, 1840

MY DEAR SISTER LUCIA. Yours of June 27 /39 rec'd with the rest & as I have written to all the others, I will not neglect you. I often think of you all & of br. J.C. & wish that I might see you, but we are far separated & what Providence will order concerning us we know not. We may be permitted to meet again on earth, but this we know not. It would be pleasant indeed could we spend our lives together. I feel the need of such society in this distant land. I used to think of your spending your lives with us as teachers, but this field does not promise enough to warrant your coming here. Indeed I feel that the opportunity of doing good here is not sufficient to compensate for the sacrifices we have made. One half of the year we are almost entirely alone. In the summer we could not sustain a school for want of scholars. In the winter the greatest number that has been here is only 275. The prospect of the people settling is dark, so that we can have but little access to them. It is not then such a field as I could invite you to enter. Were we at the Sandwich Islands, we could find abundant employment for you.

I often feel anxious respecting you & sometimes almost regret that I had not remained at home till brother J. could have completed his studies & labored as a minister at home. In this way I might have assisted you all very much & when brother should have completed his course, we might have gone together to some field. Nothing would indeed have been lost for I should have been better prepared for a missionary life after 3 or 4 years experience in the ministry.

But the Lord knew what was best & he will overrule all things for the promotion of his glory. Had the subject presented itself to my mind while at home as it does now, I should have taken that course & I should have felt that the object was one of sufficient importance to detain me. But it is now too late to think of that. What the Lord will do with me or with you I know not, but he will do all things right. Had we made such plans, they might have been frustrated. We may devise one way but the Lord alone directeth the steps. I am too far away to assist you at all. Br. J. is the one to whom you must look & I hope he will not be in so great haste as not to think of you.

Where he will select his field, I know not. Should the Board wish to send more to the Sandwich Islands, that would be a favorable place & there we might be near, if not in the *same* field. There too, you & Sister M., should you remain as you are & wish so to remain, might do immense good as teachers. Ministers & teachers are still needed in that field to secure the harvest & put that people in a situation to take care of themselves. I shall write him about this but what will be the result I know not.

We may not remain here long in this field.[79] Sarah's health is such & our destitute situation such that we cannot stand it long. Should we find it necessary to leave here for want of domestic assistance, we may go to the Islands where our situation would be utterly different & we could devote all our time to the great work. I have spent too much time to be a mere *farmer.* What the Lord will order concerning us we know not. The Islands are only 4 weeks sail from Vancouver. These are our nearest neighbors.

Pray much for us that we may be guided in all our ways. Yes, I feel the need of wisdom from on high. Write me often & tell me all your heart.

Your affect. brother.   A. B. SMITH

Addressed to Miss Lucia Smith with postmark "Ship" and "Phila-delphia, Sep. 30."

DEPARTURE FROM KAMIAH – 1841

We have little information about how the Smiths and the Clarks spent the winter of 1840-41 at Kamiah. Only four letters of Asa's are extant written from his lonely mission station in 1841. The first of these was to his parents on February 19th. This letter follows. On February 22nd Asa wrote to Elkanah Walker and to Secretary Greene. These were published in the author's Diaries and Letters of Spalding and Smith.[80] *The fourth was to Levi Chamberlain in Honolulu under date of February 23rd.*[81] *In his letters to Walker and Greene, Smith refers to the company of the Clarks as being "very pleasant" and "a great comfort to us in our lonely situation." The Clarks left Kamiah on March 3rd. Among those who came up from Lapwai to act as escort was Rogers.*

It seems most probable that when Rogers and Smith were together at Kamiah, they talked over their common woes. By this time Rogers had decided to leave the Mission. On February 27th of that year, he

[79] Editorial italics. By this time, within two years of their arrival in Oregon, the Smiths were definitely planning to leave. Sarah's declining health was indeed sufficient reason for them to ask for a transfer to the Hawaiian Mission.

[80] *Op cit.,* pp. 188 and 205. The letter to Walker is erroneously dated 1840 instead of 1841.

[81] Coll. Ha. Smith in this letter commented on the arrival of Roman Catholic missionaries in the Oregon country. He also said: "Mrs. Smith's health is still feeble."

had written to Greene telling of his decision. He then declared: "I will simply say that Mr. Spalding is felt by me to be the principal cause of my course." [82] Although Smith had not as yet indicated to the board his intention to leave, this was known by the members of the Mission.

Elkanah Walker wrote to dissuade Smith from going. He felt that it would be a disgrace for any member of the Mission to leave, thus implying a lack of faith. Walker was very pointed in his comments: "This mission has had troubles on your account . . . & for you to run off & leave us would be unjust. . . Furthermore you are in the field of your choice & one you was determined to have & if you cannot be satisfied with your own choice when & where will you be satisfied?"

Asa felt that such a letter was both unkind and un-Christian. Walker clearly did not appreciate the frail condition of Sarah's health. "Imagine yourself in my situation," wrote Asa, "alone with a sick & feeble wife, subjected to do your own wife's washing as I have sometimes been, & with your hands so tied that you had little or no opportunity of doing good & yourself ready to sink under your despondency, & should receive such language as this from a Christian brother. . ." Regarding being a trouble-maker in the Mission, Smith commented: "If it is true . . . . then is this [not] a strong reason why I should be out of the mission?" [83]

In his letter to Secretary Greene of February 22nd, Asa made reference to a request previously made that he be transferred to the Hawaiian Mission or to have permission to return home. "If it is the wish of the Board that we go to the Islands," he wrote, "Mrs. S's health is such as to render it advisable, we are ready to go. If it is their [i.e. Prudential Committee's] advice that we return home, we shall acquiesce." Such a comment at that time was rather futile as it would have taken two years to get a reply. Possibly Smith was thinking of intercepting a letter from the Board at the Islands which would give him permission to remain there or to return home.

Following the Clarks' departure on March 3rd, Sarah's health took a turn for the worse. She became confined to her bed. After a month of this, and seeing no signs of any improvement, Asa decided that they would have to go. Sarah was unable to ride horseback so plans were made to descend the Clearwater in a canoe. No doubt their few personal belongings were sent by horseback under the escort of some friendly Indians to Fort Walla Walla.

---

[82] Coll. A.

[83] For Walker-Smith correspondence, see SS, 211ff.

*Asa and Sarah left Kamiah on Monday, April 19th. No account re-
mains of their last Sunday with the natives or of their emotions on
leaving the beautiful valley which had been their home for nearly two
years. They reached Lapwai on Wednesday morning about ten o'clock,
having camped out two nights along the way. Kamiah was sixty miles
overland from Lapwai but by river it was much farther. It so happened that both Mrs. Spalding and Rogers became seriously ill and
Spalding had sent for Dr. Whitman. He arrived at Lapwai shortly
before the Smiths. Since Gray was also there, this meant that five of
the seven men of the Mission were at Lapwai.*

*Spalding in rather unsympathetic words commented in his diary:
"Mrs. S[mith] is not able to sit up much; but I am fully persuaded
that this is not the principle reason of Mr. Smith's leaving the Mission.
He says he will go home in disgrace before he will remain longer in
the Indian country. He considers the Indian race doomed to destruction. Especially this people he considers a hopeless case for two reasons, one their disposition & their language." Writing to Walker from
Waiilatpu on May 7th, Gray said regarding Spalding's reaction to
Smith's departure: "Mr. Spalding is now in ecstacy — having accomplished one of his 'darling objects'." [84] At the annual Mission meeting
held in June, Spalding again commented on Smith's leaving by writing
in his diary: "I fear that bro. Smith has been hasty in leaving the Mission but I hope he knows his own business & will not offend his God."*

*Regardless of all of the difficulties which arose out of personality
conflicts and differences in mission policies, Sarah's serious illness more
than justified their departure from the field. In his letter to Greene
written from Walla Walla on April 29th, Smith explained: "Soon after
I wrote [i.e., referring to his letter of February 22nd], her health began
to decline more rapidly so that by the first of March she was completely
prostrated & from that time to the present she has been confined almost
entirely to her bed." [85] Yet Smith was criticized by some of his brethren
because he left without first having obtained permission of the Mission.*

*It took the Smiths from April 19th to May 17th to make the four-
hundred-mile journey down the Clearwater River to the Snake and
thence to the Columbia and from there on to Fort Vancouver. This
included two weeks spent at Fort Walla Walla. Although the Smiths
travelled in their own canoe as far as Walla Walla, it is probable that
from there they were passengers in some larger boat of the Hudson's
Bay Company.*

---

[84] Original in Coll. Y.   [85] SS, 210.

The Smiths' connection with the Oregon Mission of the American Board was officially terminated when the following action was taken at the October 1842 meeting of the Mission held at Waiilatpu: "Resolved: That in view of the circumstances of Mr. Smith's family, this Mission do not feel to censure or approve of his course in leaving the country." [86]

KAMIAH, OREGON TER.   Feb. 19th, 1841

MY DEAR PARENTS &c.   Since I last wrote I have rec'd two letters from sisters dated Nov. 20th /39. I was much disappointed that I had no letters across the mountains either by the [Hudson's Bay] Express through Canada or by the way of St. Louis. My last dates to you were Aug. 27th, 28th, 29th, /40, one to each of the family. Since that time our situation has been somewhat different. In Oct. Jack, who left us in June, returned, having been engaged by Doct. McLoughlin for us two years longer, so that we have not since that time been in so lonely & destitute a condition. The Indians too as you may have heard from bro. J.C. made us not a little trouble in Oct. so that we came near leaving this place. The disturbance was made by the two principal Indians, who pretend to own the land in this valley & who have made us difficulty before tho' not of quite so serious a nature. It arose from a determination on their part to get property in some way, to force me to pay more than the usual price of the country & to compel me to make them presents, to pay for the land &c. The attempt was made on the 13th of Oct. Those two individuals came friendly as usual for ought I knew & commenced a conversation & soon began to make their demands to which of course I refused to accede. The principal demand was for pay for the land. This by the way had been given to me in the most solemn manner before witnesses in two instances, the second time after they had made difficulty about it once before.

It would of course be a most unjust thing for us to pay them for the land we occupy being unimproved & of no value to them before we took it. But this is not the worst of it, if we pay once, paying will not answer. If their wants are satisfied once, they will come again for their wants to be satisfied another year & so on. They are never satisfied as long as they are in want of any thing. They think a white man is under obligation to give to them because they are poor & this is all they wanted of missionaries & accounts for all their goodness about wh. so much has been said. At my refusal to pay for the land, they ordered

---

[86] Coll. A, File no. 366.

me to leave the next day; and repeated it in the most threatening &
insulting manner till we began to fear that there might some evil come
upon us as one of them attempted to hold the door so that Jack could
not come in after Mrs. S. had called him. I seized the latch & Jack put
himself in very soon.

I told them I would leave but must have time to get away, that I
could not go the next day. They left the house repeating the order to
leave the next day. They went to their lodges & told the people that
they should take possession of the house the next day. I stopped all
business immediately & that night sent Thomas, the Indian boy who
had been with us last winter & had come with Jack, with letters to the
other stations letting them know of our situation.

The next morning several Indians who were friendly to us came to
the house to inquire about it & soon the two came. The door was
fastened & they threatened to break the door unless it was opened.
The door was opened & they came in & such a scene I never witnessed
in my life. They wished to know what was going on when the conversation commenced between them & those who were friendly to us
& it was carried on with savage heat & fury till about noon. Those who
were friendly threatened to tie & whip those who had made the disturbance, at which they threatened to fight with guns. At length they
cooled down somewhat & left the house. Mr. Spalding & Doct. Whitman came as soon as they heard of the disturbance & we made preparations for moving, i.e., made a canoe. In the mean time things became
quiet. One of the villains left & spent the winter in the lower country
& we concluded to remain during the winter. We then invited Rev.
Mr. Clark & wife, Oberlin missionaries who came out last spring on
their own responsibility, to spend the winter with us. Their company
has been a great comfort to us. They expect to leave here soon. They
are so disappointed that they will probably return home.[87] Whether
we shall remain here or leave when spring opens will depend on circumstances. We cannot tell at present. If we find in the spring that the
same determination remains on the part of those Indians, we shall
leave. But if they pretend to be ever so favorable, we cannot trust
them at all. They have no regard for their word but have lied to me
repeatedly respecting the land. As Paul says they are "covenant
breakers."

---

[87] See SS, 19ff for list of five independent missionary couples who went out to
Oregon in 1839 and 1840. Clark was a Congregational minister. After spending
the winter of 1840-41 with the Smiths at Kamiah, the Clarks moved to the Willamette Valley.

They were set on last autumn by an ugly Indian who headed an assault against Mr. Pambrun, the trader [at Fort Walla Walla] a short time before the mission was established in which Mr. P. was taken in his own fort & tied & was in danger of his life. That was an attempt for property. The same was meditated, I suppose against me. The people have behaved but a little better at the other stations. They are waxing more & more & soon, we have reason to fear, we shall be unable to live with them at all. They live without law & restraint & we cannot expect any thing very good from them. This you will perceive is a different story from what was told before we arrived but *beware* of such favorable reports of Adam's fallen race.

Yours truly,   A. B. SMITH

[Postscript] Sarah's health has been rather better this winter, tho' still poor & the difficulty in her spine is not removed. I shall write to Br. J.C. & direct home as he will be through his studies when it arrives, so you must forward it to him if he is not at home. Sarah sends love to all. The barrel is still at Vancouver. Do not send us any thing more till I write for it. We are now quiet & comfortable & you must not feel anxious about us for doubtless all things will work together for our good. The Lord's hand is in all these things. He reigns, in that I rejoice.

Addressed to Mr. Asa Smith, East Williamstown, Vermont, U.S.A., via Canada, and postmarked "Sault de St Marie, Mic. Jul 29."

FORT VANCOUVER,   June 3d, 1841

MY DEAR SISTERS.   Last week we rec'd from you all seven letters, 6 to myself & one to Sarah. The dates were as follows: Jan. 5th, March 27th, May 21st, July 26th, & 29th, & Sept. 8th to myself & Sept. 11th to Sarah. We had waited a long time for letters & were glad once more to hear from you. My last letter to Father was Feb. 19th via Canada. I have written to brother J.C. via St. Louis April 29th.[88]

Since my last to Father, Sarah's health has been very poor, as you will have learned if those letters via St. Louis arrive safe. For more than three months she has been confined almost entirely to her bed & before we left Kamiah I had begun to feel extremely anxious about

---

[88] This letter is not known to be extant. It is truly remarkable that so many of Asa's and Sarah's letters survived the hazards connected with the transmission of the mails across the continent of those days, and the vicissitudes of time. Only rarely do we come across a reference to a letter known to have been written during the years which is not extant. Here is one such instance.

her. It became necessary for us to leave our home & obtain medical
assistance & accordingly we left Kamiah April 19th in a canoe & after
staying at Walla Walla two weeks arrived here May 17th. Sarah's health
seemed to improve a little by the journey tho' she suffered somewhat
in consequence of exposure. At the portages, she was carried on a
hammack suspended to a pole & borne on the shoulders of two men.[89]
The longest portage was a mile & a quarter.

We have here an excellent English physician in whom we have
much confidence & hope to receive much benefit from him. Already
there seems to be a little amendment & I hope she may again be able
to be about the house, tho' I always expect she will be feeble & exposed
to be brought down again by a little exposure. The exposures of this
country are very unfavorable to her & I feel that it is not safe for her
to winter again in this country. She needs to be where she can enjoy
all the comforts & conveniences of civilized life & evidently she must
be differently situated from what she has been since she has been in
this country or her life will be short.

We are pleasantly situated here & have abundance of company. Two
English vessels have left since we have been here. One has come in
since we have been here & is about to sail for the Islands. An American
Brig from Salem is now lying here waiting for a cargo of salmon. The
American Squadron consisting of 4 men of war is now at or near the
mouth of the river.[90] Commodore Wilkes & Mr. Drayton are now here,
having come across by land from Nisqually. I have had a very interesting time with them. They are both friendly to missions & all improvement. Mr. D. is a pious man from Philadelphia from Mr. Barnes
church.[91] He attends to drawing. He has been very busy since he has
been in [Vancouver] in drawing fish, snails &c. He is a fine man, very
intelligent & interesting in his conversation. The Squadron is from the
Sandwich Islands direct. They have been out three years exploring in
the Pacific & are to return by Singapore. A part of the Squadron are
expected at this place soon. This gives much interest to our visit here.
We shall remain here for the present. Capt. Varney [92] expects to sail

---

[89] No more convincing description is needed to indicate Sarah's feeble strength.

[90] By an act of Congress dated May 18, 1836, an exploring expedition was
authorized to locate and survey islands of the Pacific and to explore the Northwest
Coast of America. Lieutenant Charles Wilkes, u.s.n., was given command. The
fleet of six ships sailed from the East Coast in August 1838 and was gone for four
years. Joseph Drayton was one of the artists who was attached to this expedition.

[91] Dr. Albert Barnes was a noted New School Presbyterian minister with a
church in Philadelphia, and the author of Biblical commentaries.

[92] Unidentified.

within two months & I shall write again by him which perhaps may be the vessel to take this from the Islands.

Sarah sends her love to all, is unable to write. You must not give yourselves too much anxiety about us for we are very comfortable here & find pleasant society. We have reason to be thankful that we are still alive & have so many favors.

I remain very affect. your bro.   A. B. SMITH

To Miss Laura Smith, East Williamstown, Vermont, U.S.A. Post-marked "New Bedford, Ms. Feb. 17."

CLATSOP, MOUTH OF THE COLUMBIA RIVER
Sept. 30th, 1841

MY DEAR FATHER. My last letter home was one to Sister Laura written at Vancouver June 3d which gave an account of our situation at that time, having come to that place on account of Sarah's health which had become very poor. At that time I acknowledged the receipt of several letters rec'd a short time previous. Since that time I have rec'd no letters from home except one from Mr. Green by the U.S. Ship Peacock which was wrecked the 18th of July on the bar at the mouth of the river.[93] No lives were lost but almost every thing else. Probably some of our letters were lost & perhaps other things.

We remained at Vancouver till the last of July. Doct Barclay was exceedingly kind & attentive & rendered every assistance in his power. Sarah's health improved slowly, but still remains very feeble. She is able to sit up no more than 1/3 of the day in an easy chair & can walk short distances. She sews some but it is mostly lying on her bed. By doing a little at a time she has been able to take care of ourselves thus far so that we have not suffered. I think I mentioned in my last a difficulty which I had in speaking on account of an elongation of the uvula or palate. This I have had cut off, ⅜ of an inch. It has relieved me some but still I can preach but once on a sabbath & that a short discourse. Reading aloud very soon produces such an irritation &

---

[93] The bar at the mouth of the Columbia River is now known as Peacock Bar. A party of thirty-nine, including some of the officers, men, and scientists from the "Peacock" made the overland journey from the Columbia to San Francisco Bay in September and October 1841. The author, finding the diary of Titian Peale in the Library of Congress, published it in 1957 as one of the series on Early California Travel issued by Glen Dawson of Los Angeles under the title *The Diary of Titian Ramsay Peale*. Titian Peale, a son of the famous artist, Charles Wilson Peale, was famous for his pictures of wildlife. He was one of the artists attached to the Wilkes expedition and was aboard the "Peacock" when she was wrecked and made the long march to San Francisco.

hoarseness as to render it impossible for me to proceed. I hope to be better but still I have some fears.

We have been advised on account of our health to go to the Sandwich Islands, & the last of July took passage in the Brig Thos. Perkins from Salem, but on arriving at the mouth of the river the Brig was sold to the government to take home the crew of the Peacock so that we have been detained. We expect to sail in about six weeks in one of the Company's vessels. Whether we shall remain at the Islands I know not. What instructions we shall receive from the Board, I cannot tell. Our situation in this country has been very trying. It is hard even for persons in good health, but for invalids it is severe.

We hope to be in a much more comfortable situation at the Islands & it is hoped that the climate there will be favorable. We know not what is before us, but we are reminded often that this world is not our home. We have but a little time to stay here, & did we keep this constantly in view & live as if we were "looking for a better country even a heavenly," happy should we be.

The next time I write you I expect will be from the Sandwich Islands. The passage from here is only from 3 to 4 weeks. Then we shall not be quite so much out of the world as we have been in this country.

With kind regards to all in which Sarah unites. I remain, yours very
truly,   A. B. SMITH

HONOLULU, OAHU, Feb. 3rd, 1842

MY DEAR SISTERS. You will see by the date of this that we are in a different part of the world from what we were when I wrote you last, which was Sept. 30th at the mouth of the Columbia River. We arrived here on the 25th ult. after a long & tedious passage of 35 days after leaving the river. The usual passage is only 20 or 25 days. We were on board 57 days. Three weeks we lay at the mouth of the river waiting an opportunity to cross the bar. It is a dangerous place in bad weather & vessels are sometimes detained 6 weeks before they have a smooth sea & favorable wind. We came out very smoothly at last. The three first days out we had a rough sea & a gale of wind. The next morning after getting out we began to be seasick which lasted me 3 days & Sarah some longer. However we suffered I expect much less than many from sea sickness. It is very unpleasant & I much prefer being on land. Still I found it much better than travelling across the mountains, for I could improve my mind when not sick & not too much sea, & so it was much less dissipating & injurious to one's religious feelings. Our Sabbaths we could spend in reading & meditation & the sickness & trials are profitable if rightly improved.

Sarah suffered considerably in the passage, had much pain in her spine & when we arrived here found herself rather more feeble than when we left the Columbia. Still she is much better than when we came to Vancouver, & I think the voyage will prove a benefit rather than an injury. She seems to enjoy the climate here & I think is improving slowly tho' we have not been here long enough to know what will be the effect. Still I have strong hopes that she will enjoy better health here. The difficulty in my throat still remains & gives me considerable trouble, yet I hope to be relieved in this mild atmosphere. The atmosphere is so mild & bland that it cannot irritate. The only irritation here I think is from speaking. I have preached once since I arrived in the Seamen's Chapel & since that have felt more irritation. I hope with care I may be relieved from this difficulty.

We are in Mr. Hall's family, a pleasant, lovely family. They have been in Oregon for Mrs. H's health where we became acquainted with them. Mrs. H. has a spinal difficulty but is now much better. They live in a part of the old house first built here, the frame of which was brought out from the States by the first company of missionaries. We occupy a chamber with a verandah or portico. This is winter here but the weather is warm much like our summer tho' not as hot as it is many times in the States. At this season there are occasional showers of rain. The temperature here varies very little between summer & winter. The heat is never so great as it is sometimes in the Columbia or in New England. The thermometer stands today at 78° & never rises but a few degrees above this even in the summer season.

FEB. 4th.   Since writing the above I have visited Ewa, 14 miles from this & staid over night. At Ewa, Mr. Bishop is stationed who is an able missionary & an interesting man. Mr. Hall rode out with me. The road was very muddy & the little mountain torrents much swollen, but we had an interesting & pleasant visit. Here we found Mrs. Emerson from Waialua on her way to Honolulu & she accompanied us to this place today. Missionary work assumes a different character from what it does in the Oregon. Every one has enough to do & that of direct missionary labor. Every thing seems quite interesting here & I feel that I should like to engage in the work with these brethren.

Still I would by no means convey the idea that all is gold here. There is much [apparently the last page with address is missing. The following postscript is written on the margins of the first page:]

You mentioned in one of your letters something about sending some more dried apples. Should we remain here we shall be very glad of it every year. I think of nothing else I would care about your sending. You need not send me any clothing untill I write for it. I am well supplied for the present. Do not pay out any money for articles for me unless it is something you know I need. If you have any thing to spare, I may hereafter wish to have a small sum laid out sent in books for me, but not this without my direction. The barrel of clothing I found at Vancouver & have brought it here & shall find use for it to help defray our expenses here wh. will [———?] so much help the Board. But cloth unmade is usually about as good.

Here the manuscript abruptly ends.

Hawaii and Home Again

Hawaii and Home Again

THREE YEARS IN HAWAII

Asa and Sarah Smith arrived at Fort Vancouver on May 17, 1841, where they were made welcome while waiting for passage to Honolulu. Reporting to Secretary Green, Asa said that they were "pleasantly situated" and that Dr. Forbes Barclay, who was attached to the Fort, was 'exceedingly kind & attentive." Since Asa had never called upon Dr. Whitman to minister to his wife, now at Fort Vancouver, Sarah for the first time was under the care of a qualified physician. Asa also needed the doctor's help as he was suffering from a growth of the uvula in his throat which was making it difficult for him to speak. Dr. Barclay performed the necessary operation.

On August 2nd, a couple of days after the Smiths boarded a vessel bound for Honolulu, Dr. Barclay addressed a letter to Secretary Greene in which he said: "Mrs. Smith's case is a spinal affection and that a very distressing one, more especially considering the way she has been situated, exposed to the hardships of travelling in a rugged and un-civilized country. Indeed, I am fully convinced that the health of both Mr. Smith & Mrs. Smith has evidently been much impaired by the variableness of the climate to which they have been exposed. It is my opinion as well as that of other medical gentlemen that while Mr. & Mrs. Smith remain in this country, they will be incapable of rendering any assistance to the Mission & no chance whatever of recovering their health. I have therefore advised them to repair to the Sandwich Islands or some other salubrious climate." This opinion was endorsed by Dr. A. S. Whittle, Assistant Surgeon of the U.S. Navy, who happened to be at Fort Vancouver when Dr. Barclay was writing.[1]

The lack of regular sailings between the Pacific Northwest and the Hawaiian Islands is well illustrated by the difficulty and long delay that the Smiths experienced in obtaining passage for Honolulu. Finally, after a wait of two-and-a-half months at Fort Vancouver, passage was secured on the brig "Thomas Perkins." The Smiths went aboard on

---

[1] Coll. A. Dr. Whittle was attached to the Wilkes exploring expedition.

July 31st. However, when the ship reached Astoria near the mouth of the Columbia River, she was commandeered by the United States Navy as a replacement for the "Peacock." This vessel, a part of the Pacific Exploring Expedition under the command of Lieutenant Charles Wilkes, had been wrecked on July 18th while attempting to cross the bar at the mouth of the Columbia. The Smiths had to disembark. They found accommodations in the home of the Rev. and Mrs. William W. Kone of the Methodist Mission. There they remained for nearly four months waiting for another opportunity to sail. Finally passage was secured on the bark "Columbia" which they boarded the last of November. Because of inclement weather, the ship waited another twenty-two days before attempting to cross the bar. The fate of the "Peacock" no doubt made the captain doubly cautious. A successful crossing was made on December 21st but, due to adverse weather conditions, the voyage to Honolulu took thirty-five days instead of the usual twenty to twenty-five days. As has been noted, both Asa and Sarah suffered from seasickness. Sarah, especially, found the voyage most trying. With great relief, they went ashore at Honolulu on January 25, 1842. It had taken them nearly six months to travel from Fort Vancouver to Honolulu and over nine months, including their several delays, to make the complete journey from Kamiah. Such were travel conditions back in 1841-42 in the Pacific Northwest.

The Smiths were received into the home of Mr. and Mrs. Edwin O. Hall who had spent a year in the Oregon Mission. Thus Asa and Sarah were with friends. The Halls lived in the first frame house built by the missionaries in Honolulu in 1821. Most of the lumber had been brought around South America in the "Thaddeus" which had landed the first party of missionaries in the Islands in the spring of 1820. The house is still standing with other old mission buildings on the original site on South King Street, Honolulu. In one of his letters Asa referred to the little veranda which opened off of the room they were occupying.[2] The picture of this house, reproduced in this volume, shows the veranda.

Levi Chamberlain, the secular agent of the Hawaiian Mission, was keeping a journal at the time the Smiths arrived in Honolulu.[3] On Wednesday, January 26th, the day after their arrival, Chamberlain made the following entry: "The weekly social meeting was more fully attended this evening than usual. Mr. Smith of the Oregon mission was present and gave some account of the Indians among [whom] the mis-

2 See Asa's letter to his sisters, Feb. 3, 1842, Coll. Y.
3 Original in Coll. Ha.

The Old Mission House — Oldest Frame Building in Honolulu

Erected by missionaries of the American Board in 1821. The building to the right, erected in 1823, housed the mission printing press. See text page 214.

THE LILIUOKALANI CHURCH OF HALEIWA, WAIALUA DISTRICT, OAHU

The building was still in process of construction when the Smiths arrived. Here Asa served as pastor, 1842-1845. See text pages 219-220. The building was replaced in 1890. From a painting by C. Furneaux, 1880, in the Hawaiian Mission Children's Society.

sionaries of the Board are laboring. He thinks the whole number of the Nez Perces does not exceed 2,400 and they are not as promising as they were supposed to be."

In a letter to Greene written at Honolulu on February 25th, Asa said that his wife had "suffered considerably on the passage [from Oregon] & found herself somewhat weaker on arriving here than when we embarked." He felt that the climate at Honolulu was beneficial to her health and made the following rather surprising reference to what might be the forerunner of the rickshaw [4] which later missionaries to Japan are reported to have invented: "She enjoys the benefit of a morning ride in a small carriage drawn by a native which seems to invigorate her. Still she is very feeble & can endure but little." On March 10th the mission physician, Dr. G. P. Judd [5] wrote to Secretary Greene: "The Rev. A. B. Smith and wife having been obliged to leave their missionary field in Oregon, I have freely expressed my opinion to them as I now do to you, that the health of Mrs. Smith is more likely to be benefited by a residence in this climate than by a long sea voyage and a residence in the vigorous atmosphere of the U.S." Dr. Judd recommended that the Smiths be assigned to the Hawaiian Mission. On April 4th, Chamberlain noted in his journal: "Mrs. A. B. Smith is too ill to leave home at present."

Since it was clearly evident that it was not wise for the Smiths to depart for the States, some arrangements had to be made for their residence in the Islands. About thirty miles across the island of Oahu, to the northwest of Honolulu, was the Waialua district where a thriving mission station had been established. The Rev. and Mrs. John S. Emerson settled there in 1832. During the years, 1836-37, a spiritual revival quickened the native church throughout the islands. By 1842 "over 19% of the population" were church members.[6] At that time the Sunday morning congregations at Waialua often numbered over 500. In August 1841 construction began on a new "stone and mortar" church at Waialua which measured nearly 100 feet long. The new building was dedicated in September 1843. About 1860 Queen Liliuokalani presented a large steeple clock to this church and as a result the building became known as the Liliuokalani Church. Although the original structure has been replaced in recent years by a modern building, the church now

---

[4] According to the *Encyclopedia Americana,* the rickshaw or jinrickshaw was invented by a Baptist missionary to Japan, the Rev. Jonathan Goble, in 1871.

[5] A distant cousin of Dr. Walter Judd who served as a congressman from Minnesota, 1943-62.

[6] Emerson, *Pioneer Days in Hawaii,* p. 126.

located in the community of Haleiwa in the Waialua district is still known as the Liliuokalani Church.

The Hawaiian Mission, at its annual meeting held during the latter part of May and the first two days of June 1842, voted to transfer the Emersons to Lahainaluna school on the island of Maui and assign the Smiths to Waialua. The Emerson home, built in 1834 and called Waipuolo, was made available to the Smiths. To this place Asa and Sarah moved sometime during the summer of 1842 and there they lived until shortly before they left the Islands in the fall of 1845. The mission house at Waialua provided much more comfort for the Smiths than they had ever experienced during their residence in Oregon. Gradually Sarah's health was restored, although there were times in 1843 when she was very sick. In his 1843 report to the Hawaiian Mission, Asa wrote: "Mrs. Smith has at times been very low & feeble & ready to give up all hope, but she is at present in quite as good health as she was a year ago. Still she is feeble & has the prospect of remaining so." [7] By 1844 Sarah was able to ride horseback again.

ECHOES FROM OREGON

Several members of the Oregon Mission are known to have written to Smith when he was in Hawaii. Dr. Whitman wrote at least once, which letter is included in this volume. Gray seems to have been the most faithful correspondent. The 1842 annual meeting of the Oregon Mission was held at Waiilatpu May 26-June 7 when all were present except Mrs. Spalding. By that time Spalding had learned of the several letters of criticism that had been sent to the Board about him. At this meeting a full and frank discussion was held of all their difficulties. Explanations were given, apologies made, and reconciliations effected.

Writing to Chamberlain from Waialua on August 2nd, after receiving word about this meeting at Waiilatpu, Smith said:

> Yesterday I rec'd letters from the Oregon [Mission]. The difficulties in the mission they think are settled & they are anxious to see Brs. Paris & Rice & myself.[8] From my acquaintance with the

---

[7] This report and all letters from Smith dealing with business within the Hawaiian Mission from which quotations are taken in this chapter are in Coll. Ha.

[8] In November 1840, the American Board sent two more couples to the Oregon Mission — the Rev. and Mrs. J. D. Paris and Mr. and Mrs. W. H. Rice. They went by sea. When they arrived in Honolulu on May 21, 1841, they were detained there because of the discouraging reports of conditions within the Oregon Mission. Evidently someone in the Oregon Mission had written to Smith suggesting that the time might be opportune for the 1840 reenforcement to continue on to Oregon and even for the Smiths to return.

members of the mission, I have some fears that matters will not remain settled. Still things may be different from what things have been heretofore. . . As for myself, I see not why I should leave a field of 5,000 for one of 300 even if we were in a situation to go. But with Mrs. Smith's feeble health, I cannot feel it our duty to return. It is as much as we can endure here where we have far more comforts & she can get along with much less trial & care & fatigue.

Then in the following paragraph, Smith threw some new light upon the Spaldings, especially Eliza, when he wrote: "It seems that they have settled all the old difficulties & are hoisting sail to start anew. I hope they may remain settled, but as to that I have my fears. It seems that Mrs. Spalding was not present at the meeting when the settlement took place. Instances have occurred before when he [i.e., Henry Spalding] has been very easily managed alone but when with his wife, very difficult."

Incidentally, Smith reported in this letter that "The meeting house is coming on slowly. The plastering will be completed I hope next week." He also added: "I am hardly prepared to purchase a carriage for Mrs. Smith at $60.00. It would draw very heavily on the remainder of our present year's allowance."

Two copies of the Board's order of February 1842, which called for the dismissal of Spalding and the closing of the stations at Waiilatpu and Lapwai, were sent to Oregon. One was carried overland by Dr. Elijah White. This copy reached Dr. Whitman on September 9, 1842. A second copy was sent by sea. Whitman, knowing that the Board's correspondence would be channeled through Chamberlain's office in Honolulu, wrote to him suggesting that the Board's letter be kept from Smith's eyes.[9] Whitman's letter, however, arrived too late. Since Greene's letter was addressed in general to the members of the Oregon Mission, Smith had taken the liberty to open and read it. This is the background of the following letter which Smith wrote to Chamberlain on November 29, 1842:

The news from the Oregon [Mission] is just what I expected. I am not at all disappointed. Knowing the man [i.e., Spalding] as well as I did, it was not difficult to prophesy what would be the result. But as to the Doct's fears respecting my seeing the letter, he has shot wide of his mark this time. I should have supposed

9 The original Whitman letter was not located. The existence of such a letter is based on Smith's letter to Chamberlain.

that he had been well enough acquainted with me to know that I should not turn quite so easy as a weather-cock towards Oregon again.[10] His precautions were wholly useless. But poor man, he is in a peck of trouble & knows not what to do & the general letter will come on him like a thunder-clap. I wish he had a little more decision to enable him go through with the work assigned him in a proper manner.

Knowing that the order also called for the dismissal of Gray, Smith made the following surprising suggestion: "As for Mr. Gray, I know not what he will do; if he were in this mission he might be made use of. He might supply the place of a physician at such a place as Hilo for instance & would be quite an acquisition if a regular physician cannot be obtained. Still I am unwilling to take any responsibility in proposing such a thing."

When the astounding news reached Smith that Whitman had gone East to intercede with the Board for the cancellation of its drastic order, he again wrote to Chamberlain on December 2nd: "Oregon affairs have taken rather an unexpected turn. What the result will be I can hardly guess. But it appears to me that Doct W's excursion to the States will not be altogether pleasing to the Board. Still it may be just the thing. But what has he gone home for & what does he expect to accomplish? Is it to reconcile the Board to Mr. Spalding & obtain a reenforcement? If so, I fear he will not succeed. I hardly know what to think of the doings there. I am heartily glad that Mr. Gray has shipped out so neatly & is out of his troubles." The whole tone of the letter shows that Gray and Smith were still on friendly terms and no doubt it was Gray who was keeping Smith informed of developments.

The following letter from Smith to E. O. Hall dated December 28, 1843, evidently refers to a letter written by Whitman to Hall in which Whitman had reported on the success of his eastern trip.

I return the Doct's letter & I am much obliged for the perusal of it. There is more of Doct. Whitman in that letter than we usually get in one sheet. He was evidently in more than a usual fluster. I expect he is going to turn settler in Oregon. As to the mission & Spalding, I hardly know what to think. How the Board can return him after all they know about him, I do not see. All that the Doct's visit has amounted to so far as I am able to see is to get Spalding safely fixed again in his nest. But they must take care of their own concerns. I am thankful that I am out of it.[11]

---

[10] Perhaps Smith's correspondent in Oregon had suggested that since Spalding had been dismissed, Smith would want to return. Evidently Whitman was fearful of this possibility.

As will be noted in Whitman's letter to Smith of May 1844, Whitman wrote of his interest in obtaining Christian settlers for Oregon but discreetly made no comment regarding Spalding. The Board's cancellation of its order of February 1842 and the harmonious relationships which existed within the Oregon Mission after the crisis of 1842 must have been an unending cause of wonderment to Smith. How were such things possible? Was he able to appreciate the fact that he himself was the cause of much of the difficulty and that when he was gone, things were bound to be different?

AGAIN IN TROUBLE WITH HIS ASSOCIATES

Asa Smith was unfortunate in that he possessed personality traits which were always getting him into trouble with his associates. Such was his experience in the Oregon Mission and such likewise marred his service in Hawaii. When the Smiths moved to Waialua, they found that Mr. and Mrs. Edwin Locke and their three little girls were also living there. Locke was in charge of the school which had both a boarding and a manual training department. Mrs. Locke died on October 9, 1842, and about a year later, or on October 28, 1843, Edwin Locke died.[12] The Smiths took the three girls — Lucy, Martha, and Mary — into their home and cared for them.

The Mission appointed Mr. Abner Wilcox to take over the principalship of the school at Waialua left vacant by Edwin Locke's death. Within a year serious difficulties arose between Smith and Wilcox. Smith had but an imperfect knowledge of the Hawaiian language. Wilcox, on the other hand, was at ease in it and in addition to his school duties had carried on some religious instruction for the adult natives. Smith was offended. He accused Wilcox of intruding upon the rights and privileges which by Congregational polity belonged to him as the pastor of the church. There were other points of friction which also arose out of Smith's supersensitivity to his ecclesiastic rights.

---

[11] This letter of Whitman's likewise could not be located. The tone of Whitman's letter to Hall, as reflected in Smith's comments, is much the same as that found in Whitman's letter to Smith which is given in a subsequent section of this volume.

[12] The Lockes lie buried in the old Mission cemetery next to the Kawaiahao Church, sometimes called the "Westminster Abbey of Hawaii." The author visited their graves on April 8, 1965. A census of the birthplaces of the missionaries who lie buried there gave the following statistics: from New Hampshire-2; Massachusetts-5; Connecticut-4; New York-3; and Pennsylvania-3. For the most part these missionaries of the American Board who joined the crusade to evangelize the natives of the Hawaiian Islands and who literally gave their lives for this cause were New Englanders.

The situation at Waialua became so distressing that the Mission delegated two of its members — Rev. Richard Armstrong and Rev. Artemas Bishop — to visit the station and see what could be done to correct the situation. In spite of all efforts to work out an amicable settlement, tensions between Smith and Wilcox continued. Smith's mental attitude was adversely affected by recurring ill health including throat trouble. He was not as effective in his work with the natives as his predecessor, John S. Emerson, had been. His Sunday congregations had declined until, according to his annual report for 1843, they numbered between 160 and 200. Disciplinary cases increased, and forty-one natives were excommunicated, according to this same report. Added to the difficulties of health and problems arising on the field, Asa learned in the first part of 1845 of the death of his father on the preceding December 14, 1844. The combination of such problems and discouragements made him think of returning to the States.

On May 28, 1845, Armstrong wrote to Smith and after making reference to the official visitation to Waialua authorized by the Mission, he commented: "Then you talked strongly of going to America. . . You said repeatedly during that visit & said it with emphasis that your work at Waialua was done, that you could do no more. Your health was very poor." Regarding Smith's attitude to Wilcox, Armstrong wrote: "You were inflexible, though no doubt conscientious in the course you pursued. Mr. W. did consent to drop the whole affair & be reconciled, this being rejected . . . you ought to have yielded & been reconciled." [13]

In this letter Armstrong frankly stated his belief that the Smiths should return to the States, if for no other reason than that of the health of both of them. He then penned the following frank analysis of Smith's qualifications to be a missionary: "Upon your own admission and according to the opinions of your brethren generally, you are vastly better adapted to be useful among your own countrymen than among Hawaiians. I believe you are generally regarded among us as a good brother, a good scholar, would make with health a useful minister among your own countrymen, *but you are not calculated to be so useful or happy among natives. It seems to me I heard you say that you discovered that you were not adapted to mission life before you reached Oregon.*" [14]

---

[13] Original in Coll. Ha.

[14] Editorial italics. Evidence indicates that Armstrong was correct in his judgment. Neither in Oregon nor in Hawaii was Smith as effective in his work with the

Shortly after receipt of this letter, Smith informed his brethren of his desire to resign his work at Waialua and return to the States. The Mission accepted his resignation and reassigned the Emersons to their former work at Waialua.

RETURN TO THE STATES AND CLOSING YEARS

The Hawaiian Mission Children's Society has in its collection a document dated October 13, 1845, which shows that the Mission paid the captain of the "Leland," *"Eight Hundred Dollars* in full for the passage of the Rev. Asa S. Smith and wife and three children of the late Mr. Locke . . . from the Port of Honolulu . . . to the Port of New York . . . via China." The "Leland" with her passengers sailed from Honolulu on October 15th. She dropped anchor in the harbor of Victoria, Hongkong, on November 18th.[15] She sailed from Hongkong on January 21, 1846, and after fifty days arrived at Cape Town, South Africa. After encircling the globe, being the only ones attached to the Oregon Mission to do so, Asa and Sarah Smith with the three Locke girls arrived in New York on May 4, 1846. After an absence of more than eight years, the Smiths were back in their native land, a development they had not anticipated when they left for Oregon in the spring of 1838.

On July 20th Smith wrote to the American Board requesting that his connection with the Board be terminated. "It was my intention & expectation to have remained in the service of the Board for life," he explained, "but Providence now clearly indicates that such is not my duty. It has been with much sacrifice of feeling on my part that I have been obliged to abandon the object to which I had devoted my life." Smith added: "As yet I have found no opening for me where I can obtain the means of support" and requested that the Board grant $75.00 a year for the support of the Locke children. It is not known if this grant was made. The American Board, acting on Smith's request, officially cancelled his appointment on August 11, 1846.

Asa and Sarah, naturally after so long an absence, spent some weeks visiting relatives and friends. Asa's brother-in-law, Ira Tracy, writing from Hudson, Ohio, on May 21, 1846, warned him not to dwell on his troubles while at "Father White's" as "it would probably be easy to talk him into excitement, & bitterness, & misery & that without telling

natives as were some of his associates. Smith was too impatient for results and had no liking for the natives, either Indian or Hawaiian.

[15] A twenty-four page manuscript of notes and observations made on this voyage by Smith is in Coll. A.

him any thing but what is true." [16] The letter implies that both of Sarah's parents were still alive. Undoubtedly Asa and Sarah then went to Vermont to see his mother and other members of his family.

There was some delay before Asa was able to find a church. Information is lacking regarding what he was able to do in the interval to support himself and his family. He accepted a call to a Congregational church in South Amherst, Massachusetts, in November 1846 where he remained for a little more than a year. He was then invited to the pulpit of the First Congregational Church of Buckland, Massachusetts, where his ministry began on March 22, 1848. Here Sarah found her greatest happiness during her married life. After eight years of traveling and living in such isolated places as Kamiah and Waialua, she was with her own people again. Shortly after their arrival back in New England, the Smiths took the necessary legal steps to adopt the two older Locke girls, Lucy and Martha.[17] Mary, the youngest, was adopted by relatives on her mother's side. In 1850 Asa and Sarah received into their home two little boys, ages six and four, who were orphaned by the death of Asa's sister, Marcia. With four children in the home, life took on deeper meaning and greater responsibilities for both Asa and Sarah.

In an undated letter to her sister Roxana, written from Buckland, Sarah commented: "I love this place. It would, methinks, be a sweet place to die in." [18] Her wish came true for there the end came on May 27, 1855, when she was only forty-one years old. According to the memorial sketch of her life, she died "of consumption." She was buried in the church cemetery. Surely no other American missionary woman of her generation had traveled so far and had endured so much physical hardship with so frail a human body. Her Polyglott Bible, which had been printed in Concord, New Hampshire, in 1836, and which bore her maiden name, "Sarah G. White," stamped on the cover, was given to the Hawaiian Mission Children's Society in 1931 by her niece, Miss Alice J. White.[19]

---

[16] Original in Coll. Y.

[17] Included in the Asa B. Smith correspondence in Coll. Y. is a letter from William Locke, a brother of the deceased Edwin Locke, dated July 3, 1846, giving his approval of the Smith's desire to adopt two of the Locke girls.

[18] Hodge, *Memorial Sketches.*

[19] The title "Polyglott" refers to the fact that this edition contained two English versions of the Bible. Since the pages measure only 3½ x 5¾ inches, of necessity the type is small. A person needs good eyesight to read the text without the aid of glasses. It may be assumed that Sarah carried this Bible with her across the continent and to Hawaii.

A year or so after Sarah's death, Asa married Miss Harriet E. Nutting thus providing a stepmother for his four children. Asa's eleven-year pastorate in Buckland was terminated by an unhappy controversy with some of his parishioners. The dispute was referred to a Congregational ecclesiastical council which met at Buckland on May 17, 1859. Although Asa was exonorated from the charges made, the council recommended that he resign his parish. Pastoral relationships were dissolved on August 1, 1859.[20]

From 1860 to 1871, Asa had another eleven-year ministry as pastor of a Congregational church at Southbury, Connecticut. He and his wife then moved to Rocky Hill, Connecticut, "where he bought himself a home with a view of supplying different churches in that region." [21] Asa lived to see some of the prophecies made by Samuel Parker and Henry H. Spalding regarding the development of the Oregon country come true. When the first transcontinental railroad was completed in 1869, did he then remember how he had ridiculed such a proposal back in the years when he was a missionary in Oregon? In a letter to Greene dated September 3, 1840, he had said that any one who suggested the possibility of a railroad crossing the Rockies "must be strongly beside himself to make such a remark.[22]

There can be no doubt but that Smith kept informed about developments in the Oregon Mission through the pages of the *Missionary Herald* and perhaps from correspondence with Gray. With the departure of the Smiths and the Grays, peace reigned within the Mission but after the arrival of the first great immigration in the fall of 1843, there was increasing suspicion and hostility from the natives. This came to a dramatic and tragic climax on November 29-31, 1847, when Dr. and Mrs. Whitman and twelve others lost their lives. This brought the Oregon Mission of the American Board to a sudden end. News of the massacre was received in St. Louis on the following May 17th. The Eells, the Walkers, and the Spaldings escaped and moved to the Willamette Valley. No record has been discovered which tells of the reactions of Asa and Sarah Smith to this dreadful news. It is easy to imagine that they were deeply stirred by it.

In the fall of 1871 Spalding returned to Lapwai as a missionary of the Presbyterian Board of Foreign Missions. Associated with him was the Rev. Henry T. Cowley who was sent to open a school at Kamiah.

---

[20] The original minutes of this council is in Coll. Y.
[21] Hodge, *op. cit.*   [22] SS, 159.

Under the leadership of these two, a great revival swept through the
Nez Perce and Spokane tribes which resulted in the baptism of about
one thousand and the establishment of several churches for the natives
which continue to this day. Smith must have been amazed when he
read the accounts of this revival. His old teacher, Lawyer, was among
the converts and when the First Presbyterian Church of Kamiah was
organized on Christmas day, 1871, Lawyer was set apart as the first
elder. Also among the converts was Tack-en-su-a-tis, also known as
Rotten Belly, who when baptized was given the new name of Samuel
by Spalding.[23] Among those who followed Spalding in the work among
the Nez Perces was Miss Sue McBeth who arrived in Lapwai in the
fall of 1873 and who settled in Kamiah a year later. There in Kamiah
she began a theological class in her modest home which had been built
very near the place where Asa and Sarah Smith had their humble
dwelling. Out of that one-woman faculty "theological seminary" came
ten Nez Perces who were ordained to the Presbyterian ministry during
the years 1879-94.[24]

One of these native pastors was James Hines who remembered how
as a boy he "rode one of Mr. Smith's four horses when he began to
plow." He also recalled helping to take care of the Smith's cow.[25] Another of the ordained Nez Perces was Archie Lawyer, son of Chief
Lawyer. Even though Asa and Sarah were unable to see much evidence
of Christianity taking root among the Nez Perces at Kamiah during
the short time they lived there, yet in the fullness of time the seed
planted took root and bore fruit.

The last letter written by Asa Smith extant is one dated from Rocky
Hill, Connecticut, March 10, 1882, and was directed to Miss Kate
McBeth, who became associated with her sister Sue in the Nez Perce
field in 1879. In this letter, he made the following inquiry:

> Please inform me in regard to your work — to what extent this
> has been carried in the native language & what has been done in
> instructing them in the English language. Those whom I knew as
> children 40 years ago are now the men and women you have to do

[23] Drury, *Spalding*, 402. The name of Tack-en-su-a-tis is the second on the
census list of leaders of the various Nez Perce bands. See illustration, p. 181. See
also, Drury, *A Tepee*, 53.

[24] Drury, *A Tepee*, 127, gives a picture of the ten ordained Nez Perce ministers
who received their training from Miss Sue L. McBeth during the years 1873-1893.
Included are Archie Lawyer and James Hines. The training received in this school
met the needs of that generation but would not be acceptable to Presbyterian
standards of today.

[25] McBeth, *The Nez Perces Since Lewis and Clark*, 60 and 158.

with. James, the Lawyer's son, I well remember as a little fellow practising with his little bow & arrow in his father's lodge. I am glad to hear that he is now a useful man & also in regard to others mentioned by Mr. D[iffenbaugh] who said that they remember me. Please remember me kindly to them & also to Ims-tom-wai-kim if he still lives & the Lawyer's wife also if still living.[26]

No doubt Asa was here refering to Utes-sen-ma-le-kin, one of the ring-leaders who had ordered him and his wife to leave Kamiah in the fall of 1840. There was a Utes-sen-ma-le-kin who was a member of a Nez Perce delegation of four chiefs who visited Washington, D.C., in 1867 and who died there of typhoid fever on May 25, 1868.[27]

Smith's letter suggests that he had mellowed in his old age. Kate McBeth in her *The Nez Perces Since Lewis and Clark* commented: "Mr. Smith must have been a man of a good spirit, for more than twenty [should be forty] years afterwards he wrote, inquiring in the kindest way after some of the leaders of that trouble. With heads bowed, and shame-covered faces, they heard of his inquiries." [28]

Asa and Harriet went to Sherwood, Tennessee, in 1883 to visit relatives. While there Asa was invited to organize a Congregational church, which was effected in January 1884, and to serve as pastor. There he remained until his death from pneumonia on February 10, 1886, in his 74th year. An obituary notice which appeared in the March 11th issue of the *Religious Herald* of Connecticut reported: "He was a man of marked sincerity of purpose and consistency of effort. He never lost the missionary spirit with which he began. Sound in the faith, scholarly, conscientious, he put everything upon the altar of personal consecration to Christ."

Smith's body was taken back to Buckland, Massachusetts, where it was laid beside that of Sarah's. Today a modest monument marks their resting place.

---

[26] See Drury, SS, 221, for full text of this letter. The Rev. George L. Diffenbaugh was one of the missionaries associated with Sue McBeth in the Nez Perce field.

[27] See fn. 77, Smith letters.   [28] McBeth, *op. cit.*, 61.

Journal of William Henry Gray
May 24 to July 10, 1838

Journal of William Henry Gray

INTRODUCTION

William Henry Gray was born at Fairfield, New York, on September 8, 1810. His father died when he was sixteen years old and about that time he was apprenticed to a cabinetmaker in Springfield, New York, with whom he remained until he reached his majority in 1831. Gray's education was limited. After attending the grammar schools, he spent six months in the Oneida Industrial Institute at Whitesboro, New York, where his teachers remembered him as being "an extremely dull scholar." As a cabinetmaker, Gray seems to have possessed some ability but he was ambitious and aspired to be a doctor. In the fall of 1835, he "commenced reading with a practising physician" in Utica who likewise found him to be very dull.[1]

JOINS THE WHITMAN-SPALDING PARTY, 1836

When Dr. Whitman returned to his home at Rushville, New York, after his exploring trip to the Rockies in the summer of 1835, he began an active search for associates to go with him to Oregon in 1836. Secretary Greene suggested that he get in touch with the Rev. Chauncey Eddy of Utica who was then serving as a field agent of the American Board. Whitman wrote to Eddy in the early part of 1836 asking if he knew of anyone who might be willing to go as a missionary to Oregon. It so happened that Eddy and Gray were boarding at the same place and that Eddy had been favorably impressed with Gray. William Gray had a brother, John, who was pastor of the Presbyterian Church at Southport, New York. John had been in correspondence with Eddy about his brother and was seeking Eddy's influence to get William to study for the ministry. Although William was a member of the Presbyterian Church and active in its work, he was not interested in being a minister. Rather he then wanted to be a doctor.

On February 15, 1836, shortly after Eddy had received a letter from

---

[1] These comments on Gray's qualifications are taken from letters sent by those who knew him to the American Board at the time of his application for an appointment. Coll. A.

Whitman, Eddy talked with Gray about the possibility of going to Oregon with Whitman. The time was then very short. The Spaldings were already on their way to Cincinnati. Marcus and Narcissa were to be married on the 18th of that month and would then start for Oregon. And yet on this extremely short notice an associate was being selected with little or no investigation by the Board as to his fitness. On February 17th both Eddy and Gray wrote to the Board. Gray said that he was ready to go on two days' notice, "or less if necessary."

In addition to the letters from Gray and Eddy, the files of the American Board contain only one other letter regarding Gray before he was appointed to go out with the Whitmans and Spaldings. This was from Gray's pastor, the Rev. Ira Pettibone, and was dated simply "Feb. 1836." The letter was also signed by two of the elders of the church. Among the statements made were the following: "We think him possessed of ardent piety, such as fills his heart with a strong desire to do good. He has a tolerable share of what may be called common sense; though not as much acquaintance with human nature as many young men of his age. He evinces an unusual share of perseverance; and a confidence in his own abilities to a fault, yet this very confidence often gains him success in an enterprise where one of greater talents and less confidence might fail. . . His literary acquisitions are slender owing to the fact that he is a slow scholar. . . He is a skillful mechanic; a cabinet maker, but would readily turn his hand to almost any kind of work in wood that would be useful to the Mission. He has good health and a firm constitution."

Pettibone closed with the following warning which the Board would have done well to have heeded: "Brother Gray has by no means the qualifications that we think desirable for such a station." He added, however, the following comment: "But perhaps as many [qualifications] are combined in him as in any young man of our acquaintance who is willing to go." Feeling the urgent need of sending at least one layman with the Whitman-Spalding party and since no one else had applied, the Board appointed Gray to the Oregon Mission sometime during the latter part of February or the first part of March. Gray left soon after he received word of this action and caught up with the Whitmans and the Spaldings at Liberty, Missouri, on April 19th. In a letter to Whitman dated March 9th, Greene said regarding Gray: "He is highly recommended, and we hope that he will make a valuable assistant." There is no question about the importance of the assistance Gray was able to render to the Whitmans and the Spaldings during *their journey to Oregon and during the fall months when they were establishing their stations at Waiilatpu and Lapwai.*

RETURNS FOR REENFORCEMENTS

Before the winter of 1836-37 had passed, Gray became restless and unhappy. He was not content to continue as a laborer. He dreamed of being in charge of a mission station of his own. Moreover he had become engaged to a young lady, whose name is not known, before he started for Oregon and he wanted to get married. Gray got the idea of taking a small band of horses to the States, selling them in Missouri and then with the money buying cattle and sheep which could be driven back to Oregon. Horses could then be purchased in Oregon at prices varying from $8.00 to $14.00 apiece.[2] Without seeking any formal vote of the Mission, although he did discuss the project with Spalding, Gray started back to the States in the spring of 1837 with four Indian companions and a band of fourteen horses. He was at the 1837 Rendezvous during the latter part of June. Here one of his Indians turned back. Although warned by such experienced mountain men as Jim Bridger, the headstrong Gray started out for the States in advance of the returning caravan. He was attacked on August 7th by the Sioux Indians at Ash Hollow, in what is now western Nebraska. His Indian companions were killed and his horses stolen. Gray narrowly escaped being killed when a bullet went through his hat leaving only a superficial scalp wound. Writing to Greene from St. Louis on September 15th, Gray gave an account of the incident. He put in a claim to the Government for $2,096.45 but there is no evidence that such was ever paid.

The American Board, although displeased with Gray's unauthorized return to the States, was impressed with his glowing reports of the reception given the missionaries by the natives and of the prospects for the future. Two questions in particular seem to have been raised. First, was it feasible to send another party with women overland to Oregon? And secondly, what would be the costs? Gray strongly recommended sending the reenforcement, including women, by land rather than by sea. In his letter of November 11, 1837, to the Board, he said: "Dr. W. & Mr. S. both advise associates to cross the Mountains." In view of the fact that Spalding had written to Greene from the Rendezvous of 1836 strongly advising the Board never again to send women

---

[2] The Cayuse Indians, among whom the Whitmans lived, were rich in horses. They had a type of horse still known as the Cayuse pony.

overland, it seems that Gray was presuming too much when he claimed that Spalding favored sending women by this route.

In his eagerness to persuade the Board to send out a reenforcement and knowing that costs were of primary consideration, Gray was much too sanguine in his estimates. The total cost of sending the five members of the Whitman-Spalding party to Oregon, including the amounts paid for livestock, was $3,063.00. Gray may not have known this figure but the Board certainly did. Writing to the Board on this subject on November 22, 1837, he itemized the basic necessities as follows:

First, say each person wants one horse, saddle and bridle — which will cost say for the horse $50, saddle & bridle $20. Two blankets at 4 dollars each, $8. Every male of the company should carry a good gun which in fact we are required to do in traveling with any Mountain Company. If they have to purchase, it will cost from 20 to 22 dollars. Then to pack his provisions & luggage, he wants a second horse, or mule which is the best, $50 or $55; for saddle and halter, $6; for provisions say $25. Add to this amount say $15.00 for ammunition and Indian articles such as awls, knives & articles to purchase moccasins of the Indians as he may want.

According to these figures, the cost per couple would be about $350.00 including $35.00 for the gun and ammunition. In addition would be the cost of cattle, including fresh milch cows, and traveling expenses for each couple to the frontier. Gray estimated that cattle could be purchased for $20.00 each. All luggage except that which was needed for the overland journey was to be sent to Oregon by sea. In a letter to Greene dated March 1, 1838, Gray claimed that it would be easier for him to take a party of ten to Oregon for $3,000 than it would be to take three for $1,500.[3] He wrote: "We must either start with associates enough to help ourselves along or we must hire some men (as we did last year) to help us along."

Thus Gray committed himself to a policy of strict economy which he felt obliged to maintain even after his associates in the reenforcement of 1838 objected. Smith especially felt that the burden of physical labor which fell upon the members of the party was much more than should have been expected of them.[4]

Accepting the reassurances from Gray regarding the feasibility of sending more women overland and the low costs, the Board began to

---

[3] See Gray's financial report which follows. Actually the cost of taking the 1838 reenforcement to Oregon was $3,186.15¼ which compares favorably with the $3,063.00 paid for the party of five in 1836.

[4] See Smith's letter to Greene, July 10, 1838, from the Rendezvous. SS, 71.

make plans to send out a reenforcement in 1838 under his leadership. Early in December 1837 the Board asked both Elkanah Walker and Cushing Eells, who had been under appointment to go to South Africa, whether they and their fiancées would be willing to have their destination changed. All indicated that they would. Gray spent some sixteen weeks during the winter of 1837-38 at the College of Physicians and Surgeons, Fairfield, Massachusetts, and although he did not qualify for the M.D. degree, yet he assumed the title "Doctor" until the reenforcement arrived at Waiilatpu in the fall of 1838 when Dr. Whitman set matters straight.

When Gray called upon his fiancée upon his return from Oregon, her mother took one look at the two bullet holes in his hat and promptly terminated her daughter's engagement. In his letter of January 16, 1838, to Greene, Gray said: 'I am willing to return without a companion if it is thought best.' On the evening of February 14th, while attending a church social in Ithaca, New York, he met Miss Mary Augusta Dix. There is reason to believe that the Rev. Samuel Parker,[5] who had gone out to the Rockies in the summer of 1835 and who had but shortly before returned from his tour of the Oregon country, introduced them to each other. As far as William was concerned, it was love at first sight. He was eager to take a wife with him back to Oregon and there was no time to lose. A family tradition states that he proposed to Mary the night he first met her and that she, taken by surprise, pled for time to make her decision. William pressed his suit with such ardor that she accepted on February 20th, six days later. They were married on Sunday evening, February 25th, and left the next day for Oregon via Washington, D.C. Gray found it advisable to visit Washington in order to follow up his claim for reimbursement for losses suffered at the hands of the Sioux. While in the capital city, he picked up the passports for himself, the Walkers, and the Eells. He then knew nothing about the possible appointment of Asa Smith.

GRAY'S REPORT FROM THE 1838 RENDEZVOUS

The history of the overland journey of the 1838 reenforcement to Oregon would be incomplete without reference to Gray's letter

---

[5] Samuel Parker published his *Journal of an Exploring Tour Beyond the Rocky Mountains* in 1838 after the reenforcement had started for Oregon. Gray took proof sheets of Parker's book with him to Oregon. Whitman, in his letter to Greene of May 10, 1839 (original in Coll. A), took strong exception to some of Parker's statements. There is no reference to Parker's writings or to his map by any member of the 1838 reenforcement.

*written from the Rendezvous on Wind River, July 10, 1838, his journal
of their travel experiences, and his expense account. While at the Rendezvous, Gray had opportunity to talk with Jason Lee who was on his
way East for reenforcements for the Methodist Mission. Lee was carrying a letter from Spalding and Whitman dated April 21, 1838, addressed to the American Board. While en route to the Rendezvous,
Lee had visited Spalding and Whitman and had given them such a
glowing account of the Methodist work in the Willamette Valley and
of what he expected the Methodist Church would do, that he fired
their imaginations. They, too, dreamed big dreams. Thus inspired,
Spalding sent to Greene the following astonishing request:*

> To occupy these fields immediately, we ask as the least possible
> number which God & our consciences will admit us to name, for
> 30 ordained missionaries, 30 farmers, 30 school teachers, 10 physi-
> cians & 10 mechanics, with their wives. *This meant a total of 220
> additional workers! Whitman signed this letter which Spalding
> had written, and then added a request for* several tons of iron and
> steel . . . 2,000 gun flints, fifty gross Indian awls, 100 dozen
> scalping knives . . . two best cook stoves, six box stoves. .

*We can only imagine what Greene must have felt when he read this
joint communication. The most sensible request in Whitman's long list
was for the cook stoves, as both Mrs. Whitman and Mrs. Spalding were
cooking over open fires. Later Whitman regretted that he had joined
in this request for 220 additional workers and supplies in proportion
and was inclined to blame the extravagant nature of the requests on
Spalding.*

*Lee showed to Gray this joint letter of Spalding and Whitman. It
appears that even Gray was surprised. In his letter of July 10th to
Greene, he commented:*

> We have read the joint report of his [i.e., Spalding's] and Dr.
> Whitman which was placed in the hands of Rev. Mr. Lee. I can
> realize the situation in which Mr. Spalding and Whitman are
> now. . . Not that I would agree with the full report — as I
> find it, for were I permitted to express my own feelings now in
> reference to it, they are that they were somewhat premature in
> forwarding it, at least till they had heard something farther from
> yourself or from me. . .
>
> I agree with them in asking for laymen, farmers and mechanics
> — a greater proportion of them will diminish the expense of every
> Mission where they are sent — had you sent with us this year one
> clergyman and two Mechanics or Farmers, our expenses would

still have been less. Not but we want Clergymen, but I firmly believe that the influence of one and the action of three laymen
would have been and will be in the fields to which they go ten
times as much as the influence of the whole three on the ground.

*Here no doubt Gray was right. Actually, when established in their
respective stations, the three clergymen of the 1838 reenforcement
found that most of their time was spent in manual labor, in farming,
in taking care of their livestock, and in the multitude of chores necessary just to live in the undeveloped and uncultivated wilderness. Gray's
argument continues:*

"It is my Dear Sir action that tells. . . *Preaching the word is of
vital importance to the salvation of sinners, but my Dear Sir, has not
your experience* . . . *told you that preaching to the wild Natives
is of little service so long as they have no instruction in the first principles of Civilization?* . . . *To do the Natives permanent good, we
must put into their hands the means of becoming civilized.*" [6] *This was
the conviction of both Whitman and Spalding. Before the Indians
could be evangelized, they first had to be settled. And before they
could be settled they had to be given the tools of agriculture and
shown how to make the earth produce their food. This is the theme of
the recently discovered Whitman letter which is to be found in another
chapter of this volume.*

Gray's letter contains some references to Smith:

One point I would mention in reference to associates. It is, that
they all be cautioned about manifesting a stingy, selfish spirit.
There is perhaps no other cause that will so quickly close every
door of usefulness and shut the fountain of generosity as the mani-
festation of this spirit by one of the persons sent by the Board.
It will not answer for us to stand for small matters in . . .
the business we must necessarily transact with the Gentlemen of
the [Fur] Company. *Gray added a postscript to his letter in
which he asked:* Please inform me in your next letter whether
you told Mr. Smith while in N. York that he would be furnished
with a separate tent, travelling cases, cooking utensils &c., &c. for
the journey or what suggestion you made to him on the subject
of traveling from Independence to Walla Walla.[7]

In regard to expenses, Gray explained that "Our animals have cost

---

[6] Here Gray was touching on the basic philosophy of how to evangelize a tribe
of uncivilized Indians. Was it possible to Christianize them before they were first
civilized? See *ante,* p. 112 for Smith's views. Also, SS, 98.

[7] No answer was discovered by the author to this inquiry.

*us nearly fifty percent more than those we purchased two years ago.
Cattle we could hardly purchase at any price." And here again he referred to Smith. "There is an item of unnecessary expense in our list
which you will notice in the bill of medicine. I brought with me from
Cincinnati all the medicines necessary for the Company, in fact I took
twice as much as I thought necessary and remarked to Dr. Weed that
I had enough to supply the whole Fur Company with our own. When
Mr. Smith came on he was supplied with more than double the quantity
to the amount of $22.75, when six or ten dollars worth would have been
an abundance. We now have $30 dollars worth." Smith was no doubt
totally unaware of any interest that Gray had in medicine and since he
had pursued his medical studies with the hope that such knowledge
would be useful to him on a mission field, it was perfectly natural for
him to obtain a supply of drugs.*

*As has been noted, Smith was also writing to members of his family
and to Secretary Greene from the Rendezvous in which letters he was
far more critical of Gray than Gray had been of him.[8]*

*Gray appended to his letter to Greene the following brief journal of
their travel experiences. The author made a transcription from the
original document which was published in the July 1938 issue of the
Pacific Northwest Quarterly. This transcription follows, with some cor-
rections made of Gray's spelling, punctuation, and grammar. Gray
made no references to the other members of the party. His primary
concern was to report daily progress. For the most part his account
harmonizes with those of his companions. Gray sometimes added new
facts of interest as, for instance, when he wrote about the murder of
Dr. Satterlee, an American Board missionary to the Pawnee Indians.[9]*

GRAY'S JOURNAL OF 1838

You are sufficiently acquainted with Independence and its location,
so that I will not say any thing about it. You will have in mind that it
is about 12 miles East from the frontier town called West Port — laying
about 4 miles from the Mo. River. We left Independence on the 21st
of April & proceeded as far as West Port where we remained till Monday 23rd. The Fur Co. started on Sabbath 22nd. We arranged our baggage, etc., putting the whole, except a few dishes which we put into a
one horse wagon, upon our mules, and started about 12 O'Clock M. We

---

[8] See *ante*, Smith to his family, July 6, 1838, and SS, 70ff for the full text of
Smith's letter to Greene of July 10, 1838.

[9] See Gray's entry for May 21st, and fn. 39 of Sarah Smith's diary.

proceeded about three miles and came into the open prairie. Proceeding about 5 miles, we stopped at the first place of encampment called the Sapling Grove, 8 miles from West Port. This encampment receiving its name from a few scattered trees lining the water course running N. West into the Big Blue. The Prairies high and undulating & rich alluvial soil. Timber on the water courses in small quantities, since rock deep beneath the surface.

24th. We proceeded 25 miles over the same discription of country as on the 23, onto a little stream called Brush Creek, named properly for we found only brush & willows on it, stoping a rest time to bait [to feed] our animals, or to noon as the camp term is, in the middle of the day — The term Noon means when we stop to bait and get our dinner sometimes 9 AM, 2 PM, or 3 O'Clock as may be or wherever we make two camps a day, one is noon let it be what hour it may.

25th. We proceeded onto a beautiful stream called the Wakorousah from a root found in abundance on its banks made use of for food by the Natives — 20 miles, about 8 miles before we reached this stream, we found the Lime Rock laying over the surface. Along most of the streams, with some exceptions, we found the scrub oak and ash or Box Elder resembling the hard maple in the eastern states on the west bank of the stream in the timber.

26th. We proceeded over the high rolling prairie about 10 miles. Stopped to noon and proceeded along the top of the divide between the waters of the Wakerusak and the Kansas — called Caw River, about 10 miles farther and stoped for the night in the open prairie — gaining 10 miles on the company, they being camped at the place where we stoped to noon — At this encampment three of our horses were taken by the Kansas Indians [10] — They also came about our camp the night previous.

27th. We proceeded onto a little creek where the F. Co. had camped, 10 miles, here. we stoped to noon and proceeded about 7 miles onto a stream running into the Kansas and camped on its West bank about 9 miles East of the Kansas village — making 17 miles.

28th. We proceeded about 7 miles do [due] North till we reached the Kansas River where we found the Fur Co encamped on its South bank in a point of timber, waiting the arrival of their boat then coming

---

[10] The responsibility for the loss of the three horses must rest on Gray. He had been over the trail before and should have known that guards should have been posted at night.

up the River to meet them at that place with the outfit for the Mountains — We were kindly received by Capt. Drips in charge of the affairs of the Co. in the Mountains. Our course to this place was a little to the South of West.

THE 29th   we crossed the River with the Fur Company and camped on the North bank.[11] The timber on the River at this place is the cottonwood, walnut, and ash and some large oaks.

ON THE 30th   we proceeded about 9 miles above the Kansas Village and camped on a small stream running south East into the Kansas River, 18 miles. The country along the Kansas River is level for about 2 miles wide, of a rich fertile soil and generally well timbered near the River.

MAY 1st.   We proceeded onto a little stream called Rock Creek, 14 miles over low undulating prairie.

2nd.   This Morning Doct. Chute [12] of Westport, having come on to bring some letters and articles sent to us, took leave to return to W. Port, after letting us have his horse to supply the place of one of the stolen. We proceeded about 10 miles onto a stream called Black Vermilion to noon — proceeded about 8 miles and camp on a little stream, no name — 18 miles.

3rd.   Noon on Hoe Creek, 10 miles, camp 4 miles, again in the prairie.

4th.   Make but one camp for want of water to stop at, of 27 miles. The soil less fertile and but little timber on the water course. We camp on Burr Oak Creek, so called from the species of oak having a burr resembling a Chesnut — prairie high and rolling, camp in the bend of the creek in some timber.

5th.   We proceeded about 11 miles and crossed a beautiful stream called Black Walnut Creek, proceeding about 3 miles further, we crossed the N. East branch of a stream called the Blue and camped on its west bank, making 14 miles. At this encampment the company took the precaution to supply all the carts and wagons with extra axletrees. Our camp at this place was situated on a beautiful platt of green, skirted on three sides with small trees and shrubery. Perhaps I ought to have mentioned that the company this season have brought all their goods to this place in carts — they had 27 carts and two wagons — the

---

[11] The Kansas River was crossed in the vicinity of what is now Manhattan, Kansas.

[12] See fn. 18, Sarah Smith's diary, for reference to Dr. Chute.

wagons are owned by two private gentlemen, Mr. Clark and a man by the name of Captain Stewart,[13] an English gentleman, who spends his summers in visiting these Mountains.

6th.   Our thirteenth encampment from Westport was in the prairie, called the water hole encampment, 27 miles, over rolling prairie with but one stream, about 15 miles from our last encampment, upon which we stoped to noon.

7th.   Our 14th encampment was in the open prairie, 26 miles — stoped a short time in the middle of the day to noon on a small creek.

8th.   Our 15th encampment was on a small stream called Battle Creek, 16 miles having to stop a short time in the morning to repair one of the wagons — country open — high prairie destitute of timber, except in very small quantities on the streams.

9th.   We reached the West Branch of the Blue, 21 miles, and encamped on its North East bank. The country appearing less fertile, soil of a light gravel, with sandstone near the surface.

10.   17th encampment was on the West Branch of the Blue, 20 miles, stopped to noon.

11th.   Proceed up the west Branch of the Blue 25 miles and camp on a high bank of the River.

12th.   Our 19th encampment was on a small stream about 3 miles from the Blue, during the day we crossed the Grand Pawnee Trail meeting several Pawnees going in to their Village on the Platt. This encampment was 24 miles, about 5 miles directly out of our course to the south of our regular trail. This was a rainy wet day.[14]

On the 13th,   for our 20th encampment, we crossed from the waters of the Blue onto the Platt River, 25 miles, course Northwest — course to the Grand Pawne Trails on the Blue is a little North of West, make but one camp,[15] not finding any water on the divide. We saw but one tree during the day, this was about 4 miles to the right of our Trail. Our Ladies came into camp this day somewhat fatigued, both those who rode on horseback and those that chose the wagon. The prairie on this divide is what we call high level prairie, so much so that in

[13] See fn. 25, Sarah Smith's diary, for reference to Captain Stewart.

[14] The reenforcement of 1838 encountered much more rain while crossing the prairies than did the Whitman-Spalding party two years earlier. Myra Eells wrote in her diary for that day: "Obliged to sleep in our blankets wet as when taken from our horses." FWW, II, p. 79.

[15] Myra Eells commented: "Ride 8 hours, 25 miles — without food for ourselves or animals. I do not get off my horse during the whole distance." FWW, II, p. 79.

the wet season many acres are covered with water till it soaks into the earth which is somewhat dry and sandy, as we approach the Bluffs near the Platt, so much so that we found scarcely any vegitation. Our encampment was about 27 miles below the head of the Grand or Big Island in the Platt River on its South East Bank. The bottom of the River at this place is between 4 and 6 miles on the South E. side — nearly as wide on the North West. At this place or near as we can calculate, we are about 390 miles from Westport — 290 from the Kansas Village or Agency.

On the 14th   we proceeded to the head of the Big Island, 27 miles, encamped on the River which at this place is about 2 miles wide.

15th.   We made 27 miles, encamp near the mouth of Box Elder creek.

16th.   We make but 16 miles. Camp on the Platt.

17th.   We make 14 miles — but one camp — on the Platt.

18th.   Proceeded 27 miles, camp on the Platte.

19th.   We reached the forks of the Platt to noon this day — about 12 miles from our last encampment — 513 miles from West Port, as we make the distance. It is usually called 500 miles to the forks. We proceeded up the south fork about 15 miles and camped on the prairie about 4 miles from the River finding no wood, and had water, 27 miles. Substitute for wood, the Buffalo manure, found water from a swamp close by our camp.

20th.   We proceed up the River about 14 miles to the crossing and stoped to noon, crossed the south fork and proceeded up on the North Side the fork about 6 miles and camped on the River.

The 21st   we continued up the South fork 23 miles and camped. At this encampment we met Mr. Sarpee who gave us his opinions in reference to Doctor Saterlee's [16] death, Mr. Sarpee thinks the Dr. was killed by the Pawnees. Mr. Newel, now at this place, spent the winter with Doct. S. at Pascos [?] fort, says he does not believe a word of it. The Pawnees did not kill Dr. S. and particularly for the reason assigned by Mr. Sarpee to get his fine horse, for Dr. S. told him his fine horse had died before he left the Pawnee Village. My impression now is stronger than ever that Doct. Saterlee died by the hand of a white man. This was confirmed by Mr. Sarpee's statement, though he tried hard to throw it upon the Indians.

---

[16] See fn. 39, Sarah Smith's diary for reference to Dr. Satterlee.

23rd.   We proceeded up the South fork about 6 miles and took a N. of West course and crossed to the North. One camp of 25 miles onto the N. F[ork] at the mouth of Ash Creek. At this encampment we found timber, ash and cedar. It was five miles below this encampment that the Sioux made their attack upon me in passing down last fall.

ON THE 24th   we proceeded up along the South side of the North fork 27 miles.

ON THE 25th   we made 26 miles.

ON THE 26th   we made 30 miles and arrived at the Chimney. We camped on the 25th in sight of it. This place we call 766 miles from West Port, 193 from the forks of the Platte.

ON THE 27th   we proceeded 30 miles and encamped at the south end of Scotts Bluffs.

THE 28th   we made 25 miles and camped at a pond.

29th.   We made 24 miles and encamped 5 miles below Ft. Laramy or Ft. William at the foot of the Black Hills — where we arrived on the 30th. As near as we can make or calculate the distance, it is 790 miles. It is called when traveled with pack animals but 750.

Time will not now permit me to give you any further particulars at this time. Mr. Ermatinger [17] has arrived. We are to leave on the mor-

[17] See fn. 25, Smith's letters, for reference to Ermatinger.

row, the 11 inst. In his company we shall proceed on to Fort Hall 300 miles from this place in 18 days and 20 or 25 from thence to Walla Walla. Mr. Ermatinger has come from Fort Hall to this place for no other object than to escort Rev. Mr. Lee, Ewing & Edwards and return with us.[18] I will write on or after [——?] in reference to the affairs of the Mission &c. &c. I want to say that in case you wish a more minute & detailed discription and account of our journey, you can be furnished it by writing to Mrs. Gray's parents, John Dix, Ithaca, N.Y., either for the letters or a copy. Yours in Christ.   W. H. GRAY

GRAY'S FINANCIAL REPORT [19]

Gray's letter to Greene, written from the Rendezvous on July 8, 1838, contains a detailed financial statement of expenses to the time

[18] F. Y. Ewing, who is reported to have gone out to Oregon in 1837 for his health, was on his way back to the States. Philip L. Edwards was a lay assistant who went out to Oregon with Jason Lee in 1834. See fn. 28, Eells reminiscences, herein p. 302.

[19] Gray's handwriting in this report is so extremely difficult to read that the author found it impossible to make a full and accurate transcription.

the party started on their overland journey from Independence, Missouri. The expenditures were itemized under the following categories:

Provisions, cooking equipment & table furniture .	$94.22¼
Books, stationary, instruments & medicines . .	66.01½
Hardware, guns, ammunition, saddlery, blankets,	
tents, & Indian articles	521.69
Animals & wagons	1,444.90
Sundries, freight, soap, candles, etc. . . .	73.13½

Total $2,199.96¼

In addition to these expenditures, the four couples spent $1,086.19 for personal belongings and travel expenses from their respective homes to Independence. This brought the total cost of transporting the mission party to the western frontier and of their individual and collective outfits to $3,186.15¼. With the exception of the payments made to their hired men and of a few purchases made at Fort Laramie and at the Rendezvous the figures given by Gray covered the complete cost to the Board of sending the 1838 reenforcement from their eastern homes to Waiilatpu.[20]

Listed among the provisions purchased were the following items:

    14 lbs. brown sugar; 18 lbs. white; 16 lbs. coffee; 165 lbs. flour; 1 lb. chocolate; 57 lbs. rice; 1 box dried apples; 14 lbs. cheese; 12 lbs. butter; 64½ lbs. bacon; and an unspecified amount of bread.

These supplies were supposed to provide sufficient food for ten people, including Rogers and one hired man, for the three-week period expected to elapse before they would reach the buffalo range, and also to supplement their meat diet after they found the buffalo for the remaining period of about three and a half months before they could arrive at Waiilatpu. The food supplies taken seem to be appallingly scanty. This may have been a result of Gray's assurance to the Board that he could conduct the reenforcement to Oregon under a certain minimum cost. Here is the basis for Smith's complaint about the lack of adequate food supplies. All of the above listed items weighed a little more than 360 pounds. A pack horse could carry up to 250 pounds without difficulty. Not more than two horses were needed to carry these food supplies and all kitchen and eating equipment. And this for

---

[20] Gray did some trading with Indians along the way with items listed under Indian goods.

an overland journey of about four months for ten people! We marvel at their foolhardiness!

Eating and cooking utensils included: 1 tin reflector for baking; 1 tea kettle; 2 brass kettles; 2 frying pans; 1 coffee pot; 1 doz. pewter plates; ½ doz. earthen plates; 10 glass tumblers, 6 metallic; 1 tea pot; 1 doz. knives & forks; 1 doz. teaspoons; 1½ doz. tablespoons; 2 tin pails; 4 pans; 6 basins; 1 stew pot; 1 dipper, 1 doz. copper saucers; and 1 skimmer.

Among the books purchased were three on "mineralogy, botany, & zoology." Perhaps these were secured on Mary Walker's suggestion as she was much interested in such subjects. As has been noted, there was some duplication in medical supplies as Smith made purchases in Cincinnati and Gray in St. Louis.

Under the third category of "Hardware, guns, etc." were listed "5 guns, $78.00"; 1 keg powder; 6 Spanish saddles and "4 plush side saddles",[21] bridles — $160.75; blankets, some blue and some white; blue tent cloth; [22] carpenter tools; Indian articles as tinder boxes, knives, and awls; and 10 pack saddles. Gray listed the purchase of 13 horses ranging in cost from $35.00 to $75.00 each and 11 mules at an average price of about $38.00. Also purchased were "6 head of cattle, 6 yearling heifers, and 2 cows" at a cost of $140.00. He also reported that Smith had purchased an "old wagon" in Cincinnati for $65.00 which was judged to be unsuitable and so was sold for $20.00. Another wagon was bought for $70.00. This was taken as far west at Fort Laramie where it was left. No other reference to the wagon which Smith got in Cincinnati has been found. It may be that Gray resented Smith's action in buying the wagon and found reasons why it was not acceptable.

Gray's financial report was also signed by Eells, Walker, and Smith, which is evidence that all four accepted the figures given.

W. H. GRAY'S "HISTORY OF OREGON"

By a most interesting anomaly the least educated member of the Oregon Mission of the American Board was the only one who published a book. In 1870 the Harris & Holman Company of Portland, Oregon, and the H. H. Bancroft Company of San Francisco, California,

---

21 Mary Walker's side-saddle is now in the Oregon Historical Society, Portland, Oregon.

22 See fn. 17, Sarah Smith's diary for reference to the women making the tents. This is the only reference discovered to the fact that the tents were made out of blue cloth.

brought out *William Henry Gray's* A History of Oregon, 1792-1849. *The book contained 624 pages and, according to a statement on the title page, the contents were "drawn from personal observation and authentic information." H. H. Bancroft in his* History of Oregon *gives the following appraisal:*

As a book of reference, when compared with other authorities, the work is valuable, containing many facts and important documents. It has, however, three faults — lack of arrangement, acrimonious partisanship, and disregard of truth. A notable instance of its mendacity is the dramatic account given of Whitman's visit to the United States, its cause and purpose, and the alleged instrumentality of Whitman in raising the emigration of 1843, almost the whole of which must be relegated to the domain of fiction.[23]

As would be expected Gray devoted several chapters to the history of missionary activities, both Protestant and Roman Catholic, in Oregon. Chapter XXIII deals with the reenforcement of 1838 of which he was a member. Drawing upon his personal knowledge of his former companions, all of whom were still living when his book was published, Gray gives the following descriptions in his own inimitable style:

Rev. E. Walker was a tall, rather spare, stoop-shouldered, black-haired, brown-eyed, rather light-complexioned man, diffident and unassuming, always afraid to say *amen* at the end of his prayers, and requiring considerable effort to speak with confidence or decision upon any subject. This might arise from habit, or want of decision of character, or fear of offending. He had no positive traits of mind, yet he was studious, and kind as a friend and neighbor; faithful as a Christian, inefficient as a preacher. His efforts among the Indians were of the negative cast. The Indians respected him for his kindness, and feared him for his commanding appearance. Not at all adapted to fill the position he undertook, — as an Indian missionary in Oregon, — yet as a citizen and settler, one of the best.

Rev. C. Eells, a short, slim, brown-haired, light-brown eyed, fair-complexioned man, with a superabundance of self-steeem, great pretensions to precision and accurateness of statement and strictness of conduct; very precise in all his actions, and about all his labors and property; with no soul to laud and admire nature, no ambition to lift his thoughts beyond the sphere of his own ideas of right, he was made to move in a small circle; his soul

[23] *Op. cit.,* I, p. 302.

would be lost outside of it. . . He had no poetry or romance in his soul, yet by dint of perseverance he was a good artificial singer. He lacked all the qualities requisite for a successful Indian missionary and a preacher of the gospel in a new country. As citizens and neighbors, Mr. Eells and his family were highly respected; as a teacher, he was unreasonably strict.

Rev. A. B. Smith, a man whose prejudices were so strong that he could not be reasonable with himself. He attempted to make himself useful as a missionary, but failed for want of Christian forbearance and confidence in his associates. As to literary ability, he was superior to his associates, and probably excited their jealousy; so much so, that his connection in the mission became unpleasant, and he found an excuse to leave the country in 1841; not, however, till he and Mr. Rogers had, with the assistance of the Lawyer, completed a vocabulary and a grammar of the Nez Perce language,[24] which was the cause of Ellis's jealousy of the Lawyer and Mr. Smith, and also of an extra effort through the Jesuits and the company to get rid of him.

Lawyer was the nickname given by white men to an intelligent Nez Perce from the Kamiah country who was for a time Smith's teacher. With Lawyer's and Rogers' help, Smith compiled the first dictionary and grammar of the Nez Perce language which is now in the archives of the American Board. Lawyer served as head chief of the Nez Perces from 1848 to 1871. There was a rivalry between Lawyer and Ellis, who was another prominent Nez Perce from the Kamiah area. Ellis had attended a mission school at Red River in Canada during the 1820s and because of this and his command of English was made the first head chief of the Nez Perces by Indian Agent Elijah White in 1842. He died in the buffalo country in 1848. In all probability there were other reasons for the rivalry which existed between Lawyer and Ellis other than that given by Gray. The last statement in Gray's description of Smith — the reference to the Jesuits and the Hudson's Bay Company — is a good example of his deep prejudice against both the Roman Catholics and the Hudson's Bay Company. There is no evidence whatsoever that either had anything to do with Smith's leaving the Mission or Oregon.

In Chapter XXIX of the History of Oregon, *Gray gives the following account of the withdrawals from the Oregon Mission of the American Board:*

---

[24] See index of SS for many references to "Nez Perce language" and to Smith's work on the vocabulary and grammar of that tongue. The work that he did in this field remains as an eloquent tribute to his scholarly ability.

Rev. A. B. Smith and wife, Cornelius Rogers, and W. H. Gray and wife had left the mission of the American Board, on account of difficulties they had become fully satisfied would ultimately destroy the mission or drive it from the country. Mr. Spalding, it will be remembered, was a man of peculiar temperament, ambitious and selfish. He could not endure an associate of superior talent, or admit himself to be inferior in understanding the native language. From the time the Jesuits arrived [in 1838], some of his own pet Indians had turned Catholics and commenced a quarrel with him. These facts seemed to annoy and lead him to adopt a course opposed by Smith, Gray and Rogers. Still he found it pleased the Indians as a whole, and was assented to by the balance of the mission.

After the passing of nearly thirty years, Gray still had but few kind words to say about his former associates. In general not one of the above mentioned, according to Gray, was cut out to be a missionary with the possible exception of Spalding. Gray's critical analysis of his associates calls to mind Mary Walker's frank estimate as found in her diary for May 27, 1838: "We have a strange company of Missionaries. Scarcely one who is not intolerable on some account." [25]

---

[25] FWW, II, p. 87.

Diary of Elkanah Walker
March 7 to May 15, 1838

Diary of Elkanah Walker

INTRODUCTION

On March 7, 1838, two days after his marriage to Mary Richardson, Elkanah Walker began a diary which he kept with fair regularity to October 13, 1848. Since Mary had been keeping a diary since January 1, 1833, it seems probable that she was the one who inspired her husband to do likewise. Neither Elkanah nor Mary wrote for publication or for others to read. Each wrote for himself or herself and consequently these records are very frank, especially Mary's. The members of the 1838 reenforcement were a literary-minded company. Five of the eight missionaries kept a diary of their journey to Oregon. Only Cushing Eells and William and Mary Gray did not, or at least no such records have been discovered.[1] After arriving in Oregon, no members of the Mission were as faithful in continuing their diaries as Elkanah and Mary Walker. Mary's diary for the full mission period, with some eliminations, appeared in Volume II of First White Women Over the Rockies. *The annotations for her diary include many parallel entries from Elkanah's. With the exception of these extracts, Elkanah Walker's diary is the only one kept by any member of the Oregon Mission known to be extant which has not been published.*

The original diaries of Elkanah Walker are in the Henry E. Huntington Library and Art Gallery, San Marino, California, with the exception of the section for January 1-November 20, 1842, which is in the Oregon Historical Society, Portland, Oregon. That part of Elkanah's diary which covers his travel experiences en route to Oregon continued for only ten weeks or from March 7 to May 15, 1838. Evidently he then found himself too busy with the multitude of duties attendant upon traveling with the caravan to keep up his daily record. He resumed keeping his diary after his arrival at Waiilatpu.

In order to round out the story of the overland travel experiences of the 1838 reenforcement, Elkanah's dairy, March 7-May 15, is here included. His account throws many new sidelights on the events of those

---

[1] W. H. Gray did keep a daily progress report of the first part of their overland journey which is to be found in an earlier chapter of this volume.

days. But even more, it illuminates the character of Elkanah Walker. We see him in this record as a mild-mannered, hard-working man. He was blessed with a peaceful disposition. Mary was far more frank in recording her feelings and opinions of others than her husband. In her diary we can trace out the story of the petty quarrels that marred their travels from the very beginning of their overland journey after leaving the Missouri frontier. Elkanah says practically nothing about this. Take, for instance, the incident of the killing of the calf which had been wounded by wolves. Mary gives considerable detail about the hard feelings which arose between Smith and Gray. Walker in his entry for May 11th comments on peace being restored and then adds, not with humor but in sadness, "Weather pleasant & that was the only thing that was so." His greatest complaint was not of others but rather of the necessity to travel on Sunday, which grievously pained his conscience.

Elkanah kept his diary for this ten-week period in a small notebook which measured 5½ x 3¼ inches. His handwriting is extremely difficult to transcribe. A few words could not be deciphered. For the most part misspellings have been retained. Some punctuation marks and an occasional word have been added to clarify the meaning. Elkanah's description of this period of their travels should be read along with the accounts written by his wife and Myra Eells, which are to be found in Volume II of this series, and also with the diary of Sarah Smith and the letters of Asa Smith given in earlier chapters of this book.

The author has had a special interest in Elkanah and Mary Walker ever since about 1936 when he first had opportunity to read their diaries now on deposit in the Henry E. Huntington Library. This interest was deepened in 1938 when he first called on their youngest son, Sam Walker, then living at Forest Grove, Oregon. Sam was the last living direct descendant of any member of the Oregon Mission, and at the time of that first visit he told the author: "My parents rode horseback over the Rocky Mountains just one hundred years ago."

TO THE ROCKY MOUNTAINS

Left home the 7 of March 1838. Spent one night in Portland with brother Hamlin.[2] Left the next morning for Boston at which place we

---

[2] Cyrus Hamlin was a classmate of Elkanah's at Bangor Theological Seminary in Maine and a close personal friend. Hamlin had a distinguished career as a missionary of the American Board in Turkey. The Walkers named their son born at Waiilatpu on December 7, 1838, after Cyrus Hamlin.

arrived the same evening. Staid in Boston until the next Thursday, March 15 & reached New York the next morning, the 16th. Remained in N.Y. till the following Tuesday afternoon when we started for Phil. Met at N. York Brothers Eells & Smith & wives who were to be our companions in our future labors among the Indians west of the Rocky Mnts.

At N.Y. we met the very kindest treatment from the friends of Missions. They did everything in their power to make our stay among them pleasant to us & did all they could to prepare us for our journey across the Mountains. We wanted for no good thing. We reached Phil. the same night about one & left P. the next morning at 8 for Chambersburgh where we arrived about 12 at night. Nothing took place on this part of our journey from N.Y. to P. more than is common in a rail road. We had a view of the great tunnel through the mountain. The length of this tunnel is said to be one mile, and is judged at its mouth to be 50 feet below the surface. Thus in the middle it must be some hundred feet. How many I did not learn.

At Chambersburgh we took stage for Pittsburg, a distance of one hundred & fifty miles. The roads were exceedingly bad owing to a great fall of snow on the Sabbath previous to our leaving N.Y. I should have said that we spent one Sabbath in N.Y. & received our instructions which was given by Mr. Green, one of the Secy. It was pronounced a good document. They were given at Dr. Spring's church.[3] We left Chambersburgh on Thursday & did not reach Pittsburgh until the next Monday afternoon. We were detained on the road for want of stage about 12 hours. This prevented us from reaching Pitts. until the Sabbath. Rather than travel on the Sabbath we chose to stop & spend the Sabbath at Greensburgh. We spent the time very pleasantly & hope by our example & other means did some good. But this we must leave until the final judgment which will soon come.

MARCH 26. Left Greensburgh in the stage quite early & rode till eleven before we took breakfast. Reached Pittsb. the same day about two P.M. after ridying 32 miles. Went directly on board a steam boat & took passage for St. Louis. Were known as Missionaries to the heathen. Delivered our letters of introduction to Dr. Riddle.[4] Received a visit from him & his wife in the evening with an invitation to take breakfast with him which we accepted, — had before leaving his house a

[3] The farewell service for the outgoing missionaries was held in the Brick Presbyterian Church of New York City, of which Dr. Gardiner Spring was pastor, on Sunday evening, March 18, 1838. See fn. 4, Sarah Smith's diary.

[4] See fn. 7, Sarah Smith's diary.

social prayer meeting, some of his church being present. Left that day
for St. Louis. Made several stops as is the practice of steam boats.
Stopped at Wheeling, Maysville, & some other places. Reached Cincinnati Thursday evening & called on Dr. [George] Weed who is agent
for the A.B.C.F.M., when it was decided that we had better leave the
boat & remain in the place over Sabbath as it would be impossible for
us to reach St. L. before the Sabbath & as there was no necessity for
us to be at Independence until the last of April as intelligence had
been received that the company would not leave until the first of May.

But we did not stay as was decided another week. News came that
the company was moving up the River & we must come on in all haste.
Left. Cin. Wednesday morning in the steamboat Knickerbocker, Capt.
Van Houten. He appears a very kind & obliging man, have received
every attention from him that we could ask. Found on board this boat
[as on] the Norfolk in which we made our passage to Cincinnati, commanded by Capt. Sim. [?], same good hearted Christians who were
traveling to the west. Some on business, some on a visit to their friends,
mostly from New Eng. The company in the Lady's Cabin are about
all hopefully pious.[5] It was suggested by a gentleman on board that we
should have evening prayers. I call on the Capt. & asked his consent
which was given very cheerfully although there is no doubt to my
mind but he is an infidel in sentiment. Some objected and one lady
was quite offended, who was a Catholic. This took place before the
boat left Cin. This was on Tuesday evening. Brother Smith lead in
prayer after reading a portion of Scripture.

Wednesday night at 12 we reached Louisville where we remained
until Thursday about 11 A.M. Louisville is quite a place & is an incor-
porated city, the largest I believe in the State of Ken. Just below the
city is what is called the falls in the Ohio River. These are not of much
note. The only thing that makes them interesting is at the low ebb of
the river. They are very dangerous to pass at some seasons of the year.
For the better navigation of the river, there is a canal constructed of
about three miles length. On Tuesday there was much gambling &
drinking on board & like to have ended in a serious affair. Two became much enraged. Some proposed to settle the whole according to
the rule of honor. One of them went so far as to threaten the other
with ripping him up if he said a word to him & actually drew a dirk for
this purpose. They both showed pistols. A physician on board advised

---

[5] This was a common expression of that generation to designate a sincere Christian. Since no one could be absolutely sure of being among the saved, there was
the qualifying word "hopefully."

the one threatened to blow the brains of the other out. It was only settled by the interference of the Captain. To the joy of many, some of the most desperate of the company left at Louisville & no gambling was seen on the boat during the next day.

FRIDAY [THURSDAY] 5. passed as usual. Made but very few stops. Time passed as in the case on steamboats. A very civil company. Have had evening prayers in the Lady's Cabin since we came on board, some few of the passengers attend them.

The lower part of the Ohio & the Mississippi are too well known to need any description. The Land looks good, but very low. Spring fast approaching. Many of the trees in full bloom. Friday night, quite a thunder storm, but pleasant to day. The Capt. continues kind & attentive. Many of the passengers are from [New England] & consequently men of good morals & some of them pious.

The Pennsylvania has just passed us while we are stopping for wood & to repair. Three or four boats have passed us since we started & the Capt. has been urged by some to put on more steam. He said to me in conversation to day that he always answered such in a very short manner. If any boat was a mind to run past him, he would let them before he would put on steam. It is now about two o'clock & just five weeks since I received notice that I must leave so soon & am now more than two thousand of miles from home or what was once my home but my home is now wherever I am.

I am not much in love with the country, should rather live in New England. Give me N.E. hills for all the western prairies.

SATURDAY 7. Nothing especial occurred. Entered the Miss. some time during Friday night, so I had no opportunity to see the junction of these two rivers, the Ohio & Miss. Some time in the night some part of the machinery gave away & we were detained some hours. Did not start till ten on Sunday.[6]

SUNDAY 8, was compelled to spend the day on board the boat which, to a lover of the house of God & one in the constant habit of meeting for the worship of God in his house, is very disagreeable not to say any thing about the great profanation witnessed on board steam boats on that sacred day. Tried to spend the day in serving God in my state room. But how can one enjoy much where he is surrounded with

---

[6] Elkanah was hesitant about making any personal references to his bride, Mary, in his diary. Mary on the other hand was less restrained. On this day she wrote: "Wish I knew whether [he] is satisfied with me or not. Sometimes I think I will try and get along one day without displeasing [him], but the first thing I know, I do something worse than ever. Still I am determined not to give up trying." FWW, II, p. 55.

such high handed wickedness. Did not take dinner from a desire not to mingle with any more company than I possibly could. Spent the eve in the Lady's Cabin in singing. Reached St. Louis during the night. Staid on board the boat until after breakfast Monday. Then went & found some boats going up the Mo. & by the advice of Capt. Van Houten took passage in the Wm. Glasgow,[7] Capt. Littleton. Capt. Van H. was very attentive to our wants & did all he could to help us on our way. Came [?] & engaged to Capt. L. to take our extra baggage free. He manifested deep interest in our welfare & even said at the dinner table in our absence that he never had any passengers in whom he felt so deep an interest as he did in ours & just before we left came to our board & bade us a very warm farewel. It was quite evident that he was much moved. It was the emotion of tender sympathy. We all felt that we had great occasion for humiliation & gratitude to the Author of all our mercies.

The Capt. with whom we engaged our passage to Ind[ependence] appears to be a very kind man & has the reputation of being such by many on whose testimony we could rely. We left St. L. at or near sun set Mon. & did not expect we would run all night but did & that too at no slow rate. There was some racing in the night. A boat left about one hour before we did & we passed her & have kept in the advance. They apply more steam than I like, but my trust is in God & he can save us amid the greatest dangers.

TUESDAY 10.   Continue to ascend at a rapid rate. The Capt. appears friendly & social. As regards room we are more pleasantly situated then in the Knickerbocker. The boat is stopping for wood & all hands are busily engaged in writing.

WEDNESDAY 11,   did not run much last night owing to the dangers of the stream, are now stopping to take in wood. Had some conversation last night & this morning with a gentleman who has spent two yrs. on and beyond the Rocky Mountains. He speaks in the highest terms of the good character of Nez Perces & Flat Head Indians & says that they are doing greater favor to the whites than the whites can ever do them. We find no difficulty in securing the friendship of all.

Two quite serious things happened this day or it might more properly be said they might have ended quite seriously. The boat took fire

---

[7] This corrects statements in FWW, II, p. 56 where the name of the river steamer which the missionaries boarded at St. Louis was erroneously given as the "Knickerbocker." Rather this was the vessel which carried them from Cincinnati to St. Louis at which place they boarded the "William Glasgow."

& another run against her. The fire was discovered in time to quench it before it made much progress. They continued to run far late in the eve. stopped part of the night.

Thurs. 12.   Passed some very pleasant places this day. I should think from the appearance of things that a more enterprising coll[ection] of beings inhabited the upper part of Mo. than the lower & I should think the country better adapted for farming than that bordering on the Miss. We are now stopping to land freight & I expect that when we start again there will be hard running for both boats are lying long side one another.

Here things assumed a different appearance. Our contending Capts. entered into a new mode of warfare & came [to] a decision that we should go on board the Howard to go up to Independence. This bargain was made without even consulting the passengers whether we should have any accommodation or not & we made a most miserable change. Could not obtain state rooms. We could not obtain but one for three families. We stowed our Ladies away in this & made the best shift for ourselves we could. We found ourselves more pleasantly situated than we anticipated. Found our Capt. a very obliging man & is a professor of religion.[8] Were known as missionaries as soon as we came on board. The deck passengers are in a most miserable condition, crowded together surrounded with filth.

Friday 13.   We are now stopping at a small village, Brunswich, landing freight. Last night saw a large fire to the east & was doubtless occasioned by the burning of prairie.

Saturday 14.   Nothing special occured to day. We continue to move on at about the same rate. There was one gentleman from St. L. sick with the headache to whom brother Smith administered an emetic & who received our special attention. He appear very grateful for the kindness shown him. Went to rest to night with the feeling that we should be compelled to spend another night aboard the boat.

Sunday 15.   If ever I felt to unite with the Psalmist in his holy aspirations for the house of God, it was on this day. Never did I long so ardently for the privilege of a New England Sabbath. So far as I could learn the conduct from the appearance of the people on this day, I should think that they knew nothing about the Sabbath, such as is known & observed in N.E. We made one or two stopping places before

---

[8] A "professor of religion" was a common term then used to designate a professing Christian. The expression had nothing to do with being a faculty member in some school.

reaching Independence. The principle was at Liberty & here I must confess that the most high handed wickedness I ever witnessed was seen here & this was remarked by most of the passengers. Boys quite small, beastely drunk & the most horrid imprecations were passing, it would seem, the imagination of the very devil himself, of which he would be ashamed to be known that he was so wicked, were continually being poured forth. I was rejoiced when we left this very seat & I might with all propriety call it the very contemplation of the lower regions. I was rejoiced feeling assured that we could not possibly be in a more debased place on the face of the earth. We had some more peace after we left this place as all the lady passengers left at this place, leaving us the full possession of the lady's cabin. We reached Ind. about 5 in the afternoon. We landed immediately, landed our baggage & ladies & stowed them away in a log hut, sent one of our company to the village to announce our arrival to brother Gray who soon came down to the River with horses for our ladies to ride up to the village, a distance of about four miles.[9] We made a grand debut into the place about 11 O'clock on Sunday night amid the roar of dogs of all sizes & descriptions & lodged in a house which had only two beds to accommodate nine persons.

MONDAY 16, arose this morning rather late after a restless night rest & began to make preparations for leaving this place by fixing our tents & purchasing horses, ponies & mules. Here we were altogether. It was the expectation that we should leave this place the next day & it continued until Friday when all mounted on horses we left the place, our ladies mounted on ponies taking the lead & [I] mounted on a black horse with a white hat, with leather belt about me, with a rifle laying before, with a powder flask hung to my side, with bullet mould attached to it,[10] leading another horse, & three mules following in the train, followed close in the rear.

Reached Westport about eight in the eve & took some time to unload our animals & when we did, I had the good fortune to obtain a bed on the counter in a store composed of rolls of cloth.

SATURDAY 21. Rose rather late this morning, was quite unwell & did not do much. Slept most of the day for it was the first time for quite

---

[9] For the first time all nine members of the reenforcement, including Rogers, were together.

[10] See description given by Cornelius Rogers of his outfit. Text, p. 274. Each of the missionary men was required by the leader of the Fur Company's caravan to carry a gun. Asa Smith was most unhappy about this. See his letter of April 22, 1838, p. 140.

a while that I had a good bed. Engaged a pack man to go with us.[11] We were now stopping with a Mr. McCoy who had formerly been a missionary of the Baptist board.

SUNDAY 22. Continued unwell so much so that I [——?] did not attend meeting for she [his wife] was more unwell than myself. Attended in the eve & heard brother Eells for the first time.

MONDAY 23. Left this day [from] Westport & have travelled 12 miles & encamped for the night & for the first time since I left home. We are now beyond the bounds of law. The will of man is the only law known. I felt much my dependence upon God & dwelt with great delight upon the words of the Psalmist — as the mountains are round about Jerusalem; so is the Lord round about them that fear him.

TUESDAY 24. Was in rather an unpleasant mood from the conduct of some of the company & especially from her who should please me above all others.[12] We travelled very hard to day & made about twenty five miles. Crossed on a branch of Osage river.

WEDNESDAY 25. Rode about 18 miles this day, encamped very early to day. Did not stop for dinner. Do not feel that I am away from home. The importance of the subject in which I am engaged & the necessity there is that everything should be done with perfect propriety, that nothing else hardly enters my mind. I find it extremely hard to sustain at all time a proper course of conduct, very much inclined to forget what & who I am. I am fearful that we shall not conduct with that Christian forbearance that we should. We are now one day's journey behind the company of traders.

Broke up encampment about seven. Travelled very fast while on the journey. Made about 18 miles. Did not stop to dinner. Strong wind from the south & extremely cold. This is occasioned by the wind blowing from the snow capped monts. in Mexico.[13] This morning Dr. Chute

---

[11] In order to save money, Gray felt that the party could get along with only one hired man to assist in packing and caring for the animals. So a man known only as Stevens was hired. Later, on May 18, a hunter by the name of Paul Richardson was also hired. Smith felt that Gray should have secured more assistants.

[12] On this day Mary wrote in her diary: "Should feel much better if Mr. W. would only treat me with some cordiality. It is so hard to please him I almost despair of ever being able to. If I stir it is forwardness, if I am still it is inactivity. I keep trying to please but sometimes I feel it is no use. I am almost certain that more is expected of me than can be had of one woman. . . May God help me to walk discretely, do right and please my husband." According to the custom of the time, Mary never referred to her husband by his first name, or any title of endearment, but rather as "Mr. Walker." FWW, II, p. 72.

[13] See Sarah Smith's entry for the same day where she too refers to the "snow capped mountains of Mexico." Thus through similar entries, we learn indirectly of the subjects of conversation within the party.

left us to return to Westport. Crossed a small stream, its name I do not know. It flows in the Kansas. Our route for the most part has been about west on the high prairies between the Osage & Kansas Rivers.

THURSDAY 26.   Did not make a very early start owing to some of our animals strolling of some distance. The weather quite warm. Made about 24 miles today & encamped in rather a bleak place & was troubled by the wind which increased very much at evening.

FRIDAY 27.   This day had a bad beginning. We found when we drove in our horses, three of the best were absent.[14] We beat up the region round about but could find nothing of them. We about came to the conclusion that they were stolen after the return of brother Eells who went half a day travel back after them. Made about 20 miles to day & encamped on the bank of a small stream rather late. The country had more the appearance of a plain than one had passed over. From the best judgment I could form of the whole, I came to the conclusion that the time has been when the whole surface was the bottom of some lake or composed the bed of the sea. If we come to the conclusion that this has ever been under water, we are compelled to admit that it has been a long time under water. We find stones of some inches thick that have holes completely worn through them, so that it would require some time to do it.

SATURDAY 28.   Did not move very far to day, 5 or six miles & came up with the fur Company, received a visit from Capt. Drips & Stewart & also from Major Harris.[15] We had some presents of corn & pork from D. & H. We were very kindly treated by all these gentlemen. En-camped on the banks of the Kansas river, were visited by some Indians today.

SUNDAY 29.   This was a day of noise & confusion. It had none of the appearance of the Sabbath. We crossed the river and encamped on the opposite shore in none of the best condition to enjoy the sacred hours of the Sabbath. Here we were again favored with the company of Dr. Chute.

MONDAY, 30.   This morning Dr. Chute left us to go up to the Kansas village in a [———?] Horses not yet found. Another man went back after them Saturday & returned late Sabbath evening. Nooned on the river opposite the K[ansas] village, while stopping had a heavy shower of rain. Made 16 miles, had a rainy night, found ourselves quite wet in the morning.

---

[14] The three horses stolen were the best of the lot. They had cost $200.00. This was a serious loss.

[15] See fn. 25 and 26, Sarah Smith's diary.

TUESDAY, MAY 1.   Started from encampment rather late this morning. Owing to the rain last evening, did not [——?] Move about 12 miles to day.[16] Were joined this evening by Dr. Chute who had the goodness to let us have his horse to supply the place of one we lost.

WEDNESDAY 2.   Had a heavy rain last night which came through the tent so fast that it was impossible to write the paper, wetting [it?].

WEDNESDAY [THURSDAY] 3.   Had a fair day to day, rode about 14 miles, encamped quite early. Had some honey sent us by Capt. D. Was called to guard to night. We have passed several small creeks the two or three days past. The prairie is more broken.

FRIDAY 4.   Had high winds to day from the north west & suffered very much from the cold & wind. Travelled about 21 miles most of the way over high hills or what is called rolling prairie. Did not stop for dinner to day. Encamped quite early & we were stationed out side the ring. Perhaps it was the result of some unpleasant feeling on the part of Capt. D. owing to our taking our station the night before without being assigned by him.

SATURDAY 5.   Started quite early this morning and travelled [to] about three o'clock. The weather more favorable than yesterday. Crossed the Big Blue & encamped near it. Passed two large mounds this day. Had half a wild turkey from our hunter, Mr. R[ichardson].

SUNDAY 6.   Started this morning very early & travelled hard all day. Stopped to dine about 12 o'clock. I longed for the privileges of the house of God for one of those days I had observed while favored with them. We encamped for the night where we had little or no wood. Our pack man took a mule & went off some distance & brought in a pack load, so that we had enough to cook our supper & breakfast.

MONDAY 7.   Started as early as usual. Stopped to dinner. Travelled 20 miles. Suffered much a few days past from loss of appetite, a sickness at the stomach. This evening at camp, took an emetic given me by brother Smith. Its operation was great and powerful. Was consoled from the thought that my friends at home were assembled & praying for me. After the operation of the emetic, took 15 grains of calomel, administered by the same kind hand. Our encamping ground was very rough & wood exceedingly scarce. Was called on guard but was excused owing to my being sick. A regular guard is kept every night composed of five men. These are changed every three hours so that 15 men are on guard every night. The last or those on the morning

---

[16] See FWW, II, p. 65 for chart showing number of miles covered each day from May 1-August 31. The average distance traveled per day after the mission party joined the caravan was twenty-one miles.

guard stand all day, their duty is to see that the animals do not stray & drive them in when we want to take them up. At night all the horses & mules are drove within the ring composed by placing the carts round on the bank of the stream or ravine where we encampt & made fast to stakes about two feet long. This is termed picketing. Some of the bad horses are hobbled to prevent them from running in being caught.

TUESDAY 8.   Started rather late this morning, made about 15 miles. Had the company of Major Harris considerable part of the day, Some improvement in health but excedingly weak owing to the operation of medicine. Brother Smith & myself drove the cattle, accompanied by our ladies. The first time since I left home that I have had the pleasure of ridding all day with my wife. Encamped on a small [stream?], water good.

WEDNESDAY 9.   Did not start as early as usual. While after the cattle, discovered three quite large springs, the first I have seen on the prairie. Made about 21 miles. Did not stop on account of not finding water, reached the camp ground about 3 P.M. Most of the way to day was a plain extending as far as the eye could reach with out seeing a tree for the eye to rest upon. Health much improved, principle food fat bacon. O how I long to feast once more on bread. If I could only come to mothers [pantry?] [——?] would be [——?] for a while.

THURSDAY 10.   Last night a small suckling calf was torn some by a wolf.[17] The wolves were heard by some of the company. We continued to follow up the west branch of the Blue and encamped on its northern bank. It was decided by some of us that the calf ought to be killed & it was done, which created some hard feeling. [——?] bottom land. Some high banks on our right. Travelled 20 miles.

FRIDAY 11.   Travelled about the same distance as yesterday — following the same stream, much unpleasant feeling, so much so that we felt something must [be done] to calm the feeling that then existed & restore peace. A meeting was proposed by our camp & willingly accepted. Peace restored & arrangements made for the future. Weather pleasant & that was the only thing that was so.

SATURDAY 12.   Strong appearance this morning of rain, travelled quite fast, high wind from the North East. Met a war party of Pawnees going out to steal horses [from the] Sioux whom they supposed had recently stole some from them. It commenced raining soon after we

---

[17] For more detail regarding the incident of killing the calf, see Mary Walker's account, FWW, II, p. 78.

stopped for dinner & rained hard all the afternoon. We came into camp wet & cold. We pitched our tents & made a cosy fire before it & prepared for a rainy night, which however did not come. We were in the hope that it would rain the next day so that we might rest on the Sabbath.

SUNDAY 13.   Had quite a good nights rest not withstanding the wet. Did not rise very early this morning. Very strong appearance of rain but the order was to start. Left the west branch of the Blue & rode from the bottom land on the prairie — took our course for the Platte. Most of the way was on a level plain. The distance 25 miles without any appearance of wood or water. Made the whole distance without making any stop, were traveling 8 hours, much fatigued by the journey. How different from the manner of spending the sabbath at home. Though we so much need the rest of the Sab — there was none for us. O how I longed for the house of God, thought I knew something what the pious Psalmist felt in his holy breathing after the house of God. We reached the P. about 3 in the afternoon, hungry & exhausted. Had a fine day for travelling, the most so of any since we started. The waters of the Platte is very muddy. Not so hard as the water in the west in general. It was very low. It is a broad shallow stream. Some places nearly 2 miles wide & so shallow that it can be forded. There are many islands. Some are quite large & covered with timber. It has but very little wood on its banks.

MONDAY 14.   Made very early start & travelled until 11 when we stopped to dinner. Made about 25 miles to day over a very level plain with some bluffs on our left hand. We were on the south side of the stream. We shall follow on this side till we reach the forks where we shall cross over the stream to the north fork. Last evening the war party of Pawenees came into camp & stayed till after sunset, afterwards they went over on the island where they commenced singing which kept up for some time much to my sorrow. When they commenced I supposed it was the howling of wolves.

TUESDAY 15.   Continued to follow up the river which gives us nearly a west course. Made about the same distance as the day before. No alteration in the appearance of the country. News went through the train that buffalo was on the other side of the stream. But [——?]

Here the first installment of Walker's Diary abruptly ends even though the small notebook contained a number of blank pages. We may assume that he was so busy and so exhausted with his daily work he found it impossible to continue his notes.

Letter from Cornelius Rogers
from the Rendezvous, July 3, 1838

Letter from Cornelius Rogers

BIOGRAPHICAL SKETCH OF ROGERS

When the Walkers, the Eells, and the Smiths were in Cincinnati, March 29-April 4, 1838, they met Cornelius Rogers,[1] then twenty-two years old and unmarried, who became so interested in their projected mission to Oregon that he joined the party as a voluntary assistant. Because of the suddenness of his decision, he had no time to apply for an appointment from the American Board. Rogers was an active member of the Second Presbyterian Church of Cincinnati of which Dr. Lyman Beecher, president of Lane Theological Seminary of that city, was also the pastor. Rogers was encouraged to join the reenforcement by Dr. George L. Weed of Cincinnati, the local representative of the Board. Since there was no opportunity to obtain authorization for travel expenses, friends in the city contributed the necessary funds. Thus the reenforcement of 1838, counting the Grays, was increased to nine.

Rogers remained with the Oregon Mission on an unofficial basis for about three years or until May 1841. He was a likeable young man and caused no trouble within the Mission. Even Gray had good words to say about him in his History of Oregon. *Following the arrival of the reenforcement at Waiilatpu in the early fall of 1838, the Grays and Rogers were sent to Lapwai where Rogers assisted for a time in the school. In the spring and summer of 1839, he accompanied a party of Nez Perces on a hunting expedition into the buffalo country. This gave him an excellent opportunity to learn the language and he became, next to Smith, the most proficient linguist in the Mission. The records show that he moved rather freely from station to station within the Mission as need for his services arose.*

In March 1841 Rogers visited the Smiths at Kamiah. By this time he had definitely decided to leave the Mission and go to the Willamette Valley. Smith was then feeling thoroughly depressed and was on the

---

[1] Not to be confused with Andrew Rodgers who migrated to Oregon in 1846 and who was employed by Whitman to teach the school at Waiilatpu. Andrew Rodgers was one of the victims of the Whitman massacre.

point of resigning. The association of these two men at this particular time served to confirm in the mind of each the decision to resign. After leaving Kamiah, Rogers went to Lapwai where he was taken seriously ill. For a time, according to a letter dated April 17th from Whitman to Walker, he was so sick that the doctor felt he might die.[2] *He recovered, however, and then spent some time at Fort Walla Walla where Pierre Pambrun took a special interest in him. Pambrun conceived the idea of having Rogers marry his daughter Maria. The Whitmans felt, as did the others in the Mission, that since Maria was an uneducated half-breed and a Roman Catholic, she was not worthy of him. Pambrun's heart was set on the idea and he worked assiduously to win Roger's approval.*

On May 11th, when Pambrun and Rogers were riding horseback together, Pambrun's horse became unmanageable and threw him repeatedly against the horn of the saddle and finally to the ground. Pambrun suffered such serious interial injuries that he died four days later. Anticipating the marriage of Rogers with his daughter, Pambrun willed Rogers one hundred pounds sterling. This was indeed a handsome sum for that day. Rogers accompanied the Pambrun family to Fort Vancouver for the burial. There an unexpected development arose when Maria refused to marry Rogers. He, thereupon, returned the money he had received from Pambrun's will.

In September of the following year, Rogers married Miss Satira Leslie, a daughter of one of the ministers serving in the Methodist Mission. Since he had good command of the Nez Perce language, Rogers' services were in demand by government officials. On February 1, 1843, Rogers and his wife and several others were swept over Willamette Falls and all were drowned. His death was a severe loss to the small American community on the Willamette.

A few of Rogers' letters are in the archives of the American Board. The only letter known to have been written by him describing the overland trip of 1838 was published in the December 1838 issue of the Oregonian and Indian's Advocate.[3] *This appeared under the caption, "The Journey to the Rocky Mountains" and contained some excellent descriptions of their method of travel, their equipment, and of life at the Rendezvous. The letter was introduced by the following comment from the editor:*

---

[2] Drury, *Whitman*, p. 249ff.

[3] See subsequent reference to this publication. Text, p. 314ff.

The following letter is from Mr. C. Rogers, one of the missionaries of the A.B.C.F.M. to the Columbia river. It is dated, "Camp of the American Fur Company, in rendezvous, eastern base of Wind River Mountains, and junction of Popo Agie and Wind river, July 3rd, 1838." Our readers can form from it a pretty correct idea of the route and mode of travelling to which a company would be obliged to resort in crossing the Rocky Mountains. The letter is copied from the Cinncinnati Journal.

ROGERS' LETTER

MY DEAR FRIENDS: I sit down to redeem the pledge I made to write to you. I am yet far from my journey's end, and it is probable you will not hear from me in less than a year. Our company are all in good health, and this blessing we have uniformly enjoyed, with few slight exceptions, since we left the states. We are now more than half the distance from Westport, on the border of Missouri, to our place of destination on the Columbia, it being about 900 or 950 miles from this to the former place, and to Walla Walla about 800 or 850.

The most unpleasant road to travel is, of course, yet before us.[4] We have been greatly favored thus far, having received much assistance from Capt. Drips and his company. We left Westport on the 23d of April, and struck the Kansas river at the villages, about 90 miles above its mouth; thence following up the river a few days, we reached the Blue, its principal branch on the north; following up the Blue nearly to its source, which is in the high prairie land between the Kansas and Platte, we struck across to the Platte. The time of crossing was one day, being about 26 miles. Thus far we had plenty of wood; but now it became extremely scarce. Some days, while on the Lower Platte, we found a little drift wood; but frequently we had nothing but buffalo dung;[5] which, however, is a very good fuel, when dry. On the upper portions of the Platte there is more wood.

The Platte is a beautiful stream; but utterly incapable of navigation, on account of its shallowness. A boat drawing eight inches can scarcely pass down it. In many places, it is very wide. At some points, on account of sand bars, the channel is deep. The water is of a whitish clay color, from the mixture of sand and clay.

*   *   *

[4] This was true. Crossing the Blue Mountains in eastern Oregon was more difficult than crossing the Rockies.

[5] Dried buffalo dung, called buffalo chips, made excellent fuel. See FWW, I, p. 50, fn. 33.

Hitherto the face of the country has been gently undulating; but as we approach the forks of the Platte, the bluffs become more broken and abrupt, while the face of the country is one continued series of small hills and valleys, having no vegetation except weeds and short curly grass. The river flats are covered with a taller species of grass, which is in many places very salt. As the country becomes more broken, the river is proportionably narrower and deeper.

We reached the forks about the middle of May, and forded the south fork. Fording the Platte is somewhat difficult, on account of the quicksands. As soon as your foot is placed on the bottom, the water washes the sand from under it, and you are in danger of slipping and sinking.

Here we found buffalo for the first time, and plenty of them too. We sometimes saw twenty or more droves in a day, some small, but some so large that the whole plain was black for miles with them. They are killed either by approaching unseen, and shooting them, or by chasing them on horseback, and when within six or eight feet of their side, shooting them down. On account of the peculiarity of their shape, few, except those who know at what part to aim, succeed in killing them. The hump ribs, as they are called, run above the back bone: and those who are unacquainted with this fact, instead of striking some vital part, seldom aim below this bone. The tongue and meat on the side and hump ribs are eaten. When buffalo are scarce, other parts are taken. The meat is very sweet, and easily cooked. Ten minutes boiling is enough, more will make it tough. When roasted, it is very juicy, and so highly flavored, that no salt is needed. The meat is sometimes "jerked," by being dried in the sun or over a slow fire. In this state it can be kept for three or four days in the most sultry weather. The buffalo to be shot must be approached from the windward side, as their sense of smell is remarkably keen, and they run the instant they scent a man.

But to return. We followed up the south fork two days and a half, and then crossed to the north fork, and followed up its south side to within ten days' travel of this place. About 250 or 300 miles above the main forks of the Platte, a stream called Lorimer's Fork enters that river from the south. Here is a station of the American Fur Company, called Fort William.[6] There are also two other stations near, belonging

---

[6] Fort William, as Fort Laramie was earlier known, was named after one of the fur traders, William Sublette. Laramie is believed to be derived from an Indian trader by the name of Lorimier. See Ghent, *Early Far West*, 204. See fn. 17, Smith's letters.

to other traders. This is in the Sioux country. Here the Black Hills commence, and extend west nearly to Wind River Mountains, and north to the Missouri. They are a range of low, broken hills, covered with scattering pitch pines, of a small size. These give them the black appearance from which they derive their name.

The fort mentioned is a stockaded enclosure of about 200 feet square, with buildings on the inside around the square, leaving the middle an open space for work. A few men are left here to trade with the Indians, and take care of the furs. We left the fort on the 2d of June, and in ten days crossed the Platte for the last time. We left this river, and followed up a branch called Sweetwater, to within 50 miles of the Wind River mountains. We there left it, and, after proceeding about six miles, came to the Popo Agie, a stream which rises in the W.R. mountains, and runs in an easterly direction; this we followed for three days, and arrived at this place on the twenty-first of June.

Wind River Mountains are supposed to be the highest land in North America,[7] as the waters of the whole western territories take their rise in this chain; among others, the Missouri, Columbia, Platte and Green rivers. The maps of this section of country which have been published are very inaccurate. Their general outlines may be correct; but their filling up, in many instances, is incorrect.

We travel with a caravan; which, with ourselves and animals, form a company of 75 men and 150 horses and mules. Two of Gov. Clarke's sons,[8] from St. Louis, and an English gentleman, a Capt. Stewart, are with us; besides several free trappers, a set of men who hunt on their own responsibility, go where and when they please, and live and act as they like. The animals are all picketed at night, by being tied to stakes driven in the ground, about 20 feet apart. In the morning at daybreak, they are let loose to graze for two or three hours, when they are caught and harnessed and prepared for marching. At noon we stop about two hours, and then travel till five or six o'clock, when we encamp for the night on the bank of a stream, or near a spring. The carts and wagons form a hollow square facing the stream. Those who have no wagons are stationed on the bank. Our place was always in the center of the side next the stream. The animals eat under guard till sunset, when they are picketed inside the square for the night.

---

[7] This was based on Washington Irving's statements in his *The Adventures of Captain Bonneville.* See FWW, II, p. 50. The highest peak in the Wind River range, Mt. Fremont, is only 13,730 feet high while Mt. McKinley in Alaska is 20,300.

[8] See Eells account of these sons of William Clark. Text, pp. 302-303.

My equipment is as follows: — A belt around the waist, with a butcher knife attached; powder flask and bullet pouch over the shoulder; my rifle lying before me on the saddle, and a brace of pistols in my holsters. These things, except the pistols, every man and boy in the whole caravan carries; so that, in case of danger, all are ready for action at a moment's warning. Fortunately, however, we have yet had no occasion to use our arms. In fact, there is scarcely any danger in the country through which we have passed, when there is so large a company. We have yet seen no Indians except the Kansas and Pawnees. There is nothing to be feared from these, unless some of their wild young men meet a few whites alone. They then sometimes rob them. But if detected, their chiefs will compel them to make restitution.

RENDEZVOUS [9]

This is a term used to designate the place where all the trappers meet at this season of the year to bring in their furs, and obtain their future supplies. At the appointed time, they meet at some point most convenient for all. None are excluded: — free traders, hired men, &c., all come in, and procure their supply of clothes, ammunition, &c. Rendezvous generally lasts 20 or 30 days, and the whole time is spent in drinking, gambling, horse-racing, quarrelling, fighting, &c. Alcohol is the only liquor brought here, and is sold at $4 a pint. Some men will spend a thousand dollars in a day or two, and very few have any part of their year's wages left when rendezvous breaks up.

Our company are encamped about 300 yards from the main camp; so we are a little out of their noise; but they come down nearly every day to give us an Indian dance. They always treat us with kindness; but they wish to give us a specimen of mountain life. When the time for separation comes, it becomes each one to look well to his effects; for he is in danger of being stripped of every thing he possesses.

The American Fur Company must soon abandon the mountains.[10] The trade is unprofitable, and the men are becoming dissatisfied; besides, the Hudson's Bay Company will break down all opposition. Their

[9] For picture of site where the mission party camped, see FWW, II, p. 85. Rogers gives an excellent account of life at the Rendezvous. See also Eells reminiscences, text, pp. 300-303.

[10] The last known Rendezvous was held the following year, 1839, on Green River. Some evidence points to a Rendezvous for 1840 but authorities differ on whether or not this was held. Joe Meek said that he looked for it but could not find it while Father De Smet claims he was there. The change in styles for men's hats from beaver to silk brought an end to the Rocky Mountain beaver trade.

resources are boundless, and they stop at no expense. They are now establishing posts through all the country which is accessible west of the mountains; and they sell their goods for less than one-fourth the price charged by the other company. What their intentions in regard to the possession of this country are, I cannot tell. One of their officers, with some men, arrived here yesterday.[11] He came to meet and assist us on to Fort Hall, which is about 15 days' ride, with pack animals, from this place. Mr. Spaulding also will meet us on the way. Mr. Spaulding and Dr. Whitman, it is said, are well and doing well.

There are here no Indians except a few trappers of the Shawnees and Delawares. There are a few lodges of the Snakes around the point of the mountain; but they will not come here. There are two classes of the Snake nation. One is the Shoshonies, or those who have horses. They are friendly; but have some of the roving, savage disposition. The others are called Diggers, from the fact that they live principally upon roots. They inhabit the mountains, seldom venturing to the plains, and are a harmless, inoffensive people.

CLIMATE AND PRODUCTIONS

From the time we left the States until we reached the Platte, we had occasional rains, mostly cold and chilly. It is always more or less so at the season in which we passed. Sometimes hail of a large size falls; but we had none.Where we are now, and generally through the mountains, there is seldom any rain; but it is dry and hot. The thermometer stood at 120 in the sun and at about 100 in the shade a day or two since. As we approach the summits of the mountains, it becomes cooler. Very few clouds are to be seen. The rivers, whose sources are in the snowy mountains, rise and fall daily, with the alternate melting and freezing of the snow in the day and night. Cotton wood is almost the only timber found in the whole territory. Of this there are three kinds. One is called the sweet cotton wood, and is scarce. Another the bitter cotton wood, and grows in great plenty. The third is the same that is called the Balm of Gilead in the states. There is but little of it.

Of curiosities there are many; but I have time to mention but few. On the north folk of the Platte, a few days' travel above the junction, is a prominence of indurated clay called the Church, or Tower. It has the appearance of an ancient pile of buildings, in the form of a castle, with several out towers. One half day's ride above is what is called

[11] The reference is to Francis Ermatinger who escorted the mission party to Fort Hall.

the Chimney, a projection of the same kind of material as the tower, precisely in the shape if a chimney, and scarcely any larger, though it is about 70 feet high. There is a beautiful cascade on the Sweetwater, where it passes through a granite mountain. I visited it alone. The vastness of the chasm, the roaring of the waters, and the screaming of the wild birds, filled me with new and strange sensations. If ever I felt astonishment mingled with admiration, it was then. My mind instinctively ascended from Nature up to Nature's God. The rapid movement of the company prevented me from taking that notice of the country which I wished.[12]

---

[12] Here the published version of the letter as it appears in the *Oregonian and Indian's Advocate* abruptly ends.

A New Letter of Marcus Whitman
May 31, 1844

A New Letter of Marcus Whitman

INTRODUCTION

Included in the recently discovered collection of Asa B. Smith's correspondence was a hitherto unpublished letter from Marcus Whitman to Smith dated May 31, 1844. This letter was written about eight months after Whitman had returned from his transcontinental journey to Washington and Boston and the experience was still vivid in his memory. Smith had by that time been in Hawaii for over two years but Whitman knew that his former colleague would be interested in hearing about the results of the journey. The letter, therefore, throws further light on the much debated "Whitman-Saved-Oregon" story. Only rarely after his return with the large 1843 immigration did Whitman look back and comment in his letters on the objectives or results of his ride.[1] When he did so, he usually confined his remarks to the services he was able to render to the immigrants. Once, on April 2, 1847, in a letter to Secretary Greene, he wrote: ". . . the other great object for which I went was to save the Mission from being broken up just then. . ." Three years earlier, however, in this letter to Smith, he had stated this same thought when he informed Smith: "I am happy to know that I was enabled if nothing more to reverse the action of the Board in relation to this Mission." The whole tenor of this new letter of Whitman's supports the author's thesis as set forth in his biography of Henry Harmon Spalding that Whitman did not ride to save Oregon but rather to save Spalding and the stations at Lapwai and Waiilatpu.[2]

This letter of Whitman to Smith is important not only for what Whitman did say but also for what he did not say. A brief review of the background is necessary to appreciate the significance of the letter. After moving to the Willamette Valley in 1848, following the Whitman

---

[1] Drury, *Marcus Whitman, M.D.*, p. 343, gives a summary of such comments taken from five of Whitman's letters.

[2] *Ibid.*, Appendix 3, "The Cause of Whitman's Ride" presents a detailed study of the causes for Whitman's departure for the East, and Appendix 4, "The Whitman Controversy" reviews the extensive literature on the subject.

massacre, Spalding published a series of articles in the Oregon American and Evangelical Unionist *in which he accused the Roman Catholics of being the instigators of the massacre. This was of course
denied. There followed a pamphlet warfare between Spalding and his
friends on the one hand, and such writers defending the Catholics as
Father J. B. A. Brouillet on the other.*[3] *Out of this controversy there
evolved the theory that England, spurred on by the Roman Catholics,
was about to take over all of the Oregon territory. Somehow Spalding
had gotten some erroneous information about a treaty which the
United States was negotiating with England about Oregon. This was
the Ashburton Treaty which was concluded on August 9, 1842, but
which said nothing about the Oregon boundary. But Spalding believed
that by this treaty the United States was going to trade its rights in
Oregon for some cod fishing privileges off the New England coast. He
claimed that Whitman's sudden decision to ride East was inspired by
a discovery of this nefarious plan, and that he arrived in Washington
just in time to prevent the government from signing the treaty, and
thus Whitman rode to save Oregon for the Union.*

Spalding, who began developing this theory about 1864,[4] *naturally
hesitated to say anything about the fact that he had been recalled by
the American Board. Human nature does not thus shout abroad its
weaknesses and failures. Instead Spalding played up the patriotic and
political interests that Whitman had in Oregon. An extensive literature
grew out of the controversy. In 1870 the "Whitman-Saved-Oregon"
story appeared in book form when W. H. Gray published his* Oregon.
In 1871 Spalding succeeded in having his views published as Executive
Document No. 37, U.S. Senate, 41st Congress, 3d Session.[5] *Perhaps the
classic and certainly the most widely distributed version of the story
was Oliver Nixon's* How Marcus Whitman Saved Oregon, *which first*

---

[3] Father Brouillet's reply to the charges of Spalding regarding the Roman
Catholic involvement in the Whitman massacre was published in 1858 as a part
of *Executive Document No. 38, U.S. House of Representatives, 35th Congress, 1st
Session.* Spalding was deeply stirred over the publication by the government of
this document and spent some thirteen years laboring to get his views presented
to the American public in some similar manner.

[4] The first known published version of the "Whitman-Saved-Oregon" story was
written by S. A. Clarke, believed to be a friend of Spalding's, which appeared in
the Sacramento *Union,* November 16, 1864. A series of lectures by Spalding on
this subject began in the San Francisco *Pacific* on May 23, 1865.

[5] This was in answer to *H.R. Exec. Doc. No. 38* issued in 1858. For an account
of how the Senate document happened to be published, see Drury, *Spalding,* p.
391ff.

appeared in 1895. The book ran through six editions. It is still being used by uncritical writers and speakers for stories, television scenarios, and sermon illustrations. Perhaps no person in American history became the center of so many myths and legends in so short a time after his death as Marcus Whitman.

But the time came when the theory was challenged. Mrs. F. F. Victor, one of the authors of Bancroft's Oregon which appeared in 1884, was the first reputable scholar to question Spalding's thesis. About 1900 Dr. Edward Gaylord Bourne, professor of history at Yale University, and W. I. Marshall, principal of a school in Chicago, independently of each other, came to the conclusion that the "Whitman-Saved-Oregon" story was entirely without historical foundation.

In my first book, Henry Harman Spalding, Pioneer of Old Oregon, published in 1936, I accepted and expanded the view advanced by others that Whitman rode on mission business. One of the chapters of that book bears the title "Whitman Rides to Save Spalding." There is conclusive evidence that Whitman visited Washington, D.C., on his way to Boston. As a public spirited citizen and one deeply interested in the future development of Oregon, he sought interviews with prominent government officials, including possibly President Tyler, and told all who would listen about the importance of Oregon. After he returned to Waiilatpu, Whitman wrote out a proposed bill which he submitted for congressional approval.[6] This called for the protection by the government of Oregon-bound immigrants and also for the establishment of a pony express, seventeen years before this became a reality.[7] But there is no documentary evidence to support the claims made by the proponents of the "Whitman-Saved-Oregon" story that Whitman reached Washington just in time to prevent the signing of a treaty with England which would have forfeited United States claims to Oregon or that he made any promises to raise or even to lead a party of emigrants into the Pacific Northwest.

The fact that Whitman found it best to go to Washington before

---

[6] The archives of the War Department, File no. 424052, National Archives, Washington, D.C., contain a copy of this bill and a letter from Whitman to the Hon. James M. Porter, Secretary of War. Whitman's letter bears no date but carries a notation that it was received on June 22, 1844. He began his letter: "In compliance with the request you did me the honor to make last winter while at Washington, I herewith transmit you the synopsis of a Bill. . ." Here is clear evidence that Whitman was in Washington.

[7] There is no evidence that the suggested bill was ever seriously considered by any committee of Congress at that time.

going to Boston does not mean that his patriotic interests regarding Oregon took precedence over his mission business. Being pressed for time, it was more convenient for him to go that way. After giving various government officials the benefit of his knowledge and experience regarding the best ways to promote and protect the inevitable Oregon emigrations, Whitman hurried on to Boston where he arrived on March 30th.

The secretaries of the American Board were somewhat dismayed at Whitman's unexpected and unauthorized return. This explains the coolness with which he was at first received. At his first opportunity Whitman explained to Secretary Greene the reasons for his journey. In the archives of the American Board is a memorandum in Greene's handwriting, evidently made at the time of this interview, which was no doubt used by Greene when he presented Whitman's case before the Prudential Committee of the Board.[8] There is absolutely no evidence in this memorandum that Whitman had any political motive in going East. No mention is made of Washington even though Whitman must have informed Greene of the visit made there. All of this was incidental to the real purpose of his return, which was to keep Spalding on the field and to retain the mission stations of Lapwai and Waiilatpu.

The first part of Greene's memorandum contains a summary of Whitman's report as to the condition and prospects of the Oregon Mission. Greene noted:

Left the Oregon country, 3d October 1842 & arrived at Westport, Mo., 15 February & in Boston, 30 March 1843. Left unexpectedly & brought few letters. Letter of March 1842[9] — making changes had been received and acted on.

The difficulties between Mr. Spalding & the others was apparently healed. Mr. S. promises to pursue a different course. The mission wish to make another trial with Mr. Smith & Mr. Gray out of the mission. Mr. Gray requests a dismission — Has left the mission & gone to the Methodist establishment — Mr. Rogers also.

Prospects among the Indians more favorable — half the year from 30 to 100 & the other half from 100 to 300 attend worship at Waiilatpu & Clear Water each [10] — attentive & advancing somewhat in knowledge

---

[8] Coll. A., Vol. 248, no. 78. This memorandum was published in the *Oregon Historical Quarterly*, Dec., 1921, p. 357ff.

[9] Greene here refers to the action of the Board dated February 25, 1842. The order may not have been mailed until March.

— their temporal condition much improved & improving — the traders at Walla Walla decidedly friendly and accommodating.[11]

There is, however, an influx of Papists, & many emigrants from the u.s. are expected.[12] The religious influence needs to be strengthened.

After giving Greene this background review of conditions on the field, Whitman then dealt directly with the future development of the work. Although nothing is said in Greene's memorandum about Whitman's primary request regarding the rescinding of the Board's disastrous order of February 1842, yet judging from Whitman's letter to Smith which follows, this was discussed. The following notations by Greene indicate additional requests by Whitman:

1. One preacher be sent to join them to labor at Waiilatpu — and that

2. A Company of some five or ten men may be found, of piety & intelligence, not to be appointed by the Board or be immediately connected with it, who will go to Oregon country as Christian men, and who, on some terms to be agreed upon, shall take most of the land which the mission have under cultivation with the mills & shops at the several stations with most of the stock & utensils, paying the mission in produce, from year to year, in seed to the Indians, & assistance rendered to them — or in some similar manner, the particulars to be decided upon in consultation with the men.

Here we come to a new aspect which the missionaries in Oregon faced which has not to my best observation been discussed in any previous writing on this subject. Whitman had become aware, perhaps during his stay in Washington, that all of the proposed bills approved the granting of 640 acres of land to every adult Oregon immigrant, but that no provisions had been made to permit church organizations such as missions to lay claim to land. This meant that the American

---

[10] When one considers the number of natives living in the vicinity of these two stations, these figures show that the majority were in regular attendance at the worship services. The attitude of the natives to the missionary program began to change after the arrival of the 1843 immigration and became noticeably less cooperative with the ever-increasing inflow of white settlers during the following years.

[11] Archibald McKinley, a Scots Presbyterian, succeeded Pierre Pambrun in charge of Fort Walla Walla in the summer of 1841. He was very friendly with the missionaries.

[12] Whitman knew at the time he was in Boston that there would be a large emigration to Oregon in 1843. According to the usually accepted estimates, about one thousand people were in the overland party of that year.

Board would have to lay claim to such land as was occupied at Waii-latpu and Lapwai through individuals. Whitman's plan was for the Board to send a few devoted Christian laymen to each of its stations in Oregon who would file claim to the property and take over the secular affairs. According to Greene's memorandum:

The results would be 1.   Introducing a band of religious men into the country to exert a good religious influence on the Indians & the white population which may come in — especially near the mission stations.

2.   Counteracting papal efforts & influences.

3.   Releasing the missionaries from the great amount of manual labor, which is now necessary for their subsistance, & permitting them to devote themselves to appropriate missionary work among the Indians, whose language they now speak.

4.   Doing more for civilization and social improvement of the Indians than the mission can do unaided.

5.   It would afford facilities for religious families to go into the country & make immediately a comfortable settlement, with the enjoyment of Christian privileges — both those who might be introduced upon the lands now occupied by the mission & others who might be induced to go & settle in the vicinity of the stations.

6.   It would save the mission from the necessity of trading with immigrants. Those who now enter the country expect to purchase or beg their supplies from the mission for a year or two, & it would be thought cruel to refuse to provide such supplies.[13]

Eight members of the Prudential Committee, including David Greene and other secretaries, met in Boston on Tuesday, April 4th. Greene presented his report and Whitman was given an opportunity to appear before the committee. The minutes of the Prudential Committee likewise make no reference to Whitman's visit to Washington nor to any political activity on his part. The following action taken by the Committee shows that Whitman was successful in inducing it to rescind the order of February 1842 which called for the dismissal of Spalding and the closing of the work at Waiilatpu and Lapwai:

---

[13] Whitman was criticized for prices charged the immigrants for supplies. See Drury, *Marcus Whitman, M.D.,* 341. Peter Burnett, one of the immigrants of 1843, stoutly defended Whitman against the "foolish, false, and ungrateful" charges. Whitman often provided provisions for those who were unable to pay. Long before the need actually arose, Whitman foresaw the problems which he would have to face at Waiilatpu and, therefore, begged for help from the Board.

Resolved, That Doct. Marcus Whitman and the Rev. H. H. Spalding, be authorized to continue to occupy the stations at Waiilatpu and Clear Water, as they did previous to the adoption of the resolutions referred to above.

Resolved. That a missionary be sent to strengthen the Oregon mission, if a suitable person can be found.

Whitman was given permission to take out to Oregon "a small company of intelligent and pious laymen" if such could be found and if this could be done without expense to the Board. This action of the Board was somewhat of an empty gesture, for the time was much too short for him to find any assistants and be out on the frontier by the 10th of May. The Board was interested in sending ordained missionaries and not settlers to Oregon.

As far as it is possible to reconstruct Whitman's itinerary, he remained in Boston for nearly ten days and then hurried to Rushville, New York, to see his mother and other relatives. He probably remained in Rushville from April 12th to the 17th. While there Whitman secured the consent of his brother Samuel to take the latter's fourteen-year-old son, Perrin, with him to Oregon. The two were out on the Missouri frontier by the middle of May. There they joined the great 1843 Oregon emigration of about one thousand people. We have much evidence of the help Dr. Whitman rendered the members of this party, and after the emigration had reached Fort Hall he became the acknowledged leader. Whitman was back at Waiilatpu on Thursday, September 28, having been gone for almost a full year.

This is the background of the letter Whitman wrote the following May to A. B. Smith, then in Hawaii. Whitman first mentioned the prospects of coming immigrations and gently chided his former colleague for his lack of faith in Oregon. He referred to the future promise of Oregon as a manufacturing center and as a great wool producing country. Here was Whitman speaking — a prophet of the Oregon which was to be. And then he touched on the real purpose of his journey East. There is no mention of any political motive. Nothing was said about arriving in Washington at some dramatic moment just when the United States was about to sign away its rights to Oregon for a cod fishery. No claim was made of any activity in raising the great emigration of 1843. Instead, Whitman very simply and directly reported his success in reversing the action of the Board. The Mission had been saved. Remembering Smith's feelings toward Spalding and his convictions regarding the futility of missionary work among the Indians of

*the upper Columbia River Valley, we can easily believe that Smith
found little satisfaction in Whitman's accomplishments.*

*In the closing paragraph of the letter, we again see Whitman as a
prophet of the new Oregon. Here he made mention of his hope to
raise money for the establishment of "Academies & Colleges" in Oregon. This is the first reference in his letters to such institutions. Later
on two different occasions he mentions this hope of seeing a college
established in the Walla Walla Valley. In a letter to Secretary Greene
dated October 25, 1844, he wrote: "This is the place most advantageous
for the commencement of what may soon be an Academy or College."
And in Whitman's last letter to the Board written on October 16, 1847,
he again made reference to this subject. Today Whitman College,
founded by Cushing Eells in 1859, stands in Walla Walla a few miles
from Waiilatpu as a living memorial to his memory.*

WHITMAN'S LETTER TO SMITH

WAIILATPU, May 31st, 1844

REV. A. B. SMITH
HONOLULU, OAHU

DEAR BROTHER. I have a disposition this morning to write you but
I know not where I should limit myself if I entered on the full field
of communication.

Our situation in this country is becoming more interesting and more
important. The fact that Government is opening the country by offers
of bounty of lands will soon bring our stations to be the object of desire
& there will be no way to hold on under such circumstances, for
Congress would only give us the right of occupancy for missionary
purposes which would be no security but only make it necessary to
break up the Mission in order to get full possession. I know your views
of the country but be assured no one will agree with you now. The
interior of Oregon will be more sought than any part of it. And the
country as a whole is not surpassed by any on the globe.[14]

It is by no means necessary that it be according to any particular
pattern we have been accustomed to. If it were many times inferior
to what even yourself has regarded it, still with an American popula-

---

[14] Whitman was convinced that, spurred by government's offer of free land,
immigrants by the thousands would soon be entering Oregon. This was evidently
the theme of his letter to E. O. Hall written shortly after his return from the East.
See text, p. 222, where Smith comments after reading the letter: "I expect he
[Whitman] is going to turn settler in Oregon."

tion, the Commerce of the Pacific would make its occupancy of the greatest value. The interior is in every respect such a country as western men desire, when a settlement would have a vacant range for cattle & sheep &c. The most broken hills in the country take the place of barns & meadows without the labour of building & storing.

A country where a man can winter a thousand sheep easier than he could feed half the number from a well stored barn in your own native Vermont. Thus if any body are to take the cotton of the Islands & return the factories [the manufactured goods], so much needed by the Islanders, as also to carry on the domestick commerce & take their salt, sugar &c., &c. No tariff is wanted to protect manufactories in Oregon. The wool grown here & manufactured in the country would be exchanged for domestick articles, the same as a trade with the Islands, so that so far as the exchange in such articles is concerned, no foreign fabricks can come in competition.

I consider the growth of a colony here as more likely to give that kind of trade to the Islands that shall give them independence and domestic ability than all others put together.

My visit to the States was a hurried one as I was disappointed in not getting in so early as I expected. *I am happy to know that I was enabled if nothing more to reverse the action of the Board in relation to this Mission.*[15] No one knows more than yourself what & who have been the cause of those measures [16] as also of the sentiments which Mr. Lee thinks has taken more than one out of this Mission.[17] The Committee were willing to grant all our requests. But as I was necessitated to come back so soon no one could be ready to accompany me. I brought a Nephew fourteen years old with me. I do not know how long we shall be called to operate for the benefit of the Indians. But be it longer or shorter, it will not diminish the importance of our situation. For if the Indians are to pass away, we want to do what can be done in order to give them the offer of life & then be ready to aid [the immigrants] as indeed we have done & are doing, to found & sustain institutions [of] learning & religion in the Country.

[15] Editorial italics. Here, succinctly stated, Whitman refers to the great satisfaction he felt in knowing that he had accomplished his main purpose in going East.

[16] Was Whitman here reminding Smith that *he* had been the principal cause of the Board's action of February 1842, or was the reference meant for Spalding? In effect Whitman was saying: "In spite of all the undercutting that has been going on, I have been able to save the Mission."

[17] The reference is possibly to Jason Lee but we have no record as to when or where Lee expressed such sentiments.

Could I have staid at home longer, I should have tried to have raised the means of establishing some Academies & Colleges, but I trust to influence others to do so. The Mission now is in a united & harmonious state having less to fear from difficulties because her members are tried by having had their trials.[18] Mrs. Whitman's health has been very poor & at times life was dispaired of. But she is now much better. I am glad to learn through Doct. Barclay that Mrs. Smith's health is so good. Mrs. W. joins me in Christian salutations to you both desiring for you health, happiness, and usefulness.   With esteem

Yours Truely   MARCUS WHITMAN

---

[18] The "united & harmonious state" within the Oregon Mission continued during the remaining years of its history. But now, largely because of the ever increasing flow of white immigration, the Indians became increasingly suspicious of and finally hostile to the missionaries. This came to a dramatic climax in the Whitman massacre of November 29-30, 1847.

Reminiscences of Cushing Eells

Reminiscences of Cushing Eells

OVERLAND TRAVEL EXPERIENCES OF 1838

Whitman College contains in its archives some manuscripts written by Cushing Eells in his old age which contain reminiscences of his experiences as a member of the Oregon Mission of the American Board. Included in this collection are eight notebooks, each written at Cheney, Washington, dating from June 12, 1882, to May 23, 1883. There are also five papers with later dates, the last being July 20, 1892. Eells was then eighty-two and died the following year. Altogether these manuscripts contain about forty thousand words. Myron Eells, the younger son of Cushing and Myra, drew upon these reminiscences for his biography of his father, Father Eells, *published in 1894.*

Although these reminiscences, written forty-four and more years after the events actually occurred, contain some inaccuracies and are not well organized, yet they do throw some new and interesting light upon the experiences of those early days. Cross references by the use of footnotes have been made so that relevant passages in these reminiscences may be related to earlier sections of this volume and vice versa. Since much in these reminiscences is repetitious and disorganized, the material has been condensed and rearranged. Deleted sections will be indicated by the use of ellipses.

Although, of course, Eells had no personal memories of incidents involving members of the 1836 mission party, he did have opportunity to learn directly from the parties themselves some of their experiences. He wrote as follows regarding an incident which came to Mrs. Spalding during her westward journey of 1836:[1]

Mrs. S. was not strong. At one stage of the journey she seemed to be exhausted, and made request to be left. This could not be thought of. She rallied, and kept with the Company. The mission band had a small wagon. But usually the ladies together with the Gents. rode in the saddle. At one point the horse upon which Mrs. S. rode became unmanageable; the rider lost her balance, fell with her foot fast in the

---

[1] From section in reminiscences dated February 2, 1883.

stirrup. With the rapid motion of the horse, Mrs. S. was in great peril. Mr. Tho. McKay, a sharp shooter, raised his gun to shoot the horse just as the lady's foot slipped from the stirrup. There was no serious injury.[2]

The presence of two white women at a gathering of mountain men near the base of the Rocky Mts. was an unheard-of event. The object in view, the arduousness and peril of the undertaking by females, was singularly impressive. The power of cultured Christian ladies over men, the like of whom were said to fear not God or the devil, was acknowledged. . .

At that place [Ft. Vancouver] they were received with true English gallantry, and welcomed to the enjoyable hospitality of that head post. The entertainment was enhanced in value by the experience of several previous months of camp life. As heretofore, so now, the presence of two white American ladies was unprecedented. It caused a pleasant ripple on the monotony of life at the post. . .

If history shall do them justice, it will place on imperishable record the names of the two white ladies who first passed over the land from Mo. (the then western frontier) to the W.W. valley and the Col. river.

About eight years after writing the above, Eells returned to the experiences of Mrs. Whitman and Mrs. Spalding while crossing the Rockies by writing the following on October 6, 1891:

At that point [the Rendezvous of 1836 on Green River] the presence of two white women was an unprecedented event. The power of refined ladies was acknowledged. It is reported that a Rocky Mountain trapper said, 'I was a better man after looking upon those Christian ladies." Another trapper said: 'There is something the Honorable Hudson's Bay Co. cannot expel from the country." [3] They could drive out rival traders, but not Christian missionaries, and especially lady missionaries.

After referring to Gray's return east in 1837, Eells commented as follows on the personnel of the 1838 reenforcement:

---

[2] Spalding referred to this incident in an interview granted the editor of the *Chicago Advance* and published on December 1, 1870. The interview was republished in *Senate Document No. 37, 41st Congress, 3d Session,* p. 11. See Sarah Smith's diary describing a similar experience she had, August 20, 1838. Text, p. 106.

[3] Again Eells borrowed from Spalding. See Spalding Ms, File 201, p. 7 in Coll. W. Spalding attributed the remark to "The shrewd McKay." FWW, I, p. 116.

At that date Rev. E. Walker and myself were each under appointment to go and teach the Zulus of S.E. Africa. On account of war then raging between two powerful chiefs, Dingan and Maselekatsi, our departure was indefinitely delayed. The urgency of the call beyond the R. Mts. was such that the consent of Mr. Walker and myself was asked to the making of a change in our destination from Zulu land to the Indians of the N.W. It was done. Rev. A. B. Smith, already an accepted employee of the A. Board, was added.

Thus three ordained ministers (such only by the Soc's ruling are denominated missionaries, all others are classed as assistant missionaries) were commissioned. Mr. Walker was in Me. I in Mass. & Conn. We were strangers to each other. Each was married on the 5th of March, 1838, and on the following day with the treasure thus acquired, each started to cross almost the Am. continent. Mrs. E. & myself rode from Holden, Mass. to Worcester on runners.[4] From thence to East Winsor Hill, Conn., on wheels through mud. A tedious day's ride. . .

At N.Y. City the three newly formed families joined company. In the Brick Ch., Dr. Spring's, Sec. Greene, father of Judge G[reene] of W[ashington] T[erritory] in behalf of the A. Board gave instructions.[5] . . By the usual modes of conveyance, steamer, stage, & rail, the three mission families traveled to Independence landing. . . At Cinn. Mr. C. R[ogers] joined us. He was not under appointment by the Miss. Board. Friends assisted him to obtain an outfit. . . Mr. Gray had preceded us to Independence for the purchasing of horses and outfit for the journey thereafter. At the S[team] Boat landing we first met him and shortly after the newly married woman of his choice, who then and thenceforth was esteemed as a choice woman.

From a section dated February 13, 1883, Eells had the following to say about their experiences at Independence:

The steamboat landing was, according to my recollection, about a mile and a half from the town.[6] At that point there were small store rooms built of rough logs, also a like dwelling occupied by a family. Soon after our arrival there Mr. Rogers started to walk to town to report to Mr. Gray, and obtain conveyance thither. Night was ap-

---

[4] In a sleigh, it being winter and snow was on the ground.

[5] Robert S. Greene, son of Secretary David Greene of the American Board, was made Associate Justice in Washington Territory in 1870 and Chief Justice in 1879.

[6] Writing many years later, Eells underestimated the distance which separated the landing from the village. His wife writing at the time noted that the distance was four miles. FWW, II, p. 57. See Smith letter, April 16, 1838. Text, p. 138.

proaching, and there was no apparent locomotive to be used for our benefit. The possibility of our being obliged to remain there during the coming night was thought of; consequently inquiry was made if we could be furnished with lodging. The reply was, "Yes, if you have blankets." To ladies recently from N[ew] E[ngland] those words had a peculiar ring — produced unwonted sensation; by after experience practical familiarity was had with such accommodations. Before dark Mr. Gray appeared with three horses appropriately caparisoned for the use of females. The question was more readily asked than answered — can those unaccustomed to the use of the saddle ride by night on horse back over a road of Mo. and the ruts in the month of Apr.? With a footman holding the rein in close proximity to the mouth of the steed the gentle riders made the first stage of a journey of near 2000 miles in the saddle.

Suddenly the members of the mission party were exposed to a new manner of life that was utterly different from the sheltered existence they had enjoyed in their eastern homes. For this there had been no period of training which would have prepared them for the harsh realities ahead. Their long horseback ride was to be no picnic excursion. There would be no turning back. The alternatives were grim — either adapt or perish. Looking back over many years, Cushing Eells recalled:

The Gents. no less than the ladies were not well fitted for the . . . new demands upon strength and patience. Student life in Academy, College and Sem[inary] had not been a well adapted training school for the successful performance of the work of camp life.

While I was walking in a street of Cin[cinnati] I observed an article to myself new and of unexplained utility. I paused, looked but asked no question. It was the wood part of a pack saddle with an unusual appendage thereto. At Independence the sight of a pile of pack saddles padded and riged for the use of our party informed me regarding the use of the afore seen article in Cin. . .

The nine riding saddles with a blanket above and beneath were readily placed upon the appropriate horses. The pack saddles were not easily adjusted to the backs of Spanish mules that were not altogether remarkably tame. Then followed the putting on of loads. There were eight trunks, bedding, tents and tent poles, food, medicine, and all the paraphennalia of four young families about to start on a land journey of said to be 1900 miles to an unknown home.

At the commencement, the laboring oar was emphatically with Mr. Gray. Three novices with willing hearts offered ready hands. But their awkward doings were not invariably and entirely helpful. Slowly the loads of the pack animals, small wagon, and riding horses were placed. There was forward movement in the direction of Westport, distant 12 miles more or less. The caravan had not gone far before there was disarangement of packs. The unwelcome disclosure was made that the horse, attached to the wagon, was unreliable. This load must be improved, that modified. The call was for Mr. Gray here, Mr. Gray there, Mr. Gray everywhere.

In an attempt to ascend a hill the wagon horse refused to pull. With all my might I lifted at the rear end of the wagon. This was oft repeated. The disobedient animal was stubborn and the vehicle thereby was demoralized. My strength was exhausted. Night was near. A house with kind occupants was found where Mrs. E. and myself were comfortably entertained. A portion of the Co. reached Westport a town on the W[est] border of Mo. Next day repairs were made. Another horse and wagon were obtained.[7] Sabbath came. On that day the Fur Co's train of empty carts started. Their goods were taken by water to the crossing of the Kansas river where they were met after about a week's travel. We ventured to delay our departure till Monday Ap'l 23.

The last Sunday the missionaries were to spend in civilization before starting on the long journey across the plains was observed by going to a church service held in a log house. A Methodist missionary preached in the morning and Cushing Eells took the afternoon service. The next day they began their overland journey.

With the benediction of a few new made acquaintances, we passed beyond the restraints of law, invoking the protection of the supreme law-giver. The sensation of the first night of sleep in a tent was new. Satisfactory progress was daily made. Early on Sat. we came up with the caravan of the Fur Co. Six day's travel without their protection had been disastrous. Three of our more valuable horses had been stolen by the so-called friendly Indians.[8]

---

[7] Mrs. Eells in her diary for April 20th stated that their wagon broke down and that they were obliged to leave it "two or three miles this side of Westport." FWW, 'II, p. 59. No reference has been found in the contemporary writings of any of the party to another wagon being purchased to replace the one that had broken down. In all probability, repairs were made and the same wagon was used.

[8] Mrs. Eells in her diary tells of her husband looking for the lost horses the next day and returning to camp "so tired that the ground makes him a soft bed." FWW, II, p. 73. Actually the monetary loss was of less importance than the loss of the availability of the animals to carry their baggage. Since they left the frontier with the minimum number of pack animals, they could ill afford to lose even one horse.

Dr. Chute,[9] a graduate of Yale, an excellent Christian gentleman residing at Westport, was a real helper. He was with us at different points during that first week. In our need he, for a reasonable consideration, transferred for our use his large choice riding horse. . . In Capt. Bonneville's [10] trip to the R. Mts. many years before the Sioux Indians stole from him a serviceable mule. Subsequently the Pawnee Indians stole it of the Sioux. It was purchased of the Pawnee's for our use.[11] In such like manner the loss from Indian depredation was mostly repaired.

Special vigilance was needful in the care of my wife's riding animal. When grazing it was well to use both a trail rope and hobble. As the horses and mules of the Fur Co. and mission band were gathered preparatory to their being driven into the water for swimming across the river, the order was, "Tie up the trail ropes." Hurriedly I obeyed. Unphilosophically I passed it round and round the neck of the treacherous animal of my care. Land on the opposite bank being gained, the beast readily comprehended the unrestrained freedom enjoyed, and took position in the outer edge of the grazing herd. Then larger liberty was taken. The exercise of my skill to apprehend the animal was to no purpose. In my discomfiture, application was made to our hunter Richardson, formerly of N[ew] H[amphire] but skilled in R[ocky] M[ountain] tacts. He proposed the plan of marking the animal, as he called it, viz, the propelling a rifle ball with precision so that it [would] pass through the upper part of the neck. . . We two, he with rifle in hand, each mounted, rode in search of the creature. . . At some distance from camp and alone we discovered the object of our search. On nearing the spot, the expected disposition to elude us was not exhibited. The experienced mountaineer readily discerned that the roguish eye was subdued. Considerately he approached, and found that the rope around the neck had become tightened to such a degree as effectually to tame, but not injure the beast. The unskillful manner

---

[9] Dr. J. Andrew Chute, a native of Maine, was evidently practicing medicine in Westport. Being much interested in missions to the Indians, he rendered timely help to the mission party. He died on October 1, 1838, when twenty-seven years old. FWW, II, p. 59. Among the drafts made out by Gray and paid by the American Board is one dated May 2, 1838, for $75.00 to Dr. Chute for a horse. Original in Coll. A. See fn. 18, Sarah Smith's diary.

[10] Capt. Benjamin L. E. Bonneville succeeded in taking twenty loaded wagons through South Pass to the Green River Rendezvous in 1832. Evidently it was at this time that the Sioux Indians stole the mule which eventually passed into the hands of the missionaries.

[11] Mrs. Eells in her diary for April 30th stated: "Buy one mule." FWW, II, p. 76.

in which I [had] wound the trail rope turned to our account. The irrecoverable loss of that animal at that time would have been seriously embarrassing.

In simpler words, Eells could have said that Richardson planned to shoot the horse through the neck in order to subdue it. The loss of another horse to the mission party would have been most serious at that time. He recalled the incident to illustrate how dependent all were on their animals. He then gave the following description of the caravan.

When the caravan was in motion,[12] the guide mounted on a large and distinguishably white mule led the way. Those acting in part as scouts were in advance, or not according to circumstances. Next to the guide was the wagon of Capt. Stewart [13] with four mules attached thereto. The owner of this outfit was an English Gent. traveling for pleasure. Then followed the cart of Capt. Drips [14] hauled by three mules harnessed in single file. Said Gent. was viceregent of the Fur Co.

Next in order was a train of 2 doz. more or less carts carrying the goods of the F. Co. To each cart two mules were attached, one before the other. Then came the one-horse wagon and loaded pack animals of the mission band, with their drivers. The neat-cattle [15] were in the rear. The appropriate place for the ladies was with those following the packs, but they were not restricted.

Encampments were sought near a stream. Wagons and carts were drawn so as to form a semi-circle upon the bank of the stream.[16] At about 6 P.M. such like location was occupied. The animals were turned

---

[12] See Mrs. Eells' description of the caravan in FWW, II, p. 75. "When we are fairly on our way we have much the appearance of a large funeral procession in the States."

[13] Captain (or Sir) William Drummond Stewart spent several years in the west as an independent adventurer. He was with the 1836 caravan when the Whitman-Spalding party crossed the Rockies. A recently published life of Stewart by Mae Reed Porter and Odessa Davenport is *Scotsman in Buckskin,* New York, 1963. See fn. 25, Sarah Smith's diary.

[14] Capt. Andrew Drips was in charge of the 1838 caravan of the American Fur Company which consisted of about 200 horses and mules, 17 carts and wagons, and about 60 men.

[15] In old English the word "cattle" included all live stock. "Neat-cattle" referred to those of the bovine genus. The expression is now archaic. The mission party of 1836 started out with 17 head whereas the party of 1838, although nearly twice as large, had only "twelve horned cattle." FWW, II, p. 75.

[16] See Walker's comment in his diary for May 7th. Text, p. 264. Also FWW, II, p. 75. The men of the caravan had learned from experience the necessity of maintaining a strict watch over their animals and property while passing through the Indian country.

loose attended by a sufficient guard. Near dark they were driven up each caught and picketed within the inclosure formed by wagons and carts. A guard was detailed to watch with relief by successive stages. Each man was expected to be on guard a portion of every fourth night. At the dawn of day, in stentorian tone, the order was "Loose the animals." Continuously both day and night, they were under guard.

The men of the mission party took their turn standing guard as their animals mixed with those of the Company. The men found that such duties combined with the manual work required in packing and unpacking and in making the daily marches taxed their physical strength to the limit. The lack of proper food added to their difficulties. Regarding these trying experiences, Eells wrote:

The labor of loading and unloading pack-animals twice each day, of pitching and striking tents by the mission band was heavy. The strength of Mr. Walker was unequal to the demand. He said, Help must be had or we should not have him. A packer was employed.[17] Soon after 6 A.M. camp moved. At 11. there was a halt of two hours.

Mrs. E. expressed the opinion that I averaged about four hours sleep per night. This was however compensated by occasional days of delay when we would sleep somewhat continuously. One such resting place was at Ft. Laramie, estimated to be distant from Mo. 700 miles. Our wagon was taken as provision for expected contingencies or possible necessities. Inability to ride continuously in the saddle was not unexpected. Thus far the use of the wagon had been convenient but not indispensable. We were near an ascending grade. For this and other reasons, the wagon and harness were exchanged for a riding horse.[18]

Mr. Gray had estimated that 400 miles of travel would bring us to the region of buffalo.[19] The quantity of food was gauged accordingly.

---

[17] Smith and Walker quickly discovered that the physical labor involved in packing and unpacking, together with other duties attendant upon their manner of life, was too much. They demanded that Gray hire an assistant, and therefore the services of Stevens were secured. He remained with the party until it reached Waiilatpu. FWW, II, p. 117. Sometimes the name was spelled Stephens.

[18] Mrs. Eells mentions in her diary for May 31st, while at Fort Laramie, the transfer of their wagon to Capt. Drips. It is possible that Gray advised this and recommended that the baggage be carried on the backs of animals from that point.

[19] Evidently Gray underestimated the time when the party would be able to obtain buffalo meat. According to Mrs. Eells' diary, FWW, II, p. 81, they did not get to buffalo until May 18th. Thus for some 25 days, or from April 23rd, they had to live on such provisions as they had with them. Not only was the food insufficient in quantity, there was little variety. Instead of traveling 400 miles before reaching buffalo, it was closer to 475. Here was one of the major reasons why the

But expectation was not realized. Rations were short, but the lack was bearable. A special inconvenience was that when a supply of buffalo meat was obtainable there was not much besides to use with it. The sudden change of diet was so great that weakness and slight sickness were thereby caused. I have a distinct recollection that late one P.M. I felt unable to sit in the saddle. I was in the rear. I dismounted, reclined upon mother earth, became rested and alone reached camp.

In Conn. by the kindness of affectionate lady pupils, two not large cakes were prepared considerately adapted for use on my projected journey. They were placed in my trunk. When suffering from the disproportionate use of fresh buffalo meat, a small piece of cake from Yankee land dissolved in water was specially palatable and helpful. My heart could feel more gratitude than my words could utter.

Only rarely do the writings of the members of the mission party of 1838 indicate laughter or humor. In the following account of the experiences of Asa and Sarah Smith in fording a stream while riding in a wagon, we find one of these instances. The horse's name was Steamboat. No doubt this anectode was often retold with many a chuckle. Eells also describes another river crossing and then relates one of the best known incidents of their travel experiences — that when Mary Walker sat on her baggage and wept when she remembered how comfortable were her father's hogs! Here too we find the missionaries laughing in the midst of their trials.

The wagon horse was strong and lazy. His name was Steamboat. Mr. & Mrs. Smith were in the wagon. Following the carts, Steamboat and his load passed into the [Platte] river and stopped. In vain the small whip at hand was applied. Those acquainted with the water and bed of that river need not be told that to stop in the quick sand is hazardous, — to remain long stationary is to go down. I was in my place in the rear. The helplessness of the occupants of the wagon was apparent. I left my post, pressed to a convenient point and vigorously applied a severe scourge to so called Steamboat. Steam power was not thereby generated but locomotion was caused to that Steamboat and the craft in tow. . .[20]

---

other members of the party criticized Gray's management. After reaching the Rendezvous, Smith became outspoken in his criticisms of Gray in his home letters. But he was the exception.

[20] See Mrs. Smith's diary for May 20th, text, p. 79, where she merely states: "We have today forded the south fork of the Platte." It was the general practice of the members of the mission party when writing back to their loved ones to gloss over many of the trials and dangers of the journey.

At the time we reached the N[orth] P[latte], dissolving mountain snow had rendered the river not fordable. This was anticipated; therefore, hunters had been instructed to bring skins newly taken from buffalo. Wicker work of willows in the form of a deep boat was made. The skins, sewed together with sinew, were stretched flesh side out over the prepared frame. Then drying process followed by exposure to the sun. Two such boats were prepared.   . .[21]

Water from above and beneath saturated the ground of the encampment. Tent covering was protection from falling rain; but in spite of the use of oil cloth on tent floor, the beds were wet. Mrs. Walker was a farmer's daughter — a country cultured lady. She was strong and cheery. Her common sense and her Christianity were practical. In her tent water was uncomfortably abundant. She considerately piled the bedding. Sitting upon her heels she thought and wept. Mrs. Smith entered the tent, and saw the tears. Seemingly surprised she said: "Why, Mrs. Walker, what is the matter?" The reply was: "I am thinking how comfortable my father's hogs are." [22]

Cushing Eells alone of the 1838 mission party is the authority for stating that the American Fur Company held its Rendezvous of that year east of the Rockies for purposes of "secrecy." With others he mentions the notice written on the door of the old trading post at Green River about "rum, trade, and white women" being at the Popo Agie river.

I have stated that the usual rendezvous of the Fur Co. was on the Green river, a tributary of the Colorado. In 1838 a change of location was made. The point chosen was on the Popiazua [Popo Agie] or Wind river. If I mistake not, the place was near a 100 miles northward of the usual point of meeting.[23] The object was secrecy, and thereby to pre-

---

[21] The boats were covered with skins from large buffalo bulls. Hence the name "bull-boats." They had to be towed. De Voto in his *Across the Wide Missouri*, 116, describes one as being 18′ long and 5½ feet wide. Several skins would be necessary to make such a craft. Mary Walker in her diary tells of the mission party making a boat by covering the box of their wagon with skins. FWW, II, p. 92.

[22] See Sarah Smith's comment in her diary for June 11th. Text, p. 86; also Mary Walker's FWW, II, p. 92.

[23] The caravan left the Sweetwater on June 19th and arrived at the Rendezvous on Wind River on the 21st, a distance of less than fifty miles. Again we see an excellent example of how fallible memory can be after the lapse of so many years. The terrain was most rugged and perhaps in memory the fifty miles seemed like one hundred.

vent the H[udson's] B[ay] Co. from interfering in their trade.[24] Had
this plan been entirely successful, it might have resulted disastrously
to the mission band. On Mr. Gray's eastern trip the previous season,
Mr. Ermatinger in charge of Ft. Hall had promised that he would meet
Mr. G. and expected associates at the Am[erican] Rend[ezvous] in
1838. Faithfully with guide and another man, he rode to G[reen] river
disappointedly. . .

Dr. Newell,[25] of R. Mt. fame, had performed repeated acts of kindness to Christian missionaries. I am not sure but I believe Dr. N. possessed more or less knowledge of the arrangement made by Messrs.
G[ray] & E[rmantinger]. Report was that he wrote upon the door of
the old store house at G[reen] river rendezvous: "Come on to Popiazua
and you will find plenty rum, trade, and white women." [26] But he
[Ermantinger] was behind time. The mission band at Po. were in
painful suspense. The period was nearing for the Fur Co's caravan to
return. What shall we do? Must we return too? [27] We could only pray
and wait. In that hour of extremity, Mr. E[rmantinger] arrived. There
was hallowed joy. This was not all. We were informed that food forwarded by Messrs. W[hitman] & S[palding] to Ft. Hall awaited our
arrival there. Tears of gratitude flowed.

Accompanying Mr. E. was Rev. Jason Lee of four years experience in

---

[24] See section in Sarah Smith's diary, "At the Rendezvous," text, p. 90. There
is evidence that the American Fur Company was trying to keep the location of
the Rendezvous a secret from the Hudson's Bay Company so that it could monop-
olize the fur trade.

[25] Robert Newell, one of the best known of the mountain men, received the
nickname of "Doctor" although he never had any medical training. After spending
the years 1828-40 in the mountains, Newell moved to the Willamette Valley where
he was prominent in civic affairs for some twenty years. He had a Nez Perce wife.

[26] Mrs. Francis Victor in her *River of the West,* 58, drawing upon the reminiscences of Joe Meek, states that the notice on the storehouse door at Green
River read: "Come to Popoazua on Wind River and you will find plenty trade,
whiskey, and white women." The reference to white women was clear evidence of
the presence of the missionaries. Mrs. Victor also wrote that the American Fur
Company had changed the location of the Rendezvous because it "had become
vexed at the Hudson's Bay Company." The location on Wind River was much
more inconvenient to the H.B. Co. than that on the Green. She gives no indication
that there was any effort to keep the location a secret. See Mary Walker's comment,
FWW, ii, p. 101, and text herein at page 90.

[27] There is no evidence in any of the contemporary writings of the missionaries
that they considered turning back if Ermatinger had not arrived. Gray had been
over the trail that lay before them on two occasions and after leaving the Rendezvous, there would be no serious danger of marauding Indians. The arrival, however, of the Hudson's Bay Company was most welcome.

mission work among the Indians of the Willamette.[28] Under the guardianship of Mr. Lee were the McKay boys going to Mass. to be educated. The present Dr. Wm. McKay of Umatilla Agency was one of that number.

The Rendezvous was the great social event of the year for the trappers in the mountains. In addition to trading furs for supplies from civilization, there was much drinking and carousing. Eells comments on this and incidentally throws some light upon the antipathy some of the mountain men had for W. H. Gray. Eells also tells of the two sons of General Wm. Clark who were with the 1838 caravan.

The goods of the F[ur] Co. shipped from St. L[ouis] consisted largely of clothing, blankets, tobacco, whiskey or rum. Said articles were sold at fabulous prices. The strong drink was $30. per gal. High price did not restrain [men] from its use, so long as it was obtainable.

One night after we had lain down to sleep, two intoxicated men came to our tent. They called for Mr. Gray — said they had come to settle with him.[29] In a low tone he asked if my rifle was loaded? As usual the barrel was empty. That, together with his gun, was prepared by himself for use if necessary. At the tent door I met the disturbers of our sleep. With wisdom given from above, I was enabled to quiet the intruders. They departed and did not return.

Two sons of Gen. Clark of St. L. accompanied that expedition of

---

[28] When the Jason Lee party went overland to Oregon in 1834, P. L. Edwards, a lay assistant, was a member. Now he was returning to the States. In 1842 he published his *Sketch of the Oregon Territory or Emigrant's Guide.* With Lee also was F. Y. Ewing, who is reported to have gone out to Oregon in 1837 for his health, and five Indian boys who were being taken East to be educated. Two of the Indians were Chinooks from the Willamette Valley, one of whom, William Brooks, died on May 29, 1839, and the other, Thomas Adams, returned to Oregon with Lee's great reenforcement which sailed on the "Lausanne." Three of the boys were sons of Thomas McKay, the half-breed son of Alexander McKay. One of the three was William C. McKay, then thirteen years old, who later on Dr. Whitman's advice studied medicine at the Fairfield Medical College in New York, where Whitman himself had studied. Dr. McKay was physician at the Pendleton, Oregon, Indian Agency for many years.

[29] Myra Eells wrote in her diary for July 5, 1838: "Four men came swearing and blaspheming inquiring for Mr. Gray. . . They said they wished to settle accounts with Mr. Gray." FWW, ii, p. 99. The point at issue was Gray's responsibility for the Sioux Indian attack at Ash Hollow the preceding year. Contrary to the best advice of the mountain men, Gray had set out with his band of horses and his Indian helpers without waiting for the protection of the returning caravan. There is abundant evidence to show that Gray was unpopular with the mountain men.

the F. Co. The father of those sons in company with Lewis made exploration in the years 1804-6 to and beyond the R. Mts. The younger of those sons was a graduate of Yale. The use of alcoholic drink was to him ruinous. It was hoped that exclusion from customary modes of temptation would be favorable. Measurable it was so. The journey, the scenery, the simplicity of diet in camp life, were advantageous. A genial educated gentleman was infrequent in that crowd. . . He was worth the making of effort to save him. . . The devotion of the accompanying brother was sincere. The effect of the journey was salutary, [but] the use of the drunkard's drink at rendezvous was destructive to the otherwise choice young man.

Eells included in his reminiscences the following account of a disagreeable experience suffered by his wife while crossing the Sweetwater River. Here is a good example of the trials and dangers endured by the women in their travels. Mrs. Eells wrote:

On the 15th of June we crossed Sweetwater. I rode along the bank, saw the carts across the water and thought it about three feet deep, though many of the loose horses were swimming. I felt a little afraid and said to Mr. Gray: "We will stop until our husbands have taken the mules across, and return for us." as Mr. Eells had gone to lead the way for the pack animals, the other gentlemen to drive them. Mr. Gray, the last after the mules, said: "The ladies come directly after us." Mrs. Gray went first and I followed her.

My horse mired, entering the river. I somehow managed to dismount and wade through the water and mud on to the bank again, but saw no one coming to my assistance. As soon as I could I went back and tried to help my horse out, but he struggled so that I could not reach his bridle, when Mr. Smith came to my help. As soon as we were both out, I saw Mr. Eells — and myself covered with mud and found my strength nearly all gone. Mr. E. asked if I was hurt. I said: "I thought only frightened." By this time the company were all over and gone, and we must not stop. Mr. E. had a tin cup fastened to his belt, and he rinsed the mud off my cloak, and then set me on my horse again, and we went safely across. We then rode four and a half hours without getting off our horses. By this time the upper side of my clothes were nearly dry while the under side were wet as when we came from the river. At noon I changed my shoes and stockings, dried my other clothes on me as well as I could and in the afternoon rode three and a half hours again. This to me was a pretty sorrowful day, though I had great reason to be thankful that I was not hurt.[30]

(Her husband then added the following comment):

One person, on seeing Mrs. E. in a pitiable condition in the mud, laughed at her sad plight. That in her exhaustion and discomfort grieved her much. Never before had I seen her weep to such a degree. This fact touched my heart, and possibly warped my judgement so that I have consumed an unreasonable space of time in relating it.

The average age of the six men of the two mission parties of 1836 and 1838 at the time they journeyed overland to Oregon was about thirty-one, not including Cornelius Rogers who was only twenty-three. The ages of the six women ranged from Mrs. Smith's twenty-five to Mrs. Eells' thirty-three with the average being twenty-eight. Mrs. Whitman was thirty-nine at the time of her death. Mrs. Smith and Mrs. Spalding, both of whom were in frail health during their journey to Oregon, died at the ages of forty-one and forty-three respectively. The other three women, in spite of all the hardships suffered during their travels and in spite of all the privations endured during their mission life, lived far beyond the average life span of that generation. Mrs. Gray and Mrs. Eells lived to be seventy-one and seventy-three respectively. Mrs. Walker was the last of the mission band to die. Her death came on December 5, 1897, when she was eighty-six. In summing up his account of the overland journey of 1838, Eells wrote in his reminiscences:

Thus the distance between Mo. and W[alla] W[alla] valley was traveled a second time by white women on an overland journey, from the Atlantic States to Washington Territory, embracing a period of nearly six months. . . Forty-five years ago [*he was writing in March 1883*], since I commenced it. Thus obedience to the command, "Go ye into all the world and preach the gospel to every creature," was attempted, and thus the promise of him who said, "Lo I am with you always," was remembered by. those who gave and those who trusted it.

---

[30] Myra Eells made no reference to this distressing experience in her diary.

First White Women over the Rockies

Was it Wise?

First White Women over the Rockies —
Was it Wise?

Was it wise for the American Board of Commissioners for Foreign Missions to send six women on that long and hazardous journey over the Rocky Mountains in 1836 and 1838? Even though such a journey might have been feasible for men, was it right to subject "delicate females" to the fatigues and dangers attendant upon such an undertaking, especially when they would have to ride about 1,900 miles from Westport, Missouri, to Walla Walla on side-saddles? Was the Board guilty of acting upon imperfect knowledge of the difficulties involved in such an undertaking when it sent two parties of missionaries overland to Oregon? What did these missionaries themselves say about their experiences after they had reached the Rendezvous or their final destination? Were they willing to recommend that others, especially women, follow them?

Such questions have prompted the author to make a thorough examination of the extant writings of the twelve members of the two parties, together with those of Samuel Parker who crossed to Oregon by land in 1835 and returned by sea in 1837, to find their appraisals of their experiences. The result of this study shows that opinions were divided. Four of the thirteen — Dr. and Mrs. Marcus Whitman, W. H. Gray, and Samuel Parker — approved the plan. Five — H. H. Spalding, Elkanah Walker, Myra Eells, and Asa and Sarah Smith — were definitely opposed. No expressions of opinion have been found from Mary Gray, Eliza Spalding, Mary Walker, or Cushing Eells. But if it may be assumed that their ideas would be the same as those of their respective spouses, then the final tally would indicate five in favor of the overland journey and eight opposed. Certainly those who opposed were much more emphatic in their objections than those who tacitly at least approved. Cornelius Rogers made no comment on this subject.

THOSE IN FAVOR OF TAKING WOMEN OVERLAND

Marcus Whitman was the first to suggest to the American Board the feasibility of taking women across the Rockies. He had gone to the

Rendezvous of 1835 in company with Samuel Parker and had observed that wheeled vehicles had been taken over the mountains. He reasoned that wherever a wagon could go, a woman could go. If she grew weary of riding on a side-saddle, let her ride in the wagon. It was a convincing argument and upon his return East that fall, Whitman notified the Board of his desire to get married and take his bride with him overland to Oregon with at least one other married couple. Writing to Whitman on December 5, 1835, Secretary Greene asked. "Have you carefully ascertained & weighed the difficulties in the way of conducting females to those remote & desolate regions. . . ?" In his reply of December 17th, Whitman wrote: "We can go as far as the Black Hills [i.e., Fort Laramie] with a waggon for the convenience of females, and from that to the rendezvous." The implication is clear, wherever a wagon could go, a woman could go. Actually Whitman and Spalding took their wagon beyond the Rendezvous. It was reduced to a two-wheeled card before they reached Fort Hall and this was taken across the sage-covered desert of what is now southern Idaho as far west as Fort Boise. Accordingly, the Board approved and sent Whitman and Spalding *and their wives overland across the Rockies in 1836.*

In a letter to Greene dated July 16, 1836, from the Rendezvous, Whitman commented: "I see no reason to regret our choice of a journey by land." Although confessing that the hardships of traveling had been "somewhat fatiguing to Mrs. Spalding," he claimed that his own health and that of his wife had been improved. In a letter written from Fort Vancouver on October 24th to Mrs. Samuel Parker, Narcissa enthusiastically endorsed the overland route. "Do you ask whether I regret coming by land?" she queried. "I answer NO! by no *means*. If I were at home now, I would chose to come this way in preference to a seven months sea voyage." She praised the purity of the mountain air, the exhilarating effects of outdoor living, and the "healthful exercise of a horseback ride." She pointed out also that the overland route had another advantage over going by sea: it was much cheaper. This was a potent argument in the Board's consideration.

William H. Gray, who went out to Oregon in 1836 and returned to the East for reenforcements in 1837, also favored the overland route. No doubt his strong recommendation to the Board in favor of sending women overland was the basis for his somewhat extended arguments in justification of that decision. Writing to Greene from the Rendezvous on July 10, 1838, Gray claimed that the disciplinary values of overland travel were most important in conditioning the missionaries for their pioneer life on the mission field. The whole experience was a school. "That it is a severe school," he wrote, "none will deny and that it requires self denial, patience & perseverance there can be no doubt." He felt that the missionaries should see life at the Rendezvous and thus become acquainted at first hand with the evil influences the mountain men exercised over the natives. He wrote: "In passing these Mountains, he [the missionary] sees the fountain head of an influence he must counteract, in every branch of his labor, to do this effectually he must know from whence it comes and what it is." Gray also felt that the experience of traveling overland enabled the missionaries "to learn each others dispositions and qualities better than in any other way, or in any other place." Therefore his conclusion: "I firmly believe this is the way they should come."

Gray, like Whitman, was fortunate in having a wife in excellent health and who seemingly endured the hardships of the long ride very well. Both Narcissa Whitman and Mary Gray became pregnant on the journey. Mrs. Whitman gave birth to a daughter on March 14, 1837, about six and a half months after her arrival at Fort Walla Walla. Mrs. Gray had a son on March 20, 1839, a little less than seven months after her arrival at the Whitman station. No comment has been found in the writings of Mary Gray regarding her opinion of her overland travels. It may be assumed, therefore, that out of loyalty to her husband, she agreed with him in favoring this route.

The fifth person to endorse the overland journey in preference to a voyage to Oregon by sea was Samuel Parker. No one of the missionary group was better qualified to make comparisons than he for he had gone both ways. It is true that Asa and Sarah Smith, who left the Oregon Mission in 1841, had after spending three years in Hawaii, returned to the States by sea. They arrived back in New England in May 1846, being the only ones of the Oregon missionaries to circumnavigate the globe. Their return was by the unusual way around South Africa, and even if some opinion had been found in their latter writings regarding the relative merits of going to Oregon by land or sea, such would not be relevant to our study as they did not go around South America.

Only Parker had tried the two routes — overland across the Rockies and by sea around Cape Horn. When Elkanah Walker turned to Parker for advice regarding which was the better way to go to Oregon, Parker on February 19, 1838, replied:

By all means go across the continent by land. I had rather go across the continent three times than around the Cape [Horn] once, and probably it would not take more time, nor be attended with half the dangers and hardships, as to go by water. . . A lady can go with far more comfort by land than by water.[1]

Thus five of the thirteen approved the Board's decision to send women across the Rockies to their mission field in Oregon.

On the basis of such favorable reports, the American Board decided to send the 1838 reenforcement overland. Turning to Elkanah Walker's correspondence with the Board, we find that he made inquiry of Greene on January 3, 1838, concerning the advisability of taking women overland in preference to going by sea. Greene replied on January 11th saying in part:

> The expense of the two routes compared, I cannot give pre-cisely. Probably the expense of the water route to Fort Vancouver would be not far from $600 for a missionary & his wife. The land route, including everything, may not vary far from the same sum. It is quite uncertain when a passage could be found for the com-pany by water. You might be detained till next autumn.
>
> Although the land route seems to be a hard one, and doubtless not a little of hardship, exposure, & self denial is involved in it; yet I believe that most persons, even females, soon become accus-tomed to such a mode of life, & the peculiarities of it soon become pleasant rather than otherwise. All who have crossed the continent as missionaries have, I believe, had their health much benefited by it.[2]

OPPOSING THE OVERLAND ROUTE

The majority opinion of the mission band, however, was to the con-trary. No persons connected with the Oregon Mission of the American Board were more outspoken in their criticisms of the Board in sending women over the Rockies than were Henry H. Spalding and Asa B. Smith. The frail health of their wives no doubt influenced their final judgment. Both women had the experience of being thrown from the animal she was riding and then being dragged for a distance because a foot had been caught in the stirrup.

---

[1] Original in Washington State University Library, Pullman, Washington.

[2] Drury, *Walker*, 62. If Greene were correct in his estimate, then the four couples could have been sent to Oregon by sea for $2,400 plus the expense of getting them up the Columbia River to Waiilatpu. According to Gray's financial report, the cost of going overland was a little over $3,000 which included the cost of their live-stock. If the missionaries had gone by sea, they could have taken more personal belongings. No doubt a sea voyage would have landed them in Oregon several months later than the time they arrived by taking the overland route.

In an article that Spalding wrote for the December 1, 1870, issue of the *Chicago Advance*, he reported that his wife had fainted on July 4, 1836, when the party was crossing the Continental Divide and that, as they laid her on the ground, she said: "Don't put me on that horse again. Leave me and save yourselves." On July 12th, while at the Rendezvous, Eliza wrote in her diary: "My health is a little improved." Such is the background for Spalding's statement in his letter of July 16, 1836, to Greene: "Never send another mission over these mountains if you value life and money."

With the exception of the Grays, all the members of the 1838 reenforcement who commented in writing on their overland experiences were critical of the Board's action in sending them overland. They referred to the severe physical hardships they were obliged to endure. Smith complained about how destructive their mode of traveling was to their "piety." Without exception, all found the necessity of traveling on Sunday, or the Sabbath as they called the day, particularly trying. Not only were they breaking one of the ten commandments, they were also being denied a weekly day of rest. Even though traveling by river boat or ocean steamer often included Sundays, conscientious Christians of that generation would on such occasions spend the day in their cabins. But while traveling with the fur company's caravan, they found no seclusion and no opportunity for rest or worship.

In a long letter to Greene written from Waiilatpu on October 15, 1838, Walker reviewed their travel experiences and gave the following judgment:

> I suppose too that a lady who undertakes to go to the Indians west of the Rocky Mountains is as much a lady as one who undertakes to go to the Sandwich Islands or any other station & I suppose that a regularly educated & ordained Minister is about the same, let him go where he will under the direction of the Board. It is a pretty well attested fact that human nature is the same whatever be the condition in which it is placed & I suppose that there is but little difference between mountain sailors and sea sailors. . .
>
> It appears to me that if it is not proper or right for Missionaries who go abroad by sea to be compelled to work their passage & be exposed to all the hardships & sufferings incidental to a sailor on a voyage, neither is it right or proper that Missionaries should make the voyage across the Mountains & in such circumstances as will compel them to perform as much or more & the same kind of labor as the hired men of the company.

The same may be said in regard to ladies. If it is not right & consistent with female delicacy for the wives of Missionaries who go by water to their various stations to act as cooks for their husbands & all who may be in their company, living on deck under a miserable shelter, liable to be drenched at every passing shower & awake in the night & find that they were sleeping in water & often sitting on the deck in the open air without any thing to shelter them from the scorching rays of the sun in presence of the whole ships company — if it is not consistent with christian propriety & female delicacy for the wives of the Missionaries to do all this — then it is not right for them to cross the mountains where they will be compelled to do it. It is true our [ladies] were not compelled to do all the cooking but a considerable part of it was done by them out of necessity.

Another subject about which there is complete silence in the writings of the missionaries is the provision for the women to perform their toilet. Often when the caravan moved through the plain or desert country, there was not a rock or a tree or a hollow in which a person could find privacy. This must have created embarrassing situations for sensitive women.

In this same letter of October 15th, Walker gave his conclusions regarding the advisability of sending women overland. "So far as my opinion goes," he wrote, "it would be against their so coming, & I believe that most of our company would, if they were to come to this country again, & could, would prefer to come by water. . . I cannot think that it is proper for any company to come in the manner we did."

Walker had reason to be concerned because his wife became pregnant soon after their marriage and gave birth to a son at the Whitman station on December 7th, about three months after their arrival at Waiilatpu. Mary also had the experience of being thrown at least once from her horse while crossing the country. Any such violent incident might have induced a miscarriage.

When the Board was making plans to send its 1840 reenforcement to the Oregon Mission, the letters of Spalding and Walker were on hand advising against sending missionaries overland. It is possible that their advice was heeded, for the two couples, the Rev. and Mrs. John Davis Paris and Mr. and Mrs. William H. Rice, sailed from Boston in November 1840. By the time the four arrived in Honolulu in 1841, such discouraging reports of conditions in the Oregon Mission had reached the Islands that the second reenforcement was advised to remain there.

No expression of opinion on the propriety of women making the overland journey has been discovered in the writings of Cushing Eells. But the following quotation from one of his wife's letters gives a vivid description of the hardships endured and indicates that she would not recommend the journey to other women:

There is much more danger attending the journey than we had supposed. Since we left the States, we have found that horseback riding in imagination and in reality are two different things. We rise at half-past three in the morning. During considerable part of the way, we are liable to be met by war parties of wild Indians; and if we are not sufficiently strong, our animals may all be stolen,[3] and we left to wander in the wilderness with savage and wild beasts. . . I believe we agree that no pen can paint the realities of this journey so that any one who has not tried it will understand.[4]

Of all who offered advice to the Board on this subject, none was more emphatic in his criticism than Asa B. Smith. Looking back on his trans-continental travel experiences, he wrote as follows to Secretary Greene on February 6, 1840:

Respecting the sending of missionaries across the continent, permit me to say that I hope it will never again be done. The more I think of our journey, the more fully satisfied I am that it is improper for missionaries, especially females, thus to travel, certainly where there is access to the field by sea. The trials, hardships & perplexities of such a journey no one can realize but those who have undertaken it. We suffered from hunger & thirst, cold & heat, parching winds & severe storms in an unprotected situation, flying sand & dust & poisonous insects and musketoes, extreme hardship & fatigues & more than all were deprived of sabbaths & means of spiritual improvement.

I can assure you that it requires more grace than any of your missionaries whom you have sent across the Rocky Mountains possess, to bear up under such trials & not have their piety seriously affected. I am fully satisfied that the influence of this journey has been decidedly unfavorable on the religious character of every one who has undertaken it. I doubt whether it is possible for any to live too long without sabbaths & not have their religious character grow into deformity. I never could be induced to undertake

---

3 Mrs. Eells was remembering the fact that the reenforcement of 1838 had three horses stolen by the Pawnee Indians.

4 From Eells reminiscences, Coll. W.

this journey again under the same circumstances, in preference to a voyage at sea, on any consideration whatever.

Sarah fully endorsed her husband's feelings. On May 13th she wrote in her diary: "I hope we are the last missionaries that will ever attempt to cross the Mountains. I should advise to go around [the Horn] unless they are willing to lose all their piety." And in the closing section of her diary, as has been indicated, she wrote: "I almost hope that none will ever cross them [the Rockies] again, for I think it is a tremendous journey. . . It does seem to me that it is improper for a female to undertake it." [5]

THE JUDGMENT OF OTHERS

When the Rev. Jason Lee of the Oregon Methodist Mission met the 1838 reenforcement at the Wind River Rendezvous, he was told about the dangers and difficulties of taking women overland. This information may have influenced the decision of the Methodist Board to send its large reenforcement of 1839, consisting of fifty-one men, women, and children, to Oregon by sea. A ship, the "Lausanne," was chartered for this purpose. The Methodist Church never sent any of its women missionaries overland to Oregon. The five men under the leadership of Jason Lee who went out to Oregon by the overland route in 1834 were the only Methodist missionaries to go that way.

The news of the successful crossing of the Rockies by six missionary women had some unexpected and far-reaching repercussions throughout the northern and eastern states. Whereas Marcus Whitman had once argued, "wherever a wagon can go, a woman can go," now the refrain was picked up, "where these missionary women have gone, other women can follow." Oregon emigration societies began to be formed as early as 1838 and 1839 in such widely separated places as Illinois and Massachusetts. Here we see the first signs of the outbreak of the "Oregon fever" when hundreds and then thousands of adventurous and land-hungry people began dreaming of migrating to the Pacific Northwest. California, under the Mexican flag until 1846, was not then included in their dreams.

One of these societies, regarding which we have considerable information, was the Oregon Provisional Emigration Society with headquarters at Lynn, Massachusetts. This Society was formed by a group of Methodist ministers and laymen on August 30, 1838, for the purpose

---

[5] See Sarah Smith's diary, September 14, 1839 (herein p. 124), for her extended comments on this subject.

of encouraging hundreds of Christian settlers to migrate to Oregon. The promotors dreamed of establishing settlements in Oregon from which influences would emanate to evangelize and civilize the natives. The society sponsored a monthly publication called *The Oregonian and Indian's Advocate*.[6] The first issue appeared in October 1838 and the last in August 1839. Only six complete files of this rare publication are known to be extant.

An examination of this magazine shows that the editor made good use of the accomplishments of the Oregon missionaries of the American Board to popularize his cause. In the very first number he referred to Mrs. Whitman and Mrs. Spalding who, he wrote, were "believed to be the first white women who have traversed these mountains." The fact that "delicate females" had successfully crossed the continent was a potent argument in favor of other families undertaking the same journey. He concluded by saying: 'Thus has vanished the great obstacle to a direct and facile communication between the Mississippi valley and the Pacific ocean." In his December 1838 issue, the editor referred to the American Board's reenforcement of 1838 which included four women. It was this number which carried the letter of Cornelius Rogers, written from the Rendezvous on July 3, 1838, which has been reproduced in an earlier section of this book.

The editor referred again to this party in the January 1839 issue of his magazine, again with the implication that what these missionary women could do, other women could do. In this number he wrote:

Six white women, (the ladies of the missionaries of the A.B.C. F.M.) have already crossed the prairies to Oregon; not with a company of emigrants, who travelled leisurely, and regarded comfort equally with time; but with a caravan of traders, who travel as fast as the strength of their horses will permit, and know no day of rest; and who are as wicked and licentious a set of fellows as ever caroused over the midnight bowl. With such companions did these ladies and their husbands make the passage of the Mountains, and we are assured by their own testimony that they were in better health and spirits at the end than at the beginning of their journey, having found it extremely pleasant, notwithstanding the circumstances named. This shows, we think, the feasibility of this route for ladies, and even children.

It is evident that the editor was painting a rosy picture from the information gleaned from Rogers' letters and that he knew nothing of

---

[6] See article by the author on "The Oregonian and Indian's Advocate" in *Pacific Northwest Quarterly*, October 1965.

the reactions of Asa and Sarah Smith, for instance, to the hardships and perils of the journey.

Word reached the editor, when he was preparing the July 1839 issue of *The Oregonian and Indian's Advocate* for the press, of the successful arrival in Oregon of the 1838 reenforcement. This news gave him the occasion to remind his readers again of the fact that women had made the overland journey. He drove home again his main argument:

> Now if these ladies, making the tour in this manner, retained and improved their health, to what conclusion must we come? Must we not say that a larger company of families, who would move more slowly, be better provided, and take advantage of circumstances which these could not control, could, with the most perfect safety to health, pass from Missouri to Oregon?

Some rivalry developed in Methodist circles between Jason Lee's plan to send a colony to Oregon by sea and that of the Oregon Provisional Emigration Society's proposal to have emigrants go overland. It seems evident that by the summer of 1839 some of the initial supporters of the emigration society had transferred their sympathies and financial support to the official project of the Foreign Board of the Methodist Church. As a result the society found it necessary to give up its grandiose scheme of sending a colony of two hundred families overland in the spring and summer of 1840. After the suspension of its publication in August 1839, nothing more is known of the activities of the society. It is possible that some of the people who were thinking of going overland to Oregon with the proposed colony sponsored by the emigration society actually became members of Jason Lee's reenforcement which went by sea.

THE BEGINNINGS OF OREGON EMIGRATION

The first women to go overland to Oregon following the American Board's reenforcement of 1838 were the Rev. and Mrs. John S. Griffith and Mr. and Mrs. Asahel Munger who made the overland journey in 1839. They had no connection with any established missionary board and expected to establish a self-supporting mission among the Oregon Indians. They were followed the next year by three more couples, the Rev. and Mrs. Harvey Clark, Mr. and Mrs. P. B. Littlejohn, and Mr. and Mrs. Alvin T. Smith, all independent missionaries. These five couples soon discovered the impossibility of establishing self-supporting missions among the natives of Oregon. Their slender financial resources were soon exhausted and they moved on into the Willamette

Valley. The arrival of these five women brought the total number of white American women who had made the hazardous journey over the Rocky Mountains by horseback to eleven. These were the forerunners of that great company who followed in covered wagons.

In the fall of 1840 a party under the leadership of Joe Meek, one of the most famous of the mountain men, took wagons over the Blue Mountains. These were the first wheeled vehicles to be taken over these mountains. In this party was Joel P. Walker, his wife, sister, three sons, and two daughters. These two women were the first non-missionary women to cross the Rockies. The barrier had been broken and soon thousands were pouring through that same South Pass gateway to Oregon each year.

No Rendezvous were held after 1840 and hence no caravans were going to the mountains each year which could provide protection to Oregon-bound emigrants. Even so a party of twenty-four went out to Oregon in 1841. In this party were two families with little children. They did not have any wagons when they arrived at the Whitman mission. On October 6th of that year Narcissa in a letter to her parents wrote regarding a mother with six children: "It was very pleasing to see such a mother with so many children around her, having come so far — such a dreadful journey."

In 1842, 114 men, women, and children migrated to Oregon. Although this party started with several wagons, none was taken west of Fort Hall. They too completed the last part of their journey on horseback. Included in this party was the former Methodist missionary to Oregon, Dr. Elijah White, who was returning as the first U.S. Indian Agent to Oregon. He carried with him that fateful order from the American Board which called for the dismissal of Spalding and the closing of the stations at Lapwai and Waiilatpu. As a result of this order, Whitman started east on October 3, 1842. He returned the following year with an emigrant train of about one thousand people. This was the first great wagon-train to roll through South Pass, seven years after the Whitman-Spalding party had crossed in 1836.

When the 1843 emigration arrived at Fort Hall, Captain Richard Grant, the Hudson's Bay official in charge, sought to dissuade them from taking their wagons any further. It was then that Whitman stepped forward and assured the members of the party that it was possible to proceed with wagons. He told how he and Spalding had taken a cart through to Fort Boise and no doubt mentioned the fact that wagons had been taken over the Blue Mountains as early as 1840. The large number of women and children in this 1843 emigration demanded wagons. They could not have made the remainder of the journey into Oregon on horseback. Whitman became the acknowledged leader of the 1843 emigration after it left Fort Hall.

Regardless of whether or not it was wise for the American Board to send two parties including women overland to Oregon, this we know — the fact that these women were able to make a successful journey, riding horseback, side-saddle, over the Rockies, had far-reaching consequences. What these women had been able to do under adverse conditions, others could do when they could ride in covered-wagons.

These missionary women were the vanguard. Their names should be remembered with honor, and the epic story of their achievements should not be forgotten.

Bibliography and Index

Bibliography

Drury, Clifford M. *Henry Harmon Spalding, Pioneer of Old Oregon.* Caldwell, Idaho, 1936

——. *Marcus Whitman, M.D., Pioneer and Martyr.* Caldwell, Idaho, 1937

——. *Elkanah and Mary Walker, Pioneers among the Spokanes.* Caldwell, Idaho, 1940

——. *A Tepee in His Front Yard: H. T. Cowley and the Founding of Spokane.* Portland, Oregon, 1949

——. *Diary of Titian Ramsay Peale.* Los Angeles, 1957

——. *The Diaries and Letters of Henry H. Spalding and Asa Bowen Smith relating to the Nez Perce Mission, 1838-1842.* Glendale, California, 1958

——. *First White Women over the Rockies. Diaries, Letters, and Biographical Sketches of the Six Women of the Oregon Mission who made the Overland Journey in 1836 and 1838.* 2 volumes. Glendale, California, 1963

Eells, Myron. *Father Eells.* Boston, 1894

Emerson, Oliver Pomeroy. *Pioneer Days in Hawaii.* New York, 1928

Gray, William Henry. *A History of Oregon, 1792-1849, drawn from personal observation and authentic information.* Portland, Oregon, 1870

Hodge, A.C. *Memorial Sketches of Rev. Asa B. Smith, Sarah G. Smith, and Harriet E. Smith.* Boston, 1889

Hulbert, Archer B. and Dorothy P. *Marcus Whitman, Crusader.* 3 volumes. Denver, 1936-1941

McBeth, Kate C. *The Nez Perces since Lewis and Clark.* New York, 1908

Missionary Album. Honolulu, Hawaiian Mission Children's Society, 1937

Victor, Frances Fuller. *River of the West.* Hartford, 1870

PERIODICALS

Missionary Herald
Oregon Historical Quarterly
Oregon Pioneer Association, Transactions
Pacific Northwest Quarterly
Washington Historian

In addition, there are a few incidental references to other publications which are fully identified in footnotes.

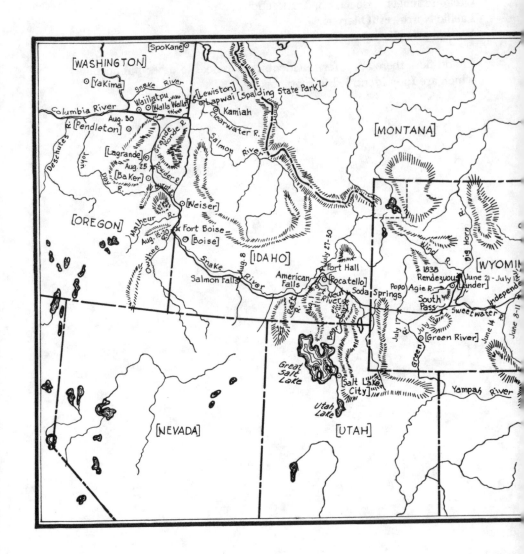

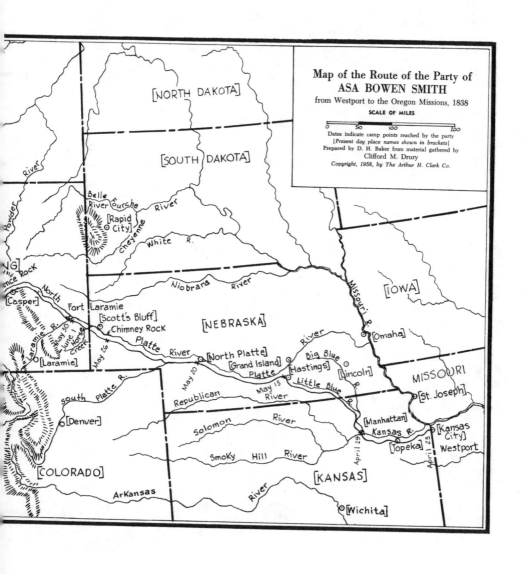

Map of the Route of the Party of
ASA BOWEN SMITH
from Westport to the Oregon Missions, 1838
SCALE OF MILES

0   50   100   200

Dates indicate camp points reached by the party
[*Present day place names shown in brackets*]
Prepared by D. H. Baker from material gathered by
Clifford M. Drury
Copyright, 1958, by The Arthur H. Clark Co.

Index